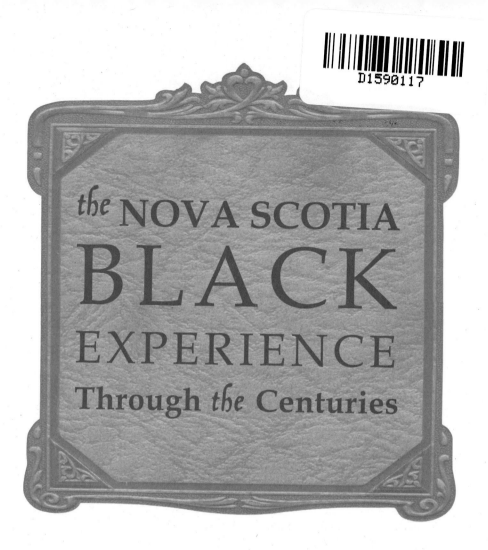

the NOVA SCOTIA
BLACK
EXPERIENCE
Through the Centuries

Bridglal Pachai

NIMBUS
PUBLISHING

DEDICATION

Saluting the memories of
Reverend Drs. William Pearly Oliver and Donald D. Skeir
who saw progress and opportunities where so many
saw obstacles and compartments.

Nimbus Publishing Limited
PO Box 9166, Halifax, NS B3K 5M8
(902) 455-4286   www.nimbus.ns.ca

Printed and bound in Canada

Front cover: Loyal Wilberforce Lodge, No 7336, I.O.O.F Halifax, Nova Scotia, 1917. Seated front row centre is C. H. Johnston. Back row, eighth from the left, is Rev. W. N. States. (Photo courtesy of the Black Cultural Centre).

Cover inset: Black pioneers making their way along a road near Halifax, as painted by Robert Petley, c.1835. (Photo courtesy of Nova Scotia Archives and Records Management).

Library and Archives Canada Cataloguing in Publication
    Pachai, Bridglal
    The Nova Scotia Black experience through the centuries / Bridglal Pachai.
    Originally published in 2 v. under title: Beneath the clouds of the promised land.
    Includes bibliographical references and index.
    ISBN 13: 978-1-55109-621-6   ISBN 10: 1-55109-621-8

1. Black Canadians-Nova Scotia-History. 2. Blacks-Nova Scotia-History. 3. Nova Scotia-History. I. Title. II. Title: Pachai, Bridglal. Beneath the clouds of the promised land.

FC2350.B6P3 2007   971.6'00496   C2007-904640-1

We acknowledge the financial support of the Government of Canada through the Book Publishing Industry Development Program (BPIDP) and the Canada Council, and of the Province of Nova Scotia through the Department of Tourism, Culture and Heritage for our publishing activities.

Contents

Image Sources

Black Business Initiative: 329

Black Cultural Centre of Nova Scotia: (cover), 29, 39, 58, 61, 111, 113, 122, 126, 127, 139, 147, 155, 160, 164, 166, 170, 179, 190, 202, 208, 253, 273, 281, 290, 296, 297, 301, 302, 319 (top)

Black Loyalist Heritage Society: 333, 339 (bottom)

Government House: 338 (top)

Nova Scotia Advisory Council on the Status of Women: 181

Province of Nova Scotia: 257

Public Archives of Canada: 47, 141

Nova Scotia Archives and Records Management: cover inset, 315

Saint Mary's University: 303

Ricky Anderson 334; Vincent Audain 340 (left); Michael Bedford 309; Beverley Bonvie 336; Evangeline Cain-Grant 324; Jack Desmond 203; Mike Doherty 163; Doris Evans 332 (right); Edith Gray 196, 198, 199, 200, 267, 286; Tracey Grosse 331 (bottom); Joan Jones 331 (top); Don MacLean 319 (bottom), 341; Peter Marsman/Dan O'Brien 326, 327, 338 (bottom), 339 (top); Bridglal Pachai 155, 234, 288; Norman Paris 337 (top); Percy Paris 337 (bottom); Sylvia Parris 328; Craig Smith 327, 335 (top); Eugenia Sojka 335 (bottom); Herman Ssebazza 340 (right); Coulter B. States 232; Gertrude Tynes 332 (left)

Note on terminology and spelling:

Reference to the black population over the centuries included words such as Negro, Colored, Black, Afro-Canadian. The first two are still used in conversation by older members but the usage is limited and no longer considered proper. They are used in this volume in direct quotes only. The spelling of Colored and Coloured have appeared in sources in both forms. For consistency, the first form only is used in this volume.

Author's Note and Acknowledgements

Volumes I and II of *Beneath The Clouds of the Promised Land: The Survival of Nova Scotia's Blacks* now appear in this book with slight modifications as Sections A and B. The first volume appeared in 1987 and the second was launched four years later.

Speaking on the occasion of the launching of the first volume on February 20, 1988, the Reverend Donald D. Skeir said: "There is and must be a determination to go beyond acquiescence and acceptance. The price we must pay should be ever seeking, ever striving, personal pride, determined effort, sacrifice to achieve, positive attitudes. Today we want to be woven within the fabric of national and international aspirations. The leaders of the past have left us with this dream, now we must strive towards it. We cannot fall back into slumber by the tokenism of a little. A little here and a little there......"

The good reverend, who followed this up with a warm personal letter to me six days later, died on October 10, 1999. He deserves pride of place, alongside the Reverend Dr. William Pearly Oliver, who died ten years earlier, as my mentors in black history and in my understanding of Nova Scotia's black experience.

In thirty-one years of living with this subject, researching it, writing about it, and teaching it in Canada, Africa, and the United States since 1975, my list of thanks grows by the day. In the early decades, some of the elders who helped me have since gone to their resting places: Deacons John Pannill, Sydney Jones, and Jack Desmond; Calvin Ruck, Coulter States, Noel H. Johnston, George Davis, Q.C., Ruth Johnson, and Winston Ruck. Others were H. A. J. Wedderburn, Gertrude Tynes, Doris Evans, Lemuel Skeete, Edith Gray, Zina Williams, Charlotte Colley, Pearleen Oliver, and Angela Cromwell. My former colleagues at the Black Cultural Centre were unfailing in their support and advice: Wayne Adams, Henry Bishop, Maxine Brooks, Ramona Hill, and Anne Johnson, as were my former colleagues at the Nova Scotia Human Rights Commission: Irma Farmer, Patricia Grosse, and David States. One-time professional teachers themselves, Peter McCreath, Glenda Redden, John Grant, and Richard Rogers have stood by with tremendous goodwill and support.

This revised and updated version is my sixth book on aspects of Nova Scotia's black history—including one on the Maritimes. Those whom I have thanked in the pages of those books, who are not mentioned here, will bear with me in my difficult task of preventing the list from becoming unwieldy. I continue to be grateful to them all.

I must now express my thanks to those who are helping me to fill gaps and take this book into the twenty-first century: Cpl. Craig Smith, Percy Paris, Geraldine Browning, Dr. Patrick Kakembo, Herman Ssebazza, Rev. Tracey Grosse, Rustum Southwell, Starr Francis, Staff Sergeant Don McLean, Elizabeth Mills, Sylvia Parris, Delvina Bernard, Mike Doherty, George and Darril Fosty, Dan Soucoup, and his colleagues at Nimbus Publishing in Halifax for their continuing cooperation, Dan O'Brien of Design North, and the Black Loyalist Heritage Society. Finally, my wife, Leela, has been a tower of help and strength in more ways than I can ever list. Thank you for freeing up so much time.

When the volumes of the original title, *Beneath The Clouds of The Promised Land: The Survival of Nova Scotia's Blacks* appeared between 1987 and 1991, it was a visionary initiative of the Black Educators Association that made it possible. On an expanded scale it was this Association that was the catalyst that heralded the appearance of the Black Learners Advisory Committee, The African-Canadian Services Division, and the Council on African Canadian Education. To that extent, its pioneers deserve special mention.

Bridglal Pachai, C.M.,
Halifax, Nova Scotia,
December 31, 2006.

SECTION A
THE PERIOD 1600-1800

INTRODUCTION

During the 18th and 19th centuries, people of African ancestry, whose for-bears had been brought to the Americas and the Caribbean in captivity as slaves, entered Nova Scotia and other parts of Canada either voluntarily or involuntarily. Most of them cherished one abiding hope: they were entering a promised land in which they and their descendants could live out their lives as free citizens. They came in different streams of immigration, in small and in large numbers, and under varying conditions and circumstances. They brought to the promised land their skills, their labour, their determina-tion, their buying power. Above all, they brought their loyalty. In the prom-ised land they were prepared to give all they had in the name of God and country in return for shelter and opportunity.

Their individual and collective experiences in Nova Scotia have influ-enced the title as well as the subject matter of this book. From the begin-ning, clouds gathered over the promised land, blotting out most of the promises and blurring the rest. The result was that the newly-arrived resi-dents as well as their descendants faced an uphill struggle for survival. Together, the imagery of the clouds above and the notions of a life-and-death struggle below present the main features of the picture of the Nova Scotian Black experience.

However, the Nova Scotian experience must be placed in the context of the preceding and the contemporary developments that influenced it. For this reason, a chapter has been devoted to the African side of the story. Nova Scotian Blacks, and indeed Blacks of the African diaspora, were deemed to be part of the African wastelands. They were labelled as primitive, backward, lazy, incompetent, barbaric, irreligious and unworthy members of the human race.

The stereotypes have defied correction for centuries. The facts of history do not support such labels and stereotypes. The history of Africa has suffered much from misinformation and misrepresentations. One important consequence of the treatment of the history of Africa has been that everyone associated with Africa has suffered from similar damnation. The African heritage has to be correctly stated, rationally assessed, properly understood and fairly disseminated. To achieve this, the history of Africa and its peoples should be given the same respect and understanding as the history of any other continent and its peoples. History should be seen as the story of organic progression through time and space. Things happened as they did for good reasons. The facts will always reveal the reasons.

One factor more than any other which has been responsible for the durability of the negative image of Africa was the factor of slavery. A people who were subjected to slavery for over 400 years and who were transported to the far ends of the globe in shackles and in humiliation became the subject of overt and covert derision. This derision outlived the legal era of slavery and was passed on to the contemporary scene where it has continued to thrive under different guises. One needs to look dispassionately, if this is possible, at the slave trade, at slavery itself, at what the slave culture produced and what all these features have meant for both the victims and the victors, the oppressed and the oppressors, the exploited and the exploiters. The relationship between these two groups was for the most part but not exclusively a relationship between Blacks and Whites. Because of its importance, a chapter has been devoted to the West African slave trade whose articles of commerce were the forbears of the Nova Scotian Blacks. Nor should the story of this trade stop outside the borders of the promised land. What happened within the borders of Canada is fundamental to a proper analysis and evaluation of race relations in Canada.

The first two chapters deal mainly with background material while the third chapter deals with events in Nova Scotia up to 1800. In a subsequent volume, the period after 1800 will be covered, thus bringing the story up to date. With the passage of time the experiences of the black loyalists, the black refugees, the black fugitives, the black communities, begin to unfold: the institutions they built as lifelines, the leaders they produced as pillars and beacons, the in-roads they made into the larger society which had been reluctant to receive them for so long. When the history is traced from beginning to end it would be possible to say that while many successes have been achieved, many challenges still lie ahead.

The lessons learned from the stirring and often times heartrending saga of the black experience in Nova Scotia over the centuries can contribute in some measure to a more informed understanding of the factors and circumstances that have shaped the society in which Nova Scotians of all persuasions and backgrounds live and work. When this happens, everybody will be the wiser for this knowledge, whether in the classroom or the playing field and the working place, or in the corridors of power. Canadian society can then be said to be truly acknowledging the dignity and worth of the human person regardless of the artificial barriers of colour, origins, language or creed.

THE AFRICAN HERITAGE

THE FALLACY OF THE NOTION OF A DARK CONTINENT

Africa is the ancestral home of Nova Scotia's black population. The distant ancestors of all the black people can be traced to Africa. Their descendants were removed from Africa at the beginning without their consent and transported to near and distant parts of the globe. This is the story of a forced migration which has become part of the story of the slave trade. Later, peoples of African origin emigrated from Africa and from other parts of the world by chance or by choice in search of adventure and opportunities for advancement. Not all persons of African descent who made their homes in different parts of the world, on all five continents, were descended from slavery. Indeed, many were free persons who served in the armies and navies, were both skilled and unskilled persons, who made a living as traders, scholars, missionaries, artisans, domestic labourers, farmers, professionals and public servants. Peoples from all continents, whether Europeans, Africans, Asians, Americans or Australians have moved from place to place throughout history as part of that fascinating human drama which may properly be labelled the international migration. This way the different colours and cultures became scattered throughout the globe, each contributing in some measure to development and change.

Africa's first contribution to human progress was in the very area of the development of the human species to the level of thinking beings or *homo sapiens*. On the basis of the evidence available, anthropologists are agreed that Africa was in all probability the home of the first human beings. Richard Leakey, the son of Dr. Louis S.B. Leakey and Dr. Mary Leakey (famous anthropologists from Britain who devoted more than half a century to research in East Africa) has given us an excellent account of the origins of all humankind in these fine words:

"Close to three million years ago on a campsite near the east shore of Kenya's spectacular Lake Turkana, formerly Lake Rudolf, a primitive human picked up a water-smoothed stone, and with a few skilful strikes transformed it into an implement. What was once an accident of nature was now a piece of deliberate technology, to be used to fashion a stick for digging up roots, or to slice the flesh of a dead animal. Soon discarded by its maker, the stone tool still exists, an unbreakable link with our ancestors; together with many others, that tool is preserved in the National Museums of Kenya in Nairobi. It is a heart-quickening thought that we share the same genetic heritage with the hands that shaped the tool that we can now hold in our hands and with the mind that decided to make the tool that our minds can now contemplate."[1]

To appreciate the heritage of Africa one needs to understand the size, the variety and the complexity of Africa. Further, one needs to understand that Africa has made important contributions internally and to the outside world. Finally, one needs to know something about the problems Africa has faced in its long history so as to appreciate the position of Africa in the modern world.

In 1985 the population of the continent of Africa was estimated to be about 400 million. The continent is made up of 50 countries. There are over 800 different languages in Africa. From extreme north to extreme south the continent is almost 8050 kilometers long (5000 miles) while the narrowest distance from east to west is about 3220 kilometers (2000 miles). Its land area comprises 30.30 million square kilometers, (11.7 million square miles) three-quarters of which lie within the tropics. The heaviest rainfall occurs in the equatorial region (average of 1524 mm-2032 mm or 60-80 inches annually) but reduces sharply as one moves away towards the north or south of the equator. Desert areas account for 40 per cent of the land area of Africa though only 8 per cent of the land mass can be said to be wasteland truly

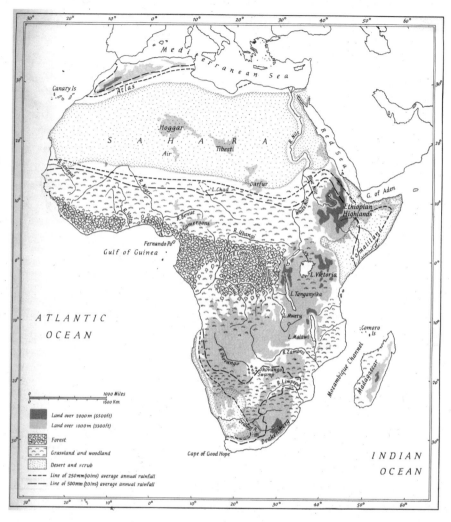

Map of Africa

devoid of any vegetation. It must be mentioned that the world's largest desert, the Sahara Desert, is in Africa. It has played an important part in creating the pattern of the African past and present. Some ten thousand years ago it was a fertile area which boasted of the finest vegetation produced in Africa. Its agricultural land mass was criss-crossed in all directions bringing human beings and beasts together, transmitting cultures and economic influences. By about 3000 B.C. the Sahara still supported a large stone-age agricultural population. Rock engravings still show evidence of the life-styles of

8

these people. Then the climate began to change and slowly but surely the region dried up and the desert grew. Some four to five thousand years ago it began to take its present form. A barrier was created across the heart of Africa dividing the north from the south. It slowed down the process of Africa's progress making trade, travel and contact within Africa and with the outside world more difficult.

Other natural factors, too, have impeded Africa's march towards progress. Water shortage has been a limiting factor in at least three quarters of Africa south of the Sahara Desert; poor soils in tropical Africa have hindered agriculture. Any civilization depends upon a surplus of food to enable division of labour to take place and make possible the accumulation of material wealth. The advancement of learning skills is then facilitated. Tropical soils are poorer than soils in temperate regions. Another limiting factor in Africa's human activity and progress is the existence of diseases such as sleeping sickness (which affects human beings and animals), malaria, yellow fever, pneumonia, plague, typhus, leprosy, worm parasites and diseases due to malnutrition (kwashiorkor). A final limiting factor is that of internal transport and communication by which Africa could be penetrated from all directions linking one part to another and the African continent with other continents. Africa has no gulfs and seas that extend deeply into the interior. No major river in Africa (Nile, Niger, Congo, Zambezi) is navigable except for a few kilometres. The rapids or cataracts impede navigation; the river mouths are blocked by sand bars or terminate in deltas which make it difficult for ships to enter. There are few good, natural harbours.

The above facts and figures about Africa are important because they help to explain the African past and why things happened as they did. They show that Africa is a complex continent of immense size—the second largest in the world. Africa is made up of many languages, many cultures, many races (Negroid, Pygmoid, Caucasoid, Bushmanoid and Mongoloid). It is the probable cradle of humankind and it was from Africa that human migration and dispersal began. The subsistence economy of Africa passed through the stages of hunting, gathering, fishing, pastoralism and agriculture. Africa has more distinct peoples and cultures than any other continent. As well, it had its own regions of early civilization, its kingdoms and its empires. When the Greeks and the Romans came to North Africa some three hundred years before the birth of Christ they took from Africa the learning, the skills, the labour and the resources which became the early foundations upon which western civilization was constructed. Indeed, to the Greeks and the Romans,

North Africa was known as "Libya." It was from here that they took gold, ivory, precious stones and slaves. They had heard of one other country south of the Sahara—"Ethiopia." By the first century A.D. traders from Greece, Arabia and India were actively trading along the east coast of Africa as far south as present Mozambique. From this time onwards written accounts began to appear in Greek, Arabic and Indian sources about the observations of these traders. There was little doubt that they found what they saw attractive. But what they saw was limited to the coastal areas. These foreign interests and activities in Africa were overrun in the fifteenth century by western interests spearheaded by the Portuguese, followed in quick succession by the Dutch, the British, and the French, and later by the Belgians, the Spaniards and the Italians. At first Africa was of interest and of service because it provided a staging ground for the voyages from Europe to the east. Later it provided its own natural products and human resources in the form of slaves. This exploitation was followed by the European partition of Africa into colonies set up in the interest of Europe. By the last decade of the nineteenth century Africa was dominated by Europe. This domination lasted a further seventy years on average.

In one form or another foreigners, mainly Europeans, interfered in the affairs of Africa for at least three centuries before the opening of the Christian era. It is true that they recorded what they saw and what they understood, which was naturally limited since they had little or no knowledge for many centuries of Africa's languages, Africa's cultures and Africa's geography. Europeans came to Africa in the later centuries to exploit Africa's human and natural resources. These resources, in the form of labour and raw materials, were needed to service the increasing demands of European factories and capital from the eighteenth to the twentieth centuries.

Before the last quarter of the nineteenth century (when the European partition of Africa took place) European interests in Africa were sporadic and limited to coastal contact. Africa happened to be of passing interest while Asia, Australia and America were of greater interest and value. Africa was the last continent which was opened up to the outside world by Europeans. For this reason it was labelled as the "Dark Continent" — dark because Europe knew so little about it and not because it was grossly backward or primitive. After all, Africa had much to show for what had happened in the continent: there was the great civilization of Egypt; the civilization of Islam; the great kingdoms of Kush and Axum; and the kingdoms and empires of Ghana, Mali, Songhai and Zimbabwe—to repeat the outstanding

landmarks in Africa's ancient history. Some writers and observers have persisted over the years in calling Africa a dark continent. Their persistence
does not mean that the continent deserved the label. Some writers once
labelled the Middle Ages in European history as the dark ages. The label
stuck. Some books still bear references to the dark ages. It is important to
ask from whose point of view and why the Middle Ages in Europe were
described as the dark ages. Similarly, it is important to ask why Africa was
labelled the dark continent by those who knew no better. The facts of
African history, societies, cultures and contributions refute the notion that
Africa, more than any other continent and judged by the same standards of
time, place, factors and circumstances, deserved the label of the dark continent. If this fallacy is laid to rest, Africa's notable contributions can now be
discussed.

THE EARLY CONTRIBUTIONS OF AFRICA

The civilization of Egypt which goes back to about six thousand years ago
was one of Africa's earliest and most famous achievements. The agricultural revolution in Egypt was among the first in the world. Wheat and barley
were grown. Goats, sheep, pigs and cattle were domesticated and reared.
Large villages developed in the valley of the Nile and religious and political
systems were introduced. The idea of priests and kings developed to hold
society together to respect heavenly and earthly authorities. The pyramids
were built to provide the last resting ground for the dead rulers or *pharaohs*.
The title of *Pharaoh* was introduced about 3500 B.C. (or about 5,500 years
ago) when the two states of Egypt were united under a single ruler. Pharaoh
Cheops built a pyramid near modern Cairo. This is the largest stone monument in the world. It was built mainly with slave labour about 3000 B.C. with
some two million three hundred thousand blocks of stone each weighing
about 2.3 tonnes (2 1/2 tons). Nothing of its kind so magnificent and so
huge was ever built since. The pyramids provide evidence of the advanced
stone technology of the Egyptians. In addition, Egyptian astronomers gave
to the world the solar calendar made up of 365 days in the year divided into
12 months of 30 days each, with 5 extra days each year. They needed a calendar to provide information on the annual floods of the Nile river which
made possible the irrigation of the dry lands and thus made possible the
production of food. The Egyptians were the first people to divide the day
into two parts of 12 units or hours each. They invented a water clock made

up of a stone bowl which was filled with water. The water filtered through an opening in the base of the bowl at a rate which was fixed. They also invented writing called *hieroglyphics* or picture writing. Writing material was produced from the papyrus plant. Finally, Egyptian doctors and chemists were highly skilled. Dead bodies were preserved by a process called mummification. When Egypt was conquered by the Greeks, the civilization described above was copied, improved and spread to other parts of the western and eastern world. The credit for this high level of civilization belongs to Africa since Egypt is in Africa. The majority of the people who migrated into Egypt when the Sahara began to dry up were Africans of Negroid origins. It was only later that immigrants from across the Mediterranean Ocean and the Red Sea settled in Egypt and lived together with the earlier inhabitants of Negroid origins.

The Egyptians not only influenced the Greeks, the Romans, and other Europeans but their southern neighbours, and the rest of Africa, as well. To the south of Egypt the kingdom of Kush emerged. It became famous for its iron goods and its iron technology. The use of iron became common in the Nile valley about 500 B.C. It spread southwards and westwards creating a revolution in agriculture, food production, trade, military conquests and migrations. To the south of Kush (whose capital was called Meröe) another famous kingdom emerged. It was named Axum and is today known as Ethiopia. The Ethiopians of later generations believed that the Queen of Sheba, who became the wife of King Solomon, was an Ethiopian and that their son became Emperor Menelik I. Axum became the first country in Africa to be converted to Christianity in the fourth century A.D. Further south, and a thousand years later, evidence appeared of a magnificent stone building with conical towers and a huge surrounding wall some thirty feet high. Known as Great Zimbabwe, this complex bore testimony to the skill of African builders whose rulers carved out a large empire and traded in gold with both the Portuguese and the Arabs.

Nor was the early greatness and achievements of Africans limited to the north, east and southern parts of the continent. Between the seventh and the sixteenth centuries important developments took place in what was called the Western Sudan. Here the famous African kingdom of Ghana was founded around 800 A.D. in the very year when Charlemagne was crowned emperor of the Holy Roman Empire. The King controlled a large army as well as valuable deposits of gold. Traders crossed the Sahara Desert to barter gold which was then exported mainly to Europe. Ghana was for a time the main supplier of gold to Europe. For almost three centuries the kingdom of Ghana flourished until it was conquered by Muslims who set up the kingdom of Mali. By then a number of cities had grown into prominence in the region, such as Timbuktu, Gao and Agades. They began as trading centres which attracted caravans carrying copper, salt, beads from Venice and swords from Damascus and elsewhere in Europe. These goods were exchanged for African slaves and African gold. In the midst of these developments, the civilization of Islam made its appearance and left its imprint: universities were set up in places like Timbuktu, itinerant scholars carried the message of the Holy Koran whose teachings regulated every aspect of life, culture and institutions. When the cities of the Western Sudan were thriving in trade and in religion much of Europe was engulfed in wars and destruction. Timbuktu produced doctors, artisans, priests, judges and administrators. Men of learning inspired the trade in books. These developments in Ghana were passed on to Mali and then to Songhai. In 1324 Mansa Musa, one of the greatest emperors of Mali, went on a pilgrimage to Mecca by way of Cairo. He was accompanied by an entourage of thousands. His display of wealth in Egypt where he made lavish gifts of gold drew attention to the greatness of Mali. Mali had a highly centralized political system in which the Sultan was held in high esteem. It was also very wealthy. We have evidence of this in a report produced by a famous Arab scholar and traveller, Ibn Battuta, who visited the capital of Mali in June, 1353:

"The Sultan's usual dress is velvety red tunic...he is preceded by his musicians, who carry gold and silver guitars, and behind him come three hundred armed slaves. He walks in a leisurely fashion, affecting a very slow movement, and even stoops from time to time. On reaching the dais he stops and looks round the assembly, then ascends it in the sedate manner of a preacher ascending a mosque pulpit. As he takes his seat the drums, trumpets, and bugles are sounded."[2]

From the western Sudan, civilization spread to West Africa. Kingdoms rose and fell; empires expanded and contracted. One notable civilization in West Africa deserves special mention: the civilization of Benin which produced the most magnificent art work in bronze. The arts and crafts of Benin became famous by the thirteenth century A.D. When Europeans came to West Africa in the fifteenth century they were fascinated by the artistic quality of Benin bronze.

By the end of the fifteenth century A.D., Africa was not any more backward than any other continent during the same period. Indeed, the facts of history show that much that was of value had taken place. If Africa had been allowed to build upon these early foundations the pattern of progress would have been maintained. Unfortunately for Africa, the slave trade intruded in the fifteenth century. When it was ended in the nineteenth century, colonialism intruded. When colonialism ended in the later years of the twentieth century, neo-colonialism replaced it with international capital, manipulated by multi-national corporations which began to strangle the economies of the independent African countries to ensure their dependence on the western world. For the purposes of this book, the colonial and post-colonial periods will not be discussed. The slave trade is, however, important and will be discussed in chapter two.

EARLY AFRICAN CULTURES: A SUMMARY

Culture is the way of life of a people and includes their behaviour, their actions, their material goods. The way of life includes language, religion, art, politics, trade and recreation. Culture is not acquired naturally or instinctively; it is learned from day to day by observation, by instruction and by practice. It is never static. It changes from period to period and from group to group. Considered in the light of this discussion and definition, African culture had its own attributes. However, much of European thought and actions had for long condemned Africa to backwardness and barbarism. In the European context, African culture was rejected as being inferior. It was only after World War II when the decolonization process began that serious attention was paid to Africa, its peoples and its cultures. Before that the western world portrayed Africa as the home of the naked savage. Missionaries deplored such institutions as religion, marriage and warfare as practiced by the Africans. They condemned such practices as initiation ceremonies, land holding, monopolies and communal behavior as primitive, un-Christian and anti-colonial. The European authorities held that these practices were opposed to European notions. The truth is that African societies were highly organized from the beginning of time: they had social, political, economic and religious systems which regulated their lives and gave purpose for human conduct from childhood to old age.

The facts of Africa's cultural past produce interesting information. Linguistically, Africa is one of the most complex areas in the world. Its 800 or so languages are divided into five language families of which the Niger–Congo family alone comprises several hundred languages, followed very closely by the Afro–Asiatic family. Of this latter family, the Hausa language of northern Nigeria is the best known, comprising the largest speech community in West Africa. Of the Niger–Congo family, the Bantu languages are spoken in one-third of Africa south of a line drawn across Africa from the Cameroons in the west to Mombasa in the east. Two examples of Bantu languages are Swahili in East Africa and Zulu in South Africa. The spread of Bantu languages is associated with the story of Bantu origins, migration and settlement in one-third of Africa.

The languages of Africa have been influenced as a result of contact with Arabs and Europeans. Though a few Arabic and European words have found their way into African languages as a result of borrowings, African languages have maintained their continuity. In the post-independence period of the last quarter of the twentieth century, African unity, African nationalism and African economic development all cry out for a greater measure of linguistic unity. In the meantime the diversity of languages continue as a constant reminder of the rich linguistic heritage of Africa.

In the cultural area of art, the oldest forms are found in the rock drawings and paintings of northern and southern Africa. The materials used in the paintings were ochre, red earth, charcoal and white clay. Ancient art in stone abound in West Africa as do terra cotta forms found in Ife and Jos in Nigeria and dated to before 2000 B.C. Iron art forms were produced everywhere in Africa as the use of iron replaced stone but they have not survived due to oxidization. Copper, silver and gold were also used as were copper and zinc (which produced brass) and copper and tin (which produced bronze). The bronze and brass ware of Yoruba, Benin and Nupe origins in Nigeria depicting figures and weapons were very popular in the west. Wood and ivory carvings were also very common.

The art forms described were produced mainly for religious purposes, either to emphasize the power of the deities or as part of the rites of ancestor worship. Masks were used in puberty rites or in ceremonies intended to enforce social and religious sanctions. In addition to masks, other art forms emphasized aesthetic and utility functions. Pottery and weaving are examples of these functions. Pottery produced water storage pots and cooking utensils while weaving produced exquisite decorations and designs which served to satisfy aesthetic needs. Materials were woven from simple raffia and dyed in various colours.

Much of the art forms in painting, weaving, carving, sculpture and building have undergone changes over the centuries. Cross-cultural influences as well as cultural adaptations have changed the patterns of the old forms. What remained constant in the history of African arts and culture was that a variety of forms, designs and colours graced the continent over the centuries and were used more in the service of societal customs and ceremonies than in support of art for art's sake.

In other forms of cultural expressions ranging from music to politics much can be written to explain the African way of life. Music, for example, played an important part in many aspects of culture. It appeared in praise songs, in the beating drums, in rituals associated with birth, initiation, marriage and death. In the field of labour, songs promoted co-operative effort; in the preservation and dissemination of history, songs were often used as the medium of narration of oral traditions. In politics order and organization were introduced to regulate the conduct of individuals, families, clans, communities, nations and empires. The political organizations in Africa ranged from acephalous states to centralized states; from military states to economic empires. Africa, too, has produced powerful rulers who, until recently, were ignored in history books, Names such as Usman dan Fodio, Bishop Crowther, Shaka, Lobengula, Mosheshwe, John Chilembwe, are now more common than before. They were as important in the history of their continent as other continental leaders like Elizabeth I, Charlemagne, Napoleon are to the history of their continent. African resistance to colonialism produced stirring episodes in African history, such as the *jihads* or holy wars of West Africa, the *Maji Maji* and *Mau Mau* movements of East Africa and the Ndebele and Shona risings, the Xhosa and Zulu wars of Southern Africa. When the more recent leaders appeared in the 1950s—men such as Abubakar Tafawa Balewa, Nnamdi Azikiwe, Albert Luthuli, Kamuzu Banda, Kenneth Kaunda, Julius Nyerere, Jomo Kenyatta, Kwame Nkrumah, Felix Houphouet-Boigny, Mohommed Ben Bella—they were the later generation of leaders from a long line in the history of Africa.

For over two million years the continent of Africa has produced revolutionary changes. Starting with the evolution of man to the level of *homo sapiens*, Africa produced revolutions in the use of stone and iron technology. The revolution in agriculture and food production led to the urban revolution which was responsible for the civilization of Egypt and the rise of states and kingdoms in the Western Sudan and elsewhere. Long-distance trade produced enterprising traders like the Arabs who straddled the trans-Saharan trade routes, the Hausa who infiltrated every part of West Africa and the Nyamwezi and the Yao whose caravans were common features of the East African economy. Trade goods were exchanged for European and oriental goods. The Greeks and the Romans who came to North Africa as conquerors centuries before the birth of Christ and extended their stay for scores of years after Christianity, interacted with Africans, borrowing from Africa as well as contributing to Africa. Africans were recruited in the Roman army and many rose to high ranks. Besides their interests and activities in Egypt, they became involved in the trading city of Carthage in North Africa, situated a few miles from the modern city of Tunis. It was to Carthage that the Phoenician ships first came to open up trade between Africa and Europe. One famous Carthaginian general, Hannibal, was an African who led a Carthaginian army into Europe. In his army were battle elephants taken from Africa. When Hannibal was defeated by the Romans in 146 B.C., the Romans seized Carthage and destroyed it.

Carthage was later re-built and later re-named Tunis. In the *Decline and Fall of the Roman Empire*, Edward Gibbons described what Carthage was like under Roman rule:

"Carthage contained the manufactures, the arms, and the treasures of the six provinces. A regular subordination of civil honours gradually ascended from the procurators of the streets and quarters of the city to the tribunal of the supreme magistrate, who, with the title of proconsul, represented the state and dignity of a consul of ancient Rome, Schools and gymnasia were instituted for the education of the African youth; and the liberal arts and manners, grammar, rhetoric, and philosophy were publicly taught: in the Greek and Latin languages. The buildings of Carthage were uniform and magnificent..."[3]

It was in Carthage, therefore, that an African branch of Roman civilization was developed in the same way as centuries before an African branch of Greek civilization was developed in Egypt.

Despite these developments, Africa was labelled for long as uncivilized. This was due to the cultural bigotry of the western world. The Europeans went beyond the biological definition of race to stigmatize Africans as inferior. Having exploited Africa in the slave trade since the fifteenth century,

Europeans perceived all Africans to be slaves: different skin colour, the texture of hair, the facial features were all associated with the status of slaves. In this way, the notion of "racial" superiority developed. European culture was deemed to be technologically superior; consequently, the European "race" was held to be culturally superior. The converse applied to Africa. When culture became equated with race, and the races became classified on the basis of skin colour, a rigid and immutable dividing line was created. This dividing line began to be questioned in the nineteenth century. A doctor by the name of Winterbottom who had worked for many years in Sierra Leone in West Africa questioned some of the old myths that suggested differences between Africans and Europeans. Examples of some of these notions will show how the racial dividing line was extended to include physical and mental attributes: that African women felt no pain in child birth; that African eye sights were better developed but in other respects their nervous systems were less sensitive than Europeans; that the brains and bones of Africans were of a different colour. A scientist by the name of James Pritchard questioned the basis for racial classification, arguing that no physical limit could be placed on the potential achievement of Africans. In spite of the shifts in the scientific position of race and culture in the nineteenth century, especially after the appearance in 1857 of Charles Darwin's book, the *Origin of Species*, European cultural prejudices remained. In the thick of the anti-slavery movement in Britain, humanitarians justified their actions by claiming that they had to do what they were doing because Africans were inferior and therefore incapable of helping themselves. The notion of the "white man's burden" gained ground. Even though more and more Europeans penetrated the interior of Africa in the nineteenth century and saw for themselves the standards of African culture and civilization, they remained tied to the existing prejudices. In their reports, they stressed the negative features of African life and denied that Africans had achieved anything. They went as far as to say that where notable achievements had been made in the past in Africa they were due to the efforts of fair-skinned persons. This marked the beginning of the "Hamitic hypothesis" which argued that any progress worth its name in Africa was attributable to foreigners. This position was echoed by prominent persons and soon gained ground to such an extent that generations were brought up to believe that it was true. The German philosopher, Friedrich Hegel told a conference in Europe in 1831 that Africans were a "people without a history." Ten years later, Thomas Arnold, Regius Professor of History at Oxford, said in his inaugural address that the force of world history had come from four creative races: the Greeks, the Romans, the Germans and the English. His successor a hundred years later, Professor Trevor-Roper, described the history of Africa as the "unrewarding gyrations of barbarous tribes in picturesque but irrelevant corners of the globe."

On February 10, 1961 Dr. Louis S.B. Leakey, world-renowned anthropologist who devoted a life time to scientific research in Africa, delivered a public lecture at the University of Oxford on the topic "The Progress of Man in Africa." A short excerpt from this lecture will show how a scholar like Leakey was trying in the 1960s to put the record straight:

"From what I have said, it is clear that I belong to the school of thought that does not blame racial factors for African stagnation, during the period which commenced about 5000 B.C. and which continued until a few hundred years ago. I lay the blame, rather, upon certain other factors; factors which were beyond human control....Africa led the world in matters of progress throughout the early years of man's development. Africa is again awakening and is destined, I feel sure, to play a major part once more in world progress. A better understanding of the problems is therefore vital."[4]

Students, teachers and concerned Canadians would do well to heed Dr. Leakey's call for a "better understanding of the problems." It is important to refer to the historical facts; to analyze the facts in the context of the factors and the circumstances of any given time. The history of Africa has passed through some two million years of human experience. It is not possible to understand this experience by referring to generalizations and stereotypes. Nor is it fair to this vast and complex continent to pass negative judgements on it and its peoples, as well as all those descended from it, without reference to objective facts and figures.

Leakey reminds us that up to about 5000 B.C. Africa experienced revolutionary changes in agriculture, in the invention and perfection of stone tools such as the hand axe and the spearhead. These appeared much later in Europe and Asia. Then Africa lost the lead that it had enjoyed for over half a million years. The decline had nothing to do with the dark-skinned races of Africa but to climatic and geographic factors which have already been discussed. Again, when Europeans arrived to introduce western civilization to the peoples of Africa, Dr. Leakey holds that Africa had already experienced centuries of "civilized" existence. By way of examples he mentions the areas of family planning, the imposition of the death penalty only on persistent murderers, rights given to African women,[5] widespread prohibition of drunkenness except in the cases of the very old, and social responsibilities in the care of orphans, widows, the destitute and the elderly. If civilization is equated to science and skyscrapers, then Africa was left behind for long. While the advancement of the western world in science stemmed from a long heritage of training, Africa was denied the opportunity of similar training since it was subjected, in addition to its climate and geographic handicaps, to some five hundred years of European exploitation and domination which are covered in part in the next chapter.

CHAPTER TWO

THE WEST AFRICAN SLAVE TRADE

Long before Europeans made their appearance along the coast of West Africa in the fifteenth century AD, slaves were already being removed by European, Arab, and Asiatic traders from North Africa and East Africa. Their main destinations were places in Arabia and Asia where they were made to serve as domestic servants, as concubines in harems, or as slave-soldiers. A few were destined for islands in the Mediterranean, the Aegean and the south Atlantic. The scale and severity of this traffic were of lesser proportion than the West African trade in slaves to the Americas which lasted for some four hundred years between about 1450 to about 1850. During this four hundred-year period three stages can be identified, each representing a greater escalation than the one before: in the first stage Africans were enslaved by pirates; in the second stage African slaves were obtained through war-like alliances entered into between European adventurers and African allies; the third, and most devastating stage, was built upon a more or less peaceful and lasting partnership between European slavers and African suppliers. This last phase lasted from about 1650 to 1850 and is the main concern of the first part of this chapter. It is commonly referred to as the Atlantic slave trade or the peak of the West African slave trade to the Americas.

The number of African slaves shipped to North America, South America and the Caribbean between c. 1450 to c. 1850 range from 11 million to 15 million gleaned from the works of such scholars as Fage, Curtin and Inikori. If the figures for North and East Africa are included, a further 8 to 10 million must be added. Taken together, then, a minimum of about 19 million and a maximum of about 25 million persons were forcibly removed from Africa and settled in the Middle East, Asia, Europe, North America, South America and the Caribbean. Today over 100 million persons of African descent live in these places, of whom an estimated number of 300,000 live in Canada. They have contributed in no small measure to the development of these regions. In spite of their contributions, they have suffered many disadvantages because of the stigma attached to their slave ancestry and slave experience. These disadvantages have been accentuated by the fact that the enslavement of persons from Africa was the last large-scale operation of its kind. Consequently, the image of the black man as a slave became a lasting one since it was the one that was most referred to. The fact that the West African slave trade lasted four hundred years did much to reinforce that image.

The stereotype gained ground that since Africans were taken in slavery for so long this was due to their own weaknesses and to weaknesses in Africa. It was a common feature in the past to blame Africa herself for this development. The argument was that slavery was endemic in African society; that Europeans simply participated in an ongoing activity; that the process provided benefits for Africa and that the overall operation was not as bad as it was made out to be in most studies. The facts do not support such analyses.

The first point that must be made is that slavery was not peculiar to Africa. The institution of slavery in one form or other has existed since time immemorial. While a dictionary would classify a slave as chattel that could be bought or sold like any other thing or moveable property, a slave as a human person is a complex being who is part and parcel of society. What is understood by the word "slave" differed from one society to another and from one country to another. In the Roman empire the slave of an important person could rise to a higher position than an ordinary freeman. In some African societies, too, a slave who rendered meritorious service could marry in his master's household and rise to the rank of a military commander. Indeed, in the history of the Niger delta in Nigeria a famous oil dealer, King Ja Ja of Opobo, was once a slave. In Islamic law a fellow believer could not be enslaved. In other circumstances, war captives were taken as slaves; destitute persons were also taken under protection as "slaves" or wards; debtors could be enslaved until their previous debts were cleared. These are but a few examples of what constituted "domestic slavery" in Africa. The word itself was used interchangeably to describe what is commonly understood in other situations as "serfs," "wards," "servants" and "captives." The fact that domestic slavery existed in Africa over the ages is not disputed. What is in dispute is the equation of domestic slavery with plantation slavery or commercial slavery. Worse still is the reasoning that justified the Atlantic slave trade on the grounds that it was founded on the pre-existing domestic slavery in Africa. Domestic slavery was a part of the social organization of African societies. As such it served a useful function. It did not depopulate Africa or weaken the social and economic fabric of African society. It provided for social mobility and for individual advancement if those who had temporarily lost their full freedom applied themselves to remove the deficiencies. There was no such thing as a pre-determined permanent condition.

It was Europe's demand for sugar that marked the beginning of the rise of sugar plantations worked by slave labour. In the thirteenth and fourteenth centuries the headquarters of the European sugar industry was the island of Cyprus. The labour force was a mixture of free European labourers, local serfs, war captives, slaves obtained from slave dealers and slave markets in the Mediterranean and Black Sea areas, and slaves from Africa shipped from North Africa. This last-named group was bought or captured mainly in West Africa and transported across the Sahara desert. By the early fourteenth century, slaves from West Africa began to appear in Europe in small numbers. When the Turks captured Constantinople in 1453, the Black Sea market was closed to Europe as a source for slaves, leaving North Africa as the main supplier.

Up until now the scale of operations was small: the sugar plantations of Cyprus, Crete, Sicily, Spain and Portugal were relatively small operations. However, during the fifteenth and sixteenth centuries a number of far-reaching changes took place with the result that the sugar industry was expanded and more labour was needed. West Africa was required to supply this labour on a scale previously unknown.

The first factor responsible for this change was the development in European maritime technology which made it possible for European ships to navigate near and distant places. The second factor was the introduction of new sugar plantations by the Portuguese in the south Atlantic islands of Madeira, Canary, and São Thomé, and worked by cheap slave labour obtained from the nearby coast of West Africa. By the mid-sixteenth century the south Atlantic islands still produced twice as much sugar as the newly-acquired areas of the New World (Hispaniola (Haiti), Puerto Rico, Jamaica and the coast of Mexico). The third factor was the emergence of Portuguese Brazil as the main centre for sugar production by about 1580. The composition of Brazil's estimated population of 57,000 ten years later gives some idea of the people engaged in the sugar industry: Europeans, 44%; Indians, 32%; Africans, 29%. Thus West African slaves were now a permanent part of the plantation economy of the New World. When cotton production in the southern part of the present United States became as lucrative as sugar, African slaves were commandeered to service both sugar and cotton plantations of the Americas. At the beginning of the nineteenth century (1800) there were approximately one million African slaves in each of the two countries of Brazil and the United States. However, about the time of the American Civil War the number had increased to about four million in the United States as compared with 1.5 million in Brazil.

The buying and shipping of slaves to the Americas soon developed into big business, contributing significantly to the expansion of international trade. Many countries made huge profits by responding to the attractions made possible by the slave trade. Western European countries dominated trade, finance, transportation and manufacturing. The middle and northern parts of North America dominated the production of foodstuffs to be sold on the slave plantations of the Caribbean islands as well as shipbuilding, lumber trade, fishing and, later, manufacturing. The West Indian islands produced plantation crops (coffee, cotton, indigo, sugar cane) as did the southern states of North America (specializing in tobacco and cotton) and South America (mainly Brazil specializing in sugar). The slave trade and the consequent superstructure put into place to cater for the burgeoning international trade based on the plantation economy of the Americas, created an economic revolution unheard of before. While many partners in the trade made huge profits, Africa alone suffered a tremendous setback for over 400 years, a setback from which it has yet to fully recover.

Some writers have gone so far as to say that Africa did not suffer as much as it has been made out; that there were positive aspects that did much to neutralize the detrimental effects. These arguments need to be considered. Firstly, the supporters of cost-benefit analyses hold that the calculations should be based on what the slave population removed from Africa would have produced in the subsistence sector had slaves remained behind, as opposed to the total value of the import goods received in Africa in exchange for the slaves. If the latter exceeded the former, the material welfare of Africans in Africa did not suffer from the trade in slaves. There are

many reasons why such an analysis cannot be measured either scientifical-
ly or morally. Another argument is that it was the slave trade that made possible the importation of food crops from the Americas to Africa (mainly man-
ioc, sweet potato, maize, groundnuts). This argument is untenable since the
crops were introduced by the Portuguese in the sixteenth century when the
Portuguese interest in slaves was less than their interest in gold, pepper and
such items. A third reasoning is that African slave dealers made huge profits. This argument is not borne out by any evidence relating to capital formation by which economies in Africa profited. There is no evidence that
profits made by slave dealers were of such a nature that they were ploughed
back into African development. Such a situation was certainly true after the
abolition of the slave trade when capital accrued as a result of profits from
the palm oil trade. A fourth factor concerns demographic considerations:
whether the population of Africa suffered from the slave trade. Here authorities are in disagreement over whether West Africa suffered from depopula-
tion. There is agreement that this did happen in the Congo–Angola region
but not in West Africa to the same degree. What this argument ignores is the
associated or consequent loss of numbers far in excess of the slaves actually shipped off—those who were victims of wars, raids, the long march to
the coast, incarceration in warehouses and dungeons. These and related
losses, some argue, could at least match the actual numbers transported
across the Atlantic. There is also the question of the reproduction capacity
of the slave population as a crucial factor affecting African demography.

Professor Joseph E. Inikori of Ahmadu Bello University, Zaria, Nigeria,
has made a close study of the population census relating to the external
West African slave trade. His conclusion is that, with all factors considered,
had the 19 million Africans not been exported they would have produced a
population of at least 99,420,000 by about 1870. Worse still, argues Inikori,
the long-term disadvantages resulting from the exportation of African slaves,
did irreparable harm to Africa to such an extent that the Africa of today has
not recovered from it. Professor Inikori's main argument is that the initial
loss to Africa of 19 million of its inhabitants deprived the continent of the
opportunity to build on these numbers. Had they remained behind, normal
increases in population over centuries would have contributed to more profitable utilization of land resources. The following quotation from Inikori is
important for greater understanding and for further discussion as the need
arises:

"The inescapable conclusion to be drawn......is that the extremely low ratio of population to cultivable land which prevailed in Africa south of the Sahara up to the present century was the direct repercussion of the external slave trade from Africa.

This underpopulation prevented for several centuries the growth of a virile market sector in the African economies by eliminating population pressure that would have led to internal colonization, taming the forests, and greater population concentration...... Because the ratio of population to land remained extremely low, population remained largely dispersed, the forests remained untamed, extensive, rather than intensive, cultivation was encouraged, and subsistence production and local self-sufficiency remained the rule. Because land was never a scarce resource no market for land developed and agriculture generally remained uncommercialized. The land-tenure system which became hardened under the conditions produced by the slave trade is one of those institutions inimical to the growth of capitalism which took root in Africa as a result of the external slave trade. In most of Africa, this system is often talked about as if it were something inherently African, without it being realized that the persistence of the system has its history in the slave trade, which prevented the growth of demand for land that would have made it a scarce, and, therefore marketable resource."[1]

Whatever argument is used to explain the extent of the devastation in West Africa caused by the Atlantic slave trade, it is recognized that the slave trade did result in the rise of powerful states and kingdoms. The rise of Oyo, Benin, Dahomey and Ashanti in present Nigeria, Benin and Ghana are the best examples of states and kingdoms in West Africa that matched the power of the earlier states and empires of the Western Sudan. The rulers of these territories became partners in the slave trade. They obtained their captives from distant places in the interior and sold them off to the European traders all along the West African coast. The fact that lucrative markets existed along the coast contributed to the intensity with which individual rulers waged their wars of conquest, expansion and domination. The seventeenth, eighteenth and nineteenth centuries were times of chaos, plunder, bloodshed, and misery in the entire region of West Africa affected by the slave trade. By mid-nineteenth century, the combined effect of the anti-slavery movement and the uneconomic nature of slave labour and the plantation system resulted in the decline of the slave markets. By the end of the nineteenth century the states and kingdoms of Oyo, Benin, Dahomey and Ashanti had collapsed or were on the verge of collapse. While it is true that their rise had been linked directly with the slave trade, their decline was, however, only partly due to the closure of the slave markets. By then the dynamics of internal politics, the competition from rivals, and the focus on new opportunities combined to overthrow the 400-year old organization geared to service the slave trade. Africa looked within to heal its wounds. The legacy left behind in Africa was one of hurt and hardship while the legacy of the slave trade implanted in the new world was the creation of a folk culture rooted in the institution of slavery.

SLAVERY AND THE RISE OF A FOLK CULTURE

It is a remarkable fact that millions of African slaves survived the miserable transportation experience from West Africa to the Americas and the Caribbean. This journey, commonly described as the Middle Passage, was so brutal in all its details that it remained a lasting scar in the memories of those who experienced it and also those who heard it in the traditions passed down from generation to generation. The famous abolitionist, William Wilberforce, once wrote that "never can so much misery be found condensed into so small a space as in a slave-ship during the Middle Passage."[2]

This experience, added to the life on the plantations, combined to create a society which of necessity turned out to be different from that of the original home as well as the host country. The fact that these marginal people retained aspects of their original culture and used these footholds to survive, overcome, and eventually challenge their limitations, is a tribute to their courage and resourcefulness. The patterns of culture that emerged took on various characteristics influenced by existing circumstances. In Jamaica, for example, the Akan culture of the Gold Coast dominated in the Creole speech on the island even though the number of slaves from the Gold Coast was far smaller than those from the Bights of Benin and Biafra, a little to the east of the Gold Coast. On the island of St. Dominique, the dominant culture was that from Dahomey even though the immigrant population was about equally divided between Dahomey and Angola. In the United States, on the other hand, it was difficult for any African culture to gain predominance because the increase in numbers was due more to natural increases than to continuous additions from Africa.

Slave owners took great pains to ensure that the slave links to Africa be severed as far as possible so that a loyal and docile labour force could be cultivated. To this end, new arrivals were placed in the hands of older slaves whose duty it was to break the spirit of the new arrivals and to arrange for the separation of the tribes and the teaching of the masters' language. The aim was to de-personalize the slaves and to create dependent personalities.

It is difficult to quantify the degree of success or failure of this policy since the experience varied from plantation to plantation, from country to country, from owner to owner and period to period. It is easier to state some generalizations from which conclusions may be drawn. The West Indies had more absentee landlords than the Americas, with the result that slaves were accorded greater responsibilities and were subjected to relatively less brutality. There was a difference in the reactions of Creole slaves born in the West Indies and slaves born in Africa. The latter were more inclined to meet violence with violence. In Jamaica alone, there were twelve slave revolts during the eighteenth century. Maroon colonies sprang up all over the island and maintained an independent existence until they were finally overcome in 1796. The Trelawny Maroons were expelled first to Nova Scotia and finally to Sierra Leone in 1800. Some maroons remained behind in Hispaniola (Haiti) as a separate entity up to 1790 when they joined hands with the mainstream of slave freedom fighters seeking independence from the French and later from the Spanish. They contributed in no small measure to the emergence of the independent republic of Haiti — the first black country to emerge from the shackles of slavery in the new world in 1804.

The maroons of Jamaica and Haiti were not the only rebels to set up independent settlements. Earlier escaped slaves from the plantations of Guiana set up settlements along the South American coast where they were free from the influences of western culture. Ten such settlements were set up in Brazil in the seventeenth and eighteenth centuries. One of them was Palmares which remained free until its conquest in 1694. Mention must be made of one of the earliest and most daring examples of an independent settlement. This was the classic case of slaves shipwrecked off the coast of the modern republic of Equador in 1570. They escaped, conquered the local Indians, intermarried, and set up an independent Afro-Indian community.

One conclusion that can be drawn from these activities is that African slaves and their descendants were far from broken in spirit in spite of the rigours of their captivity, removal, settlement and indoctrination. The creation of independent settlements during the height of slavery and the slave trade was a forerunner of their will to adapt to the new circumstances and to prepare to recover their freedom.

In the United States of America a mixed picture emerged: in the South they were portrayed generally as docile and loyal, epitomized by the classical figures of the Black Sambos, and their loyalty to their masters during the Civil War. Conversely, there are accounts of slave revolts and slave protests, the latter covering such ground as negligence, sabotage, use of secret language, theft, self-mutilation, poisoning food, attempting escape and singing veiled spirituals which camouflaged their real convictions and message. The verse of one such spiritual was:

"Go down Moses!
Way down in Egyptland!
And tell old Pharaoh.
To let my people go."

Their preoccupation with freedom was seen in the large numbers of runaways and uprisings. One account has listed six uprisings between 1663 and 1700, fifty during the eighteenth century and fifty-three between 1800 and 1853. Another report estimated that by 1855 no less than 55,000 slaves fled from the southern states to the north in search of freedom. Such figures can only be regarded as estimates and probably on the low side since not all cases were reported or publicized.

One revolt which was heavily publicized was the Nat Turner revolt of 1831. Nat Turner was a slave on a plantation in Virginia. On Sundays he acted as a priest-exhorter to fellow slaves, preaching his divine mission of freedom for slaves. On August 22, 1831 he led some sixty Blacks in rebellion against their masters, over 50 of whom were killed. Though the effort ended in failure and Nat Turner was himself killed in an act of retribution, the rising provided important lessons for both slave owners as well as slaves. The slave owners were reminded that time was running out for slavery as an institution. Slaves were reminded that difficult days still remained ahead of them.

Another experience which made a powerful contribution to the moulding of the slave folk culture was that of religion and the church. Clergymen saw nothing wrong with the institution of slavery. Indeed, many church ministers owned slaves. They deemed it unwise to allow slaves on plantations to receive the teachings of Christianity for fear that such teachings would

Captured Slaves
Slaves were considered to be extremely valuable to their owners. Escaped slaves were hunted, captured, and returned to their masters and the harsh world of slavery.

lead to opposition and rebellion. However, some owners allowed pastors to minister to slaves while others prohibited such practice, causing slaves to worship in secret. Those denominations, such as the Methodists and Baptists, which adopted a style of group participation instead of emphasizing rituals, earned the support of slaves. The fact that religious education and free worship were generally denied to slaves made them the more determined to imbibe the message of the scriptures. If they were to be denied freedom on earth, they were willing to sacrifice to prepare to enjoy the fruits of freedom in heaven.

Slaves were also denied formal secular education by legislative enactment. One Ordinance passed in the South stated that "any person that teaches a person of colour, slave or free, to read or write, or causes such a person to be taught, is subjected to a fine of thirty dollars, or to be imprisoned for ten days and whipped thirty-nine lashes." Fortunately, this prohibition was not uniformly carried out with the result that by the time of emancipation in 1863 one slave in fifty was said to be literate.

Some ex-slaves who, through remarkable efforts, acquired a sound education, have written accounts of the domestic life of slaves on the North American plantations. Outstanding among them were the distinguished Frederick Douglass and the Revd. Josiah Henson. From these accounts we read of the food they ate (mainly corn meal), the gardens they kept (in which European and African vegetables were grown), the clothes they wore (and the particular embellishments on the Sabbath day), the quarters they lived in (generally huts measuring some 4.8 metres (16 feet) by 4.4 metres (14 feet), the work they did (mainly cotton cultivation and domestic work in the South but also semi-specialized work such as lumbering, mining, road-making, blacksmithing, shoe-making, weaving and spinning).

Sexual relations between slave owners and their slave concubines, contributed to the emergence of a new breed of persons. By 1860 it was estimated that there were nearly half a million mulattos or persons of mixed descent in a total slave population of nearly four million — one out of eight had some European blood. As one approaches the present day it is estimated that almost one-third of the black population of the United States is derived from mixed parentage and only a small fraction, perhaps 25%, can be said to be of full-blooded African descent. The separation of families, the exploitation of women, the degradation and humility inflicted on males, have led to the emergence of a matrilineal pattern in the societal norms: mothers were the ones most remembered by slaves and their descendants. Frederick Douglass tells us that his mother was sold to a neighbouring plantation when he was just an infant; that he saw her only on a few occasions and that at night. She died when he was seven years old.

These, then, are the outstanding identifiable features of the folk culture that emerged in the Americas and the Caribbean as a result of the Atlantic slave trade. A hundred years after the end of the slave trade—and indeed up to the present in 1986—a recognizible Afro-American, Afro-Caribbean culture remains. The descendants of slaves brought out from Africa are distributed unevenly. They constitute the majority of the population in Haiti, Jamaica and Barbados; comprise some 37% in Brazil (Blacks and mulattos), 10% in the United States and about 1% in Canada. In all these countries, the heritage of slavery lives on. No country is as yet totally free of racial prejudice, to which has been added cultural and class prejudice. Persons of light skin and disposed to European culture are in a different category to persons of dark skin and African in culture. While in Jamaica, for example, it is argued that a three-caste society exists in relative harmony (white, coloured and black), in the United States the relations between Whites and Blacks are still fraught with difficulties in spite of the considerable advances registered in civil rights, education, employment and politics.

This section began with a consideration of the West African slave trade. It has looked at various sides of the issue. One side remains and is best expressed in the following excerpt with which the section closes:

> "Is there nothing on the credit side? Was the American 'peculiar institution' all undiluted evil? Did the Negro race in America gain anything from the centuries of slavery? Three things they gained but none of them, one hastens to emphasize, was sufficient to justify their sufferings: the Negroes made a civilization out of a wilderness: their offspring grew in health and stature, for the very harshness of their lives weeded out the weaklings, and today the American Negro is two or three inches taller than the average West African; and finally - though this was still hidden from them — they were helping to create a land in which these same descendants could hope to enjoy the blessings of freedom and wealth, each of a standard unknown in their native Africa."[3]

SLAVERY IN CANADA

As previously mentioned, slavery was a well-established institution in Europe at least as far back as the days of the Greek and Roman empires. Europeans as well as non-Europeans were taken into slavery during the many wars fought in Europe and outside. As already noted, when the first Europeans reached North Africa and, later, West Africa, slaves were acquired and shipped to Europe and the Americas and the Caribbean. It is no wonder, then, that when the French and the British obtained colonies in North America, slavery was practised here as it was in other parts of the world under their influence and control.

The French led the way in the creation of European settlements in what was to become Canada. In the French settlement of Acadia, Governor de Monts was said to have had a Black named Mathieu da Costa as a slave in 1608. It was reported that two years before this a Black had died of scurvy in the same settlement.

Blacks were not the first slaves in Canada. The first Portuguese explorers who touched the shores of the Atlantic maritime regions enslaved the

Amerindians who were unlucky enough to be captured. One such explorer enslaved fifty such men and women in 1501. The French who occupied the Acadia and Quebec settlements about a hundred years later followed this practice. Thus the practice of taking persons in slavery in parts of Canada goes back to as early as the sixteenth century.

The early records show that a black boy of about six years old was brought out to the French settlement of New France (later Quebec) in 1628 from Madagascar. He was given the name Oliver Le Jeune (acquired from a head clerk and a religious teacher). When he died in 1654 the burial register listed him as a domestic servant. Some time between 1628 and 1654 he had obtained his freedom.

To the French up to this point the presence of Blacks in Canada was more a matter of chance rather than design. This changed in 1689 when King Louis XIV of France granted official permission to the French in New France to import slaves into Canada to augment the much-needed labour resources. It was understood that in the process the French would be performing a useful service converting heathens to Christianity. The prospect of converting heathens to Christians was an attractive theory. In practice, however, there was little economic justification for importing slave labour into Canada: the fur trade did not lend itself to promotion through slave labour; there were no plantation industries in Canada and the weather was not supportive. The Company of the Hundred Associates (which ruled over the French settlements in Canada up till 1663) did little to import slaves. The French government in Paris which took over from 1663 and ruled until the French were defeated in Canada in 1760 followed suit. Slave labour did not appear to suit the development of French economic interests in Canada. However, when governments changed hands in 1760, the institution of slavery was accorded legal recognition and was incorporated in the treaty by which British rule replaced French rule. At this time there were about 4000 slaves, of which about a quarter were Blacks. Slaves made up about 2% of the total population which was about 60,000 in 1760. Mention has already been made why slavery did not gain an important foothold in Canada under French rule. The economic factor has already been mentioned. The climatic factor was commonly advanced but was also strongly disputed on the grounds that black slaves in the United States were able to withstand the cold climate. A third factor was the indifferent role of the Roman Catholic Church. While it did not campaign openly to abolish slavery, it did nothing to support it and felt that slavery was irrelevant. This position was in sharp contrast to the Protestant churches who saw nothing wrong with it and could even find justification for it in the scriptures. Finally, the number of black slaves in French Canada was a small fraction of the total number. The result was that the prejudice that later developed in British Canada against Blacks did not reach the same scale. After all, there were more Amerindian slaves than black slaves. An important side effect was that Blacks were treated much better than in other situations that were to develop later.

It was under British rule in Canada that slavery was confirmed, extended, condemned and ended. The episode went full circle. The confirmation was done without difficulty: the British were still slave dealers and slave owners; the famous court judgement of 1772 by Lord Mansfield setting slaves free on British soil had not yet been issued when British rule began in Canada in 1760 (and even when it was issued it had no legal effect in the colonies).

On the basis of this confirmation, then, slavery was legally recognized in British North America, including Nova Scotia. Slavery was extended by a British imperial law introduced in 1790 which encouraged British immigrants to come to British North America, the Bahamas and Bermuda with their slaves and other property.

As in Upper and Lower Canada (created as constitutional units in 1791), there were both free and slave Blacks in Nova Scotia from the beginning of European settlements. There are clear references to black slaves in Halifax since 1749 and before that in French Louisburg. In September, 1751, for example, the following advertisement appeared in the *Boston Evening Post*:

"Just arrived from Halifax and to be sold, ten strong, hearty Negro men, mostly tradesmen, such as caulkers, carpenters, sail makers and ropemakers. Any person wishing to purchase may enquire of Benjamin Hallowell of Boston."[4]

There were quite a number of similar advertisements in the eighteenth century announcing the sale of slaves by auction in Nova Scotia. At least one Black was reported to be in Saint John River area and he was most probably a slave. In 1768 there were some 2,217 black slaves in the British possessions in North America, Newfoundland, the Bahamas and Bermuda. Twenty-years later between three to four hundred black slaves were transported from Bermuda to work in the Newfoundland fisheries.

While it is clear that since the sixteenth century Amerindians and Blacks were kept as slaves in the European settlements in what was to be later known as Canada, and that the institution of slavery was practised by both the French and the British conquerors of Canada, the number of black slaves in Canada increased considerably between 1783 and 1784. With this increase other things happened. The use of slave labour was more strongly championed. Black slaves replaced Amerindian slaves (or panis as they were called). The black slaves who were brought in during these years were skilled in many ways. It was not easy to distinguish between free Blacks and slaves since both categories lived virtually side by side. There were more free persons than slaves yet in the racially-prejudiced climate of those and later years, all Blacks were stigmatised as slaves and discriminated against because of the stigma attached to slavery.

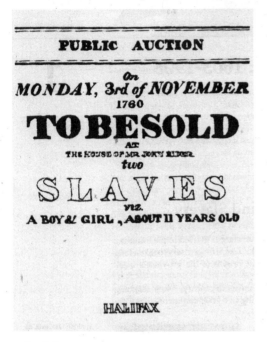

Sale of Slaves
Treated as property, black slaves were bought and sold at the will of traders and owners. Frequent advertisements for the sale of slaves appeared daily in newspapers and on posters in Nova Scotia and elsewhere in the Americas.

Between 1783-4, some 1232 black slaves were brought by British masters into Nova Scotia, New Brunswick and Prince Edward Island. Of this number, 26 went to Prince Edward Island and 441 went to New Brunswick. The number of slaves in Upper Canada during the Loyalist immigration was estimated to be about 500 while Lower Canada accounted for 304. Of a total of some 2000 slaves who entered Canada in 1783-4, more than half that number were distributed in the Atlantic provinces, with Nova Scotia receiving the largest consignment, Annapolis Royal leading with 230 and Digby second with 152. T. Watson Smith provided a break-down of the distribution of 1232 slaves in Nova Scotia, New Brunswick and Prince Edward Island. He accounts for 1194 of this number and makes no entry against Shelburne (Birchtown). If the difference is allotted to Shelburne the number will stand at 38, making "a total of twelve hundred and thirty-two persons, to nearly all of whom must have belonged the appellation of 'slave'."[5]

Canada, then, shared with the United States, South America and the Caribbean islands the invidious distinction of being a slave society. Slavery in Canada had all the traits associated with the de-humanizing treatment meted out to human beings in bondage. However, Canada in general lacked the economic base upon which slavery could flourish. In addition, in Canada there were those who supported slavery as well as those who opposed it. The result was that slavery as an institution received a mixed reception of greater proportion than in the United States.

As stated earlier, the British government passed a law in 1790 permitting prospective immigrants to bring in their slaves with other property. This provision was strongly opposed in the new British colony of Upper Canada created in 1791. Both Lieutenant-Governor Simcoe and Chief Justice Osgoode had scant respect for slavery. These two officials, supported by the solicitor-general, were responsible for the introduction of a bill in 1793 to "prevent the further introduction of slaves" and also to "limit the term of contracts for servitude within the province." While the bill guaranteed the rights of existing owners to their property, it provided that children born of mothers in bondage should have their birth registered and would be entitled to their freedom upon attaining the age of 25 years. Any children born to such persons at any time before the age of 25 were automatically deemed to be free citizens. The bill was passed into law but not without stiff opposition, thus once again confirming the pattern of Canadian ambivalence towards slavery and, later, towards racial discrimination. The end result was that slavery lived on in Upper Canada in its restricted form and elsewhere in British North America until all slaves were emancipated by an Act of the British Parliament as of August 1, 1834.

The story of slavery in Canada is replete with accounts and details which are now accepted as forming the hard core of this institution, viz., the harsh treatment of most of them; instances of runaways; public auctions; transfers of slaves and bequests of slaves in wills. There can be little said in appreciation of any humane features in an inhuman system. It is true that there was opposition to slavery by men like Osgoode and Simcoe in Upper Canada, by Chief Justice Andrew Strange and his successor Salter Blowers in Nova Scotia, by attorney Ward Chipman in New Brunswick, later to become Chief Justice of New Brunswick, but these gentlemen of revered memory were in the minority. It served little good for the plight of those persons who continued to remain in bondage when cases testing the legality of slavery came up every now and then in Nova Scotia and New Brunswick. Those who escaped this bondage by running away, however, profited from the attitude of the law courts. Slave owners found it extremely cumbersome to satisfy the courts that they were in legal possession of their slaves by providing original proof of purchase as well as the right of seller to clear ownership.

In sum, slavery began to decline in the opening decades of the nineteenth century because of the combination of factors which made slavery uneconomic in Canada, to which must be added the opposition of the law courts throughout British North America from the third quarter of the eighteenth century. When slaves were legally emancipated as of August 1, 1834, there were very few slaves in British North America who had not already obtained their legal freedom. On that date 781,000 slaves were set free in the British empire. A hundred million dollars were appropriated by the British government to compensate the slave owners. Not a single dollar was paid in Canada since no claims for compensation were submitted. The institution was no longer of consequence.

A number of conclusions bring this chapter to a close. Slavery existed in Canada from the early years of the seventeenth century. Black slaves were among the main body of slaves long before the white Loyalists from the United States immigrated with their human cargo in 1783-4 and other white immigrants were encouraged to do so after 1790. Slave labour contributed to the economic development of Canada since those slaves who were brought in were skilled in various occupations. White Canadian society was split on the merits and demerits of slavery and in the end a combination of economic realities, helped along by supportive decisions and attitudes of the judiciary, put an end to slavery. After 1834 Canada could pride itself that legally it was a free society rid of the institution of slavery. With this attitude, it opened its doors to runaway slaves from the United States in the wake of the Fugitive Slave Law of that country of 1850 and the "Dred Scott" decision of 1857 by which escaped slaves could be pursued and recaptured. Canada became the promised land to American slaves. Whether Canada could equally prove to be the promised land to its own Blacks of whatever ancestry remained to be seen.

CHAPTER THREE

ARRIVAL, SETTLEMENT, DEPARTURE

THE FIRST FREE BLACK SETTLERS OF NOVA SCOTIA

The story of black people from the time they left Africa to the time they reached Canada is a long and poignant one. In the first chapter we have read about their ancestral continent. In the second chapter we have an account of slavery in Africa and outside Africa, particularly in Canada, including Nova Scotia where slavery contributed to the creation of a slave society with its notions of superiority and inferiority, preferences and prejudices. These notions lived on for tens of decades after slavery was legally dismantled. There was no future for slaves for as long as they remained enslaved. Nova Scotia was at first the promised land for white immigrants from Europe and North America. It was later perceived by black immigrants, too, as their promised land.

In 1749, white immigrants arrived in Halifax in small numbers, adding to those who had preceded them as the founding settlers of the new British colony of Nova Scotia which had been taken over from the French in 1713. In 1749 each settler was promised fifty acres of land for himself and ten acres for every member of his family. They were provided with arms and ammunition, as well as material for farming, fishing and house-building. Soldiers received grants of land according to rank ranging from eighty acres to six hundred acres for the head of the family and proportionate allocations for members of the family. Artisans were given the same conditions as for

38

soldiers and sailors. In addition, settlers were to receive free rations for one year.

These terms clearly show that the government of the day realized that attractive and realistic conditions were necessary to attract and retain the pioneering settlers. Those who responded to these terms in England in 1749 "were largely the poor of London, a rabble of cockneys wholly unfit for a life in the American wilderness, attracted simply by the promise of free victuals. Among them were fifty or sixty former officers of the army and navy, unable to resist the generous offers of land."[1]

The same terms applied to Blacks. At least 15 Blacks were reported to have received rations in Halifax in 1750. They were among the newly arrived settlers of Nova Scotia who had come from the New England colonies or from military service to take advantage of the immigration opportunities opened up in 1749. Ten years later, the Nova Scotia government opened up new lands, confiscated from the exiled Acadians, to settlers from the New England colonies which were later to become part of the United States of America. Once again free Blacks arrived on the same terms to take up the offers. They were reported to have taken up residence in Halifax, Liverpool, Bridgetown, Annapolis, Onslow, Cornwallis, Falmouth and Amherst. In 1770 there were seven free Blacks in the town of Annapolis Royal. One of the black settlers of Liverpool around 1760 was a person by the name of Barbara Cuffy. She held a share in the township at a time when townships were being opened up through large land grants. In the period 1759-1765, 19 allotments of lands were issued, ranging from 40,485.8 hectares (100,000 acres) to 121,457.5 hectares (300,000 acres). A total of over 890,744.9 hectares (2,200,140 acres) of land was allotted for townships during this period. Individuals combined to form a kind of company which acquired the township allotment of 40,485.8 hectares (100,000 acres) or more. The township became a collective unit and the occupation and ownership of the land was based initially on the collective principle and only later were individual apportionments demarcated. In this way, Barbara Cuffy could be said to have been one of the founders, and shareholders, of the township of Liverpool.

According to the census of 1767, the population of Nova Scotia was 13,374 of whom 302 were English, 52 were Scottish, 853 were Irish, 264 were German and 104 were Blacks, made up of 55 males and 49 females. There were at least more Blacks than Scots in the Nova Scotia of 1767. Even

Pioneers with a mission
Robert Petley painted this scene of Blacks making their way along a road near Halifax during the early nineteenth century.

in French Cape Breton, which was later to become a Scottish stronghold, there were free black soldiers, labourers and masons before 1749.

This is sufficient basis to conclude that Blacks, together with the natives, the Acadians and the English, were among the first settlers in Nova Scotia; that they were among the founders of the first townships; that their presence and contribution must be dated to the pre-Loyalist period even though the number was small. After all, in the pre-Loyalist period, the numbers were small all round.

When the former French possession of Acadia became part of English Nova Scotia in 1713, British colonists from the neighbouring New England colonies entered Nova Scotia with their slaves. An estimated number of 500 free and slave Blacks in Nova Scotia in the pre-Loyalist period places the black population at between three and five per cent of the total population of some 10,000, a proportion which has remained fairly constant over the years.

The Black Loyalists: 1782-1792

The first black loyalists to come to Nova Scotia were members of the "Company of Negroes," a separate Black fighting unit in the American War of Independence, who were evacuated from Boston in 1776 together with the British soldiers. There is not much known about their numbers and what eventually became of them. For a time they were even considered to be used in exchange for prisoners taken by the Americans. They were the first to arrive while the war was still going on. The second group to arrive owed their fate to the time when Charleston and Savannah in the south fell to the American troops in the War of Independence in June, 1782, leaving some 4000 black loyalists waiting to be evacuated to a free land. There were other Blacks, too, with similar hopes but they were not free to seek their own salvation. These were the estimated 6000 slaves who would be ultimately evacuated with their white loyalist masters. For the moment, in June 1782, the black loyalists were given priority. The majority of them were taken from Charleston and Savannah to Jamaica, Trinidad, England or moved to New York. About 500 of the Charleston refugees, both white and black, including the famous Baptist preacher, David George, came to Halifax. It took twenty-two days to travel to Halifax as it took time to make the travel arrangements. They arrived in Halifax in December, 1782.

The immigration to Nova Scotia of these two pioneering groups of black loyalists from Boston, Charleston and Savannah, in 1776 and 1782 respectively took place before formal arrangements were made between the British Government and the United States Government by which the Loyalists, both white and black, were offered certain terms and conditions to settle in Nova Scotia. The war was still in progress and formal peace was only concluded in 1783.

Long before peace was concluded, Blacks were drawn into the conflict. When the American War of Independence broke out in 1775 there were about a half-million black slaves in America, including Nova Scotia. The British looked upon them as useful allies. The slave Blacks, too, saw in the British an opportunity for them to win their independence from slavery. They made up one-fifth of the population but in the southern state of Virginia the slaves made up two-fifths of the population. The British Governor of Virginia, Lord Dunmore, had barely 300 troops at his disposal to fight against the American rebels. It is understandable, then, why he issued a proclamation in November, 1775 that......"I do require every person capable of bearing arms to resort to His Majesty's standard......and I do hereby further declare all indented servants, Negroes, or others......free......".

Almost 2000 Blacks responded immediately to Dunmore's appeal. Dunmore's plan was to raise two regiments, one white and one black. The black regiment was named the Ethiopian Regiment. In one month about 300 Blacks were in uniforms on which were stitched the slogan "Liberty to Slaves." Among them were some who later came to Nova Scotia and moved on in 1792 to Sierra Leone. Following Dunmore's appeal, another overture was made in 1776, this time by the British Commander in New York, General Sir William Howe, after the American army began recruiting free Blacks. Three years later, in 1779, the American army, in desperation, took steps to recruit slaves. The British replied by way of a third appeal, this time by the commander of the British army in America, Sir Henry Clinton, offering freedom to any slave who crossed over to the British side. Thousands of Blacks, free and slaves, joined the British side, a small proportion as fighting men in the separate black regiments, while the majority were non-combatants. But between 1779 and 1782, the tide turned against the British. Many strongholds were captured by American troops and the British army, including their black allies, had to be evacuated. In May, 1782, for example, 5000 Blacks had to be evacuated from Savannah. The majority were sent to East Florida and Jamaica. David George was among the 5000. With his wife and three children he escaped to the nearest British stronghold of Charleston (where Boston King, another famous black loyalist who came later to Nova Scotia, had gone before him). Both David George and Boston King wrote accounts of their experiences during the war.

Another famous black personality who played an important part in the war was Thomas Peters, later to earn a reputation as one of the leaders of the black loyalists who came to Nova Scotia and New Brunswick, and afterwards left for Sierra Leone. Thomas Peters, at age 38, was a sergeant in a British brigade named the Black Pioneers which was formed in 1776. When the war ended 67 of the Black Pioneers, made up of 21 men, 28 women and 18 children, emigrated to Nova Scotia.

A number of arrangements had to be concluded before the black loyalists were formally sent to Nova Scotia. In November, 1782, a provisional peace agreement was entered into between Britain and the United States. Article vii stated that the British would withdraw their army but would not remove American Blacks from American soil. In April, 1783 the British began to implement the provisional agreement. On the position of Blacks and their right to leave the United States, the British interpretation was that those Blacks who had crossed over to the British side before November 30, 1782 in accordance with the promises made in the three proclamations were free to go and could not be considered to be American property. The first proclamation was issued by Lord Dunmore, British Governor of Virginia in 1775. The second proclamation was issued a year later by General Sir William Howe, British Commander in New York while the third proclamation was issued in 1779 by Sir Henry Clinton, Commander of the British Army in America. This interpretation was at first disputed by the Americans but finally agreed to in May, 1783. The British Commander-in-Chief, Sir Guy Carleton, kept a register of all the Blacks who were being sent away from American soil as free persons. This was Carleton's "Book of Negroes." It contained the personal details of the Blacks who were selected for emigration. This register listed 3000 individuals made up of 1336 men, 914 women and 750 children. Of this number 2775 were headed for Nova Scotia while 225 were bound for the West Indies, Quebec, England and Germany. The majority who were bound for Nova Scotia sailed during the months April–November, 1783. Their immediate destinations were Port Roseway (later named Shelburne), Annapolis Royal and Port Mouton. Of the 2775, 1423 were designated as army persons sailing as members of "Black Companies."

This contingent of 2775 black loyalists was the largest number of black settlers to be transported to Nova Scotia as a group in the 1780s. They traveled as free passengers in eighty-one vessels in a shuttle service between New York and the ports of Nova Scotia over a ten-month period. Most of them had originally been born in Africa and had been moved from there against their will to a foreign land. Now they were being transported as free persons to a new land where they could live out their lives as free persons.

These new members of Nova Scotia's indigenous black population were talented and skilled. Though two-thirds of them came from the South, and the remainder from the middle states of New York, New Jersey and Pennsylvania, there were few field hands and common labourers among them. From the information available in Carleton's register, many had specialized occupations and skills, including blacksmiths, coopers, tailors, carpenters and bakers. Some were cooks, orderlies, waiters. In addition and more importantly, they were determined not only to win their freedom but to keep it and to build upon it.

We have already noted that David George was not in this large group, having left a year earlier. Sergeant Thomas Peters was in it as was the blind and lame, thirty-six year old, Moses Wilkinson. Colonel Stephen Blucke, thirty-one years old, who was born free in Barbados, was accompanied by his wife, Margaret, and Isabel Gibbins, possibly a daughter. Peter French was the senior black loyalist. He was ninety-three years old, attached to the wagonmaster-general's department and described as "remarkably stout of his age."

The first large contingent of loyalists which left New York in April, 1783 comprised over 20,000 persons, whites, free Blacks and slaves. They sailed in a fleet of almost 300 ships led by two men-of-war. The fleet dropped anchor in Port Roseway on May 4, 1783. That was a historic day in the history of Nova Scotia. More arrived in the next few months. By December 31, 1783 the total loyalist immigrant population stood at 23,347. In the next few years, when the immigration was finally over, it was estimated that about 30,000 loyalists and troops arrived in Nova Scotia. Among them were about 3,500 black loyalists and 1232 black slaves belonging to white loyalists. Nova Scotia's population was dramatically increased from about 10,000-18,000 to about 40,000. Blacks comprised ten per cent of the new immigrant population. This was destined to be the highest proportion ever.

Nova Scotia was not prepared to receive this large influx of immigrants. Some background information on pre-loyalist Nova Scotia has already been given. Between 1749 and the time of the arrival of the loyalists, liberal land grants to settlers had resulted in half the available land area in the colony being allotted to the first colonists, mainly from the New England colonies. Some 5,555,520 hectares (13,722,134 acres) of land out of a total 10,526,316 hectares (26,000,000 acres) were available for the new arrivals, both loyalists and troops, white and black, while the government made efforts to re-acquire land previously alienated. At the time, Nova Scotia included the wilderness area to the west of the Bay of Fundy which, in 1784, was created as the separate, loyalist-dominated, province of New Brunswick.

In Nova Scotia a new governor, Lieutenant-Colonel John Parr, was sworn in at Halifax on October 9, 1782. Among his first instructions he was notified of the large number of evacuees who were expected to arrive in Nova Scotia shortly and advised that land should be reserved for them of the average size of 202.4-242.9 hectares (500-600 acres) per family. Nova Scotia was selected because it was located barely 966 kilometres (600 miles) from New York; it was a naval base; it was sparsely populated; three-quarters of its

44

population was already made up of New England colonists. It held out much promise as an ultra-royalist British colony offering refuge to thousands of ultra-royalist loyalists. The first number of evacuees whom Governor Parr received in December, 1782 in Halifax were the Charleston–Savannah loyalists led by General Patterson. This group included David George and his family.

Governor Parr was given definite instructions on how to distribute land to the 30,000 immigrants who arrived between 1782 and 1784: those who lost the greatest property in the United States were to be served first; they were to be compensated with extents of land which matched the property lost in the United States. Then came the military men whose grants were determined by their military rank, ranging from 40.5 hectares (100 acres) for a private to 404.9 hectares (1000 acres) for an officer. Their families were to get the same allowances as for ordinary loyalists. The ordinary loyalists were to receive grants of 40.5 hectares (100 acres) for the family head plus 20.2 hectares (50 acres) for every member (wife, son, daughter, slave). The procedure laid down was that the grantee had to apply (petition) for a specific land or simply state the maximum the petitioner was eligible for. Troops and civilians could apply as a group. The governor would then request the surveyor-general to arrange for the land requested to be surveyed. Once this was done the governor forwarded the report to the surveyor-general of the King's Woods (whose business it was to protect the timber stands for the Royal Navy). If there were no objections up to this point, the approval papers were sent to the Provincial Secretary who passed them on to the Attorney-General. The actual grant was then made out and signed by the governor. The grantee then took the oath of allegiance and the land granted was at last the property of the grantee.

The significance of these rules and regulations must not be dismissed. The leap overnight from a population of about 10,000-18,000 to one of about 40,000 caused havoc in the civil service while the resources were far too meagre. Funds were extremely limited and trained and paid land surveyors were too few. Employment was not easily available to provide alternatives to land grants. The waiting list was a long one and Blacks were placed at the end of it. Some lands were tied up by absentee landlords while other lands had to be re-acquired for distribution and this took time. The weather in December, 1782 for the Charleston, Savannah evacuees was too hostile for the new arrivals to settle down in winter; even in May, 1783 when the majority arrived in Port Roseway, the climate that confronted them was quite different from what they had been accustomed to mainly in the southern parts of the United States. The net result was that the procedures laid down caused much unrest, considerable delays and great hardships.

Between 1782 and 1784 some 3550 Blacks arrived in Nova Scotia. The records indicate that 3548 individuals were distributed as follows:

Birchtown (1784): 1521
Chedabucto (1785): 350
Preston (1780s): 300
Halifax (1780s): 400
Shelburne (1787): 200
Liverpool (1787): 50
Brindley Town (1784): 211
Little Tracadie (1787): 172
Little Tracadie (1788): 50
St. John (1784): 182
McNutt's Island (1787): 12
Annapolis (1780s): 100
Small centres (1780s): unknown

From the very beginning clouds began to gather over the promised land. The British government had agreed to the scheme to settle the loyalist patriots in Nova Scotia in acknowledgement of their loyalty and to provide free land as well as rations for three years. With land and rations the new settlers were expected to overcome their initial problems of resettlement. Once the lands were cleared, the first crops planted and the first harvest reaped, the settlers would become reasonably self-sufficient, thus reducing the financial obligations of the British government.

The reality turned out to be different: many black loyalists did not receive the free food provisions for even a year though they were promised these for three years. Thomas Peters and his Digby settlers received provisions for a few months while David George received his for six months only.

Housing was another serious problem. The loyalists were housed in the thick of winter in tents, bark shelters, public buildings, transport vessels, dilapidated church buildings and single apartments built with sods. It was a trying time for all the poor loyalists whether black or white but increasingly so for the Blacks who had to wait longer for their provisions, housing, employment and land.

Wage employment was easy to come by since the black loyalists were skilled in many forms of labour. In the largest black settlement of Birchtown, Blacks comprised thirty-eight occupational categories. They were offered little in return for their labour even if they could get a job. Wages were as low as $40.–$60. a year. Some received food only and no wages. They travelled long distances for poor returns. In his autobiography Boston King wrote: "Many of the poor people were compelled to sell their best gowns for five pounds of flour, in order to support life. When they were parted with all their clothes, even to their blankets, several of them fell down dead in the streets through hunger. Some killed and eat their dogs and cats; and poverty and distress prevailed on every side."

Poor whites blamed the poor blacks for devaluing wages by providing cheap labour. The poor Blacks blamed the government and the system for their deplorable plight. In this atmosphere of grinding poverty, deep hate and bitter distrust, racial riots erupted in Shelburne on July 26, 1784. Whites set upon the Blacks, driving them out of Shelburne and pursuing them into Birchtown where many of their homes were destroyed. The official version was that the riots were due to the surveyor's delay in laying out the plots of land for allocation. While it is true that grievances associated with the issue of land allocation must remain as one of the most important complaints of both whites and blacks, the racial riots were due to more than one single factor. Racial hostility certainly spilled over from the existing practice of slavery both in the United States and in Nova Scotia. In a depressed economic situation, competition led to racial hostility and violence. The Shelburne–Birchtown racial riots of 1784 were an ominous reminder of the looming dark clouds.

The majority of the black loyalists received no land at all. Only one person received 81 hectares (200 acres) of land. He was Colonel Stephen Blucke. Even in this case Blucke had to wait for four years to receive it in 1787. Between 1784 and 1789, only 167 grants of land were issued to Blacks and 327 warrants (or preparatory documents) were prepared. Thus, in the six-year period since arrival, only 494 Blacks had received—or were in the process of receiving—land grants. Of the 3,548 individuals identified as the black loyalists from 1782 to 1784 those who received any land at all were as follows:

Birchtown: 184 individuals received a total of 2,586.6 hectares (6382 acres)

Brindley Town: 76 individuals received a total of 30.8 hectares (76 acres)

Little Tracadie: 74 individuals received a total of 1,214.6 hectares (3000 acres)

Preston: 51 individuals received a total of 1,035.4 hectares (2557 1/2 acres)

This allocation to a small minority represented an average size of about 12.1 hectares (30 acres), a far cry from the promised allocation of 40.5 hectares (100 acres) per civilian family head and 20.2 hectares (50 acres) for each family member, and far less than anything that was deemed to be realistic in the land allotted to the first Nova Scotian settlers in the pre-loyalist period.

It was clear from the start that the black loyalist Nova Scotians were in for much trouble. The fact that all of them survived the first decade (1782-1792) and half of them became part of the permanent population of Nova Scotia is a tribute to their resilience and to their faith. Some features of these

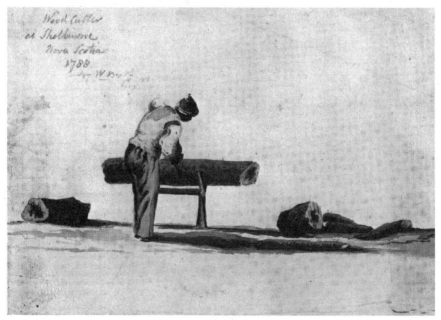

William Booth painted this extremely rare view of a black woodcutter at work in Shelburne, Nova Scotia, in 1788.

foundation years need to be reviewed. The first settlements and the first institutions deserve special mention.

The settlement of Birchtown (named after General Birch, the commanding officer in New York who signed the freedom papers of the black evacuees) was the largest Black settlement. It lay on the north-west arm of a heart-shaped bay in the Atlantic. On the north-east arm lay Shelburne (formerly Port Roseway). A short ferry ride or a 4.8 kilometre (three-mile) walk separated these two settlements. The free Blacks lived in Birchtown; the slave Blacks and black servants lived in the otherwise white-dominated town of Shelburne. The Shelburne–Birchtown area had the highest concentration of Blacks in the province in 1784, forming about 40 per cent of the population. The census of that year showed 38 occupation categories among the Birchtown residents but not a single storekeeper or baker. There were 31 farmers and 46 carpenters (the notable ones were Boston King and Cato Perkins). With some 1522 persons resident in 686 households, Birchtown was perhaps one of the few towns outside of Africa in 1784 with a black population of that size. One contemporary report on Birchtown shows how the outside world was informed about this town and its inhabitants. This was by an aide of Prince William Henry (later King William IV) visiting Nova Scotia in 1788. His description makes painful reading:

> "The place is beyond description wretched, situated on the coast in the middle of barren rocks, and partly surrounded by a thick impenetrable wood. Their huts miserable to guard against the inclemency of a Nova Scotia winter......I think I never saw such wretchedness and poverty......"[2]

Birchtown was not an isolated case. A contemporary observer arriving from England said the same things about the Blacks in Halifax in 1784. John Wentworth, Surveyor of the King's Woods in 1783, later to become governor of Nova Scotia, admitted that the black loyalists "had not as much attention as otherwise they might have had, and which was more necessary for them......"

The wretchedness was equally bad in another black settlement, Preston, not far from Halifax. Very few Blacks were included in the land grants of 1784. In 1786, 40 grants were issued and none was more than 20.2 hectares (50 acres) while no white person obtained any grant in Preston which was less than 40.5 hectares (100 acres). None of the grants made to the black residents in Preston was surveyed and divided into lots since the government stopped the pay of the surveyors. The whites made arrangements to pay for their own survey costs. Only two or three Blacks, were able to pay the fees. Many of them did not even know specifically where their lands were since all they had was a document authorizing a land grant of a certain size. It was up to the surveyor to locate the land and issue a certificate of occupancy. About 150 Blacks lived among some 600 whites in Preston but not all of them lived on the lands allotted to them since the process of survey had not been completed. Their status was that of squatters. They murmured and they complained but in their poverty-stricken state they could do no more.

One notable black loyalist was prepared to take his complaints to the highest authority. He was Thomas Peters who landed at Annapolis Royal with other Black Pioneers on May 25, 1784 after being driven by storms to Bermuda where they spent the winter months of 1783-4. Annapolis county then included Digby which had the largest black community in the county. In Digby there were 500 white families and 109 black families. Peters and his fellow sergeant, Murphy Steele, submitted a petition for land for the recently-arrived Blacks. Through the complicated procedure already described, Governor Parr instructed the surveyor to grant 12.1 hectares (30 acres) each to the three Black Pioneer sergeants (Peters, Steele and Abram Leslie) and one-acre town lots to the rest. When the surveyor finished his work he discovered that, except for the one acre town lots, the other lands had already been granted to the Church of England for purposes of building a school and a church. The Black Pioneer sergeants never obtained any land in Nova Scotia for all their devotion to the British cause. The other complaint by Peters and his followers was that their provisions of free flour and meat were held up by a white ex-army chaplain because they refused to provide free labour for road construction. This was a form of forced labour which was not stated in the terms and conditions previously drawn up.

In their first ten years in Nova Scotia most of the black settlers found life to be very trying. They were the worst hit by economic difficulties caused by delays and frustrations in their efforts to obtain land. When they did obtain land it was usually insufficient and unsuitable land. Since they could not make a living by farming, they had to sell their labour for poor wages. The result was that their means of livelihood were extremely limited, causing them to live in poor housing conditions. It was sometimes made out by their critics that they were not working as hard as they should, that as recently-liberated slaves they were still victims of a dependency syndrome. Many white officials attributed their difficulties to the hostile climate. Blacks themselves, however, hardly complained of the weather as their main concern or handicap. Their single most important grievance related to the failures and delays in getting land. Even when a few did obtain land, the size was far too small and the quality was much inferior to the lands granted to whites. The other complaints related to broken promises on such matters as free provisions and free survey fees and titles. The black loyalists had come willingly to Nova Scotia believing in the British sense of justice. Their experiences turned out to be quite different from their expectations.

In their difficult days what sustained them most of all was their deep sense of trust in a divine providence. In their pursuit for religious salvation and nourishment, they were equally disappointed in the behaviour and the attitude of their white compatriots. As in the economic domain, they soon found themselves discriminated against in the religious domain. The result was that they turned inwards to themselves and their communities for individual and collective upliftment.

When the black loyalists were arriving in Nova Scotia between 1782 and 1784, a religious awakening had already taken place through the work of Henry Alline, the Congregationalist preacher, who founded "New Lights" chapels everywhere in the province, offering believers free and full communion, without regard to conventional church procedures and organization. This movement was in conflict with the Church of England, the religion of the government establishment. The Methodist church was similarly under government suspicion. The conventional churches had regional strengths: the Anglican church was dominant in Halifax and in the areas settled by the white loyalists; the Presbyterians were dominant in the north and west of the province while the Roman Catholics were strongest in Sydney county. The Baptists were organized in the south-west.

The experience of the black loyalists soon brought them to the realization that the existing churches were only prepared to receive them as special members, with separate seating and service facilities. In Halifax, for example, a special gallery was reserved for Blacks in St. Paul's Church in 1784. Soon, even this was taken away and they were advised to meet in private black homes served by black instructors. In the Digby area, black Anglicans were admitted in a separate congregation in the black settlement in Brindley Town served by a black preacher named Joseph Leonard. The same situation existed in the Shelburne area where black Anglicans were served separately in their settlement at Birchtown under a fellow Black named Isaac Limerick. In Little Tracadie, the black preacher, Thomas

Brownspriggs was in charge of the black Anglican congregation. In other parts of the province, such as Preston, Windsor, Annapolis, Wilmot, Cornwallis, Granville, Blacks were considered part of the parish in which they resided. They were, however, not allowed to attend the services except under separate conditions in the homes of black members. In Preston, for example, separate services were held in the home of an literate black woman, Mrs. Catherine Abernathy who was also a school teacher.

The Anglican church, then, had the best resources in the province but it failed to use them at the opportune time to admit the newly-arrived black loyalists to its fold as equal co-believers. It is not surprising that many Blacks began to lean towards those church organizations which received them in a more friendly manner. Among these were two off-shoots of the Anglican church — the Countess of Huntingdon's Connection and the Methodists. The former was headed by a black person, the Rev. John Marrant. Marrant was born in the United States. He served with the British Navy during the American war and was discharged after being wounded. He entered the priesthood in London and was ordained under the auspices of the Countess of Huntingdon in 1785. He came to Birchtown at the invitation of his brother who was one of the black loyalists already settled in Birchtown. Accompanying Marrant as his assistant was another black loyalist resident of London, William Furmage. For the first time since the loyalist immigration, Blacks in Nova Scotia were to receive the religious services of fellow Blacks brought out especially to serve the church. Marrant's work at Birchtown turned out to be a great success. After ordaining two local preachers to carry on the work (Cato Perkins and William Ash) Marrant and Furmage went on a preaching tour using Henry Alline's New Light chapels whenever possible. In this way, the Huntingdons made good progress.

The Methodist church, supported by the Wesleyan Mission Society, also recorded noteworthy success, partially through the work of two white ministers in Shelburne district (Rev. William Black since 1783 and the Rev. Freeborn Garrettson) since 1787, but mainly through the efforts of Moses Wilkinson, the blind and lame black loyalist. Soon the Methodists could boast of having the largest single congregation in Birchtown. The other distinguished black Methodist preacher was Boston King whose work took him from Shelburne district to Digby, Halifax and Preston where he was placed in charge of the church. As the Methodists increased their activities they assumed a position similar to that taken by the Anglican church: the first contact was made by the white preachers; then black pastors were placed in charge of the black congregations; church worship was arranged in separate venues at different times. The only organization which had no room for this formula was the Roman Catholic Church whose age-old stricture demanded complete integration or nothing at all. Since the Catholic Church was not prepared to integrate Blacks in the congregation, it did not arrange for separate congregations.

Another organization which had no room for this formula was the black Baptist church whose work in the loyalist period (1782-1792) is associated with the name of David George, one of the founders of the first black church in America in 1773, The Silver Bluff Baptist Church in South Carolina. David George's arrival in Halifax in December, 1782 and in Shelburne in August, 1783 has already been noted. Here was a man who had been a Baptist preacher for at least ten years before coming to Nova Scotia. On arriving in Halifax, he found very few Blacks to whom he could minister. In Shelburne the situation was different. He had a large potential following of Blacks in the Shelburne district but he also had the potential distrust and hostility of many whites who were still slave owners and unaccustomed to being preached to by a black person. There was also the situation of unemployment, food shortage, pioneering problems of new settlers, to inflame racial sentiments. David George first organized camp meetings in the woods in Shelburne bordering between the white and black settlements, drawing attendance from both camps until the outbreak of the racial riots in Shelburne in 1784 caused him to be driven out. He took shelter in Birchtown for about six months, baptizing about twenty and preaching in private homes. He returned to Shelburne in December, 1784 only to find that his former meeting-house had been turned into a tavern. From Shelburne David George went on a preaching tour which took him to Liverpool, Saint John and Fredericton. He returned to Saint John after a journey which brought him from Shelburne to Halifax by water. On another trip he came to Preston where he baptized five persons and left an elder, Hector Peters, in charge.

David George ranks high in the annals of the Baptist church of Nova Scotia. He is credited with founding six churches (Shelburne, Birchtown, Ragged Islands, Saint John, Preston and Halifax). More than that, he has remained a rallying point for the black Baptists of Nova Scotia for his pioneering work, for his strenuous efforts to overcome many odds. His preaching in the woods, his experiences in Shelburne where his house was torn down, his chapel entered into while he was preaching and his being beaten in his own chapel by sticks and driven into a swamp, all these symbolize for Blacks the clouds that darkened their promised land.

Next to the church, educational institutions were another community prop. In the eighteenth-century world it was not unusual for most of the inhabitants to be illiterate. Blacks were no exception. Most of the early settlers could not read or write. The only commonly-known book was the Bible. Two societies, both related to the Church of England, took the lead in providing what little schooling there was for the children of black immigrants: one was the "Associates of the late Dr. Bray" and the other was the "Society for the Propagation of the Gospel" (S.P.G.). The first of these founded four schools (Brindley Town under Joseph Leonard; Halifax Orphan House under William Furmage; Birchtown under Colonel Blucke and Preston under Catherine Abernathy) and the second founded one school at Little Tracadie under Thomas Brownspriggs.

The children studied reading, spelling and sewing. Writing and arithmetic were passed over since they "were considered unnecessary accomplishments in children who would subsequently be required to perform the meanest tasks." The schools were not set up to provide for equality between the races.

In 1791, there were about 136 pupils in the Bray schools and about 25 in the S.P.G. school. Between three to four hundred black children received an elementary education between 1785 to 1791. These were the first pupils in the first black schools in Nova Scotia. Their teachers were black people and with one exception these teachers were all involved in the separate black congregations of the Anglican church. They were all segregated schools since they were founded in the five main black settlements of the province. The schools were founded on the principles of western civilization but their objective was not to create an integrated society but a parallel society. This pattern of a parallel or segregated society begun in the eighteenth century was consolidated in the nineteenth century.

BACK TO AFRICA

On January 15, 1792 fifteen ships left Halifax harbour carrying 1196 persons to Sierra Leone in West Africa. These emigrants were part of the 3550 black loyalists who had come to Nova Scotia (and later New Brunswick) in the period 1782-1784. By their departure, almost half the original black persons of Nova Scotia had returned to their ancestral continent. The loss of this half comprising preachers, teachers, soldiers, craftsmen and patriots was a severe loss. Their departure impoverished Nova Scotia and left behind a reminder of broken promises and a fragmented society for the remaining half to redeem in future years.

The background to their departure is traceable to the catalogue of broken promises over the years that spread a cloud of distrust over the promised land. When the first available opportunity came to leave, 1196 chose to go. This opportunity came as a result of the founding of the colony of Sierra Leone in 1787, five years before this departure. Sierra Leone was founded by a group of philanthropists as a home for free Blacks. Ever since the famous legal judgement handed down by Lord Chief Justice Mansfield in 1772, no person could be kept in slavery in England. Consequently, public-spirited people decided to pool their resources, obtain a grant of land, form a company and establish a free colony. The Sierra Leone Company was incorporated in 1791. What the company needed to make the settlement viable was more settlers. At the time when the company began to recruit for more settlers, Thomas Peters was in London reaching out for help from the British government for the promised land for himself and his followers in Nova Scotia and New Brunswick.

As already noted, Peters had petitioned for land, without success, on three occasions between 1784 and 1790. (Brindley Town, Fredericton, Saint John.) He organized his fourth and last petition on behalf of 100 black families in Saint John and 102 black families in Annapolis county. The 202 petitioners asked him to go to London to deliver it in person to the Secretary of State. The Secretary of State took action by requesting the governors of Nova Scotia and New Brunswick to investigate the grievances and instructing them to appoint agents to visit the black settlements and place before the black loyalists the option of free passages to Sierra Leone or an opportunity to serve in the army in the West Indies. The Sierra Leone Company sent its own commissioner, John Clarkson, to canvass for settlers. Peters acted in a similar role. Over a period of just over three months, the recruitment exercise succeeded in obtaining 1196 names.

The exercise was not easy. The white population opposed the emigration proposals. It realized that the province would lose useful citizens and that the economy would suffer. For selfish reasons they placed as many obstacles as they could in the way.

Thomas Peters was even physically assaulted in Digby for his role in recruiting emigrants. Rumours were circulated that the scheme was really aimed at re-enslaving the Blacks and that they would pay rents and taxes on their lands. Some Blacks could not produce their freedom papers while others were falsely certified to be in debt or to be serving indentures. Since only those who were able-bodied, certified to be free in status and unencumbered in any way, were eligible to emigrate, the obstacles were not easy to overcome. The white population which had for a decade ignored the grievances of the poor Blacks had at last woken up to the impending economic decline that would be triggered by this mass exodus. The realization came too late for a growing number of enlightened people had already begun to throw in their support for black emigration to Africa. One such person was a distinguished white West Indian Quaker, William Thornton, who was educated in London and Paris. In 1785 he inherited half a sugar plantation and immense wealth, some of which he devoted towards founding a colony to settle free Blacks in Africa. In 1787 he wrote prophetic words which summed up the aspirations of the deprived Blacks of America (among whom must be numbered the black loyalists of Nova Scotia):

"......the Blacks of America will seek an abode in some region of independence where their own laws alone are to be regarded......where all are upon an equality; and where a man that Nature clothed with a white skin, shall not, merely on that account, have the right of wielding a rod of iron."[3]

For the Nova Scotian Blacks this was a new experience. In the United States they were forced to go to the British camps for shelter, for protection and for the opportunity to emigrate to a land of freedom. Now the roles were reversed. Commissioner John Clarkson visited them in their homes appealing to them with kind words and explaining the approved terms so that they could be helped to consider emigrating to another land of freedom.

All the notable Nova Scotian leaders left with the single exception of Stephen Blucke. It must be said that their determination to leave was so strong that many who were in possession of land and other property were prepared to leave everything behind. David George was one such person. Joseph Leonard was another. He left behind a 40.5 hectares (100-acre) farm in Digby. Mrs. Catherine Abernathy left her school behind in Preston. This famous black loyalist settlement was deserted by all its settlers who chose to return to Africa. The entire black population of six towns or villages emigrated (approximately 600 from Shelburne and Birchtown; 200 from Preston and vicinity; 180 from Annapolis–Digby; 200 from New Brunswick). 72 per cent of the emigrants were in the valuable age group of thirty to fifty years. They would have had much yet to offer to Nova Scotia; instead Nova Scotia's loss became Sierra Leone's gain.

FORCED MIGRATION: THE MAROONS[4]

The third group of black immigrants to come to Nova Scotia in the eighteenth century were the Maroons. Some 550 of these immigrants arrived in Halifax in July, 1796. They came from Trelawny Town in St. James' Parish, Jamaica, and all of them were of African descent.

The Maroons earned their name (fugitive slaves taking to the woods) as well as their reputation from their age-old struggle in Jamaica against the slave system. Their ancestors had been taken as slaves in the period associated with the West African slave trade (c. 1450-c. 1850) and transported to the Caribbean. In Jamaica, runaway slaves took to the mountains in an heroic attempt to gain their freedom. From these mountainous hideouts, the Maroons waged a struggle against colonial oppression for 140 years. They finally gained their freedom in 1738 when formal peace treaties were signed between them and the government. It was not easy for a quasi-independent black community to live in peace side by side with an oppressed black community in a slave society under colonial domination. There were many Maroon communities on the island. The largest single group was the Trelawny Town Maroons. In 1795, war broke out once again between them and the colonial government. During six months of fighting they endured heavy losses and agreed to a cease-fire in December, 1795 in which three conditions were laid down: they would ask for pardon; they would agree to re-locate on land to be pointed out to them on the island; they would give up all runaways. It was understood by both parties that they were not to be sent off the island.

Once they laid down their arms on January 1, 1796 this understanding was breached on the grounds that they had not given up all runaways. The Jamaican government decided to deport them as quickly as possible, arguing that their presence on the island was not in the interest of peace and order. No final destination was worked out and they were loaded on to what really were prison ships and sent to Halifax. These deportees arrived in Nova Scotia when the Napoleonic wars were under way in Europe, on the high seas, and in the colonies — wherever British and French interests were represented. French ships had been sighted off the shores of Nova Scotia. The governor, John Wentworth, and the military commander, Prince Edward, were in need of sturdy manpower to build new fortifications and to renovate the old ones.

The arrival of the Maroons opened up two possibilities: they could be employed as labourers or as military men. They were capable of being both. In Jamaica, their experience as fugitives who had to be highly organized to win and keep their freedom, had led them to organize themselves on military lines, under designated leaders bearing military ranks. They kept themselves in superb physical condition through exercises obtained in hunting and marching exploits. Their last leader in Trelawny Town was Colonel Montague James who had become a Captain of the Trelawny Town Maroons as early as the 1770s. He also held the title of assistant superintendent in Trelawny Town. He was the recognized leader of the Maroons in Nova Scotia.

These facts on the Maroons are recalled since they had a considerable bearing on their Nova Scotia experience. The governor and the military commander were quite happy to release the Maroons from detention in the prison ships in return for their services in rebuilding the fortifications on Citadel Hill in Halifax, an assignment which lasted three months. Since the cost of maintaining the Maroons in Nova Scotia was being borne by the government of Jamaica, the province was benefiting handsomely at little cost to its own coffers.

It was not only the Nova Scotia government that was interested in the services of the Maroons. The white settlers and merchants were in dire need of labour, especially after the exodus of the 1196 black loyalists in 1792. For their part, the Maroons had newly arrived from a country where they had struggled long and hard to break from the shackles of oppression, had organized themselves on the lines of military units, and had worked hard at being an independent society. They were not prepared to compromise their group identity and pride by accepting servile positions. They were the first group of black immigrants to Nova Scotia who dictated their own terms. Those who received them and dealt with them respected their wishes. For the first time in the history of Blacks in Nova Scotia a black community was not being dictated to.

Since the Nova Scotia government was now interested in keeping the Maroons in the province, accommodation had to be arranged. In the initial

Leonard Parkinson: Maroon Captain
**Under the supervision of Commissary General
Quarrell, the Maroons arrived in Nova Scotia in
1796; however, due to the harsh conditions of the
land, the climate, and the treatment they
received, the Maroons left Nova Scotia for
Freetown (Sierra Leone) in 1800.**

months they were housed mainly in the centre of Halifax, close to their place of work. Now the surveyor selected Preston as the settlement for the majority. There were many good reasons for this choice: the lands previously granted to the black loyalists were available for re-allocation since all of them had left Preston for Africa in 1792; the surveyor (Theophilus Chamberlain) had land of his own which he was anxious to sell at a considerable profit since the price was being met by the Jamaican government; Governor Wentworth had his own farm in Preston; finally, Preston was close to Halifax and could be reached by boat.

The Maroons who had arrived in Halifax in July, 1796, moved to Preston in October of that year. The ensuing winter was hard for them compared to their accustomed climate of Jamaica though their presence and their needs generated much revenue for both the government and the merchants. While the Jamaican government provided for the upkeep of the Maroons it was the government of Nova Scotia as well as some individuals who profited from the situation. The provision of food, clothing, blankets and shelter, generated much revenue. While the government and certain individuals used the Maroons to promote their vested interests, the Maroons felt uncomfortable with the arrangements that were being made. They felt that their life-style was being changed and their group identity and cohesiveness were being destroyed through the introduction of Christian teachings, churches and schools. Brought up as members of a polygamous society they were now being introduced to the virtues of monogamy. Their previous adherence to traditional religion was now challenged by Christianity while their communal way of life was now being subverted in favour of individual advancement.

Between December, 1796 and June, 1798, 27 adults and 42 children were baptised. A school was started in the settlement of Preston and a new Christian Maroon settlement was established at Boydville (now Maroon Hill in Sackville), thus giving two Maroon settlements. The first was determined to retain Maroon culture. The older members were unhappy with their lot. They wanted to leave Nova Scotia as quickly as possible. They did not object when the younger members went to the new school designed to inculcate in them western standards and virtues. Indeed, a document uncovered shows a school boy named John Thorpe of the Maroon School, Preston, writing about the word of God on August 15, 1799:

"God gives us the greatest Encouragement to be good, by promising us more Happiness than we can express, or all the world can afford; and he also declares, that if we continue in Sin, and disobey him, he will punish us for ever and ever......".[5]

Christian teachings were beginning to make small inroads.

The Boydville community on the other hand took to farming on lands granted to them. They were more disposed to stay on permanently because of being tied to the land.

However, whatever the divisions within Maroon society, and whatever the attempts of the government to break up the cohesiveness of this society, the Maroons in general remained disgruntled and dissatisfied. As early as the first winter of 1796-7, some of them had informed the governor that they would not stay on permanently. The following year, in April, 1798, they informed the agent who had brought them to Nova Scotia that they wished to go elsewhere in the British empire. They made the point that "the Maroon cannot exist where the pineapple does not." Led by their traditional leaders and others like one of the Jamaican commissioners, the Maroons adopted a policy of non-co-operation, refusing to work on public projects and growing the barest minimum of food crops just to survive. The Jamaican government, which continued to foot the bill, had hoped that by then the Maroons would have become self-sufficient and the Jamaican government's subsidy could be stopped. In 1797, that government made its last payment of 6000 pounds. After that, the Maroons would be the responsibility of the Nova Scotia authorities. This point was not heeded by the Nova Scotia governor who continued to spend lavish amounts against the Jamaican vote of money to support the Maroons until he was reminded by London to desist or be held personally liable for the expenses incurred. At this point it was clear that the dilemma of the Maroons in Nova Scotia could not be resolved internally for as long as the Maroons maintained their posture of passive resistance.

Once again, as in the case of the black loyalists eight years before, the Sierra Leone Company stepped in by offering to take the Maroons. They had been afraid of the militancy of the Maroons at the beginning. Now the company was reassured by the British Government who were determined to relocate the Maroons as a body. The black loyalists in 1791-2 were given a choice; the Maroons in 1800 were given no choice. In August, 1800 almost every single Maroon was shipped off to Sierra Leone. Physically, biologically and culturally, the Maroon chapter closed for Nova Scotia in August, 1800. Politically and emotionally, the legacy of the Maroons re-surfaced in the 1970s and later when black power, black pride, black identity and black consciousness became key concerns in the changing circumstances of those years. For Nova Scotian Blacks to identify with the Maroons, to claim descent (however unlikely this certainly was) from the Maroons was to say that here were a people who had been treated with respect and dignity: They were an example worthy of emulation by succeeding generations of black Nova Scotians. Therein lies the significance of the Maroons in the history of black Nova Scotians.

Montague Road and Maroon Hall, situated not far from the Black Cultural Centre in Westphal, Halifax County, and the grounds on which stood Governor Wentworth's private estate in East Preston and Maroon Hill in Middle Sackville, are all contemporary reminders of the Maroon interlude in Nova Scotia. For the Maroons, Nova Scotia was never the promised land. With their departure, the nineteenth century was born, introducing a new era in Nova Scotian black history.

The story of Nova Scotia's Blacks traced in this publication ends with the departure of the Maroons in August, 1800. How many, if any, of the

Maroon Hall was built by the Nova Scotia government for the Jamaicans who were deported from their homeland due to their opposition towards the British Government on the island. They became known as Maroons and settled in Preston. The Dartmouth Memorial Gardens now occupies the site that housed Maroon Hall.

Maroons remained behind it is difficult to know. What is clear is that the British government wanted all of them to be removed so as to close that chapter which had not been successful either politically or economically. With their departure it is convenient to draw the curtains on the history of Blacks up to the end of the eighteenth century.

In the two-hundred year story of Blacks in Nova Scotia, falling between 1600 and 1800, important landmarks can be identified. In the seventeenth century, the first Blacks made their appearance. They were without exception slaves or bound in such strict servitude ("indenture," "servants") as to be virtually slaves. In the previous century, as members of European ships' crews, Blacks plied the ocean routes of the world, stepping ashore at ports of call. It is no wonder, then, that Mattheu da Costa was reported to have had some knowledge of the Micmac language when he was in the Acadian settlement in 1608. He, or others like him, must have met Micmacs before.

The story of the slave Blacks has been told in this study. When one reads this story it is not the fact of numbers or treatment or attitudes of employers, politicians or law courts, that matters in the end. It is the legacy which outlived the institution that is far more important. What respect can the hunter be expected to have for the hunted except to ensure that the roles are never reversed? Disadvantaged through the degradation suffered from having once been slaves, Blacks were expected to remain permanently disadvantaged. Europeans had once been slaves of other Europeans. There was nothing permanent about this situation.

But the unequal relationship between whites and blacks was forged on a permanent basis. The self-proclaimed superiority of the "Anglo-Saxon (British) race" had much to do with the consolidation of this relationship. In the mercantile period of European expansionism and adventurism abroad, which thrived in the seventeenth century onwards, notions of superior physical and mental attributes were widely held and equally widely practiced. Since one-quarter of the world was for centuries under British domination in particular (and European domination in general), these notions were given wide currency. What these notions conveyed were that there were specimens of higher (white) breeds and lesser (black) breeds, cultured (white) breeds and savage (black) breeds, beautiful (white) breeds and ugly (black) breeds. The British novelist John Buchan made the point clear in *Prester John* that the white hero was alive to the duties and responsibilities of his "race":

"He has to take all risks, reckoning nothing of his life or his fortune and well content to find his reward in the fulfillment of his task. That is the difference between white and black, the gift of responsibility, the power of being in a little way a king; and so long as we know this and practice it, we will rule not in Africa alone but wherever there are dark men who live only for the day and for their own bellies."

Others, like Rudyard Kipling, in *The White Man's Burden*, and Cecil John Rhodes in his "Confession of Faith" have made similar allusions. It is against this background that the story of Blacks in Nova Scotia in the period 1600-1800 must be read, understood and interpreted. Alongside the slaves who lived and toiled to build the province, which became more and more British in character from 1713 onwards, there were free Blacks, too, who came either by choice or in response to promises.

Those who came by choice during this period were very few. These were the pre-loyalist immigrants or settlers who happened to be in the service of the French or British warring factions in the period between 1713 and 1782 in the main, or free residents in the neighbouring New England colonies. Like other entrepreneurs of their age, they responded to the new frontiers that opened up fresh opportunities. Land was abundant and settlers were in great demand. The few hundred Blacks who made Nova Scotia their home were the first Black founders whose contribution cannot be ignored or minimized. Because of its size and impact, the loyalist immigration which followed completely overshadowed the pre-loyalist few.

The 3550 black loyalist immigrants who came to Nova Scotia (and in 1784, New Brunswick) did not really come by free choice. They were removed to a land which held out promise for freedom from slavery. They could have gone to the far ends of the earth in the quest for freedom from slavery. Nova Scotia was a conveniently-close British colony for British loyalists to be shipped from a recently British-ruled territory. The fact that free passages were provided, free provisions and free grants of land were promised, were normal and practical arrangements operative at the time in other parts of the British empire. What was uncommon about this immigration scheme of 1782-1784 was that both white and black immigrants were part of the subsidized colonization scheme (for such it was since Nova Scotia then and New Brunswick later and Prince Edward Island last of all, needed immigrants badly). In no other part of the British empire at that time or later were white and black British subjects sent out in comparable numbers.

This scheme ran into trouble from the very beginning largely because of the very fact that it was mixed and because there was no precedent to help out. The rules of the game clearly worked to the disadvantage of the Blacks. In their wretched circumstances (and with the ever-present fear of being re-enslaved) the black loyalists were in a hurry to get out from the United States. They could have had no premonition of the scale of impending injustices in a British colony that awaited them. After all, it was the British who, through their proclamations, had freed the loyalists from continued slavery in return for patriotism to the British flag. Blacks had been used as pawns in the American war to defeat the anti-British forces. For the British, the gamble didn't payoff. They were, therefore, saddled with, what was for them, "The Negro factor." Nearly two hundred years later the British would gamble again to preserve the integrity and power of a declining empire by granting citizenship to British colonial subjects. This time they would become saddled with "the Asian factor" as overseas Asians sought to redeem the promises of citizenship. The British, acting in desperation, introduced a citizenship law in 1968 which conferred on these British subjects of Asian descent second class citizenship.

The parallel was not far removed when the black loyalists attempted to redeem the promises under which they had been removed to Nova Scotia. The promises were not redeemed. They, too, became second class citizens. Church and State acted in unison against them. The ten-year history of the black loyalist interlude in Nova Scotia must certainly constitute one of the dark spots in the story of the province. A great opportunity presented itself for real commitment to the cause of the evangelical revival which had become a powerful lobby in British politics and society. The humanitarians were active; Lord Chief Justice Mansfield's famous judgement was still re-echoing its clear message of British morality; missionaries and explorers were setting out to discharge the "white-man's burden" in Africa. All this was happening in the closing years of the eighteenth century at the same time as David George, Moses Wilkinson, Thomas Peters, Boston King, Catherine Abernathy, to name a few, were in the vanguard of the black struggle for survival in Nova Scotia and for the redemption of the promises which took them to the promised land.

Ignored as members of a common society by Church and State and driven to exist as a segregated segment, half of the black loyalists left Nova Scotia for Sierra Leone in 1792. The white hierarchy in both Church and State had no room in the eighteenth century to redeem the promises inherent in *freedom*. Dr. James Walker, foremost Canadian historian of the Black Loyalists, describes this picture in vivid prose:

"The Baptists by intent, the Huntingdonians by coincidence, the Methodists and Anglicans by default, all created what were in effect independent black branches only loosely tied or, in the first instance, completely untied, to any white hierarchy."[6]

Those black loyalists who chose to remain in Nova Scotia and New Brunswick in 1792, never became much of a factor in their own right. All their leaders had left; all who were free of debt and free in status chose to leave. Those who remained were in the main the terribly disadvantaged who had yet to redeem themselves from real or inflicted debts or other disabilities. Their fortunes later merged with the black refugees of 1813-1816. That is a part of the story of the nineteenth century and is not included in this section.

Finally, the Maroons arrived four years later in 1796. They stayed on for just four years. They came as deportees; they left as deportees. They had no choice in coming to Nova Scotia; they had no choice in going to Sierra Leone. It was the British government which decided both destinations. The Maroons left a valuable legacy behind: while in Nova Scotia they did their utmost to remain untied, to preserve their culture, to foster their group identity and to nurture their pride. Towards the end their cohesiveness was temporarily fractured when the Maroon settlement of Preston was splintered by the creation of a smaller settlement in Boydville. That was a pointer to the future: to the difficulties inherent in maintaining group identity; to the problems and challenges present in adjusting to a new land and to new circumstances.

The story of Nova Scotia's Blacks from 1600 to 1800 means much for that informed understanding of the present that can only come from an equally informed understanding of the foundation years upon which the rest was built. The contribution of Blacks in the past must be measured in both tangible and intangible terms. In the first category, Blacks must rank among the foundation members of Nova Scotia; in the second, their many trials and few triumphs provided useful lessons for the future. If the nineteenth century, and most of the twentieth century, saw a confirmation of attitudes on the part of the majority leading to the setting up of segregated societies based on racial discrimination, the eighteenth century experiences of Nova Scotia's Blacks are an important pointer to the shape of things to come. For that reason alone the facts must be stated and understood. The contemporary scene can only be understood by reference to what preceded it.

SECTION B
THE PERIOD 1800-2006

THE PERIOD 1800–1853

NOVA SCOTIA IN 1800

By 1800 the major single event in North America, the American War of Independence, had officially ended seventeen years earlier. These seventeen years, however, had been crucial for Nova Scotia. Some forty to fifty thousand immigrants, of whom about ninety percent were white persons, arrived in what was then British North America. They brought with them their loyalty to the British flag and became part of the history of Canada as the Loyalists. Approximately two thousand settled in Quebec and seven thousand settled in Ontario and a few thousand settled in what became New Brunswick. The majority of them, numbering approximately thirty thousand, settled in Nova Scotia.

The society, as well as the economy, of Nova Scotia went through a trying period during these seventeen years. Competition for social mobility in a class-conscious society was deeply rooted in economic advancement: politics and privilege controlled the purse strings.

Among these immigrants were free black persons numbering some 3500 or roughly ten percent of the total. Like their white counterparts, the majority of them settled in Nova Scotia. But unlike their white counterparts, they had no share in politics or privilege. While the white population was divided in this competition of politics and privilege between the older immigrants or the pre-loyalists and the newer immigrants or the loyalists, the only discernible division in the ranks of the black population was between the one hundred or so black pre-loyalists who had been resident in Nova Scotia since the founding of Halifax in 1749 and the 3500 free blacks and some 1200 slave blacks of the loyalist era.

While Governor Sir John Wentworth who administered Nova Scotia from May, 1792 to April, 1808 favoured the white loyalists for senior positions in the bureaucracy and in politics, the only public position he took which had any bearing on the blacks occurred during the Maroon settlement. Wentworth first came to Nova Scotia in 1783 when the largest single stream of black loyalists arrived in Shelburne. He was then Surveyor General of the Kings Woods. It was Wentworth's duties to mark out small forest areas where white pine woods would be grown to supply the British navy ships with durable pine masts. Once such forest areas were created, his next responsibility was to demarcate crown lands for present and future allocation to settlers.

One of the assurances that was given to all loyalist immigrants while they were still in the British camps in the American colonies was that they would be given reasonable land grants to enable them to make a living under the British flag. This was not fulfilled in the case of most of the black loyalists, causing 1196 of them to leave Nova Scotia for Sierra Leone in January, 1792, three months before John Wentworth became Governor of Nova Scotia. His predecessor Governor John Parr had been appointed in 1782 to oversee the loyalist settlement in Nova Scotia. Parr had little interest in the mundane matters of settling in the new immigrants at a time when his attention and energies were directed by the American and French revolutions. In both these revolutions, the British and the French were on opposite sides. Nova Scotia was in the middle of this conflict and Governor Parr's meagre financial resources and inadequate administrative infrastructure made it very difficult for him to give equal attention to the problems and priorities of the new settlers. In fact, he chose to ignore them.

In this situation the Surveyor General of the Kings Woods, with an eye to his own future promotion, sided with the Governor to ignore the pressing and persistent demands of the loyalist immigrants for urgent assistance. The result was that all loyalists suffered severe hardships in crowded conditions with few opportunities to make hurried progress. None suffered more than those who stood at the end of the queue, friendless and voiceless. These were the 3500-odd black loyalists who waited long, and mostly in vain, to get a pittance of a land grant for about a third of their number. Even those who were successful received, on average, less than a third of the size of land grants given to white loyalists. The meagre land grants to black loyalists were located in barren and remote areas.

If farming opportunities for Blacks particularly were non-existent and jobs were few and scarce, there were better opportunities for those who could profit from politics and privilege. Merchants were becoming prosperous re-exporting British goods to American and Caribbean markets, when privateers became rich through plundering and capturing goods and vessels. White agriculturalists and dairy farmers in counties such as Annapolis and Cumberland made good progress while Pictou residents did well exporting cattle, sheep, horses and goods to Newfoundland. Street tax collectors, often poorly educated but always whites, earned a livelihood. The streets of Halifax were improved, a new market house was built and slowly but surely drains, slaughter houses, a poor house and hundreds of new houses were constructed. The Town Clock of Halifax was among the obvious landmarks in 1800, and the corner stones of St. George's Church, a new Masonic Hall and a new Government House were laid.

While all this was happening in the seventeen years following 1783, the major black settlements were in Birchtown, Brindley Town, Little Tracadie and Preston, where some 385 families received twelve thousand acres of land, were established. These residents lived in segregated communities served mainly by their own teachers and preachers drawn from among the Baptist, Methodist, Catholic and Anglican faiths, and with separate and private schools sponsored by philanthropic organizations such as the Associates of the Late Dr. Bray and the Society for the Propagation of the Gospel. The strength brought into Nova Scotia by determined and dedicated black artisans was considerably diluted by the departure to Sierra Leone in 1792 of a third of the community. This third included all the preachers and the teachers, all those who were not encumbered by debts and all were free citizens. Included among them were some 105 from Shelburne and Birchtown and about 75 from Preston who numbered among the few Blacks who had received their meagre land grants. The fact that over one thousand persons opted voluntarily to leave Nova Scotia after almost ten years of pioneering efforts to put down roots was a sad commentary on the lack of opportunities for the black loyalists.

While life in general for the majority of the fifty thousand or so who lived in Nova Scotia around 1800 was rough and hard, the economy was receiving a strong boost as a result of military needs and personnel. Other than the ruling oligarchy and the landed and commercial gentry, there were struggling

Acadians and Irish and Scottish Catholics for whom life in Nova Scotia in 1800 was hard too. But the Acadians had come back home after being displaced and dispossessed between 1755 and 1763 to salvage what remained, giving their labour to construct dykes and their skills in fishing to an administration which continued to exploit them. The administration had no choice but to accept them as a result of the Treaty of Paris of 1763 by which the Anglo-French war ended. Similarly, the administration frowned upon the Catholic Irish and Scots but learned to put up with their presence as religious toleration grew. In 1782, the very year in which the first black Baptist preacher, David George, arrived in Nova Scotia with the forerunners of the loyalist immigrants, Catholics in Nova Scotia were allowed to hold land for the first time. In short, whatever the historical handicaps faced by other immigrants, deliberate and durable discrimination was experienced by Blacks alone of all the immigrant groups which had settled in Nova Scotia by 1800.

Given this context, it would appear as a paradox at first glance that Governor John Wentworth made so much of a case and a fuss to keep the black Jamaican Maroons in Nova Scotia against their general will between 1796 and 1800. The Maroons were some 550 black immigrants who were brought to Halifax in July, 1796 pending the final arrangements for their settlement in a part of the British empire. Why Governor Wentworth favoured their permanent settlement in Nova Scotia, when the earlier black loyalists had received unfavourable attention and treatment, has become the subject of considerable historical debate. There are a number of possible explanations: as Surveyor General of the Kings Woods from 1783 to 1792 he had been unable to help the black loyalists or any of the thousands of other loyalists given the character of the administration and the magnitude of the problems of the day. Barely three months after he assumed office as Governor, the black exodus of 1196 immigrants to Sierra Leone had taken place. As governor, he had assured the remaining black residents of his interest and protection. Indeed, he had reason to take some satisfaction that during his governorship the practice of slavery in Nova Scotia came in for serious opposition from the judiciary. He had himself recruited a number of Blacks into the Royal Nova Scotia Regiment as infantry labourers and had approved the formation of a black company which was attached to the 1st Battalion of the Halifax militia. The arrival of the Maroons presented him with a further opportunity to use the talents and skills of fighting men who had distinguished themselves in their struggle in Jamaica. Here was an opportunity for Governor Wentworth to use their services for his own good as well as for the good of Nova Scotia. His Maroon policy throws interesting light on the Nova Scotia scene of 1800.

From the very outset the arrangements made for the Maroons were indecisive and tentative: the governor of Jamaica would have liked to send them to Port Royal Bay in Jamaica itself while their future was being worked out but Halifax was chosen because of the "great scarcity of provisions at Port Royal"; they were to be employed, if possible, "either as they wish, or in some way for the public benefit or at least in such a way as to avoid danger......"

Wentworth was more decisive: they would be employed voluntarily as labourers on the Citadel Hill fortifications at nine pence (roughly eight cents) per day and provided with provisions, clothing and lodging. He would try to make their life so comfortable that they would forget about going anywhere else. The Rev. Benjamin Gerrish Gray would minister to their spiritual needs and would teach their children. Though Wentworth was specifically instructed not to interfere in the affairs of the Maroons in Nova Scotia and to allow Colonel William Quarrell, seconded from his position as a member of the Jamaica Assembly, to be responsible for the Maroons as commissary general, he ignored these instructions and assumed control.

Governor John Wentworth's assumption of this control was rooted in both personal and political reasons. The dividing line was not always clear. The governor had obvious advantages since he had been in the province since 1783. He had a personal stake in properties and had already located in the Preston area, some eight kilometres from Dartmouth on the Eastern Shore. This location was strategically served by Cole Harbour. There was land available in this area previously occupied by the black loyalists and abandoned in 1792 when they left for Sierra Leone. Above all, the governor had no cause to bother about the financial costs since these would be met by the Jamaican Government.

So, with an eye to personal and political gain, Wentworth purchased three thousand acres (1,214 hectares) of land to settle the Maroons in the Preston area where, as noted, the governor had set up his own summer house and started his own farm in a section which represented the highest elevation. A sort of military outpost was set up on this high ground.[1] The ruins of this outpost still stand. Some five kilometres from Wentworth's summer house and farm, another summer house was built. This served as the residence of Quarrell and his deputy, Alexander Ochterlony. It was named Maroon Hall.[2]

Wentworth employed some fifty Maroons on his farm and in his house-hold. He also employed some Maroons in Government House in Halifax.

There was no question about Wentworth's high evaluation of the Maroons. He was upset when they petitioned to leave the country. He blamed this on agitators from outside their ranks, mainly a few large landowners who were envious of Wentworth's use of Maroon labour. They wanted a share in this exploitation.

Foremost among these landowners was William Cottnam Tonge but there were opponents to the governor's handling of Maroon affairs from within the ranks of the Maroons as well. Wentworth listed five names in a dispatch to London—two Jarretts, two Shaws and one Harding—and threatened to settle them individually in distant parts of the province to break their resist-ance to work and to accept government directives.

Whether one sees this threat to scatter the protesting Maroons as a strat-egy to divide and subjugate, Wentworth was already using it in his policy to settle a number of Maroon families in Boydville, at their request, in what is today Middle Sackville (Maroon Hill), so that those who were amenable to farming, acquiescence to Christianity and Western education, could be sep-arated from the other Maroons. In a letter to the Duke of Portland, Secretary of State for the Colonies, dated April 13, 1799, the governor of Nova Scotia described the situation in the following words:

> The Division of these People at Boydville are industriously pursuing their husbandry, with great cheerfulness and ingenuity and will soon be comfortably independent in their circumstance. Those at Preston are still deluded with false schemes of returning to Jamaica, where they may gratify their revenge. Wicked as these ideas are, they find some wicked enough to encourage them and to advise them not to work or plant, or to do anything toward their own support.[3]

By now a petition signed by the Maroons as well as their Nova Scotia supporters was already in London making it clear that the Maroons found it impossible to stay on in Nova Scotia. How much of their determination to leave was due entirely to their unwillingness to live in a cold climate "in which pineapples did not grow" and how much was due to Governor Wentworth's policy towards the Maroons (which also earned him hostility from among the white residents) it is not clear. What is abundantly clear is that Wentworth did not give in without a fight: he sent a private dispatch to an influential friend in the Colonial Office alleging that the petition was the work of a retired military officer, Captain Hale, who lived openly with a Maroon mistress.

Wentworth lost in the end. His last request that he be allowed to keep some of the Maroons in Nova Scotia was officially rejected. He was instructed to send them all to Sierra Leone. The British Government had reached the conclusion that Wentworth's reports to the British Government on the Maroons were unreliable.

Wentworth informed the Duke of Portland, the Secretary of State for Colonies, on August 6, 1800 that 551 Maroons were to leave on board the *Asia* the following day. Whether this number constituted all the Maroons and their offspring remains unclear to this day. In June, 1797 Wentworth had reported the Maroon population as 532; in September of the same year it was given as 542 and a month later it was 550. What intermarriages or offsprings could have come about as a result of the separate Boydville settlement, or the liaisons in the Preston area, or even the not improbable flight of adventure into the interior by individuals not quite without the tradition of adventure or daring—these were all matters for nineteenth century conjecture and reconstruction.

As far as governor John Wentworth was concerned, his Maroon policy was examined and found wanting. The British Government concluded that personal considerations had clouded his better judgement. One of these considerations, as Wentworth's biographer informs us, was that "he had one of the most beautiful Maroon women as his own mistress, and at least one child was born of the liaison."[4]

The relevance of this discussion on Governor Wentworth's Maroon policy in the context of the Nova Scotia scene of 1800 is to draw attention to the governor's championship of the Maroons as well as his championship of the Loyalists. As for the former, the verdict was a clear defeat. The issue of the racial climate cannot be ignored: the Maroons were free, skilled in fighting for survival, hardworking and reliable when they applied themselves to a cause in which they had personal stakes to uphold. But they were also Black, few in number, and strangers at the gate. Whatever championship they received, from the governor downwards, was not championship, it could be argued, for its own sake but one which was directed at promoting the vested interests of others. Where the other cause was concerned, namely, the championship of the Loyalists, the Wentworth era and its aftermath to 1830 produced enough of a success story to conclude that white loyalists, the majority of whom had few skills, little money and education, nonetheless found opportunities and props which propelled them upwards.

The fortunes of the over two thousand black loyalists who did not go to Sierra Leone in 1792 but who stayed on in Nova Scotia permanently will be traced in the other sections of this chapter and in the succeeding chapters.

BLACK LOYALISTS AND BLACK REFUGEES

The story of the Black Loyalists who made Nova Scotia their permanent home has become blurred with the passage of time. This was due to a number of factors: when the exodus to Sierra Leone took place in January, 1792, among the 1196 emigrants were most of the leaders of the time including individuals like Thomas Peters (present Annapolis County), David George, Moses Wilkinson, John Ball, Cato Perkins and Joseph Leonard (present Shelburne County), Boston King, Hector Peters and Adam and Catherine Abernathy (present Halifax County). These were the very people who provided hope and relief to the black immigrants through the church institutions of the Anglican, Methodist and Baptist denominations. With their departure both the pillars of church and school were uprooted.

Added to this was the preoccupation of the Nova Scotia administration with the internal politics of the struggle for power between pre-loyalist and loyalist white settlers waged against the background of the Anglo–French conflict in different parts of the globe. It was only when this conflict was finally resolved by international treaties in 1814-15 that attention could be paid to the plight of blacks in Nova Scotia. But before this could happen, another international conflict would intervene to affect the fortunes as well as the composition of Nova Scotia's Blacks. This latter development will introduce us to the history of the Black Refugees of Nova Scotia. Because of its impact, its numbers, its durability, this history of the Black Refugees would quickly overshadow the remaining Black Loyalists.

The Black Refugees came to Nova Scotia between 1813 and 1816 as a result of the War of 1812. This war was fought between the United States of America and Great Britain for a number of reasons which had nothing to do with the black people who resided at the time in the United States or in Canada. Many outstanding differences, mainly to do with trade, remained after the American Revolution or War of Independence. When Great Britain introduced the policy known as the continental blockade which prevented

American ships from trading with France and those parts of the European continent under French influence or control during the Napoleonic wars, Americans felt slighted once again. The relations between Britain and the United States after the formal peace treaty of 1783 were anything but harmonious. On the high seas the British navy displayed both strength and arrogance by assuming the right to search American ships for what was described as contraband trade. There was also a group within the congress of the United States known as the "War Hawks" who wanted war with Britain so that Canada could be captured. For which ever reason, the Americans declared war.

In the war of 1775-1783, American Blacks, both slaves and free persons, had been given promises of freedom, protection and resettlement in a British colony if they could cross over to the British side. In the War of 1812 a similar promise was two years late in coming because of a reluctance this time on the part of the British to incite rebellion among the slaves. In April, 1814, Vice-Admiral Alexander Cochrane issued a proclamation with similar promises. His naval forces sailed the American coastline off such states as Virginia, Maryland, North Carolina, Louisiana and Georgia, attracting fugitive slaves, many of whom were shipped to Bermuda, Trinidad and Nova Scotia. Known in the history of North America as the Black Refugees, they took their place in this history with the earlier pre-Loyalist free black settlers, the Black Loyalists, the slaves and the Maroons, and the later underground railroad fugitives of Upper Canada[4a] and the nineteenth century enterprising black immigrants to Canada, to constitute the full body of black nation builders in Nova Scotia and other parts of Canada. The Nova Scotian blacks, however, because of dates and numbers, led the way and set the pace.

Before the majority of the Black Loyalists were sent to Nova Scotia in an earlier period, Governor John Parr, who held the military rank of Lieutenant-Colonel, had been forewarned and given specific instructions to prepare for the imminent arrivals. In the case of the Black Refugees, Governor Sir John Coape Sherbrooke was neither forewarned nor prepared. As early as September, 1813 an advance party of 133 Black Refugees arrived in Halifax. The largest count in this stream of immigrants over a three-year period numbered some nine hundred in 1815. In all, some two thousand Black Refugees arrived in Nova Scotia, the majority of whom disembarked in Halifax while a few hundred disembarked in Annapolis Royal. Some four hundred were sent to New Brunswick.

Peace was signed on Christmas Eve, 1814. By then some 1200 Black Refugees had already arrived in Nova Scotia. With the end of the war the challenge for the British was to settle the many Blacks who had come over to the British side and had not been settled in any British colony. The black soldiers who rendered military service in the Colonial Marines were sent to Bermuda to do civilian duties while some of their numbers were sent from Bermuda to Trinidad. Meanwhile, the laws in Bermuda did not permit free Blacks to settle there permanently and arrangements were begun in March, 1815 to send additional numbers to Nova Scotia.

Before we pick up the story of the additional numbers earmarked for Nova Scotia in March, 1815, it would be interesting to look briefly at the 1200 who had come before the end of the war.

The first consignment of Black Refugees arrived in Halifax in several vessels in mid-September, 1813. On October 2, 133 set foot in Halifax as the pioneer refugee settlers. Of this number, 77 were men, 29 were women and 27 were children. The men were listed as labourers, farmers, and tradesmen, including shoemakers, sawyers and wheelwrights.

The following year a few hundred more arrived in Nova Scotia where the war-time economy was good and employment was readily available. White skilled tradesmen were entrenched in year-round jobs in Halifax and in the other urban areas, while black unskilled tradesmen were encouraged to go out to the rural areas where labourers could earn five shillings and upwards a day.

The new black refugee immigrants were not the only Blacks in Nova Scotia at the time since over two thousand older black settlers who had come to the province bearing the label of Black Loyalists were already settled for some three decades, eking out a living as seasonal unskilled labourers, share-croppers, farm labourers and market gardeners, domestic labourers and ship hands. Naturally, most of the competition was evident in the capital town of Halifax which had a population of 11,156 in 1818. Of this number, 745 were Blacks, 391 men and 324 women, comprising some 6% of the population.

In the first year of their stay these pioneering refugees survived on their own initiatives and labour. The government had no plans to offer assistance. There was the danger looming, as Governor Sherbrooke recognized, that with increased numbers in future, the onset of harsh winters and the decline in jobs, a crisis situation could develop quickly. In anticipation of such a possibility, the governor sought guidance from the Colonial Office.

A year later, the forebodings of Governor Sherbrooke were realized. A crisis had in fact developed. The number of destitute Blacks increased and the Commissioners of the Poor in Halifax informed the governor that they were in extreme distress and unable to fend for themselves. What had led up to this situation had been anticipated outside Nova Scotia but corrective measures were not promptly or effectively taken. Vice-Admiral Cochrane, who operated out of Bermuda, knew that the Blacks from the southern states wanted assurances that their lives would be better off if they defected from their slave masters and came over to the British side. Thus, in April, 1814, while the war between Britain and the United States was still at its peak, Cochrane issued these assurances in the form of a proclamation that the defecting Blacks would be given food, clothing, shelter and would be settled in British colonies. Months later, in October, 1814 when the crisis situation developed in Nova Scotia, Cochrane admitted to Sherbrooke that it was the proclamation that had induced the Blacks to come over and that it was the duty of the British to honour the assurances given.

While Bermuda and Britain were aware of the promises made, Nova Scotia was not. Sherbrooke learned of them only after he had taken the first step which included the preparation of a list every Wednesday morning of those who were to receive food rations for the succeeding week. The men were, to receive the same rations as were issued to the wives and children of white soldiers in similar distress every Thursday at the Government Stores. Only the aged and the infirm were admitted to the Poor House, subject to space being available. Those who were able to work were encouraged to take up employment which was generally available throughout the province during the war years.

But these were temporary measures which were reluctantly taken. The governor was concerned about funds since official sanction had not been received from London and he was obviously prudent when he reported his initiatives to Lord Bathurst, Secretary of State for the Colonies, on October 5, 1814 in the following words:

"I have to state to Your Lordship that though such of them as are industrious can very well maintain themselves as a common labourer here can at this season earn a dollar and a half per day yet the generality of them are so unwilling to work that several of them are absolutely starving owing to their own idleness."[5]

The official correspondence and reports cannot be expected to give the complete picture. What we have here is a situation in which some 1200 black refugee immigrants were consigned to Nova Scotia between 1813 and 1815 without any prior official arrangements having been made to receive and settle them in a systematic way. At the end of this period, the results of this omission became apparent over several winters. Some measures had to be taken, however tentatively, to provide some relief. In this situation, with two authorities to placate, Sherbrooke took steps to assure Vice-Admiral Cochrane that everything possible was being done, while at the same time informing Lord Bathurst that there was adequate employment to be had but that a number of the black immigrants preferred idleness to industry, and that money and clothing were needed to carry the burden from this end.

From other sources another picture emerges: the majority of the 1200 Black Refugees who arrived between 1813 and 1815 took up residence in Halifax and Dartmouth. This number included those who had already arrived in Nova Scotia or who were en route to Nova Scotia before the sign-ing of the Peace Treaty of Ghent on 24 December, 1814. Those who arrived after this date make up a different category and will be treated separately.

Of the first category of Black Refugees, 705 were reported to have taken up residence in the vicinity of Halifax–Dartmouth, 336 in Halifax, 150 in Preston, 72 on the Windsor road, 49 in South East Passage and Cow Bay and 49 at Porter's Lake on the estate of Rufus Fairbanks.

One of the members of the majority ruling community who took an inter-est in the black immigrants was a Quaker who lived in the Nantucket area of Dartmouth, one Seth Coleman who came to the province to engage in the whale fishing industry. According to Coleman, the black immigrants found it hard to get gainful employment; that in their penury some resorted to stealing as in a case involving two black refugees at Cole Harbour driv-en to this act by desperation rather than by habit. Coleman explained that the unfavourable criticism levelled by whites against blacks was due main-ly to the image that presented the blacks as beggars. He also informed the authorities of the outbreak of smallpox among them in October, 1814. A people who were poorly fed, poorly housed, poorly clothed and who were severely unemployed, were prime victims of epidemics like smallpox.

Acting on the advice of a physician, Dr. William Bruce Almon, whose findings upheld Coleman's observations, the government commissioned Coleman himself to carry out the task of vaccinating the Blacks. The govern-ment requested that the exercise be carried out in a central locality in

Dartmouth where the people from Preston could attend. Given his knowledge of the black community and aided by his own religious background, Coleman chose to go to the Preston area himself on Sundays when members of the community from as far as Halifax congregated for worship and to exchange visits. In a four-month period from October, 1814 to February, 1815, Coleman had the satisfaction of vaccinating 423 persons of whom 285 were Blacks, and stopping the spread of the epidemic.

While a contagious disease was successfully contained, the same could not be said for the anti-black sentiment which was gaining ground at the same time. The issue of the Black Refugees, also referred to as the Chesapeake Refugees, became the subject matter of deliberations in the Nova Scotia House of Assembly. It opened with a message from Lieutenant-Governor Sherbrooke on 24 February, 1815, informing the House that during its recess

> many families, principally people of colour, have arrived in this Province from the United States of America. They have fled from the calamities of War, and the misery which they were suffering in their native country, to seek an asylum under the protection of the British Government, and have indulged the hope that they will be admitted as free settlers in this Province. A great proportion of these people, active, healthy, and endured to labour, have gone to the interior of the Province, affording, I trust, a large accession of useful labour to the agriculture of the Country......[6]

Sherbrooke went on to present the negative side as well and referred to "some instances of decrepit age, helpless infancy, and unavoidable sickness, which require relief." His thrust was to seek support to make the matter a provincial responsibility rather than to continue to rely on public assistance and private charity. He asked that consideration be given to land grants for Blacks to enable them to settle upon the forest lands of the province.

This was the first time since the arrival of the Black Refugees in Nova Scotia in 1813 that the issue of provincial responsibility and land grants was raised. Predictably, the members of the House of Assembly were unprepared to deal with this issue until they were better informed. Two months later, on 1 April, 1815, they presented their response to the governor. They voted a sum of five hundred pounds sterling to prevent the spread of smallpox among the Blacks brought to their attention by the governor but that was as far as their generosity went. For the rest, they expressed "alarm and concern" at the "frequent arrival of Negroes and Mulattoes." They could not see why public funds should be spent on settlers whose "character, principles and habits" had not been previously investigated; they urged the governor to make representations to the British Government to prohibit further black immigration to Nova Scotia. As far as they were concerned "the proportion of Africans already in the country is productive of many inconveniences; and that the introduction of more must tend to the discouragement of white labourers and servants, as well as to the establishment of a separate and marked class of people, unfitted by nature to this climate, or to an association with the rest of his Majesty's Colonists."[7] The colonists also wanted the British Government to provide extra funds to meet costs related to the black immigrants.

A careful analysis of the call by the provincial politicians of 1815 to prohibit black immigration to Nova Scotia shows how deep-rooted racial discrimination and racial bigotry were in this province as they were elsewhere. When one compares this call with the employment equity programmes of the 1980s or the human rights legislation since the 1970s or the philosophy underlying the Charter of Rights and Freedoms of 1982, one is struck by the distant origins of conflicts in race relations in Nova Scotia.

Governor Sherbrooke dutifully carried out the bidding of the Nova Scotia House of Assembly delivered to him on 1 April, 1815. His task was compounded by a communication which he received the following day, 2 April, from Vice-Admiral, Sir Alexander Cochrane, stationed in Bermuda, informing him that he was about to send some 1500 to 2000 more Black Refugees to Nova Scotia. Sherbrooke notified Colonial Secretary Lord Bathurst of the ban desired by the politicians and of the entry required by the vice-admiral. Two sides were competing to determine the destiny of a people who were themselves muted by their helplessness.

It was now up to the higher authority vested in the British Government to settle this matter decisively.

While this decision was awaited, and with the House of Assembly prorogued on 3 April, Governor Sherbrooke placed the matter before the Executive Council since there was extreme urgency to provide relief to those black refugees already in the province and to prepare for the arrival of the 1500 to 2000 additional refugees. In the end, it was the arrangement put in place by the Executive Council, rather than anything new authorized by the British Government, that became the operative formula to receive and settle the new refugees expected as well as to settle the older refugees who were already in the province before 3 April, 1815.

It was decided that a government official, either the Chief Officer of the Customs or the Collector of Customs, would be the designated officer in charge of all arrangements appertaining to the refugees. This was an arrangement first started in the British colonies in 1808 to meet the situation created by the abolition of the slave trade in 1807 by an Act of the British Parliament. After the passing of this Act, ships were searched to ascertain whether any slaves were on board; captured slaves were taken before special courts to receive their freedom papers and then entrusted to the Chief Officer of the Customs or the Collector of Customs in any British colony. It was the duty of this official to take care of the welfare and comfort of the freed slaves at the expense of the British Government. The representative of the Crown in each colony was clearly enjoined to make sure that this official carried out his duties "with the utmost care and vigilance, in order that the benevolent purposes of the Act may be carried into execution in the most beneficial manner."[8]

Had the representative of the Crown in Nova Scotia, the Lieutenant-Governor, Sir John Coape Sherbrooke, put this piece of legislation into practice when the first of the immigrants called the Black Refugees set foot on Nova Scotia soil in September, 1813, their initial misery and suffering would have been prevented. The greater burden for this oversight must be borne by Vice-Admiral Cochrane and Lord Bathurst for the slave refugees had become technically free persons the moment they defected to the British side. There was no intermediary court set up to adjudicate on their freedom. These free persons should then have been sent to Nova Scotia not as refugees in search of charity and asylum but as settlers bearing the British flag and breathing British loyalty—as was the case with the contemporary assisted emigration schemes all over the British empire handling white emigrants from Europe.

The existing military prison on Melville Island, located in the north-west arm of Halifax Harbour, was converted into a depot and a hospital to accommodate the Black Refugees under the charge of the Collector of Customs, the Hon. T.N. Jeffery, in accordance with the new arrangements. The first rations for the Refugees were delivered to this venue on 27 April, 1815. Melville Island served this function until it was ordered to be closed down on 20 June, 1816, a little over a year in all. During the same month of June, Sir John Sherbrooke left Nova Scotia, taking some satisfaction from the fact that what began so badly for Nova Scotia's latest black immigrants had taken a relatively better turn by the time he left the province. He had not found his task an easy one. On the one hand, the politicians in the province demanded that black immigration be banned and on the other, the naval authorities, led by Vice-Admiral Cochrane, were planning to offload a further 1500 to 2000 black immigrants on Nova Scotia. Any extra assistance that he hoped for from the British Government was not forthcoming. The directives he had appealed for to Lord Bathurst in April, 1815 were hardly addressed seriously in the reply he received in July of that year. The problem of black immigrants which the Nova Scotia provincial legislature perceived was now a thing of the past since the war had ended. As for the plight of those already in the province, surely the hoped-for imminent opening of coal mines which the government was working on, would resolve the matter of jobs for them. Fortunately, for Sherbrooke, he was able to deflect up to the first five hundred of the new arrivals to New Brunswick, beginning with the first consignment of 376 who were landed at Saint John on 26 May, 1815.[9] Nor did Nova Scotia receive anywhere near the number Cochrane had advanced: the later immigrants numbered approximately 812 making the grand total of Black Refugee immigration around the figure of two thousand.

Unlike the experience of the Black Loyalists, when opportunities, or the lack of opportunities, to make a living remained constant, the earlier arrivals among the Black Refugees were met with good opportunities for gainful employment due to the acute shortage of labour during the war years both in North America and Europe. But by the closing months of 1814 the labour situation changed dramatically with the advent of peace on both continents, bringing in its train soldiers and other immigrants. In this climate there was no chance that black immigrants could compete for jobs in a province which was on record calling for an official ban on black immigration.

Given this reality, Sherbrooke's recommendation to the British Government was that the newly-arrived black immigrants who were willing to settle and cultivate land should be given land grants as in the case of the loyalist immigrants of the eighteenth century. He cautioned against making grants of barren land in unfavourable situations as factors that would discourage the new arrivals and advised Lord Bathurst that he had instructed the Surveyor-General "to look out for and reserve the most favourable situations now unappropriated for the purpose of locating such of the free Negroes as are willing to become settlers."[10]

These immigrants had come to Nova Scotia for no other reason than to gain freedom from slavery and settle down. They gladly accepted the offer by the Surveyor-General to settle some two hundred families in Preston on the same land earlier acquired to settle the Maroons, comprising some three thousand acres (1214 hectares) originally purchased through funds provided by the Government of Jamaica. The land had been sold or repossessed after the departure of the Maroons in 1800.

The plan was to settle a village for Blacks in Preston on ten-acre (4 hectares) plots drawn by lot. Adjoining the village would be a wood lot of 1500 acres (607 hectares) which would provide an additional source of wood supplies for fuel, fencing and building. No title deeds would be issued to the plot holders until they could provide proof that they were determined to settle permanently. In the meantime they would be given provisions, agricultural implements, construction tools and some building materials to make a start. The Surveyor-General was of the view that the village settlement would succeed if nothing unexpected happened to "discourage the attempt" since the close proximity to Halifax provided an outlet for garden produce as well as for craft products like laths, shingles, hoop poles, brooms, axes halves, oar rafters, scantling and clap boards. It is significant that the official should temper the prospects by referring vaguely to factors that could "discourage the attempt." There certainly were many factors that had deterred the Black Loyalists and the Maroons when they had occupied the same land and had been presented with the same opportunities.

By September 1815, the 200 lots were divided but the extent was nowhere near the ten-acre (4 hectares) lots originally recommended. This was due to, on the admission of the Surveyor-General himself eight years later in 1823, the situation that "in the day this settlement was forming......there was not land sufficient for half their number but they were so urgent to be placed near each other, that the Lots were necessarily reduced for their own convenience and accommodation."[11]

Here already was one discouraging factor which Surveyor General Morris himself had either wilfully or otherwise put into place. While 2000 acres (809.4 hectares) were required for 200 ten-acre (4 hectares) lots, what the government acquired in 1815 was 1350 acres (546 hectares) from six white property holders in exchange for other tracts of equivalent value. A land grant in the region of some eight acres per family in the pioneering context of 1815 was more than mere discouragement. The new Nova Scotia settlers of 1815 were off to a poor start even if 189 families out of 200 received their lots by the end of 1815.

To be given a land grant, whatever the size of land, was not the end of the matter to settle immigrants who were strangers to the environment, the economy, the culture and, above all, to the climate. How were they to fish the lakes and rivers near Preston for the vaunted trout, gaspereaux, eels and perch, supply the Halifax market with greens and vegetables and mobilise strength and family hands to make shingles, brooms and axe handles, when their dwellings were:

> made of green materials, and neither proof against the wet and cold, and having no cellars under them, and some even no floors, their diet also being dry and salt, and their not being very well clothed......?[12]

Yet, within five wintry months, most families had cleared from one-quarter of an acre (0.1 hectare) to one acre (0.4 hectare). And by the end of 1816 some 924 black settlers were settled in Preston. This was a remarkable achievement given that between September, 1815 and December, 1816 almost a thousand immigrants, or half the total number of the Black Refugee immigrant population settled in what was called the village of Preston, building their modest dwellings on the basis of community self-help and held together by no greater bond than communal fellowship and strength in race and cultural ties. Even when they were told that there was insufficient land for every family desirous of settling there on the promised ten-acre lots (4 hectares), they accepted less in order to be together. There was a value in that togetherness that was to stand the community well in future trials and tribulations.

The Black Refugee immigrants were much maligned in both official and non-official quarters as a burden on the public purse, as lacking in industry and skills. Their recent slave status was deemed to be a handicap because they were inexperienced in handling freedom. What was overlooked in this argument was that they were part of the labour force that had made the southern American states enjoy a buoyant economy. They were deemed to be sufficiently important to the British cause to be deliberately encouraged and invited to defect to the British ranks. But once they set foot on British soil in Nova Scotia they were immediately deemed to be a burden to the white society and to the white economy. Consider this assessment first published in 1893:

> They were a wretched class of settlers. On the plantations of their owners in Virginia and other of the Southern States, all their wants had

been provided for, and consequently they were unacquainted with the thrift or the reward of labour. Freedom made them idle and miserable. The government was obliged to allow them rations during the winter and otherwise to provide for their existence. For many years they experienced the wretchedness incidental to idleness and improvidence, and were a constant drain upon the benevolence of their white neighbours.[13]

As for their reception by the politicians since the first of the refugees arrived in September, 1813, it was clear that they were not wanted. We have already noted the call for a ban on black immigration on 1 April, 1815. Sherbrooke had walked the tightrope quite astutely serving the wishes of Nova Scotia, Bermuda and Britain until his departure in June, 1816. By then the immigration side was all over and the settlement side had just begun. When Sherbrooke's successor, the Earl of Dalhousie, assumed office on 24 October, 1816, the politicians would try again, for by then white immigration had also become a factor and the time had come to take sides.

The new governor wasted no time in coming to grips with the situation of the new black immigrants. Their lot had not improved during the few months since the previous governor had left. This was to be expected since there was little that could be done in a few months. Clearly, the Earl of Dalhousie was overwhelmed by the magnitude of the problem facing the settlers and the province. His first official response was of such despair that he began to consider sending them away either to their former masters as free labourers or their distant brethren in Sierra Leone. To him, the future for the black settlers was bleak: they would not make it. Like other similar first-impression observations made before his time, it was not the circumstances that were to blame but inherent defects in the black population:

Permit me to state......plainly that little hope can be entertained of settling these people so as to provide for their families and wants—they must be supported for many years—Slaves by habit and education; no longer working under the dread of the lash, their idea of freedom is idleness and they are therefore quite incapable of Industry.

This was a serious indictment of the contemporary black population, the forebears of the majority of the indigenous black population of Nova Scotia. Those maligned were in no position to defend themselves then but they bided their time for a later day to refute the stigma that slaves moulded by habit and education were permanently handicapped by that experience and status. If, as the returns indicated, 1619 of the recent arrivals were in need of rations and a helping hand in December 1816, were all contributory factors being taken into account? And how could the Earl of Dalhousie say in the same breath that "one third, perhaps, I am assured will do very well, are industrious, sober and deserving every encouragement?"[14]

Eight months later, in August, 1817, after the Earl of Dalhousie had personally visited each of the settlements of the Refugee immigrants, his negative views changed markedly. They had proved to him individually that at least one acre of land had been cleared in every instance and made ready for planting, as the Earl himself reported "against difficulties of nature almost insurmountable and opposed, abused and cheated by the old Settlers near whom they had been placed." Who the older settlers were who cheated them was not more explicitly stated. The settlers older in time to the Black Refugees were both white and black Loyalists.

There were other factors, too, coincidental with the Dalhousie era from October, 1816 to June, 1820 which provided competition for scarce jobs which favoured those competitors who were part of the system. With the end of the Napoleonic wars in Europe, demobilised British soldiers were rapidly accommodated in various parts of the British empire. Indeed, between 1815 and 1821, 19,000 passengers left Britain for Canada.[15] Depressed Newfoundland fishermen also found their way to Nova Scotia in increasing numbers. In the first season that the Refugees sowed their fields in 1815, mice ravaged the fields as never before and this serious setback was compounded with harsh wintry conditions persisting in 1816 well into July. The absence of beginners' luck had to be added to a catalogue of misfortunes. Thus it was not only the tentative and hurried manner in which these new British subjects called the Black Refugees were shipped to Nova Scotia that presented problems for survival. The reluctant reception by the provincial politicians as well as the competition from white immigrants who came at the same time—many of whom were recipients of rations, too—that combined with the ravages of mice and snow to make the beginnings of the settlement of the Refugee immigrants so difficult. But they did survive the beginnings and most refused repeated offers to emigrate to some other parts of the British world. Only 95 of their number chose to emigrate to Trinidad in 1821. The rest cast their lot with Nova Scotia, for better or for worse, and it is to that future in the new community settlements in Halifax–Dartmouth and adjacent areas that we must now turn to trace the emerging experiences.

The Black Refugees were poorly rated when they arrived and some later writers, relying on the testimonies of the detractors, have tended to give endorsement to this rating. Robin Winks, who wrote the first substantive book on the history of Blacks in Canada asked the right questions: What went wrong? Why was their story so depressing? While admitting that the opportunities for black immigrants were limited for a number of reasons, including the arrival of some sixteen thousand white immigrants during the preceding twelve years and some sixty thousand more in the succeeding twenty-five years, Winks added their geographical origins in the south, their absence of particular skills because they were slaves, inability to do domestic labour, unfamiliarity with interacting with whites, with land ownership and utilization, and also because of their deep adherence to the Baptist faith—basing the last-named handicap on the testimonies of white Protestant sources. [16]

Earlier, contemporary, and later immigrants to Canada, white or black, were not necessarily equipped with special skills to cope with the challenges which confronted them in the new country. Few pioneers ever met with familiar situations and few countries in the world have conditions similar to those which exist in Canada. Even in 1989, immigrants who hold doctoral degrees drive taxis, which was not part of their previous training; and some immigrants who were practicing doctors in their countries of origin do no better at the beginning than work as caretakers in hospitals and as morgue attendants.

The Black Refugees were invited to come to Nova Scotia and like other immigrants they, too, were prepared to rough it out until the dawn of a better day.

COMMUNITY PROFILES

The 2000 Black Refugees (the nearest rounded whole number) who were brought to Nova Scotia in the name and by the authority of the British Government between 1813 and 1816 were admitted as refugees and allowed reluctantly to stay on as settlers. The process of establishing new settlements began in 1815 and continued for the better part of the nineteenth century as the settlers and their descendants responded to market, labour and farming opportunities.

The process involved coming into contact with fellow Blacks who had come to Nova Scotia as the slaves of the white Loyalist immigrants or who were the descendants of these slaves; also with those Black Loyalist immigrants who had not left for Sierra Leone in January 1792, as well as their descendants; also with the few Maroons who had eluded the net cast to remove the entire Maroon community to Sierra Leone in 1800, and the descendants of Maroon marriages and liaisons. What began as contacts, developed into interaction and ended in integration. By the end of the nineteenth century a black community had evolved in Nova Scotia which saw no reason to fragment its ranks by identifying with different origins and different streams of immigration. The eighteenth and nineteenth century black immigrants, settlers, citizens and descendants had much in common. Together, they constituted the bedrock of black settlement in Nova Scotia— that bedrock which is synonymous with the indigenous black population of Nova Scotia. The twentieth century black immigrants from the Caribbean, the United States, and Africa are identified and acknowledged as newer and different when issues of origins and affiliations surface.

Of the first of these, the slaves, some 765 were resident in Nova Scotia with their masters in 1783-84. Originally, they were located as follows: Dartmouth, 41; Country Harbour, 41; Chedabucto, 61; Antigonish, 18; Cumberland, 21; Parrsboro, 69; Cornwallis–Horton, 38; Newport–Kennetcook, 22; Windsor, 21; Annapolis Royal, 230; Digby, 152; St. Mary's Bay, 13 and Shelburne–Birchtown (estimated), 38. This number of 765 was Nova Scotia's share of the 1232 slaves who were brought to the Maritimes in 1783-84. The remainder were in New Brunswick and Prince Edward Island.

Nova Scotia's economy could not sustain a slave population for long. Though the slave owners petitioned more than once to get the legislature to legalise slavery, they did not succeed. Neither the legislature nor the courts encouraged the institution of slavery. By the time the Black Refugees were moving into their new areas of settlement, in the period from 1815 onwards, many of the slaves had become free.

The second group was the Black Loyalists. Of the original number of some 3550 who came to Nova Scotia mainly between 1783-84, 1196 left for Sierra Leone in 1792, including some 200 who came from New Brunswick.[17] The Nova Scotia Black Loyalist exodus thus totalled 996, leaving 2654 in the province. According to John Clarkson who was in charge of the arrangements to ship the Black Loyalists, "almost the entire black population of six towns or villages" in Nova Scotia and New Brunswick left.[18] In Nova Scotia these places were Birchtown and Shelburne (600), Preston and vicinity (220) and Annapolis and Digby (180).

The majority of the Maroon population left for Sierra Leone in 1800. Very few remained behind. It is this residue of the Maroons in Nova Scotia which is difficult to establish. In the East Preston area, at least one prolific family tree is traceable to the Maroon period derived from the line of Sarah Colley, the Maroon mistress of Governor Sir John Wentworth. The son of this union, George Wentworth Colley, was born on August 16, 1804 and died on November 2, 1893. He inherited the house which was built by his father, Governor Wentworth, as the governor's summer residence between 1792 and 1796. George Wentworth Colley is the ancestor of a long line that survives to the present. The original house, which was a dwelling of some forty feet by thirty-five feet, collapsed around 1845 and a new house was built adjacent to it after 1918. The Wentworth property was passed down over the years from father to son. The third in the line of inheritance was James Alexander Colley (1874-1935). His wife, Harriett Colley, who was still alive as these lines were written in January 1989, was the head of the Colley family with fifteen children.[19] Those who came before these children since the days of the Maroon sojourn in Nova Scotia as well as those who will follow them, will all be part of the Maroon legacy and history. In the long history of the durable black settlement in the Guysborough area, which goes back to the Black Loyalist period and was not touched by Maroons or later immigrants, is not clear. It is difficult, therefore, to establish Maroon descendants in Guysborough.

So, when the Black Refugees began to be distributed and dispersed, this was the kind of situation they were to meet. They joined with the other black groups who had preceded them to form the total black population of Nova Scotia. This population numbered around 5000 in 1816.

Of this figure of some 5000, the permanent Black Loyalist community began with a figure approximating 2650, with allowance being made for births and deaths, while the slave population began with some 765, most of whom regained their freedom long before slaves were emancipated in the British Empire in August, 1834. To these numbers should be added the few dozen or so Maroon adults and children. The Black Refugees of Nova Scotia, numbering some 2000, would, after 1816, add their numbers to the 3500 or so other Blacks as they moved into existing black settlements or started new ones. The lives and times of upwards of some 5000 Blacks can best be gleaned from the communities they settled and the institutions they forged.

The largest settlement was that of Preston situated between eight and ten kilometers from what was then the town of Dartmouth. The settlement was first surveyed in 1784 by Theophilus Chamberlain for land grants to the Loyalists, both white and black. The extent of the land was some 56,772 acres (22,975.6 hectares) of which 32,000 (12,950.4 hectares) were allotted to the original grantees, including Chamberlain himself. Almost all of the original black residents left the area in 1792 for Africa but Chamberlain held on to his position of deputy-surveyor long enough to be placed in charge of the Maroons later and even to survey the lands to settle the Black Refugees.

The name "Preston" must not be confused with the name "Richard Preston," the famous black religious and community leader who came to the area around 1816 in search of his mother who had preceded him to Nova Scotia. The name was already in use before the first grants were made in 1784. Two theories have been advanced to explain its origins: the first that it could be a corruption of "Priests' Town" from the English usage of identifying a place with many religious houses; the second that it could have been named after a British military officer, Captain Preston, who was removed to Halifax for his protection after becoming embroiled in an incident in Boston which led to the death of three Bostonians in 1770. Chamberlain would have known of this officer who lived in the area and left for England before the survey and settlement of 1784.

The original land grants to Black Refugees ranged from eight to ten acres (3.2 hectares to 4 hectares). To the handicap of small size was added the problem of the poor quality of the soil. The woods on the small lots were quickly exhausted. To sustain a family on such meagre resources in rural Nova Scotia in the early decades of the nineteenth century was a difficult task indeed. The settlers tried hard to clear the land and to cultivate it. The going was rough; government aid came in the form of seed potatoes but if the harvest in a single year was ten bushels (3.5 hectoliters), how long would that quantity serve a whole settlement numbering almost a thousand bodies? On one occasion in 1833 acute food shortage resulted in temporary relief being granted by the government. The sum of twenty-five pounds sterling (approximately fifty dollars today, but worth much more in 1833) was voted to supply corn meal to the residents. There were 857 persons to feed, drawn from 189 families. Relief of this kind which was continued throughout the period covered in this chapter was hardly a permanent solution. The residents realised this and applied for more land.

One of the original Preston settlers of Refugee stock, Septimus Clarke, who went on in later years to become a distinguished officer of the African United Baptist Association, asked for 250 acres (101 hectares) in 1820. He got 120 acres (48.5 hectares) and this marked the beginning of larger grants to other applicants, ranging from 25 to 150 acres (10 to 60.7 hectares), up to 1827 when the law was changed putting an end to free land grants. By that date some 42 persons had received these larger land grants, among them were names quite familiar even today: Bundy, Sparks, Boyd, Clayton, Crawley, Deer, Evans, Grant, Hill, Johnson, Johnston, and Smith, to name a few from the list supplied by Fergusson.[20]

This development did not change the plight of the majority of the residents. Those who benefitted were a small number and even in their case the grants were not accompanied by title deeds which would have enabled them to raise loans for business and development. A further handicap to community development after 1827 was the change in the land laws introducing sales in the place of grants. In the decade following 1827 many questions were raised about the viability of the Preston settlement and the future of Blacks in Nova Scotia. The proposition that they leave for another country with warmer climate was generally rejected. They had established roots and ties and an attachment to the soil in spite of the difficulties they faced. Another proposition was more favourably received by the black residents, that they resettle in other parts of the province.

Since no free land grants were permitted after 1827, some other plan had to be devised to resettle them. In August 1837, Lieutenant Governor Campbell recalled in a despatch to the British Colonial Secretary, Lord Glenelg, that the provincial legislature was still determined to hold to its previous views on the undesirability of making more funds available to ameliorate the lot of the black population. He appealed to the British Government to introduce an amendment to the 1827 land law. This appeal was followed a year later, in August 1838, by Joseph Howe who supported Campbell's appeal that the ban on free land grants imposed in 1827 be lifted with regard to the black settlers of Preston who would agree to be relocated on unoccupied Crown lands in other parts of the province. The Colonial Secretary agreed to modify the land regulations in 1839 provided that the legislature was prepared to pay for the cost of relocation. He advised, however, that no title deeds be issued in the new settlements until some future date to ensure that the grants issued would not be disposed of before the new settlement became a reality.

As for Preston itself, the original settlers were given their lots on the basis of temporary authorizations called tickets of location and licenses of occupation. By 1840, the first settlers had occupied their lands for twenty-five years without any security of tenure. This was changed for the first time in March, 1841 when the Executive Council authorized the Surveyor-General to issue "a General Grant to these poor people of the lands long occupied by them."[21]

A year later this was done and 1,800 acres (728.46 hectares) were allotted to the pioneering black settlers of Preston who had come to Nova Scotia as the Black Refugees between 1813 and 1816 and laid the foundations for the largest and most durable black settlement of the nineteenth and twentieth centuries.

While the surveyors were working on the allocation of lot numbers covering the 1,800 acres (728.46 hectares) made available under the general grant, the residents of Preston realised that nothing would really change. They would in fact go back to those years when they had to make do with ten acres (4 hectares) of barren land with poor soil. One hundred and seven petitioners led by William Deer Snr. and Sampson Carter informed the Lieutenant-Governor of Nova Scotia in 1841 that never mind how hard they toiled there was little they could do with swampy, barren and unproductive land. They made two specific requests: that they be granted titles to their land so that those who wanted to sell and move to other areas in search of employment could realise value for their land as well as the improvements made on it; that those of them who were willing to resettle in other places should be granted larger and better lots of land on such terms as would allow them to acquire freehold rights in due course "through patient industry and frugality."[22]

Such observations and proposals hardly reflected poorly on those who made them. On the contrary, they suggest a serious sense of purpose and a determination to "rise above the level of hopeless poverty." The government was slow or indifferent on both points: the absence of land titles remained a serious problem for more than the next hundred years; and the land grants made in other parts of the province were no better in terms of size, quality and security of tenure.

Before we leave Preston for the other settlements, some idea of numbers of residents up to the middle years of the nineteenth century show that the population of Blacks declined between 1816 and 1851. In 1816 the figure was 924; in 1827 it was 708; in 1838 the number fell to 525 which included

67 on the New Musquodoboit Road while in 1851 the number stood at 496. Even looking beyond the middle of the nineteenth century, the figures hardly suggest any sizeable increase. In 1941, over a hundred years later, the figure stood virtually where it was in 1816, at 909. What this suggests is that the limits for expansion of this premier black settlement were already defined in the early decades of the nineteenth century by the size and quality of land grants as well as by the absence of freehold land titles.[23]

The fluctuations in the numbers given in the above paragraph suggest that people were on the move in search of better opportunities to eke out a living or that the census were not very accurate. Such movement is typical of a people seeking upward mobility anywhere in the world, not only in pioneering situations as in Preston but well into contemporary times. A review of the family names of the Preston black settlement listed in the 1847 census shows that bearers of those names can be found in the present divisions of the settlement in 1989 in North Preston, East Preston, Cherry Brook and Lake Loon, as well as in other places in the Halifax–Dartmouth Metro area and in adjacent parts of Halifax County. Before they came to be where they are in 1989, individuals and families moved to other places along the way, such as Africville, Hammonds Plains and Beechville. Making allowance for variations in the spelling of names, the list of family names in the 1847 census will provide leads for the tracing of family origins and also serve as an example to illustrate what was going on in the lives of black community members in other parts of the province:

Allen, Beel, Blair, Blue, Bondy, Bowers, Boyd, Brown, Cain, Carter, Carvery, Cellom, Sellum, Cephus, Clark, Claten, Colley, Collins, Craney, Crawley, Croud, Curry, Dear, Dennis, Diggs, Dillivery, Donald, Dunkins, Evins, Fawney, Fletcher, Galyard, Gasker, Gilmore, Grant, Henderson, Homes, Hopkins, Johnston, Jones, Kelly, Lambert, Lee, Munro, Nelson, Pelo, Ranger, Robertson, Saunders, Savage, Seaton, Semo, Shatten, Skinner, Slaughter, Smith, Smithers, Sparks, Spriggs, Stanley, Sye, Taylor, Traverse, Vass, Walker, Warren, Williams, Winder, Wise, and Young.[24]

Of the black settlements founded as a result of the arrival of the Black Refugees between 1813 and 1816, Preston was the largest. The others were Hammonds Plains, Windsor Road, Refugee Hill (close to the North West Arm in Halifax), Porter's Lake (just beyond Preston), Beech Hill (later called Beechville, some eight kilometres from Halifax), Cobequid Road, Prospect

Road, Fletcher's Lake and Beaver Bank (most of the last-named four areas are identified these days with the black communities settled in Lucasville, Cobequid Road, and the various geographical divisions of Sackville).

The Black Refugee settlement in Hammonds Plains began at the same time as the Preston settlement, in 1815. As in Preston, the area settled was not at first identified as separate geographical divisions based on cardinal points, topography or other designations but simply as Hammonds Plains. The origins of the pre-black settlement go to 1781 when the Lieutenant-Governor of Nova Scotia, Sir Andrew Snape Hammond, granted one Leonard Yammer and thirty others 5,000 acres (2,023.5 hectares) of land which carried his name.

A local history written in 1978 by senior citizens of the black community states that some Maroons stayed on in the area: "Those who wanted to remain were granted land and permission to settle in Hammonds Plains. They were good workers, farmers and woodsmen."[25]

As mentioned in the early section in this chapter, information on the number of Maroons who did not leave for Sierra Leone in West Africa in 1800 remains scanty. Is it possible that the Hammonds Plains Maroons were part of the Boydville Maroons of Middle Sackville settled there as a group by Governor Wentworth between 1796 and 1799? Certainly, the Preston Maroons were not described in contemporary reports as "good workers, farmers and woodsmen" while the Boydville Maroons were the favoured and praised settlers of the time.

The Black Refugee settlers began arriving in Hammonds Plains in 1815 and by June 1816, the population was 307, increasing to 504 before the year was out. The tempo of settlement matched that of Preston as did the problems associated with it. The original 75 settlers received lots of ten acres (4 hectares) through licences of occupation and a number of families were settled on the lands owned (but not occupied) by whites without receiving grants of their own. Some of them built houses and made other improvements on these lands and in 1819 thirty-six of them led by one Dominic De Broker requested that a portion of this land which had reverted to the Crown should be granted to them. Similar requests came from new settlers as well as from those in Preston who wanted more land for farming and for wood.

The story of the pioneers of Hammonds Plains is a repeat story of the pioneering black settlements in Nova Scotia during the first half of the nineteenth century: poor housing, poor heating, high incidence of illness, seasonal employment, poor harvests, food shortages, welfare grants from the provincial government, similar relief from humanitarian bodies and kindly, more prosperous, white neighbours, insufficient land for farming, and land grants by tickets of location or licences of occupation. The pattern was a familiar one broken only by the changing landscape.

The population figures for Hammonds Plains showed a greater stability once the initial strenuous first two decades were over when compared to Preston. Starting with 440 in 1827, it fell drastically to 196 in 1838 but maintained a steady growth or stability thereafter, reaching 606 in 1851, a figure which was higher than that of Preston by over one hundred.[26]

The numbers who settled in the other areas were very much smaller than Preston and Hammonds Plains. Fifty-one were originally settled on the Windsor Road, some of whom were employed on road construction linking Halifax to Windsor. Two of their number were able to acquire ten-acre lots (4 hectares) in Windsor for ten shillings (roughly one dollar today) each through a private arrangement with a white clergyman, Rev. William Cochrane, to occupy and improve the lands for seven years while a third person made a similar arrangement in exchange for the use of two acres (.8 hectares) for seven years. On the expiry of seven years, these lots had to be vacated in accordance with the agreement after a nominal sum was paid for improvements effected. Arrangements of this nature represent a form of exploitation linked to the fate of squatters, sharecroppers, labour-tenants and so on when absentee and affluent landlords with more land than they could work take advantage of the destitute in their midst.

The Refugee Hill settlement started with the small number of 23 in 1815, increasing to 76 by the end of 1816. In early 1818 twelve persons were issued licences of occupation for ten-acre (4 hectares) lots each for a period of five years after which the future tenancy would be determined on the basis of whether their conduct was "industrious, peaceable and loyal."[27]

The remaining small settlements began with modest allocations: Beech Hill, 89; Porter's Lake, 27; Fletcher's Lake, 10; Prospect Road, 11; Beaver Bank, 2.

When the census of 1851 was taken, the black population of Nova Scotia remained around the same figure as in 1816 when the Black Refugee immigrants added their number to the previous freed slaves, Black Loyalists and the few Maroons who had chosen to make this province their permanent home. A glance at the distribution of this population shows that the settlements responded to market forces, to land grants and to previous aggregations of blacks in earlier settlements. There was a natural reluctance to get too far from kith and kin as there was to pressures from the government that they could move to warm climates in such places as Trinidad and Demerera. The 95 who went to Trinidad in 1821 went almost as an extended family, mostly from Hammonds Plains. At the time, slavery was still in practice in the British empire, in the United States and in European possessions in scattered places of the globe. In choosing to stay in Nova Scotia they cast their lot with the pioneers of Nova Scotia, opting to live as free persons, loyal to the flag and establishment and God-fearing and other-worldly in their affiliation to and bearing towards the Christian church and the Christian faith. In adopting this position, these pioneers were unconsciously subscribing to the tenets of survival theology which, more than a hundred years later, would be transformed by some of their erstwhile and disappointed descendants into a form of liberation theology to free themselves from the fetters of continuing discrimination and denials.

In 1851, the total number of Blacks in Nova Scotia was 4908, with females being about 250 more than males. The largest number, 1688, was settled in Halifax county which included all the places mentioned as Black Refugee settlements; next came Guysborough county with 603, mostly of Black Loyalist stock, followed by Annapolis with 483, Digby with 454, Yarmouth with 247 and Queen's county with 213. Cape Breton had 238 of whom 162 were in Sydney alone. Those who numbered between 100 and under 200 were listed under King's, Hants, and Cumberland while Colchester, Pictou and Lunenburg were at the bottom of the list with 20 and under.[28]

One Nova Scotia black settlement associated directly with the coming of the refugee immigrants was established before 1850 and was uprooted a hundred and twenty years later. Known at different times as Campbell Road, Africville and Seaview, the story of this settlement is a sad indictment of the insensitivity shown to members of the black community. When placed in the context of the formation of pioneering black community settlements in the period up to the 1850s, the genesis of the Africville settlement is an example of black initiatives and enterprise.

Contrary to the belief held today by some of the younger descendants of former Africville residents, Africville was not one of the settlement areas which refugee immigrants were allowed to settle in 1815-1816. Nor was this area settled before this by Black Loyalists or former slaves as an identifiable black settlement area. The first black residents came to Africville, located within the municipal boundaries of Halifax on the northern side adjoining the Bedford Basin, from Preston and Hammonds Plains in the late 1830s and early 1840s to seek employment in Halifax. William Brown and William Arnold were the first two Blacks to obtain title deeds to three five-acre (2 hectares) plots in Africville which were previously owned by Whites. Their title deeds were dated 1848. The fifteen acres (6 hectares) acquired by Brown and Arnold represented the total extent of land associated with Africville. On this extent of land, other pioneering families obtained titles to smaller lots and in due course these families grew to eight in number: Arnold, Brown, Carvery, Dixon, Hill, Fletcher, Bailey and Grant—names which appeared on the lists of Preston and Hammonds Plains.[29]

One hundred and forty years later, in September 1988 when a memorial cairn was unveiled on the grounds where Africville once stood, now called Seaview Memorial Park, thirty-nine family names were inscribed to remind us that between 1848 and 1968 these names were associated with an almost all-black residential area which was utterly neglected by the civic authorities of Halifax, the capital of Nova Scotia.[30]

William Brown, Sr. is remembered in Africville lore as the founder of the settlement. His son, John Brown, was a teacher. Like William Arnold, he came from Hammonds Plains. Carvery, Hill and Fletcher came from Preston, as did Allen Dixon who became a prominent church leader and founder of a long line of famous Nova Scotians, including the world famous boxer, George Dixon, who was born in Africville in 1870 and who died in New York City in 1909. To look at why Africville was settled by persons who had already received grants of land in Preston and Hammonds Plains is to gain some insight into the efforts made by the pioneer black settlers to make headway in Nova Scotia.

Bedford Basin provided good fishing prospects; wage labour was promising in Halifax where a steamship mail service was introduced in 1839; shipbuilding, dockyard work, road construction on Campbell Road and the beginning of the intercontinental railroad in 1854 added to the prospects generated by a booming trade with the United States. When pioneering blacks were responding seriously to employment opportunities, and buying pieces of land which they could call their own, they were certainly combatting the myth that it was only welfare grants that were keeping them alive. Of course, as in other settlements, true titles to land were hard to come by. Some settlers died intestate (without drawing up wills) and their descendants lived on the land in the belief that durable occupation meant undisputed ownership, only to be disappointed later when their claims to ownership were disputed. The ongoing story of the one hundred and twenty-five years history of Africville will appear in other parts of the book.

Such local accounts as can be put together for the black settlements of Nova Scotia in the first half of the nineteenth century rely heavily upon official sources which were intended to serve the government. These sources were not concerned with details of community life and labour. Petitions on behalf of Blacks are replete throughout this period seeking relief of one kind and another, ranging from food and clothing to schools and roads. These petitions were written by white Nova Scotians, neighbours, employers, priests, teachers, civil servants or plain, public-spirited persons responding with compassion and goodwill. The petitions carried the names of the black petitioners, and in this way served to identify the earliest residents, but alongside these names were the familiar marks to indicate illiteracy, while some of the petitions phrased in excellent English and written by well-trained hands contained the signatures of the petitioners in the very same handwriting. Clearly, such documents were prepared and signed by white persons.

This is not to say that there were no literates among the earliest black settlers. There were very few and the standard of literacy for that time and circumstance was, understandably, low in both black and white communities. One petition prepared in Hammonds Plains in 1828, and reproduced in this book, is a touching example of the handiwork of the pioneers themselves, with whatever outside help they could enlist. However faulty the spelling and grammatical construction, the message, rewritten here in standard English was undeniably clear: "We are all poor people in this settlement and in want of a school house and a school master that we are not able to obtain by ourselves."[31]

Sources of this kind in pre-literate societies serve an important function to complement and balance official sources. Another example is reproduced as an appendix to this chapter to draw attention to community life as explained by the black settlers themselves.[32]

Before this section on community profiles in the early decades of the nineteenth century comes to an end, mention must be made of one distant and isolated area of settlement. Guysborough county which, in 1851, had the second largest number of black settlers. With 603, it was second only to Halifax County with 1688. In addition to the usual problems encountered by black immigrants in Nova Scotia, the problem of isolation introduced an added handicap. In Halifax and the surrounding areas, closeness to government and to humanitarian bodies made it relatively easier to receive support and relief. In the Guysborough settlements, it was a case of the old adage: out of sight, out of mind. One writer states that "racial prejudice was especially intense in the more isolated communities in Nova Scotia."[33] Why this should have been so is not obvious since economic competition and rivalry are generally more pronounced in urban areas rather than in rural areas.

Segregated black settlements developed in Guysborough as in other parts of the province. Rawlyk states that segregation did not come about "as a consciously determined policy of the white inhabitants" but that "segregation was rather an assumption reached more or less independently by both races."[34] There was no assumption that a marginal and neglected community could make it one way or other. It was not the black families living in one of the settlements on Chedabucto Bay close to what would later be known as Guysborough, that named the settlement "Niggertown Hill." It was not the black settlers already living as squatters in Tracadie who determined that 3000 acres (1214 hectares) should be allotted to them to formally constitute a settlement out of a squatter district. Blacks could not squat anywhere in Nova Scotia for long without tickets of location or licenses of occupation.

If segregation was not a consciously determined policy of the white inhabitants, it was certainly a predetermined policy of the white establishment to make land grants in such a way as to create segregated black communities which formed the settlements of Upper Big Tracadie and Sunnyville. Since these settlements maintained a continuity since the arrival of the Black Loyalists in the 1780s, the early leaders stayed on to establish durable patterns and traditions relating to labour, religion and education. The first of these leaders was Thomas Brownspriggs, a Black Loyalist, and one of those who started off at "Niggertown Hill" on Chedabucto Bay and who proceeded to press for land grants to individual farmers. It was to him and seventy-three others that the 3000 acres (1214 hectares) of land were granted in 1787 in Tracadie. From 1793 to the 1820s, the leadership was assumed by Dempsey Jordan who, like Brownspriggs before him, was a general help for his people: teacher, preacher, counsellor, tax collector, and link between the black and white communities. The tasks for these leaders were not easy given the isolation, the poverty, the racial prejudice and the conflicting forces of Protestantism and Catholicism competing for spiritual control.

In spite of these difficulties, the black settlers in Guysborough County did reasonably well to receive a favourable assessment from a British traveller in 1830 who observed:

> In many parts of the country, both east and westward, detached families of negroes are to be found, whose condition, though still miserable poor, is far better than that of their brethren near Halifax. The nearest approach to comfort I have observed among this race is in a few families who occupy the backlands of Great Tracadie......They are descendants of some slaves who came with refugee loyalists, and consequently have only experienced by inheritance the demoralizing effects of slavery. Those who are employed as labourers and servants in the towns are in better circumstances than the rest.[35]

A hundred years later, the same could not be said for black life and living in Guysborough County. In 1964, the black population of Upper Big Tracadie and Sunnyville was put at 596 where it had stood at 603 in 1851.[36]

A list of the black residents in Tracadie as of March 7, 1848 gives such names as Clike, Paris, Jackson, Bowden, Shepperd, Reddick, Day, Ash and Williams. The discerning observer in Nova Scotia will recognize bearers of these names, often spelt differently, in all parts of the province in 1989.[37] These descendants of the pioneer black settlers in the area which became Guysborough County in 1836 will do well to remember that they owe much to the sweat and toil, the patience and the bravery, of their ancestors. This is how one contemporary study records the life of the pioneers of Guysborough:

> The only shelter these unfortunate people had was some rude huts or camps as they could fashion, till trees were felled and logs were prepared for more substantial dwellings. The Government supplied them with provisions intended to last for a year, but all was consumed in half that time......and bitter privations were experienced by them as in too many of the newly settled portions of the Province. Mussels were sometimes their only food. Fish and wild animals were caught and dressed by unskilled hands......They travelled up the shore to Guysborough, and made log canoes for short voyages. They found the way to Arichat, and some of the men obtained employment there. The ladies sold their jewelry, and their clothing to provide their families with the necessaries of life. When they had cleared small fields and

planted grain, the growing crops had to be carefully guarded against the inroads of bears. If patience and bravery grow by exercise, to what heights they must have attained.[38]

Community Institutions: School and Church

Education and religion went hand in hand throughout the colonial period in Africa. White missionaries of both Protestant and Catholic denominations introduced schools so that African children as well as their parents could read the scriptures. A good Christian was a product of civilization and civilization meant those customs and institutions which originated in Europe. If a good Christian was to serve his or her community, society and country, such a person had to model European or Western standards. In time, reading, writing and arithmetic became the main components of education. The church produced the first educated African preachers, teachers and civil servants as well as generations of African leaders. The church also produced the first generation of moderate African nationalists who protested against the injustices of colonial rule as well as the later generations of uncompromising, western-educated, nationalists who ended white domination over African societies and countries. Modern African Presidents like Nkrumah of Ghana, Kenyatta of Kenya, Banda of Malawi, Nyerere of Tanzania and Kaunda of Zambia, were all products of western civilization and western Christianity.

What was true of Africa and its African peoples in the colonial period was true of earlier Africans who left Africa for other parts of the world, whether in the British Empire or in the plantations where the sons and daughters of Africa were transported to serve foreign masters. Whether in bondage or as nominally free persons, such Africans, by whatever name they were called, Negro, Coloured, or Black, were denied access to the corridors of real opportunity in the white world of exclusive membership. They set out to create their own opportunities, their own institutions, their own network— not because they loved segregation but because they had to do their utmost to survive. Religion was the centre of survival. Everything else was a means to this end.

Education was one of these means. The Black Loyalists received help from a British charity organization called the Associates of the late Dr. Bray which sent funds from 1785 onwards to start schools in the black settlements in Halifax, Preston, Brindley Town, Birchtown and Shelburne in Nova Scotia while the Society for the Propagation of the Gospel (which had been operating in the province since 1749) opened a school in Tracadie. The teachers in these schools were members of the communities as well as leaders and preachers in the local black churches, whether Methodists like Boston King, John Ball and Moses Wilkinson, or Anglicans like Isaac Limerick, Joseph Leonard and Catherine Abernathy, or Huntingdonians like Cato Perkins and William Ash, or Baptists like David George and Hector Peters. There were some who were teachers but not preachers, Colonel Stephen Blucke was a teacher in Birchtown and Thomas Brownspriggs and Dempsey Jordan were teachers in Tracadie.

These are the pioneer black teachers of Nova Scotia. All but the last three left Nova Scotia for Sierra Leone in 1792. One of them, Boston King, was sent by the Sierra Leone Company to Bristol, England, in 1794 to continue with his studies at Kingswood School. During his two-year stay at this school, he wrote his memoirs which were published in *The Methodist Magazine* in March, April, June, 1798.[39]

In his memoirs, Boston King recalled how awkward he felt at one time in Nova Scotia because of his limited education: "The Blacks attended the preaching regularly; but when any of the White inhabitants were present, I was greatly embarrassed, because I had no learning, and I knew they had."[40]

In recalling the example of Boston King in this section on education during the foundation years of black settlement in Nova Scotia, the conclusions to be drawn are many: the first teachers and preachers were barely literate; those who made headway were only able to do so when opportunities appeared outside Nova Scotia, a situation which persisted well into the 1980s for many black Nova Scotians. An eighteenth century personal testimony on race relations in Nova Scotia by a black person is a very rare, if not unique, experience. The reader may find some profound insights in this excerpt:

When I first arrived in England, I considered my great ignorance and inability, and that I was among a wise and judicious people, who were greatly my superiors in knowledge and understanding; these reflections had such an effect upon me, that I formed a resolution never to attempt to preach while I stayed in the country; but the kind importunity of the Preachers and others removed my objections, and I found it profitable to my own soul, to be exercised in inviting sinners to Christ; particularly one Sunday, while I was preaching at Snowsfields-Chapel, the Lord blessed me abundantly, and I found a more cordial love to the White People than I had ever experienced before. In the former part of my life I had suffered greatly from the cruelty and injustice of the Whites, which induced me to look upon them, in general, as our enemies: And even after the Lord had manifested his forgiving mercy to me, I still felt at times an uneasy distrust and shyness towards them; but on that day the Lord removed all my prejudices; for which I bless his holy Name.[41]

There is a spirit of forgiveness implicit in Boston King's philosophy which is difficult to endorse in the light of the further provisions for education for blacks during the early decades of the black refugee immigrants' experience. One will also see in the generation of Boston King the results of the kind of education offered by charitable institutions like the Society for the Propagation of the Gospel and the Associates of the late Dr. Bray. The example of the last-named institution's stated purpose of education for black children illustrates this point. Black children were to be "properly instructed in the principles of Christianity and that the great and necessary duties of obedience and fidelity to their masters and humility and contentedness with their condition would be impressed on their minds."[42] There was to be just enough book learning to be provided that would turn out loyal and obedient subjects who would sing their master's praises forever. Such objectives also dictated the relationship between the different classes in white society.

Nor were the laws introduced in the period covered in this section, i.e. to the mid-1850s, any more helpful to black children than was the philosophy underlying the purpose of this education. In 1766, when whites and blacks were beginning to show up in Nova Scotia, an Education Act was introduced to licence teachers who were permitted to teach in the private schools. Power was vested in the church to make the selection. In 1811 the law provided for a government subsidy if a local district with at least thirty families who held land in freehold built a school house, hired a teacher and raised between fifty and two hundred pounds sterling. This requirement was difficult for most rural Nova Scotians, let alone the black community who held no land in freehold and could not raise the money required. For some twenty-five years black children in the rural districts went without any schooling until, in 1836, the government allotted a portion of the grant available to poor districts in general to be used to set up schools for black children. This is not to suggest that no black children went to school.

A one-room school and a small house for a schoolmaster were built in Preston in 1816 with government funds for the black community which began residing there in 1815. The white teacher was provided by the Society for the Propagation of the Gospel. This provision was repeated for Hammonds Plains in the same year. In 1824 a school for black children in Halifax reopened after being shut down for some time. During these years the only black school teacher in Nova Scotia was Dempsey Jordan at Tracadie.

The schools for black children from 1816 onwards were segregated schools. Placed in historical context, this was happening all over the world under European domination at the time. In Great Britain a religious revival was in full swing aimed at improving the lot of the colonized peoples of the British Empire while parliamentarians of liberal persuasion were using their influence to pass laws which would put an end to the institution of slavery in the British Empire. The first half of the nineteenth century could well be described in colonial rule as the age of parliamentary and humanitarian reforms. While slavery as an institution came to an end in 1834 and white missionaries of all denominations opened mission stations to promote what Dr. David Livingstone, who spent some thirty years in Africa, described as the three Cs: Christianity, Civilization, and Commerce, these developments took place within the framework of segregation within both church and state.

The duty of history is to tell it as it was and not to rewrite the facts; the duty of the reader is to interpret the facts in historical context and to apply them to understand the evolution of society.

What happened in Nova Scotia in this segregated setting between 1816 and the 1850s was the emergence of modest schools for black children provided for by the Society for the Propagation of the Gospel, the Associates of the late Dr. Bray, one private school on total black initiatives, and government-aided schools in Preston, Hammonds Plains and Halifax. There was one school in Yarmouth, two in Birchtown, one each in Sackville, Digby and Beech Hill.

In the meantime the concentration of black families in the north end of Halifax identified today by such streets as Maynard, Creighton, Cornwallis, Gerrish and Gottingen reached such proportions that in the mid-1830s upwards of 300 black children under the age of sixteen were in need of education. There was one school operating since 1824 but this could not cope with the growing numbers. Through donations received in Halifax and from England a new school, called the African School, opened in 1836 and soon began to serve as a day school, a Sunday school and an evening school. Tragedy struck that same year when the school was razed to the ground by fire but the school was functional again before long. The core subjects included writing, arithmetic, geography and English grammar. Girls were taught knitting, sewing, spinning and related domestic subjects while the brighter boys were taught geometry, navigation and surveying to prepare them for positions in the merchant navy.

The Rector of St. Paul's Church was one of the most ardent supporters of the Halifax African School. In his representations to government he visualised further additions to the building so that it could be turned into a Normal or Training School to produce black teachers to serve in their own schools. Dr. Robert Willis would surely have had in mind that after Dempsey Jordan in Tracadie, there was but one other black teacher in the whole province since the late 1820s: John Pleasant in Brindley Town.

The example of the African School in Halifax served to show that black parents and black children were interested in education, that black children were capable of handling such subjects as geometry, navigation and surveying. What it also showed was that the time was long overdue to produce black teachers to replace the white teachers whose usefulness was certainly restricted by the reality of the colour dividing line which prescribed different roles for whites and blacks. One black community comprising a few families living off the beaten track at Port La Tour beyond Birchtown and near Barrington Passage, started their own small school after a visit to the African School.

Dr. Willis cited the example of the Port La Tour initiative to implore government in 1841 not to withdraw support for schools serving the black communities in Nova Scotia. He argued that "the peculiar condition of the People of Colour justly entitles it" to this special government financial support.[43]

While one would readily concede that the plea for a recognition of the "peculiar condition" of the black population of Nova Scotia was a fair and proper one given the historical context of the mid-nineteenth century, what is difficult to concede is the justification for the re-echoing of a similar refrain from various directions nearly one hundred and fifty years later.

What went wrong between 1841 and 1989? Why is the label of "peculiar conditions" still there?

Dr. Willis had implied in 1841 that adequate funding might not be forthcoming. Numerous petitions in the period up to 1850 and beyond testify to this implication. To cite the example of the Salmon River black settlement in Yarmouth County: William Turner and others petitioned as follows in 1839:

> That in your petitioners families are about forty children of an age capable of receiving instruction which your petitioners are very desirous should be imparted to them who are now growing up in ignorance, and the principal impediment in the way of their obtaining it is the want of a School House which your petitioners have not the means for constructing......[44]

Six years later, the same petitioners reported that hardly any progress had been made in this matter, that the School Commissioners "have been unable to allot your petitioners a sum sufficient to support a school for their children to which object, they, being themselves very poor, have not means to contribute......"[45]

This illustration shows that Dr. Willis' concerns were well placed: the 1836 Education Law which provided for a portion of the provincial grant to poor districts to be used to support schools for black children in those districts was ill conceived. Once the poor districts dispensed with the general needs for the majority, there was little or nothing left for the minority blacks placed in a marginal status.

The educational experience of blacks in Nova Scotia up to the 1850s covered in this section underscores the fate of a people left on the periphery and discriminated against by a combination of society and politics. There was one institution, however, to which blacks could turn to with pride and dignity and which would not subject them to the mercies and manipulations of society and politics: that institution was the black church.

The black church made an effort in a limited way during the Black Loyalist interlude between 1782 and 1792 but, as all its leaders left for Sierra Leone, all that remained was the memory of their pioneering efforts. There were lessons to be learned from these efforts. Firstly, most of the Black Loyalists joined the Anglican Church but were not accepted and served as members of the general congregation for reasons already discussed in this chapter. Their spiritual needs were attended to in the main by their own lay preachers and teachers in their segregated settlements in what were independent churches only nominally affiliated to the parent white-dominated churches. The same was true for those who joined the Methodist Church.

Secondly, two other religious groups attracted a large black membership and remained under black control and direction. These were the Huntingdonians, a splinter Anglican group, and the Baptists. Of these, the Baptists made the greatest and most durable impact in Nova Scotia, beginning with the determined leadership provided by David George in his ten-year turbulent crusade in Nova Scotia. Those sterling Baptist leaders and followers who came after David George could relate to his experiences in an action-packed decade when he preached to both whites and blacks. They recalled how he was harangued for baptising a white woman and how his house was broken into and turned into a tavern after he had been beaten and chased away. His fellow blacks turned against him. This founder of the Silver Bluff Baptist Church in South Carolina in 1773, must have wondered what price he had to pay to preach the gospel in Canada which slave blacks referred to as the promised land of freedom. Like Boston King, he left us his memoirs from which this excerpt is taken:

> Those who desired to hear the word of God, invited me from house to house, and so I preached. A little before Christmas, as my own color persecuted me there [Birchtown], I set off with my family, to return to Shelburn; and coming down the river the boat was frozen, but we took whip-saws and cut away the ice till we came to Shelburn. In my absence the Meeting house was occupied by a sort of a tavern-keeper, who said, "The old Negro wanted to make a heaven of this place, but I'll make a hell of it." Then I preached in it as before, and as my house was pulled down, lived in it also. The people began to attend again, and in the summer there was a considerable revival of religion.[46]

That revival was to endure well beyond the departure of David George and the other 1195 Black Loyalists to Sierra Leone in 1792. But there was no black successor to take over from David George though four months after David George left, a white Episcopal missionary, John Burton, came to Halifax, worked among the black residents in the town, and left for the United States to become a Baptist minister. This man, John Burton, known affectionately by his black parishioners as Father Burton, returned to Nova Scotia two years later and founded the First Baptist Church in Halifax on the southeast corner of Barrington and Buckingham Streets in 1795 with a modest congregation of some 30 black adherents. However, with the coming of the Black Refugees between 1813 and 1816, the number increased by some tenfold by 1820. Until the African Baptist Church was started on Cornwallis Street in 1832, it was Burton's First Baptist Church that ministered to the majority of the black Christian population of Halifax while Burton extended his field of mission influence to the black settlements of Preston, Hammonds Plains, Dartmouth, and similar settlements close to Halifax. Organizationally, Burton's church stood alone even though the Maritime Baptist Association had been formed in 1800 as a result of a meeting at which nine churches were represented at Lower Granville, Nova Scotia. Whether Burton's church stayed outside this organization for some years either because of the composition of his congregation or because of the practice of baptism by immersion, is unclear. The fact that his church was poor, its members were poor, and the pastor was poor did not prevent the church from surviving. Well before he joined the Maritime Baptist Association in 1811, two years after baptism by immersion was adopted, he was cautioned by white colleagues not to fraternize too freely with blacks, not to sleep in their homes, eat with them or allow "unqualified" elders to preach. Burton's white colleagues felt that such practices changed the natural order of society. If this went on and "the blacks began to think of themselves as social equals to the whites they would come to demand the rights and privileges of the white men."[47]

Such references to the place reserved by the dominant society for black people were, as already stated, common at the time and for a long time still to come. But people, like Burton, then and later, on this continent and other continents, paved the way for a new morality ahead of their time.

In 1812, John Burton was elected Moderator of the Maritime Baptist Association. The following year, hundreds of black refugees came to Nova Scotia. Their difficulties have been traced in earlier pages. What must now be added is the part played by the compassionate and caring Baptist pastor whose knowledge of blacks was second to none. The government recognized this and placed Burton in charge of the pastoral and human needs of the new black settlers in Preston and Hammonds Plains: "Brother Burton was just the man to have the care and management of this class of people. There is something peculiar in them and there was something in the preacher which qualified him to deal with them" was an observation made by a white person.[48]

What could have been the peculiarity of the blacks and the qualification of a white preacher that bridged a gulf that for so many then and later appeared to be unbridgeable? Was it only religion, since nearly all the refugees were Baptists? Or did it transcend religion to include a measure of a person's humanity to fellow beings?

The results of this relationship are astonishing. In 1815, Burton's church had 49 members. In 1819, his black congregation swelled to 300, making Burton's First Baptist Church the largest in the Association. It is not surprising, then, that an escaped slave, Richard Preston, from the Virginia tobacco fields who came to Halifax in 1816 at the age of 26 in search of his mother who was then living in the black settlement of Preston, should have been attracted to Father Burton's Church.

The coming of Richard Preston opened a distinguished chapter in the history of the black Baptist Churches of Nova Scotia and, by extension and implication, revolutionized black society, black culture, and black achievement. Amidst all the doom and gloom of 1816, a ray of hope shone.

A contemporary journal described him as a person with limited education but endowed with a keen wit, a ready sense of humour and good oratory, more than adequate qualities to become immersed in the urgent task of helping recently arrived fellow black refugees to settle in.[49]

Richard Preston's contribution to church and society in Nova Scotia from 1816 to 1861 is without parallel in the annals of the history of the black communities of this province. His leadership role was undisputed from beginning to end. He arrived at a time when the fortunes of the black population were very bleak. We have seen that black immigrants were most unwelcome in 1816. They were here on sufferance only because the British Government had seen it necessary to co-opt black slaves to defeat white Americans who had dared to challenge the might of the British Empire. His forty-five years of unstinting service in the nineteenth century may be conveniently reviewed in two parts: the period 1816 to 1832 and the period 1832 to 1861. The watershed was 1832. In that year, on May 8, this former Virginia slave and still a relatively recent Nova Scotian, was ordained in the Grafton Church chapel, London, England, by the West London Baptist Association. Also, in that same year, three weeks prior to his ordination, the African Baptist Church, Cornwallis Street, Halifax, was founded and Richard Preston was named its first pastor.

The early part of the first period found him working closely with Father Burton in the black communities of what is now referred to as the

Halifax–Dartmouth Metro area. Here, the first black Baptist congregation was in Burton's First Baptist Church in Halifax started in 1795. The second congregation was in a branch of Burton's church in Hammonds Plains. While Burton concentrated his efforts in Halifax, Richard Preston worked zealously in the outlying black settlements. This teamwork produced good results as church membership increased.

From 1821 to 1824 Richard Preston served as the first black delegate to the Maritime Baptist Association. The reception he received was mixed. He had admirers as well as opponents. His mentor, John Burton, occupied a similar ambivalent position in the eyes of the Association. We have noted that he had been cautioned for frat-ernizing with black church mem-

Richard Preston was a leader in church and society in Nova Scotia for forty-five years, beginning with his arrival in 1816. A former Virginia slave, he became an ordained Baptist minister and helped found the African Baptist Church in Halifax and the African United Baptist Association.

bers. He was also criticized for licensing unqualified black church members as elders and permitting them to preach. This criticism extended to Richard Preston also although he preached to all-white gatherings effectively. Richard Preston does not appear to have been deterred in his work though he could not have remained unmindful of the mixed reception accorded him. There was no question that with exposure to more education he would be better prepared to cope with the criticism as well as with the reception. Fortunately for him, the preparation for higher duties was made possible by extraneous developments in the white church community in Halifax.

In 1825, a controversy over the appointment of the successor to John Inglis as Rector of St. Paul's Church in Halifax caused a number of the more affluent members to leave the Anglican church and join other churches. Twenty of this number were attracted to Father Burton's First Baptist Church in 1826 but not to its dominant black membership. The future of Richard

Preston and his fellow black Baptists was now being determined by the internal split in St. Paul's Church.

These new white members were not prepared to share membership and fellowship with the predominant black congregation. When they decided to form their own Second Baptist Church on Granville Street in 1828, their action was a clear signal to Richard Preston and others that their own future would be better served by a church under their direction and management. Their previous complete faith in John Burton was no longer enough to reassure them. In failing health and 68 years old in 1828, unable to keep white and black Baptists under a single roof, and embroiled in a bitter dispute with his white co-pastor, Robert Davis, on the issue of ownership of church property, Burton's best years were behind him. For Preston and his fellow blacks the best years were ahead of them. These years could best be served by a black Baptist Church under a black Baptist pastor, neither of which existed in 1828. Within four years both became realities.[50] The groundwork was already being laid as a result of local initiatives.

By 1831, a number of black Baptist elders and leaders were in place: Richard Preston, a licensed preacher since 1823; William Henry; Jacob Allen; John Hamilton and George Carvery—all of whom were devoted but none of whom had the level of education that was required before ordination could be conferred. By then, as we learn from a February, 1833 petition submitted by Richard Preston, Prince William Sport, Joseph Campbell and John Hamilton, all black Baptists, the black Baptists had already taken steps to buy a piece of land and erect their own church, but without success. It was at that point that they decided to send Richard Preston to England for two main reasons: to educate himself to the level of becoming ordained, and to raise funds for the erection of an independent black Baptist church in Halifax.[51]

It is clear that this was an initiative taken by the black Baptists themselves with whatever financial support from well-wishers. The First and Second white Baptist Churches were in no position to become involved in this development given the history of the dissension that had already become so bitter and so divisive.

Richard Preston landed in Liverpool, England, on 15 April, 1831 on the first leg of the journey to complete his two-fold mission. The first part of this mission was completed a year later when he received his ordination by the West London Baptist Association on 8 May, 1832. The second part was accomplished when he successfully collected the sum of 650 pounds sterling (roughly 1400 dollars today) with which to build the African Baptist Church in Halifax.

In the 1830s the black population in Nova Scotia was taking its place as a part of the province's permanent population, producing its leaders, consolidating its settlements, responding to the challenges of finding jobs for the adults and education for the children, seeking spiritual guidance from those churches and church leaders who were prepared not only to accept black members but who understood them, their past sorrows, their present dreams and their future hopes. Individuals of the calibre of John Burton were exceptions to the rule which relegated blacks to the end of the line and indeed to separate lines. Thus it was obvious to the incipient black leadership of the 1830s that the time had come for a black church under black leadership and management.

The Cornwallis Street African Baptist Church was the result of this initiative and endeavour. It was formally organized on 14 April, 1832 under the pastorship of Rev. Richard Preston, a man of truly broad experience and

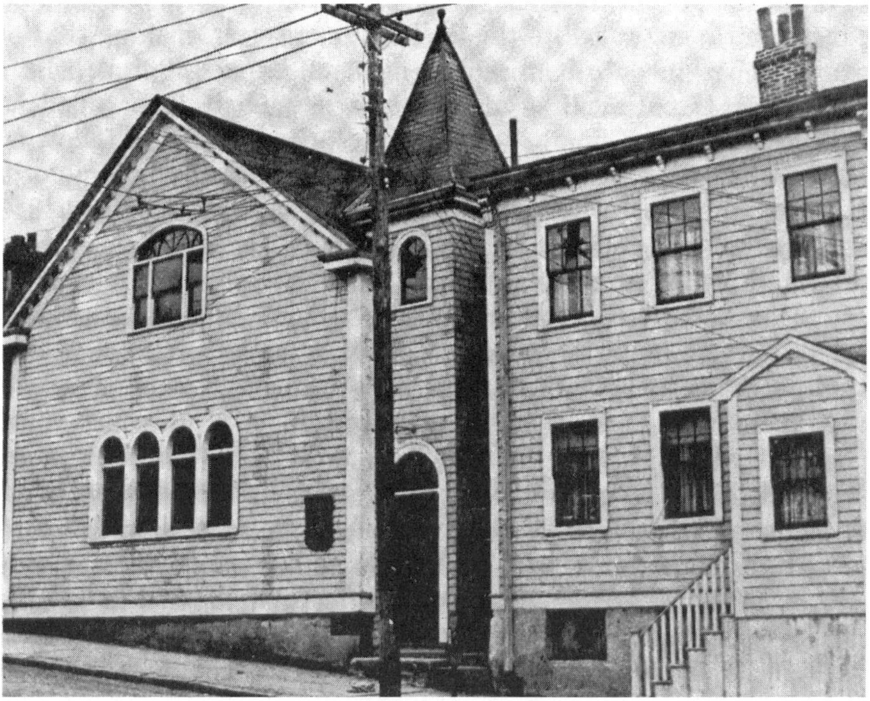

The Cornwallis Street Baptist Church, the first church in Nova Scotia owned and controlled by blacks, was built in 1832.

exposure. Preston understood not only the politics and priorities of the church in Nova Scotia but also the broader commitments and concerns of the church and politics of that time through the powerful evangelical revival and humanitarian movement in Britain. A black slave from the Virginia tobacco fields, a black refugee in Nova Scotia, a theological student in London, England, Richard Preston was personally known to such giants of the age as William Wilberforce, Thomas Clarkson and Thomas Buxton. While studying in London, he became involved in the abolition movement and lectured to British audiences in 1831-32. He was quite a man.

Richard Preston's jurisdiction extended to branches of his church which were started at the same time in Dartmouth, Preston, Beechville (known then as Beech Hill) and Hammonds Plains. Starting ten years later, these branches became separate churches: Preston in 1842; Dartmouth and Beechville in 1844; Hammonds Plains in 1845. Since the first branches were set up and extending into the era of the separate churches, the mainstay of this powerful community institution were the deacons and elders who forged that magnificent link between the grassroots and the pastors. While Richard Preston and the long line of distinguished black church leaders who came after him have a special place in the annals of Nova Scotia's black church history, an equally important place has to be kept for those dedicated deacons and elders who cared for minute details in finance and management. Some day their contribution should be catalogued in greater detail. For now, the pioneers are listed.[52]

Between 1832 and 1845, Rev. Richard Preston was instrumental in setting up five black Baptist churches. Six more were added by 1853. The Campbell Road Baptist Church, later to be called the Seaview Baptist Church in Africville, started in 1849 with Licentiate E. Carvery in charge; North Mountain Baptist Church in the Annapolis Valley, also known as Granville Mountain, started in 1853 with Deacon Charles Jackson in charge; the Greenville Baptist Church, serving the Salmon River community not far from Yarmouth, opened its doors in the same year and was for years well served by white Baptist pastors from the region. Three others, in which Richard Preston had had no direct hand, were added to the list in the same year, making 1853 of particular significance in the birth of black Baptist churches: Bear River under Licentiate Henry Jackson; Joggins, Digby, later called the Acaciaville Baptist Church, headed by Licentiate Jordan the following year; Weymouth Falls Baptist Church led by Deacon John Langford.

Founding eleven black Baptist churches between 1832 and 1853 was a remarkable achievement for one man. Given the fact that there were no other organizations to bring the black population together or to articulate the black voice, Richard Preston's contribution to the nineteenth century history of blacks in Nova Scotia is as unique in the spiritual domain as that of William Hall, V.C., about whom more will be said in chapter two, is in the secular field.

By 1853, Richard Preston had established himself as an outstanding leader, known personally or by reputation in every black community in Nova Scotia. Besides being the moving spirit behind the formation of numerous black Baptist churches in the province, he was also responsible for the organization of an Anglo–African Mutual Improvement and Aid Association in 1842 under the Cornwallis Street African Baptist Church. He advised the first committee of this organization to apply itself to political action, a feature not commonly credited to the black church leadership in Nova Scotia. Yet, at a time when the church was the only medium articulating grievances and aspirations, it was already functioning as a vehicle for political change, asking for more lands, better lands, titles to land, more schools, better schools, more jobs and a greater measure of recognition of the contribution of black folk to the development of Nova Scotia. In 1846, he was also instrumental in establishing the Negro Abolition Society in Nova Scotia. Having been involved in this movement while studying in London, England, Richard Preston was acutely aware of the fact that while slavery was abolished in the British Empire as from 1834, the institution was very much alive in the United States as well as in other European countries and colonies.[53]

Richard Preston's greatest claim to fame in the history of Nova Scotia was yet to follow: the formation of the African United Baptist Association in 1854, a subject for the next chapter.

Between 1800 and 1853 the black population of Nova Scotia was made up of a number of segments traceable to slaves or former slaves, Black Loyalists, Maroons and Black Refugees. Each of these segments has its own history and has made its own distinct contribution to the evolution, character and traditions of the total society. The collective memory of generations of black members of Nova Scotian society has a place for each one of these segments. Without a proper understanding of the part played by each of them there can be no real appreciation of how the black society evolved. Different backgrounds and different experiences contributed to the growth

116

and character of black society and explain the emotions felt, the responses made and the memories held.

If history could be rewritten, the present generation of Nova Scotians would be more comfortable with the knowledge that slavery did not exist in the province; but history cannot be rewritten and slavery did exist. But slavery did not have the necessary economic climate to sustain it. Neither did it have the law to endorse and maintain it. What it did reflect was a callous disregard for decency and morality in the dominant society which prided itself on being founded upon Christian ethics. The cruelty inflicted upon Blacks by this institution of slavery in Nova Scotia was bad enough while it lasted. What was even worse was the permanent stigma attached to a people for generations to come, making sure that it relegated them to the bottom of the social and economic order. It is this stigmatization rather than the real experience of slavery that is the more damning legacy that has continued to the present.

The first Black Loyalist decade which ended in 1792 marked the infusion for the first time of a sizeable black population. A province which could not deal fairly and squarely with ten percent of its population could reasonably be expected to do better with the population reduced by the third that emigrated to Africa after a decade of broken promises. But this was not to be.

When the Maroons arrived they were little more than pawns in the economic rivalry between the white pre-loyalists and the more strident white loyalists since their presence and their upkeep meant the infusion of funds provided by the Jamaican government. Nothing was really done to integrate them into the Nova Scotian society for to do so was to open doors then closed to other blacks. Everyone lost when the Maroons left for they took with them their cohesiveness and their values of self-worth. Later generations of black Nova Scotians saluted the Maroons because the Maroons reminded them of cohesiveness and self-worth as well as of militancy and assertiveness which were noticeably absent in their conservative environment.

It was left to the Black Refugees to negotiate all the previous hurdles as well as face new ones in their gallant efforts to set down roots. They did so through the twin pillars of education and religion. Their successes in education up to 1853 were modest but their concerns and commitment remained strong as they persisted in sending petitions to government for financial help so that their children could be educated. These petitions were often mistaken for begging as was explicit in the book written by C.D. Owen in 1852 entitled *History, Statistics, etc. of Nova Scotia* when he said that blacks "are perpetually begging and receiving charity yet in general they are neither prosperous nor useful."[54] While it is true that they were not prosperous by white standards, it is not true that they were not useful whether to themselves, their community or their province.

Their usefulness was much in evidence once they were able to organize themselves in institutions which they could control and direct as instruments for advancement. The best example of such an institution in the period covered in this chapter is the church. It was the church that provided the organization and the leadership for development and change.

The Anglican Church had the first opportunity but failed to keep the spiritually-hungry blacks within its main body. The black Anglican lay preachers, affiliated in name only, left the province in 1792 with one exception: Thomas Brownspriggs stayed on to preach and teach in Little Tracadie and was joined later by Dempsey Jordan. The Methodist Church fared no better than the Anglican Church while the forerunner of the black Baptist movement in Nova Scotia, David George, left his imprint and his legacy behind as he, too, looked to Sierra Leone after an exciting but turbulent decade in Nova Scotia.

It was to the credit of the Black Refugees in general and Richard Preston in particular that a black Baptist revival took place in the first half of the nineteenth century. Though the white missionary-turned Baptist, John Burton, is given considerable recognition for his work among his black parishioners from 1795 until close to his death in 1838, it is difficult to attribute to him and his movement the genesis of the black Baptist churches of Nova Scotia. In the last decade of his life, he stood far too discredited and far too isolated in Church politics to have launched that major thrust that was to propel the black church forward. The consolidation of the black church was no less than a major black initiative which has maintained a remarkable momentum right up to the present. This church was more than a religious organization. It was a training ground for generations of black leaders and followers, preachers and teachers, politicians and professionals.

Besides the black Baptist church one other black church initiative in the mid-nineteenth century deserves mention. This is the Zion African Methodist Episcopal Church which was started in 1842 in Halifax at the corner of Falkland and Gottingen streets in the north end of Halifax. Other localities which housed the Zion Church were Liverpool, Amherst and Yarmouth. These Zion churches were affiliated to the British Methodist Episcopal

Church rather than to the American parent body. In June, 1876, the Halifax Zion Church obtained its title deeds and was incorporated. The set of trustees registered in 1944 were Wendell Skeir, Beresford Jordan, James Grosse and Reginald Grant Barrow. This church ceased to exist in 1954. With the singular exception of the Highland African Methodist Episcopal Church which was founded in Amherst in 1874, no other African Methodist Episcopal Church exists in Nova Scotia today.

In the period up to 1853, the two black teachers who are listed and remembered are Thomas Brownspriggs and Dempsey Jordan (spelt also as Jourdan) of Little Tracadie. The teachers in this period were mostly white teachers supplied by church or missionary organizations.

As for black religious leaders up to 1853, the name Richard F. Preston stands supreme. The many lay persons who were associated with the churches he founded are listed in the narrative prepared by Peter McKerrow, Secretary of the African Baptist Association from 1876 to 1906 and entitled *A Brief History of the Coloured Baptists*. The history of this Association will be traced in the next chapter.

By 1853, the black population of Nova Scotia was no longer a transient one groping for moorings. It was already producing personalities who would earn honour in both near and far places.

THE PERIOD 1854–1918

THE AFRICAN UNITED BAPTIST ASSOCIATION

By 1853 Richard Preston had been instrumental in setting up eleven black Baptist churches in various parts of mainland Nova Scotia. One other black Baptist church had survived since the days of David George in Moose River, Cumberland County, making a total of twelve churches ready for an organizational structure which would bind them closer together and enable them to grow in strength and numbers.

Once again, Richard Preston took the lead. In 1854 it was thirty-eight years since he had arrived in Halifax as a black refugee in search of his mother. In these formative years of black settlement he had had a foretaste of what was in store for black people in Nova Scotia. He would remember how his mentor, John Burton, had been reviled for associating with black church members, how white church dissenters from the Anglican Church joined Burton's church, only to leave it soon afterwards because of its dominant black membership. He would remember his own short stint as a delegate from Burton's church to the Maritime Baptist Association which was then notably cool towards Burton and his church. With this experience behind him, coupled with his British education and experience, Richard Preston was well qualified to take the lead in the formation of the African United Baptist Association on the first day of September, 1854.

The inaugural meeting of the A.U.B.A. was held in the picturesque setting of Granville Mountain, some twenty kilometres from Inglewood

(Bridgetown). Ordained ministers of the black (African) Baptist churches, licensed ministers, deacons and elders constituted the founding members. Thirty-six delegates in all, drawn from the twelve black Baptist churches, tackled the important task of setting up an Association which would be the largest organization in the history of the black population in Nova Scotia. It would also become the oldest organization of its size. These founding fathers did their work so surely and securely that the A.U.B.A. has not had to look back since 1854 in spite of a split in the Association from 1867 to 1880. Their names and their work deserve to be recorded and remembered.[1]

Of the thirty-six delegates, there were three ordained ministers: Rev. Richard Preston, listed in the minutes of the Association as Bishop, Halifax; Rev. John Hamilton, Hammonds Plains, and Rev. Henry Jackson, Bear River. John Hamilton was born in Africa and came to Nova Scotia, like Richard Preston, as a black refugee from Virginia. Like Preston, he came under the tutelage of John Burton. Henry Jackson lived to see the ordination of his son, James Edward, in 1867. The younger Jackson then left to seek employment in the United States but returned three years later to work for the Maritime Baptist Association in various posts in western Nova Scotia. Of these pioneer ministers, Richard Preston and John Hamilton died in the same year, 1861; Preston on July 16 and John Hamilton on November 19 while Henry Jackson died some time after the ordination of his son in 1867. In 1854, when their monumental achievement was registered, they were approaching the end of their lives.

The African United Baptist Association was inaugurated at Granville Mountain on September 1, 1854 and held its first annual convention a year later at the same venue on the anniversary date with Rev. Henry Jackson as first Moderator and Septimus Clarke as first Clerk, a position he occupied until his death in January, 1859. A number of motions adopted at the first annual session have guided the Association throughout the 136 Sessions that have been held between 1855 and 1989 when the present study ends. The first of these was to confer upon the Cornwallis Street Baptist Church in Halifax the status of Mother Church of the Association.

During the lifetime of Richard Preston, the Association remained united and continued to grow. Beginning with 12 churches, 3 ordained ministers and 308 members in 1855, the numbers advanced to 15 churches, 4 ordained ministers and 443 members in 1861.[2]

Richard Preston's background, training and leadership qualities were difficult to replace. It is understandable, then, that serious difficulties arose after his death. The successor to Preston at the Cornwallis Street Baptist Church was a Welshman by the name of Rev. James Thomas who had been brought to Nova Scotia by his parents when he was 12 years old. His parents acquired a farm in the Preston settlement from where his father travelled to Halifax to carry out his fur business. James Thomas married a black woman named Hannah Saunders and consequently associated with the black community. As a founding member of the Cornwallis Street Baptist Church, he worked closely with Richard Preston. His interest in evangelical work led to his ordination by his mentor in 1857. It was thus a short step for Rev. Thomas to take up a dual responsibility in 1861 as pastor of Cornwallis Street Baptist Church and Moderator of the A.U.B.A.[3]

The pastorate of James Thomas lasted for 18 years between 1861 and 1879 during which both growth and upheavals took place. A crisis of leadership developed when Rev. Benson Smithers of the First Preston Church withdrew from A.U.B.A. in 1869 and formed a rival association. At the same time unsuccessful attempts were made to impeach Rev. James Thomas in Halifax. Since both these church leaders were competing for leadership roles in the black community, with one being white and the other black, it is a moot point whether race featured as an important issue in the divisions which rent the church between 1867 and 1880. Since the issues were manifold, it is difficult to identify a single root cause: Smithers faced charges of personal immorality; Thomas faced charges related to trust and management. When the situation led to two parallel Associations, the broader membership was drawn in and sides were taken. After more than a decade of division and rancour, resolution and reconciliation were achieved when James Thomas died in 1879. The period between 1861 and 1879 was a trying time for the A.U.B.A. with affiliates and opponents competing to preserve the groundwork laid by their respected leader, the Reverend Richard Preston.

The rivalry and the divisions traced above indicate growth within the black community. More people were being involved and more ideas were emerging. Greater accountability was required as more leaders were staking claims. Even if quarrels were disquieting, they were, after all, family quarrels. Outside the family there continued to be the more pressing matter of presenting the case of the black community for advancement in all spheres of Nova Scotian life. In his report to the annual session of A.U.B.A. in 1877, the Clerk of the Association, Peter E. McKerrow, who served in that capacity from 1876 till his death in 1906, reminded the members that Blacks in

Nova Scotia were being weighed down by racial discrimination, that while their votes were canvassed by the politicians they were receiving little in return and having "to put up with the meanest of school houses that the province can afford, which deserves the greatest censure from the educated world."[4]

On this matter of education, A.U.B.A. has always taken an active interest. In 1883, a petition prepared and signed by Rev. Alexander Bailey, pastor of the Cornwallis Street Baptist Church from 1879 to 1880, Rev. Wilton Boone, pastor of the same church from 1880 to 1881 and Peter McKerrow, was presented to the Legislative Assembly. This will be treated in more detail under education in this chapter.

Between 1879 and 1918, when chapter two closes, there were 12 pastors who served at the Cornwallis Street Baptist Church, many of them were from the United States.[5] While the majority of them served for periods ranging from one to three years, the notable exception was Rev. M.B. Puryear who served from 1909 to 1917. He came to Halifax from Harrisburg, Pennsylvania, and immediately plunged himself in developing projects and reorganizing the church. One of his more notable achievements was the groundwork laid and supported for the setting up of an industrial school for Blacks in Nova Scotia.

James R. Johnston, Nova Scotia's first black lawyer.

The credit for this idea and enterprise must go to an outstanding Nova Scotian whose life was cut short in its prime by tragic circumstances. This man was James R. Johnston who first joined the A.U.B.A. in 1886 as the holder of three important positions in the Mother Church, the Cornwallis Street Baptist Church. He was superintendent of the Sunday school, clerk of the church and president and organiser of the Baptist Youth Provincial Union. He accepted these responsibilities at a time when very few young Blacks were profiting from elementary education, let alone higher school education. He became the first in a long line of young Blacks in Nova

Scotia who have grappled with the problem of raising standards through personal examples and achievements. He was the first Nova Scotian Black to be admitted to the Dalhousie Law School from which he graduated in 1898.

Already an outstanding young man, scholar, church-goer and community worker, he stood on the threshold of greater things to come when he was called upon to assume the mantle of the Clerkship of the A.U.B.A. when his uncle, Peter McKerrow, died in 1906. James Johnston held this position until he was killed in a family quarrel in 1915.

As already noted in various places above, the Baptist churches individually and the A.U..B.A. collectively were deeply concerned about the disparities in the education system. Petitions for government aid to keep the segregated schools open brought little or no actual sustained relief. Year after year, the A.U.B.A. debated the matter of schooling in search of alternatives. The idea of starting a Normal and Industrial Institute came up from time to time. With so many pastors being recruited from the United States, American models like the Hampden Institute and the Tuskegee Institute came under active consideration. In 1908, lawyer Johnston crystallised the ideas and came forward with a definite plan to set up such an institute. The proposals received support from an influential quarter when Rev. Moses Puryear assumed office in 1909. Even then, it took five years of planning to get the proposals off the ground. In 1914, Rev. Puryear convened a public meeting to enlist the support of church and civic leaders and then took the matter to the annual convention of the A.U.B.A. in September, 1915. The Association supported the creation of The Industrial School of Nova Scotia for Coloured Children, noting that there was no institution at the time where black men and women could receive industrial, domestic and business training.[6]

These developments constitute the background to the formation of the Nova Scotia Home for Coloured Children and they show the very close affinity between the A.U.B.A. and the Home. This relationship has endured with the passage of time. Indeed, one regular item at the annual meeting of the Association ever since the Home was founded is the report by the Home to the Association.

What started off as The Industrial School included another feature from the beginning. While it is true that there was an urgent need for an institution to provide industrial, business and domestic training for Blacks, it was equally true that an institution was urgently required to place orphans and destitute black children in suitable shelter. Pearleen Oliver tells us of the case of the black baby boy born at the Victoria General Hospital in Halifax in 1914 whose mother died during the birth and who could not be placed in a single Protestant institution. The Catholic institution which came to the baby's rescue was most probably the St. Patrick's Home in Halifax.[7] The following extract, taken from a contemporary source, touches upon the problem and the attempted solution:

> As a result of the interest and humane attitude taken in the matter of the neglected coloured children of the community and province by certain of the leading citizens of the city, a home for neglected coloured children seems now an assured fact. Work in fitting up the house that will be used is under way, and as soon as the renovation is completed, it will be opened for the reception of children. An ideal site has been secured, through the efforts and faithful labor of Mr. E.H. Blois, on the grounds of the Halifax Industrial School. This building will take care of at least fifteen or more of such children.[8]

Many facts emerge from this report. The public meeting called by Rev. Puryear in 1914 led to a request to the province to introduce an act of incorporation setting up the industrial school which would also accommodate children in need of shelter. A Board of Trustees made up of ten members was drawn from the provincial, civic, community and church sectors, a truly representative body, chaired by H.G. Bauld, M.P.P. with R.H. Murray, K.C. as secretary and G.R. Hart as treasurer. The other seven members were M.B. Puryear, E.H. Blois, C. Strickland, C. Blackadar, John Murphy, J.A.R. Kinney and Thomas P. Johnson. The house leased for this enterprise is stated to have been part of the Halifax Industrial School, probably the Industrial School and Home run by St. Patrick's Church in Halifax.[9]

The Board of Trustees included three prominent black members who were active in the A.U.B.A. More will be said about them in chapter three when the story is told of what came to be known, since June 6, 1921, as the Nova Scotia Home for Coloured Children. For now, a public appeal was made by the Board in October, 1917 to launch the initiative. An editorial comment in the local paper pointed out that while it was easier to place neglected white children in homes, the same was not true in the case of black children. With an eye to the ravages of the world war then in progress, the editorial referred to the grave responsibility vested in society to nurture its human resources. Part of this comment of 1917 is recalled here to underline its relevance to the Nova Scotia scene of 1989 when similar concerns are felt in society and politics, in race and inter-personal relations:

> The wealth of a nation is its child life, so that the conservation of its youth becomes a prime matter of great importance and especially so at this present world upheaval when so much of its real manhood is being sacrificed in the cause of human freedom. It is our duty to see that all of the children, who are to be the men and women of the future, be given a fair start in life. A thrifty, intelligent and law-abiding neighbor is a greater asset to the community than a worthless dependent, regardless of his race or creed. With this as the guiding motive, this Home is established and on these principles its founders and friends appeal for active sympathy and kind consideration on the part of a generous public. [10]

It was through the efforts of Rev. Puryear that the services of one Miss Jackson from Philadelphia were engaged to run the Home. This well-qualified tutor assumed office in November, 1917 and a few weeks later, on December 6, the Halifax Explosion destroyed the building which housed the Home. That tragedy marked the end of what must be considered to be the initial chapter in the history of the Home for Coloured Children and also, for the time being, the dream of lawyer James R. Johnston that a school would be part of the Home. The second chapter would open four years later to mark the realisation of the dream.

The A.U.B.A. continued to be active and prominent in the formation and direction of the Home through the contribution of the clergy as well as laymen like James R. Johnston and J.A.R. Kinney, Sr. who held the influential position of Clerk of the Association. Kinney held this position from 1916 to 1922 and was, consequently, involved in the Home when it was initially started in Halifax in 1917 and when it was relocated on the outskirts of Dartmouth, in Westphal, in 1921.

Another layman involved from the beginning was Thomas P. Johnson who served on the foundation Board of the Home. He held the position of treasurer of A.U.B.A. for the 21 years between 1915 and 1936. The financial bequest he left to the Association is operative to this very day.

In the period covered in this chapter the A.U.B.A. developed into a powerful institution. New traditions were established and leaders in the spiritual and secular fields gained experience. Youth sections were started in the

The women's executive of the African United Baptist Association of Nova Scotia 1919–1920. Back row (l–r): Maggie Walsh, Julia Williams, Louise Bundy, Nettie Kinney, Annie Thompson; middle row: Muriel States, Margaret Upshaw, Maude Sparks, Bessie Wyse, Sophie Wilson, Isabel Diggs; front row: C. M. Saunders, Sara Middleton, Mary Saunders.

affiliated churches modelled along the lines of the Baptist Young People's Union at the Cornwallis Street Baptist Church and attributed to the initiative of James R. Johnston in 1898, the very year he graduated with a law degree from Dalhousie University. Numbers began to grow steadily, from 520 in 1880 to 648 in 1914, though Robin Winks informs us that the figure was once considerably higher: "in 1897, following another awakening, there were twenty-two churches and 2,440 members."[11] Its involvement in the establishment of the principles and the ground rules for a Home and Industrial School for black children and youth was bold and forward looking as was the involvement of women in the movement. This last-named development deserves special mention because of the pioneering nature of the work.

The first woman delegate to the annual convention of the Association was registered as Sister S. Gray from Falmouth in 1891, 37 years after the Association was formed. In successive years the few women delegates found an opportunity to speak on such issues as temperance, education and mission work. Indeed, in holding the family together, black women played a crucial part. If they were late in becoming actively involved in the

Association directly, they made up with their innovative work within a few short years. Women's groups were formed and specific tasks were undertaken in such activities as the Pastor's Aid Society in Halifax in 1895, collecting funds for the proposed Normal and Industrial Institute in 1908, the Bright Lights Mission Band in Hammonds Plains in 1909, the Women's Missionary Society in 1913 and the Ladies' Auxiliary of the A.U.B.A. in 1917. The inaugural meeting of the Ladies' Auxiliary took place in East Preston on 3 September, 1917 under the leadership of its first president, Maude Sparks.[12] Referred to in popular folklore as the Meeting of Women at the Well, after the site of the initial meeting, this event has gone down in the annals of the history of the A.U.B.A. as an historic occasion of considerable significance. Black women had organized themselves in a way which had no counterpart at the time among the male membership. It was only in 1944 that the men formed the Laymen's Council.

The work of the Ladies Auxiliary grew so rapidly that in two years' time there was need for a full-time worker to promote women's activities and participation in the work of the Association. Margaret Upshaw, a vice-president of the Auxiliary, was the first holder of this position. This development

The executive committee of the African United Baptist Association of Nova Scotia 1919–1920. Back row: Jas A. R. Kinney, secretary; Rev. W. N. States, assistant secretary; front row: Thomas P. Johnson, treasurer; Rev. A. A. Wyse, moderator; Rev. (Capt.) W. A. White, vice-moderator.

must rank among the notable and durable achievements of the A.U.B.A. covered in this chapter.

EDUCATION

As reviewed in Chapter 1, the major burden of providing education to black children in Nova Scotia (between 1800 and 1850) was borne by white missionary societies and churches, notably the Associates of the late Dr. Bray (1785) and the Society for the Propagation of the Gospel (1796). The limitations of the Education Act of 1811 have been discussed. The amendment introduced in 1836 to mitigate the main difficulty of funding to establish and maintain separate black schools in the segregated black settlements provided for a ceiling of seventy pounds sterling to be disbursed for this purpose throughout the province.

To see just how far seventy pounds sterling (roughly 150 dollars today) would go on a provincial basis, one need only look at the cost of running a special school for black children which opened in Halifax in 1836 at the corner of Gerrish and Maynard streets, called the African School. Dr. Robert Willis, Rector of St. Paul's Church submitted a petition in 1840 on behalf of the black community of Halifax for continued provincial support and listed the income and expenditure as follows:

Income: Fees by scholars—17 pounds, 5 shillings; Donation by Dr. Gray's Associates—50 pounds; Provincial grant—100 pounds; Private subscriptions—5 pounds, making a total of 172 pounds, 5 shillings.

Expenditure: Fuel—22 pounds, 1 shilling, 6 pence; Contingency expenses—5 pounds, 19 shillings, 4 pence; salary of the master—110 pounds; salary of the mistress—40 pounds, making a total of 178 pounds and ten pence. (One pound sterling is roughly two dollars in Canadian currency today and one shilling is roughly ten cents.)

Many points of discussion arise out of this information. Fees paid by the students represented some 10% of the total cost. The proportion of grants obtained and the disparity in salaries of the sexes were notable features. The crucial one for our purpose is the utter inadequacy of the amount of money made available in the 1836 amendment.

Regulations introduced in 1864 provided that school fees would no longer be paid by children attending the common schools set up under the terms of the 1811 Education Act, provided that they resided in the school district. Once again, this excluded the majority of the black children since they resided outside the white school district. Worse was to follow a year later when the Council of Public Instruction was authorized to set up separate departments under the same roof or set up separate roofs for children of different sexes and colours. It was only in Halifax that three separate schools were set up for black pupils, the African school at the intersection of Gerrish and Maynard streets being one; the second school stood on what was called Poplar Grove, "a street which ran north to south between Jacob and Procter Streets, probably bisecting the Trade Mart......"[14], while the Africville school was the third one. In the rest of the province, wherever Blacks were in sizeable numbers or in the majority, separate schools were provided for black children with all the attendant problems of keeping them open on a regular basis comparable to the common schools. Separate provisions meant inferior standards and these ranged all the way from the calibre of the teachers recruited to the quality of the facilities provided. From this time onwards a pattern of irregular, interrupted and inferior education developed throughout the province where separate schools existed.

The black communities of Nova Scotia, scattered as they were in isolated pockets throughout the province, with a variety of backgrounds and experiences, could not be expected to be united in their response to separate schools. Responding pragmatically to local situations, some were in favour while others were opposed. Taking the province as a whole, however, without regard to race, the majority of petitions received opposed separate schools. The Committee on Education reported as follows to the House of Assembly in 1869:

> "The committee have had before them a large number of petitions in favour of the present law and against separate schools, and are of opinion that so serious a change in our present educational system as the introduction of separate schools would be injurious......"[14a]

In Halifax, there was strong opposition to the two separate schools described above and for the reasons already stated. Excluding the Africville school which served that community, the two Halifax schools served a community of some two hundred families living in the city with a school-age population of some 560 children. The community response to these two schools is of special significance and is embodied in the petition of 1883.

The petition, bearing 106 signatures and carrying the names of Revs. Boone and Bailey, pastors of the Cornwallis Street African Baptist Church—

itself located in very close proximity to the two schools—and Peter McKerrow, Clerk of the A.U.B.A., drew attention to the steps taken by the government to circumvent the spirit of its own earlier legislation:

That on or about the months of December, 1876, your petitioners learned for the first time, that a minute had been passed the Council of Public instruction, in defiance of the whole tenor and general spirit of Act establishing free schools in Nova Scotia and which enabled the Commissioners of Schools for this city to exclude all coloured children, so called, from the common schools and to establish separate schools for said children. That the alleged minute of Council was passed on the recommendation of the Inspector of Schools for the County, which recommendation your memorialists have reason to believe was not only never made by the Inspector of Schools for the County, but the sentiments therein contained is utterly opposed to the sentiments of said Inspector, both then and now, as well as abhorrent to the views and feelings of your petitioners, and that it is utterly false for any man to say that the coloured people of this city ever concurred in such an arrangement, especially when the said minute of Council assumes an inferiority which we deny.[15]

This petition contains an important testimony, a testimony on how the bureaucracy is manipulated for political ends. In western democracy, the civil service is lauded for its impartiality but the black experience in Nova Scotia has shown that politicians and bureaucrats have often combined to ignore the plight of black Nova Scotians.

Separate schools sprang up in Halifax, Preston, Hammond's Plains, Birchtown, Port Latour, Brindley Town and Liverpool. Their category was that of "private" schools as opposed to "common" schools, the funding for which could by no means come by way of the Education Act of 1836 or the Education Act of 1811—that of 1836 was too small to go around while that of 1811 required a community contribution which was just not available. The channel used by the provincial government was that of a charitable donation, the kind of provision which consigned the recipient to a lower order of citizenry.

Besides the lowly status of the private schools, the curriculum emphasized the bias of their sponsors, stressing religious education and church music, basic literacy, arithmetic and carpentry for boys and needlework and domestic work for girls. Nor was this the only distinction. The common or public schools in white school districts were superior in quality to similar category schools in black school districts as a result of larger budgets for salaries, books, and equipment. The overall results, as Walker tells us, were utterly debasing: "Inevitably, the education received by blacks was inferior. School buildings were often overcrowded and ramshackle, creating an environment that was not inclined to encourage blacks to attend. Teachers willing to work for low pay in isolated communities tended to be underqualified, and some were barely literate."[16]

The debate on the merits and demerits of the colour line in education finally reached the floors of the Legislative Council and Assembly in 1884 after simmering since the colour line was introduced in 1876. It opened with a delegation comprising black and white members which called on the Committee on Education. The black members on the delegation were Rev. Henry H. Johnson, William Johnson and Peter McKerrow. According to the press report of the proceedings, the following account deals with the case presented by Rev. Johnson:

Rev. H.H. Johnson was not there seeking equality socially of the coloured people with the white, but seeking their rights as citizens to equal educational advantages with the white children on the ground that the coloured people were British subjects and had equal rights; because the press of Canada has condemned the color line; because the press of the United States has condemned the same; because best men in Halifax have signed to blot it out; because City Council was in favour of equal rights for the coloured men; because with the exception of a few anonymous communications nothing has been said against it; that in many of the schools coloured children are now attending—none of the whites have left or have any complaints come to the fore. He wished to impress the importance of the fact that temporizing with prejudice is a sure way of increasing its importance. He stigmatised this color line as a relic of slavery, and asked for justice for the coloured people.[17]

This report is recalled in some detail to enable the reader to draw a comparison between what is stated in this report with what was reported in the local press over a hundred years later, in 1989, and attributed, for example, to the Parent–Student Association of Preston or the Afro–Canadian Caucus of Nova Scotia in another education crisis in Nova Scotia associated with racial conflict in the Cole Harbour District High School and dealt with in the concluding chapters of this book.

In summary, what Rev. Johnson was saying was that the perspective of the broader community was not reflected in the policy pursued by some politicians. One of them, Robert Hockin, Conservative member from Pictou County and a member of the Education Committee, was impressed by the case presented by Johnson and his fellow members of the delegation and agreed to introduce an amendment to the colour provisions in the law of 1876. This was how a full-blown debate ensued in both chambers of the legislature during March–April, 1884.

From the outset, it was clear to Council members in the so-called colour line debate that the critical area was the city of Halifax where the black children attended four schools mainly, identified in the speech made by the member from Yarmouth as Africville, Lockman Street (between Gerrish and North Streets), Maynard Street and the National School (located at George and Argyle Streets where the Five Fisherman's Restaurant stands today). A few attended St. Mary's School (on Grafton Street). This member argued that what was perceived to be a problem in Halifax city was hardly a problem at all where no more than a hundred black children on the whole were concerned. There was no need for a colour line in education, he argued, and the matter should be left to the trustees of the different sections in the province and the Board of School Commissioners in the city of Halifax to act with uprudence, tact and judgment." The member (Loran E. Baker, Liberal) concluded with a call for justice and fairplay and for an extension of the educational advantages enjoyed by white children to black children as well.[18]

The statement attributed to Dr. Daniel Parker, (Conservative) who supported the position taken by the member from Yarmouth, deserves detailed mention as a commentary on racism and bigotry and what the consequences of such behaviour are for both the perpetrators and the victims:

In this Province civil rights, religious rights and educational rights were for every man and every man's child, and yet they were striving or some persons in the city would strive, to exclude these people from the privileges which the law was supposed to confer upon every citizen. These coloured people were citizens performing the duties of citizenship. When the tax collector came to their doors he did not pass

by them without first collecting the taxes due by them as taxpayers......He had listened with a great deal of attention......to the statements made by some of the coloured men who had come before the
committee......They had come here as educated men, and their desire
was to elevate those to whom they were sent as preachers, and they
had done much towards that end......but they saw this distinction and
they saw that children living in the northern end of the city had to pass
the doors of the school situated in their section and perhaps walk a
mile or miles, because the color line excluded them from the schools
which they ought properly to attend. One of them had very well put
it to the committee, that they would not allow the child of a
respectable coloured man, who was obliged to pass the school, while
the child of a prostitute might enter and receive an education
there......[19]

This speaker asked what his fellow legislators were there for: to pander
to popular prejudice or to uphold the principle of the constitution that provided for every person equal rights and privileges before the law. He asked
his fellow legislators, especially the supporters of the colour line in education—the exclusion of black children from the common schools—to put
themselves in the position of the oppressed. Would they like their children
to be excluded? He produced a letter he had received from the Principal of
the National School, a common school, which contained the following statement:

I have been teaching about seven years, and for the past two years as
principal of the National School. A short time after taking charge of the
school, I was asked to allow some of the coloured boys to attend. I
consented and since that day six have attended the different departments of the school. They have all behaved well and no disagreeable
results have followed their attending the school. Before they came I
told the boys they were coming, that they wanted an education, and
as their parents paid taxes like other people they had the same right
there as white children. They sit, play and recite with the other boys,
and I have never heard anybody object. The attendance has not fallen
off, and last of all one of the boys will be ready for High School next
summer.[20]

Despite the eloquent and persuasive arguments presented in the Legislative Council to reject the colour line in education, the efforts were defeated by eight votes to seven. A compromise amendment was then introduced by Samuel Creelman from Truro, himself a one-time school teacher, and adopted. The operative sentence stated that "colored pupils shall not be excluded from instruction in the public schools in the section or ward where they reside." With this amendment the Council of Public Instruction was free to provide separate schools for the sexes and for black children.

As far as legislative procedures went, the matter was not yet settled. The debates and decision of the Legislative Council are only part of the story. At a time when Nova Scotia had two legislative chambers, there was always the possibility that conflict between the different chambers could lead to a polarisation in which issues could be affected. Unhappily for the supporters of desegregated schools in 1884, conflict between the two chambers was one of the determining factors. When the Conservatives were in government from 1878 to 1882, the Liberals in the Legislative Council, led by Thomas F. Morrison, used the upper house to thwart government legislation. In 1884, the reverse held true. There was a Liberal government in office and high on the Liberal agenda of the day was the introduction of separate schools for black children. Morrison's defence of the proposed legislation drew forth the wrath of the Conservatives in the Council who remembered Morrison's obstructionist strategy in 1878-1882.[21] Had a bi-partisan spirit pervaded the debates one might have been better informed on the racial attitudes of politicians of the day. The political conflict between the two chambers blurred the debates.

The two key figures in the Legislative Assembly debates were the Conservative member from Pictou County, Robert Hockin, and the Liberal member from Halifax County, William S. Fielding, managing editor of the *Halifax Morning Chronicle.*

Though segregated schools were not an issue in Hockin's constituency, he opposed such a provision on principle, describing it as an outmoded barbarous law. Its strongest advocate, William Fielding, was no doubt representing the general attitude of his constituents, a position which found kindred echo more than a hundred years later in the Assembly debates relating to the Cole Harbour District High School racial incidents of January, 1989 discussed in the concluding sections of this book.

Fielding's position was that it was the duty of legislators to make laws "for the greatest good of the greatest number." Excerpts from the reported account of Fielding's views make for interesting discussion in the light of the evolving attitudes on racial issues:

> From the standpoint of theory we would perhaps say that colored children were entitled to admission to the public schools of the city, but there was a prejudice so deep that it could not be suddenly uprooted. It might be admitted that men should be regarded for what they were worth, regardless of color and creed; but even in the neighbouring republic—where if anywhere all men were supposed to be equal—the prejudice existed, and, although all men were equal in the eye of the law, they were not equal in matters of social life. He thought that if time was afforded the School Board would be able to relieve to a large extent the grievances at present complained of......From the stand point of taxation the colored people had no grievance. It was a fact that, in proportion of the numbers attending these schools, the education of colored children cost much more than the education of white children. They were not paying money for which they received nothing. The question was not one that was entirely confined to Halifax. He believed that the rule was in force elsewhere......[22]

Fielding had spoken of deep-rooted prejudice that needed time to work itself out. He argued also for time to allow the school board to resolve the issues, that equality before the law did not necessarily mean extending its implications to include a just social order. Fielding's position was that services should match taxation contributions. These were points articulated in 1884. The reader in 1989 and beyond will measure these postulates against the actual performance over more than one hundred years.

The motion to abolish the colour line in education was argued vigorously in the House of Assembly and was narrowly defeated by 17 votes to 15. Perhaps the deciding point lay in the expressed fear that if public schools were opened to black children, white parents would withdraw their children and send them to private schools, even though one member pleaded that this could be averted if the Education Act of 1883—providing for compulsory attendance—was invoked.

It was the measure adopted on March 28, 1884 in the Nova Scotia House of Assembly establishing segregated schools for black children that was sent to the Legislative Council where, as reviewed in earlier pages, it was amended to read "but colored pupils shall not be excluded from instruction in the public school in the section or ward in which they reside."

The amendment became the subject of further debate and varied inter-pretations in the House of Assembly before it was finally adopted by 15 votes to 10, with William Fielding being one of the ten. Four months later, in July, 1884, William S. Fielding, strong and unrelenting advocate of sepa-rate schools for black children in Nova Scotia, became Premier of the Province—a position he held till 1896—ensuring that during his tenure the pattern of segregated schools would endure, except for the marginality of the amendment squeezed in against his will which allowed black students to attend public schools in the section or ward in which they resided.

In the history of race relations in Nova Scotia, the colour line debate pro-vides interesting grist for the historical mill: Fielding's philosophy of the greatest good for the greatest number and Hockin's retort that if legislation was to be governed by phrases one needed to throw in the phrase that it was a fundamental principle of all law that there was no other bound to the liberty of a subject, excepting where it trespassed on the liberty of another. Hockin's point was that in providing for separate schools for black children, Nova Scotians were trespassing on the liberty of the black people of Nova Scotia. Jason Mack, a lawyer from Queen's County and supporter of Robert Hockin, reminded his audience of the conundrum of a colour law: "It was difficult to tell from the law what degrees or shades of colour would be included."23

The Education Act which became law in April, 1884 stipulated that a black child could not be excluded from attending a school in the ward or section in which the child resided but the government would continue to provide for separate schools for the sexes and the colours. The result was that segregated schools were strengthened in areas of high black concentra-tion and weakened in areas where a few black families resided.

The Education Act of 1918 reaffirmed the principles and the formula of the 1884 Act with the further provision that the Council of Public Instruction could receive recommendations from school inspectors to establish separate buildings for different sexes and different races in Nova Scotia, again with the proviso that black children would not be excluded from the section in which they lived.

For all practical purposes, the majority of black children who went to school in Nova Scotia in the period covered in this chapter went to segre-gated schools, mostly one-room schools in which they received a modicum of education compared to the situation in the majority of the public schools.

137

One cannot agree more strongly with Robin Winks' perceptive comments that "Between 1918 and 1954, when the racial reference was dropped from the statute, the Negro schools continued to fare badly, and the most blind of school inspectors could not have pretended that separate education was equal education."[24]

While the city of Halifax was a glaring example of iniquities in education, the town of Dartmouth took pride in being more progressive. The warden and town councillors received a pat on the back from the town's School Committee:

Your committee beg to congratulate you upon your being the first school board in this Province to adopt the new amendment in the education act allowing any school Board to see to it that all children under its jurisdiction are receiving an education somewhere. It is also a subject of congratulation that while in the neighbouring city the question of a color line has been agitating the people, the town of Dartmouth has been enjoying the reward of having treated its colored inhabitants in the spirit of fair play, by giving them every educational advantage enjoyed by others. And now your committee has just engaged for them the first colored teacher who has ever succeeded in this province in obtaining a first class license.[25]

The identity of this black teacher has not yet been established, though it is clear that since the 1880s teachers assigned to schools for black children were holders of Permissive Licenses. For example, the inspector of schools reported in 1892 that in four school sections in which segregated black schools existed: Beech Hill (later Beechville), Halifax African, Cobequid Road and Lucasville, all the teachers were in possession of permissive licenses. The report acknowledged that the teachers were not necessarily incompetent but they lacked training and experience. When plans were laid to open the Partridge River School in 1892, many things were lacking, including a suitable school house, finances and teachers.[26] A year later the school in Beech Hill was burnt down and was not replaced for at least two years.

The report on "Colored Schools" in Halifax County for 1895-96 paints a depressing picture:

Out of the eight sections in this County only one had school during the year. The African section above Hammonds Plains, with a school

CHAPTER TWO: THE PERIOD 1854-1918

population of upwards of 50, has been without a school for the last
five years. After much laudable effort they have succeeded in providing suitable accommodation, and will commence a section in August,
1894. The Lucas Settlement has a comfortable house and kept a school
for the year. Maroon Hill, with a poor school house, kept a school
open for only one term in the last seven years. Beech Hill, with some
aid from the Commissioners, has put up a small house, and will shortly open a school. Lake Loon, with a pretty good house, has been
closed. Preston, with children enough for a large school, has no school
house, and has had no school open for the last fifteen years. I have
repeatedly visited this section, and done my best to create an interest,
but have hitherto utterly failed. Partridge River (Preston), with upwards
of 60 children, had their house destroyed by fire in 1892, but at the last
annual meeting they voted money to erect a new school. But suppose
we had in each of these sections a well equipped school house, the
question arises, how are we to get good teachers, such as these poor
people require; for unless such special aid is given as will induce competent teachers to take charge, the colored people, of whom there are
upwards of 300, will be left to struggle on in their ignorance.[27]

The above detailed excerpt is a fair, if depressing, commentary on the
standard of education available for the black people of Nova Scotia. A hundred years ago there was talk of special aid to prevent generations from lan-
guishing in ignorance. It is no small wonder that the same cry is being
repeated a hundred years later. What went wrong and who was responsible? Government policy and the lack of will to foster the creation of a just
society based on fair opportunities, must shoulder a large part of the blame.
But so must the African Baptist churches and the Baptist Association, especially at a time when hope and leadership, guidance and innovation, were
left to them and indeed accepted by them as falling within their domain.

It was not that individuals lacked the fortitude or good sense to march
forward. Since the middle years of the nineteenth century, success stories
began to emerge: in the neighbouring province of New Brunswick, Arthur
Richardson became the first black university graduate in 1886 and Mary
Matilda Winslow, the first black woman graduate in 1905, while in Nova
Scotia, James R. Johnston, already mentioned in earlier pages, graduated in
Law in 1898 and opened his law office in Halifax at 197 Hollis Street, oppo-
site the Legislature. The first black teacher to obtain teaching qualifications

Members of the Odd Fellows Lodge pose before the Gerrish Street Hall in Halifax, around 1919–1920.

in New Brunswick in 1886 was William Gosman. All three of the New Brunswick graduates left that province to work in neighbouring and distant places. Winslow certainly worked in Halifax County for some time.

These pioneering examples were followed by Nova Scotian blacks like Selina Williams, later Jefferson, of Fall River and Fred Jemmot of Africville. These small beginnings were important milestones in the challenging road which lay ahead. The names which have come down of black teachers in Nova Scotia in the period covered in this chapter are few in number. This is not unusual in pioneering contexts anywhere. What is important is that the examples of such pioneers as Thomas Brownspriggs, Dempsey Jordan, Selina Williams, Fred Jemmot and Margaret Upshaw—all of whom had been associated with school teaching in this period and a few years preceding it— not only endured but went on to inspire many later generations of dedicated black teachers whose contribution will be discussed in later chapters. In turn, teachers in the formal school system owed much to the example and inspiration of the black Baptist churches, other churches, as well as the African United Baptist Association. The Sunday School was the training ground for teachers as were such organizations as the Masonic orders, all searching for ways and means to forge ahead.

The Masonic organizations go back to the middle years of the nineteenth century. In 1856 the Negro Lodge of Free and Accepted Masons was founded and in the next four decades it was joined by the Independent Order of Odd fellows, the Loyal Order of Wilberforce and the Lodge of the Ancient Foresters, all "serving the mystical, psychological and social needs of Black adults. Those organizations not only performed supportive functions, but by their very existence acted as a safe haven through which skills, knowledge and social graces, observed while working in the white community, could be introduced, refined and acted out without obstruction by members of the White community."[28]

While many Masons have contributed to the improvement in the quality of life of black Nova Scotians, one name is advanced at this early stage to illustrate the force of masonry. Clarence H. Johnston was born in Halifax in 1892 and began his working life as a station porter at the North Street station in Halifax in 1911. In later years he became active in three masonic orders while his association with the Cornwallis Street Baptist Church never wavered. He served the church in many capacities and notably as the Superintendant of the Sunday School for 35 years. On March 11, 1915 Clarence Johnston, then 23 years old, wrote to the Prime Minister of Canada, seeking a position in the public service. Four days later, a reply was dispatched from the Prime Minister's office:

Your case is being placed before several of the Ministers with a view to having some provision made for your entrance into the public service. I shall be glad to assist in any reasonable way. Mr. Regan, who has written to me on the subject, is being informed that your application has been commended to the attention of four departments of the Government.[29]

This personal example is used to illustrate the strength that came from a combination of factors and influences that exemplify the efforts made by black individuals, groups and organizations long ago to improve their lot at a time when there was a lot more prejudice and obstacles to overcome. The nineteenth century produced personalities from the black communities all over Nova Scotia who made their mark in near and distant places. Names such as Richard Preston and William Hall would bring pride to any place, anywhere, at any time because of the quality of their contribution to society.

William Hall, V.C.

"Canadian schoolbooks have long ignored the story of the blacks of Nova Scotia" was the opening line in an article which appeared in a prestigious United States newspaper in 1986.[30] One astonishing feature of this neglect is the abysmal ignorance on the part of generations of Canadians of the outstanding achievement of one of Canada's greatest sons. The ignorance is compounded by the fact that the memorial cairn constructed over his final resting place on the grounds of the Hantsport Baptist Church in Hants County carries an inscription which opens in small letters which read "The first Nova Scotian and the first man of colour to win the Empire's highest award for valour" but ends in conspicuous bold print which reads as follows: "his great pride was british heritage."

William Hall, as a black person, would surely have had pride in another heritage, too.

William Hall was born in the Annapolis Valley in 1828. After retiring from the Royal Navy, he settled on his farm in Avonport, where he died in 1904.

The century which produced William Hall and acknowledged him for his greatness produced others, too, some better known than others. Among the lesser known black personalities of Nova Scotia are two seamen who, like William Hall, sailed the seas to distant lands to earn fame and glory. The first was John Perry, also known as "The Black Sailor." He was born in Annapolis Royal in the early decades of the nineteenth century. His father once served in a British warship and would have most likely moved to and settled in Nova Scotia with the black loyalist immigrants. Young John Perry followed in his father's footsteps when he served in a British warship for four years, ending up in London, England, in November, 1845. Two months later, this well built man, standing six feet one and one-half inches and weighing 212 pounds made a successful debut in the boxing ring and

thus blazed the trail for a distinguished long line of Nova Scotian black boxers who followed in later years: men of courage and determination, like the
legendary George Dixon and Sam Langford, about whom more will be said
later.

The world of prize fighters was a rough and rocky one and John Perry
soon fell foul of the law, was convicted, and transported to the penal settlement of Australia for life. There, in New South Wales, he resumed his boxing exploits and on December 10, 1849, this black man from Annapolis
Royal, Nova Scotia, became the heavyweight boxing champion of Australia
in a contest which was staged in Cummings Point, Australia.[31] John Perry
went on to spend his life in Australia and earned a place in the annals of
that country's history through his personal triumph and through the triumphs of the many boxers he trained. His story exemplifies what a person
can achieve given an opportunity and a helping hand.

The other black seaman from Nova Scotia was Joseph B. Noil who was
born in Nova Scotia in 1841 at a time when John Perry was about to enter
service with the British navy. Joseph Noil enlisted in the United States navy
in 1871. In 1873, he was awarded the Medal of Honor, the highest award
that could be bestowed upon a serviceman in the United States for gallantry.
The captain of the United States steamer, *Powhatan*, submitted the following
report in Norfolk, Virginia, dated December 27, 1872, on the basis of which
Joseph Noil received his award:

I have the honor to bring [to] the notice of the Department the gallant
conduct of Joseph B. Noil, (negro) one of the crew of this vessel. The
circumstances are as follows: On yesterday morning the boatswain, I.C.
Walton, fell overboard from the forecastle, and was saved from drown-
ing by Joseph B. Noil, seaman, who was below on the berth-deck at
the time of the accident, and hearing the cry "man overboard," ran on
deck, took the end of a rope, went overboard, under the bow, and
caught Mr. Walton, who was then in the water, and held him up until
he was hauled into the boat sent to his rescue. The weather was bitter cold, had been sleeting, and it was blowing a gale from the north-
west at the time. Mr. Walton, when brought on board, was almost
insensible, and would have perished but for the noble conduct of Noil,
as he was sinking at the time he was rescued......Pierce Crosby,
Captain, Commanding.[32]

The noble conduct of one man saving the life of another man deserves the highest praise and surely represents the highest quality of human behaviour. The fact that Noil was black and Walton was white would ordinarily be irrelevant. However, placed in the context of race relations and the vilification of black people as inferior, unworthy, unreliable, immoral, dishonest, and so on, it raises questions of unfair stereotyping which has done so much damage. To most Nova Scotian whites of that period and subsequent periods, John Perry, Joseph Noil and William Hall would have been no more than upstart "niggers."

While no more is known about the lives of John Perry and Joseph Noil, fortunately for Nova Scotia and Canada the name of William Edward Hall V.C. has been immortalized through the memorial cairn erected over his grave on the grounds of the Hantsport Baptist Church. The various memorials are the William Hall V.C. Branch No. 57 of the Royal Canadian Legion which was incorporated in 1938—34 years after his death, the Da Costa-Hall Educational Programme for black students in Montreal, a gymnasium named after him in Cornwallis, Nova Scotia, and more recently in 1986 by the association of his name with the Nova Scotia Tattoo Gun Run. It is one thing to memorialize his name and fame; it is another thing to acknowledge the fact and to appreciate the significance that this great man of humble bearing and outstanding gallantry was a black Nova Scotian.

The precise location of the birthplace of William Hall has been the subject of a number of interpretations which list different locations in close proximity. These include Horton's Bluff, Hantsport, Avonport, Newport and Summerville. These variations arise because of folklore which associate the Hall family with living and working in these places at different times. Since the distances between these places are a few kilometres, the different interpretations are understandable. Consider the following account given by Dr. Phyllis R. Blakeley:

> While William was still a child, the Halls moved across the Avon River from Summerville to Horton's Bluff, a little village lying between Avonport and Hantsport, and William grew to manhood on the shores of the Avon River, living in a house that stood on the site of the Bluff Lighthouse.[33]

His father was an escaped slave from Virginia who defected to the British side in the War of 1812. William's parents were part of the total of some

2,000 black refugees who were brought to Nova Scotia between 1813 and 1816. The Halls were settled in the Annapolis Valley area described above. The most popular historical lore is that William Hall was born in Horton, near Avonport, near the site where the Horton Bluff lighthouse was later built, on 26 April, 1828. The Halls had three children, William, Mary and Rachael. The baptismal records, however, give the birthdate as April 25, 1829 and state that Jacob and Lucinda Hall had six children.

William Hall grew up in Hantsport at a time when this place was the centre of the wooden shipbuilding industry. There was little more that could influence a boy's thinking and interest given this environment and the fact that his father once worked for the famous Halifax shipowner, Samuel Cunard. Shipbuilding and sailing were part of the Hall household for father and son. Not far from their home was the famous shipbuilding yard owned by Ezra Churchill and J.B. North whose wooden ships sailed the seven seas. Here William Hall worked for some six years, sometimes on land and other times on the seas. His early boyhood days included some schooling in Avonport, some work in the shipyards and some sailing on the high seas, a combination which stood him in good stead when he moved on from a two-year service as a merchant seaman on Nova Scotian vessels plying cargo to London and Boston from about 1845 to 1847 to do a stint with the American Navy between 1847 and 1849 before enlisting in the British Navy in Liverpool, England, in early 1852.

By now, William Hall was a seasoned and well-travelled seaman. Not quite 24-years-old, this young man had already travelled the distant areas and ports of the world, including London, England, Boston, Massachusetts, and San Francisco, California. His service with the American Navy took him as far afield as the Pacific waters where, in 1848, the Mexican war was waging. He saw service during this war as a crew member of the United States battleship, Ohio.

Thus, this young black man from the Annapolis Valley who enlisted in the British Navy in February, 1852, was already a seasoned traveller, an accomplished seaman and a war veteran. If he had achieved no more, he would have still been a worthy son of Nova Scotia. But more was to follow.

The first ship he was drafted to in Portsmouth was the famous flagship, *Victory*, which Lord Nelson had commanded in the historic Battle of Trafalgar in 1805. A week later he was posted to H.M.S. *Rodney* on which he served for four years, the first two as part of the fleet in the English Channel and the remaining two in the war zone of the Mediterranean and Black Seas during the Crimean War, 1854-56. Hall saw active service during the Crimean War, witnessed valour of the highest degree, and emerged with personal distinction. His training was continuing. Dr. Bruce Fergusson, former Provincial Archivist, describes Hall's participation in the following words: "Hall took part in the bombardment of Odessa and Sebastopol. He was one of the sailors landed from the Rodney to take an active part in the siege of Sebastopol during the winter of 1854-55. At that time, when men experienced severe hardships on the bleak hills of the Crimea, on account of disease, cold and privation, Hall was captain of one of the Lancaster guns on Green Hill."[34]

It is a coincidence in the adventures of William Hall that he should have witnessed an act of extreme gallantry on the part of a fellow member of his gun battery during the siege of Sebastopol. This man, William Hewitt, disregarded an order to retreat, opened a burst of fire against the advancing Russians, sending them back and in the process winning for himself the highest award for bravery in the British Empire—the Victoria Cross. Little did Hall know that he would himself repeat this performance two years later in a distant part of the empire and become the first Nova Scotian to win the Victoria Cross.

At the conclusion of the Crimean War in 1856, Hall, now an Able Seaman, was posted to the frigate *Shannon* which was stationed in Hong Kong. About this time a nationalist movement was in ferment in nearby India in which Indian soldiers played a leading part. Most of India was then ruled by a trading company in the name of the British Government. This company, called the English East India Company, had crushed Indian troops in Bengal a hundred years earlier, in 1757 in the Battle of Plassey. In 1857 a major mutiny was being planned in the Indian army and the introduction of a new bullet coated in pig and cow fat—which coating had to be removed by biting off the cover—sparked a revolt on religious grounds (pork is objectionable to Muslims and beef to Hindus). This military revolt was not only a blow against the rule of the English East India Company: it was a blow against the British empire. Troops and warships throughout the empire were placed on full alert and many ordered to proceed immediately to the Indian towns of Lucknow and Cawnpore which were the centres of the nationalist rising.

This was how the boy from Hantsport found himself in the company of over 400 seamen and marines drawn together hastily to rush to the aid of some 38,000 British troops in India pitted against some 200,000 revolting Indian troops, as members of what is listed affectionately as the "Shannon

Brigade." This contingent was assigned the task of taking the town of Lucknow from the rebels. What stood in the path of entry was a formidable mosque, a Muslim place of worship built with thick stone walls in which were embedded positions for guns to defend the building. Muslims were once the military conquerors of India and their outposts were well constructed and ably defended. Such was the case of this mosque, the Shah Nujeef.

By the afternoon of November 16, 1857, the "Shannon Brigade" was within four hundred yards of the mosque which defied intense shelling for some three hours while many men fell in battle. It was at this point that two 24-pounder (10.8 kilograms) cannons were ordered to move closer in a final effort to break an entry in the walls. Another man was needed to work the guns and William Hall volunteered. The following description by Dr. Blakeley recounts the valour of many brave souls:

The sailors strained at the ropes and hauled their guns to within twenty yards (18.2 meters) of the wall in a hailstorm of bullets. All the men working one gun were killed, and the crew of the second were falling fast. Calmly Hall worked the remaining gun. Only his wounded officer, Lt. Young, and Hall were left, but the Nova Scotian continued sponging and loading, sending shell after shell crashing into the wall. With his own gigantic strength he brough back the gun and fired the charge which made a breach in the wall, just large enough to allow a man to climb over......[35]

It was for many acts of bravery by a seaman doing battle on land, volunteering to serve in a gun crew, singlehandedly pulling a cannon, loading 24-pounder (10.8 kilograms) shells, firing the shells, doing all this while his fellowmen were falling around him and his superior was severely wounded, that Able Seaman William Edward Hall was awarded the Victoria Cross, the first Nova Scotian, the first seaman, the first black person and the third Canadian to achieve this great distinction. The Victoria Cross was presented to William Hall in Queenstown Harbour, Australia, on October 28, 1859, on board the ship HMS *Donegal* which he was serving at the time.

By now he had reached the pinnacle of his naval career. Within four months in 1858 he rose in rank from Able Seaman to Leading Gunner, to Captain of the Mast, to Captain of the Foretop. He was discharged from the Royal Navy with a certificate of good conduct on June 10, 1876 with the rank of Quarter Master, having served the Royal Navy for 19 years and 278 days in various parts of the world. He won four medals: the Crimean Medal with clasps for Inkerman and Sebastopol; the Turkish Medal; the Indian Medal with bars for Lucknow and the Relief of Lucknow and the Victoria Cross. He was a veteran of four wars and of three navies (Nova Scotian, American and British).[36] This galaxy of achievements is difficult to match.

A newspaper reporter who interviewed William Hall in 1900 on the farm to which he retired in 1876 wrote that the small farm was located about four miles from the village of Hantsport. This eyewitness account of Hall's retirement years is a rare testimony and deserves special mention:

> The old veteran lives in a little farmhouse overlooking Minas Basin. The property is protected from heavy winds by a row of spruce trees bordering the road, so that only the upper windows can be seen when driving past. For a small farm it is well stocked with cattle and poultry, and there is a two-acre (.8 hectares) orchard of thrifty young trees adjoining the house.[37]

Dr. Bruce Fergusson, writing in 1967, noted that the farm was 'about 100 yards (91.4 meters) from the spot where he was born' and that living with him were his two sisters "Mrs. Rachael Hall Robinson and Mary Hall [who] kept house for their bachelor brother; and his pensions and his labor were for years the support of those two sisters and a niece."[38]

Except for the small community of friends and acquaintances, William Hall was little known in his retirement years. Working quietly on his farm and "far from the madding crowd's ignoble strife," his years passed by and his deeds were forgotten. For a fleeting moment three years before he died, this bemedalled man stood proudly before royalty in Halifax, Nova Scotia, and royalty took note

The Victoria Cross, the highest military honour in the British Commonwealth, was awarded to William Hall in 1859. He was the first black man, the first Nova Scotian, the first seaman, and only the third Canadian to receive the distinction.

and shook hands with this proud black man who had served the empire well. The Duke and Duchess of Cornwall and York, later to become King George V and Queen Mary, were on a brief visit to Halifax in October, 1901 as guests of the Royal British Veterans. For that brief moment his country remembered William Edward Hall, black citizen, and holder of the Victoria Cross.

William Hall died at his home in Avonport at the age of 76 on August 25, 1904 and was buried without honours, military or civilian, in an obscure graveyard at Stoney Hill, Lockhartville, midway between Hantsport and Grand Pre.

A few events connected with his property and his person took place after his death. The first relates to his medals, particularly the coveted Victoria Cross. Fergusson informs us that at the time of his death the sum of $500 was owing on the family home and his sister, Rachael Robinson, placed the medals in the custody of a family friend, Dr. Henry Chipman, of Grand Pre, to dispose of to pay the debt. The various advice that Dr. Chipman received are mentioned by Fergusson and need not detain us here. The medals ended up in England, and were loaned for display in the Atlantic Provinces Pavilion in Montreal in 1967. Today, they are in the custody of the Nova Scotia Museum in Halifax.

The second footnote in his life relates to his final resting place. In 1945, his remains were removed from the cemetery at Lockhartville and reinterred on the grounds of what is today the Hantsport Baptist Church where, two years later in 1947, a memorial cairn was erected on a plot of ground acquired by the Canadian Legion. The unveiling ceremony took place on November 9, 1947, almost 90 years to the day when this brave man had left his imprints on the sands of time on the battleground of Lucknow, India, thousands of kilometers from his birth and resting place.

The final words should be left to his contemporary friend, confidante and country resident, Dr. Henry Chipman: "Allow me to say......that I had the honor of knowing William Hall well, and a braver, truer, more modest man, white or black, never lived......"[39]

COMMUNITY GROWTH

The period 1854-1918 covered in this chapter was a time of considerable extremes for black people throughout Canada. In central and western Canada the period saw new refugees and immigrants surging into the country either because of the Fugitive Slave Act of 1850 in the United States or because of better economic prospects, especially for well-to-do black immigrants on the Pacific coast. For Canadian Blacks living in Nova Scotia, it was a period of consolidation during which many challenges had to be met. It was a time to settle down and produce results, whatever the odds. Mary Ann Shadd, Quaker-educated black, and former school teacher, later editor and founder of the newspaper, *Provincial Freeman*, published in Ontario, listed the two main challenges facing black people everywhere in British North America in 1854:

> We have two great falsehoods to live down......1st the Negro is unfit for freedom; 2nd the Negro cannot live on terms of equality with the white man on the American continent......The development, education and progress of Canadian colored men will do more to stamp those two Anglo–Saxon assertions with their native falsity than anything else this side of Heaven can do.[40]

In Nova Scotia during this period both men and women of the black community proved without doubt that they were indeed capable of using their freedom to advantage. Personalities associated with thought and action came mainly from the fields of religion and sports. They were soon joined by educators and business people, farmers and homemakers—ordinary people in a humble society of God-fearing individuals. Indeed, the church was the focal point of community life.

Take the case of the black community of Dartmouth: life was built around the Dartmouth Lake Church—as it was originally known when it was founded in 1844. It was also referred to as the African or Colored Meeting House from the very fact of its community focus. It was located at the junction of what was later Crichton Avenue and Micmac Boulevard. In folklore, Crichton Avenue is remembered as the Colored Meeting House Road. Personalities associated with this Dartmouth community during the period covered in this chapter include Revs. Richard Preston, James Thomas, Benson Smithers, F.R. Langford, James Borden and S.B. Kempton whose death in 1918 brings this list to a close. Two of the founders of the Ladies Auxiliary in 1917 came from this Dartmouth community: Sara Middleton and Edith Samuel Sparks. The burial ground close to the church on Crichton Avenue is a reminder of the oldest black community in Dartmouth before the church moved in 1906 into the Sunday School building of the Anglican Christ Church on Victoria Road.[41]

Rose Mann who was born in 1898 has described her recollections of growing up in this Dartmouth community. She attended school in the Crichton Avenue area where her father, William Riley, was a deacon in the church. Her grandfather grew up in what she described as the "coloured people's barracks" in Dartmouth in the 1880s a place which was "very prejudiced at one time. They wouldn't allow coloured teachers to teach school here."[42]

Accounts recorded by senior citizens of the Upper Hammonds Plains community reinforce the influence of the church and community. In what was, as we have seen in earlier pages, one of the most populous and black settlements in the early nineteenth century, this community has made its mark in many ways. The first mill was built in Upper Hammonds Plains in 1888 by James Allison and Deal Whiley. The partnership was later dissolved but their descendants continued to be associated with the two different mills over the years. As one respondent who was a school teacher in the area in 1925 notes: "Hammonds Plains was a lumbering community. Very few people worked outside of the area. Employment was found in cutting logs and junks. There were mills in which staves were made for barrels. Boxes were not as popular then as now for packing fruits and vegetables and fish. Loads of barrels were hauled by oxen and horses. These were the only methods of transportation for many years."[43]

Pioneer women are remembered for their courage and contribution. One of them was Mary Ann Reid from Hammonds Plains, born in 1825, who lived to a ripe old age, documented at 111 years. This grand lady married one John Gigi on New Year's Day in 1854 and worked tirelessly as a midwife for many years. Another of the pioneer women of Hammonds Plains was Florence Ann Williams, born in 1891, who is remembered in the community for service and devotion. She was one of the senior citizens who put together a booklet containing memories of community life in the area with the help of contemporaries like Stanford Allison, born 1889 in a pioneer family.[44]

The community of Hammonds Plains, now designated as Upper Hammonds Plains, some 20 kilometres from Halifax, came about as a result of various groups occupying different settlements over the years, such as the Pockwock Settlement started in 1834 when thirty black settlers occupied a six hundred acre (242.8 hectares) lot. The Camp Town Settlement was famous for the earliest saw mills. The Kehoe Settlement about which little is known was another.[45]

Another situation about which little is known is the folklore which states that some Maroons were granted land and permission to stay in Hammonds Plains and that over time they became "good workers, farmers and woodsmen."[46] This is a subject for further local investigation.

The community of Hammonds Plains, like every other black community in Nova Scotia, has its own interesting local history, its heroes, its pillars, its memories. Accounts of how individuals made it in spite of tremendous odds have lessons for both the black and the white community. The efforts of ordinary and. simple people also matter in the building of a nation. Take the example of Blois Sinclair Williams:

> I was born in Hammonds Plains in October, 1901. We were a family of 6 children. I went to school at age 5. My father died when I was 11 years old. After my father's death, my brother, Charles, and I quit school and went to work to support the family. When I left school at age 11, I had a grade 5 education. I went to work for R.D. Haverstock in Pockwock—making 50 cents per day......In 1942, I quit working for R.D. Haverstock and went to work for Standard Paving, and continued to work for them for two years. After I left Standard Paving, I went to work at the Halifax Shipyards and worked there for seven years. After I left the Shipyards, I went to do construction work. I worked on such buildings as Mount Saint Vincent, Halifax Shopping Centre, Park Victoria, St. Mary's University, Uniacke Square and Mic Mac Mall. I worked doing construction work until the age of 72.[47]

The first black teacher to graduate from the then Provincial Normal School in Truro in 1928, Madeline Francis Symonds, taught in Upper Hammonds Plains for 28 years from 1928 to 1964. In a recent book which refers to the local history of this and neighbouring communities, Viola Parsons remembers this school teacher:

> Mrs. Madeline Symonds, a school teacher who resided in Hammonds Plains, told me she was a frequent visitor of grandmother's. She loved talking with her and said their conversations were always spiritual and uplifting. Mrs. Symonds has been a long-time friend of mine and a spiritual advisor. She has written lovely poetry; I have a book of her poems. Thank God for her Christian witness.[48]

Individuals such as those recounted in this section on Hammonds Plains exemplify the efforts of members of the Nova Scotia black communities everywhere in the province to make headway since the coming of the last black immigrants from the United States between 1813 and 1816. Off the mainland, on the island of Cape Breton, black immigrants with a different background were also making an impact on community development.

In 1900, the Dominion Iron and Steel Company located in the Whitney Pier area of Sydney, Cape Breton, began steel production and attracted labourers from Europe, the Middle East, the West Indies, the United States, Newfoundland, Cape Breton and the mainland of Nova Scotia. Included in this ethnic mix of various cultures and backgrounds were Canadian Blacks from places such as Guysborough and the Preston area. A pioneering group of Alabama Blacks arrived in Sydney in 1899 but returned shortly after arrival. The largest number of black immigrants to arrive in 1900 and in succeeding years came from the West Indies, mainly from Barbados. Soon a dominant West Indian culture developed as more immigrants arrived. In a few years a distinct black community emerged close to the steel plant in what became known as the "Coke Ovens" part of Whitney Pier. This settlement has survived to the present time.

While the local black population on the mainland of Nova Scotia was still struggling to make ends meet on small-scale agricultural holdings in the closing years of the nineteenth century, the emerging coal and steel industries in Cape Breton looked to immigrant Blacks from outside the province, notably the West Indies, for labour. From the time of the formation of the Dominion Coal Company in 1893 to the opening of the blast furnaces for the manufacture of iron and steel, West Indian Blacks were actively recruited for those industries. The largest number of some 300 recruited in Barbados settled mainly in the Whitney Pier area with smaller numbers in Glace Bay and New Waterford.[49] The 1911 census listed 311 Blacks in Sydney, with 145 of that number classified as West Indians.

In the context of community growth, these developments in Cape Breton had a great impact on the Nova Scotia black society and culture. They experienced racial intolerance and discrimination as did their mainland counterparts. They started their own churches, too, like the St. Philip's African Orthodox Church at Whitney Pier, the only one of its kind in Canada and an offshoot of a parent church started in the United States in 1921. St. Philip's Church in Whitney Pier was constructed in 1927 in the wake of discrimination against West Indians who attended the St. Alban's Anglican Church in the same area. Unlike the case of the mainland where Blacks are predominantly members of the black Baptist churches, Blacks in Cape Breton belong to the traditional western churches with a modest number affiliated to the St. Philip's African Orthodox Church which is located in 1989 on Hankard Street, Whitney Pier and headed by Chief Priest Vincent Waterman.

The twentieth century history of the black community of Cape Breton, mainly of West Indian origins, tells an interesting story of individuals and institutions. In the first decades, as these immigrants became Canadians, their contribution to society as a whole became prominent. One early influence came from the life and work of the Jamaican-born Marcus Garvey who established the Universal Negro Improvement Association in his own country in 1915 and in New York in 1919-20. Soon afterwards, branches were formed in many countries, including Canada, in Montreal, Toronto, Halifax, New Glasgow, Sydney and New Waterford where the branch identified itself as the Aberdeen Division No. 303 of the Universal Negro Improvement Association and Africa Communities League. The first memberships in New Waterford were taken out in December, 1919 in the names of such individuals as N.B. Crawford, Lemuel C. Brewster, Hilton Robinson, Aubrey Braithwaite and Wilfred Smith. Many more joined in the 1920s and 1930s.

For black people everywhere in the world, Marcus Garvey had a telling message which was conveyed through speeches and through the columns of his journal, The Black Man, which he set up in London and which he edited as President-General of the UNIA. The force of his vision and its relevance for black people everywhere conveyed an important message for blacks in Nova Scotia and the newly-arrived black immigrants in Cape Breton. The following 1935 excerpt from his journal also has relevance for the contemporary scene in Nova Scotia:

> Sometimes it is good to have an individual or a group of people undergo certain hardships and difficulties to make them fully realize that which they would probably not have understood otherwise. When the Universal Negro Improvement Association 20 years ago appealed to the consciousness of the race, with the object of having each and every member thereof concentrating on the great object of economic and political redemption, very few could appreciate the force of the appeal, because conditions at that time were somewhat favourable to each and

everyone without much energy or effort to secure them. Those were the war and immediate post-war conditions. They were very inviting, but the vision of the Universal Negro Improvement Association was a correct picture of what would happen today to those who were not well prepared......This same Organization has issued its second most important appeal in its history; it is to once more organize the senti-ment of the Negro throughout the world for definite action in his eco-nomic, social, political, industrial, educational and religious freedom. There must be no mistake. The Negro is called upon to do for himself by depending upon himself to the extent that all peoples do for them-selves and depend upon themselves. The Negro must originate, he must create, he must invent, he must manufacture, he must launch out into every field of human activity, he must refuse to surrender his rights and privileges to anyone. Whilst he may co-operate with others, he must always have the independent outlook, reaching to the point of self-security as a race......[50]

This statement bears analysis even today. The term, "Negro" is, of course, not used anymore because of its connotations of inferiority and degradation. In the early days of the UNIA, the people of Cape Breton worked hard and tried hard to raise themselves to meet the standards set by Marcus Garvey for black people everywhere. Of special significance for the history of black communities in Nova Scotia in the early decades of the twentieth century is the fact that of the six branches of UNIA mentioned earlier, four were set up in Nova Scotia. The point cannot be missed that this was due in no small measure to the presence of black immigrants from the Caribbean. The impact of this presence for community development was felt in many ways as the years went by. Many examples illustrate this impact.

Take the case of the first black Canadian to be invested with the Order of Canada. Isaac Phills of Sydney, Cape Breton, who was born on the island of St. Vincent where he trained in agriculture before immigrating to Sydney in 1916. Unable to get a job in the area of his expertise, he followed the beaten track of West Indians and took up employment with the Dominion Steel and Coal Corporation which he served faithfully until his retirement in 1963. In all these years of strife and stress in industrial Cape Breton the Phills brought up seven children and made sure that through education they would make their mark in Canadian society. The achievements of their chil-dren vindicated the determination of their parents. Of the three daughters, one became a qualified secretary, the second a certified teacher and the third a graduate nurse. Of the four sons, the eldest became a minister of religion, the second a medical doctor, the third an industrial chemist and the fourth received a doctor of philosophy degree from the University of London. In between the Phills served the church, the Canadian Red Cross Society, Home and School Associations and the Canadian Cancer Society. Their example disproves the stereotype, if proof is needed at all, that Nova Scotian blacks, without exception, were a burden to the state, unable to help themselves or raise themselves, as Marcus Garvey had preached they should do. The Order of Canada which Mr. Isaac Phills received in 1967 was the forerunner of similar awards to distinguished black Nova Scotians in later years: Dr. Carrie M. Best, Rev. Dr. William Pearly Oliver, Rev. Dr. Joseph C. Mack and Dr. Marie Hamilton, to 1989.[51]

Isaac Phills became the first Black Canadian to receive the Order of Canada in 1967.

F. A. Hamilton, founder of the *Nova Scotia Gleaner*, was a lawyer awarded the title of King's Counsel.

Another first for a Cape Breton Black of West Indian descent belongs to F. Allan Hamilton. Born in the British West Indies in 1895, he graduated in law from Dalhousie University, Halifax, and then started a law practice in Sydney in 1922. Twenty eight years later, in 1950, he became the first Canadian Black to be appointed a King's Counsel.[52] Another notable first for Allan Hamilton in Nova Scotia was the first black newspaper, The Nova Scotia Gleaner, which he started in Sydney in August, 1929. He is listed as the editor and publisher. The object of the paper was to "unify the colored people of the province of Nova Scotia." A cursory reading of the third issue shows that a serious attempt was made to provide news about individuals and communities all over Nova Scotia.[53]

It was not only the professional people who must be remembered for their contribution to the growth of the black communities of Cape Breton. The rank and file, the humble folk, whether factory labourer, housewife, tradesman, entrepreneur, musician, all made their contribution and left their mark. Take the case of the couple, Daisy and Alexander Parris, both of whom were born in Barbados in the closing years of the nineteenth century. Alexander Parris came to Sydney to work in the steel plant; Daisy Parris followed in 1918 to marry him. Alexander Parris worked in the coke ovens for five years and then opened his own shoe repair shop on Tupper Street. The Parris' were among the first Blacks to acquire their own house in Sydney. Later, they opened a candy store, then a grocery store, and soon acquired an apartment building which they rented out. These achievements were made during difficult times and are a "reminder of the contribution of immigrants from Barbados to the growth and strength and achievements of Canada."[54]

Similar accounts can be put together, and indeed should be accepted as a challenge in the forty-odd black communities which developed during the period covered in this chapter, from Sydney to Yarmouth, from Amherst to Halifax, narrating chapter and verse of black endeavours and black accomplishments. This section can do no more than touch upon representative samples by way of illustration. The community of Africville, in Halifax, is one such example.

EARLY HISTORY OF AFRICVILLE

In their seminal study, Donald H. Clairmont and Dennis William Magill, produced the first detailed account of what they called *Africville, The Life and Death of a Canadian Black Community.* This study traces the history of a black settlement in the north end of Halifax from its inception around 1848 when the first land titles were acquired by William Brown and William Arnold to plots of land of six acres (2.4 hectares) each. In subsequent years, another three acres (1.2 hectares) were added to this number and the total acreage of 15 acres (6 hectares) made up the Africville settlement. This area was first owned by whites and was possibly occupied in part by Brown, Arnold and other black persons before the purchases were actually made. Since the Black Refugee immigrants who came to Nova Scotia between 1813 and 1816 were settled, as we have already seen, in various places in Halifax County, there was constant movement of individuals and families in search of better lands, employment and business opportunities. The names of the eight black pioneering families of the Africville settlement had appeared, as already noted, in official records at different times before 1848 in Preston, Hammonds Plains and Halifax before they became associated with Africville: Brown, Carvery, Dixon, Arnold, Hill, Fletcher, Bailey and Grant.[55]

The settlement was originally named Campbell Road, following the construction of that road in 1836 linking Halifax with the outlying communities. A church was built soon after the first land titles were obtained in 1848. In the words of Peter McKerrow, the first historian of Nova Scotia's black churches, the beginnings were as follows:

> The Campbell Road church was organized about 1849. This little Zion of late has been the subject of much comment, being in such close proximity to the city with a fine day school......which nearly all the schoolable age take advantage......community of intelligent young people......much is expected of them......"[56]

McKerrow's first-hand knowledge makes for an interesting analysis. From it we gather that at first there was a school in the settlement, that it was a community of intelligent young people. Such a comment does not appear for the other communities McKerrow writes about. It is likely that McKerrow was making a special case for a school in Africville. Its proximity to Halifax gave it the appearance of an urban setting while the prospects of employment in the dockyard, the Inter-Colonial Railroad, shipbuilding, and fishing and baptisms in the then clean waters of the Bedford Basin were attractions which could not be matched in the other black settlements in Halifax County or elsewhere in the province. There were obvious prospects, relatively speaking, for the Campbell Road settlers.

Unlike Preston and Hammonds Plains, the fifteen acres (6 hectares) of the Campbell Road settlement, referred to in documents as Africville since 1860, were too limited to sustain a large population. In 1851, the black population stood at 54. A little over a hundred years later, when the residents were being relocated in 1964, the population was 400. Whatever the size, the settlement developed over the years, drawing strength, cohesion and direction from the Seaview African United Baptist Church. It was in the church building that the first private school was started before the city of Halifax provided for a school on adjoining leased city land in 1883. John Brown was one of the earliest teachers, followed by the Jemmots, father and children.

158

Gordon Jemmot, Sr., belonged to the old school of teachers who adorned the late nineteenth century-early twentieth century age with limited education but unlimited zeal and dedication. Older generation of Africville residents in their seventies and eighties in 1989 have vivid memories of "teacher Jemmot" who meant so much to so many. Gordon Thomas Jemmot, Jr., followed in his father's footsteps. Residing at 37 Maynard Street in Halifax, he ran the Africville School as Principal for 18 years. He attended Acadia University, where he was a contemporary of William Pearly Oliver, and graduated with a B.A. degree while also distinguishing himself as an athlete. His career as a teacher, a coach, and a respected executive member of the Halifax Men's Teachers' Federation and the Nova Scotia Teachers Union, vindicated McKerrow's comments about intelligent young people who were associated with Africville. Unfortunately for many of them, it took years, and even many generations, before any recognition was accorded to them. The case of George Dixon, treated in some detail below, is an example of this belated, and often reluctant, recognition.

The story of the community of Africville is better known since the 1960s because of the national attention which focused on the relocation of the community. However, the earlier period is important for information on the structure and the strengths of the community. There are many personal first-hand accounts of living conditions in the early decades of the twentieth century given by persons who were born in the late nineteenth century and early twentieth century. A few excerpts are given below to enable the reader to form a mental picture of the human side. The first is a testimony by Elsie Desmond, born in Africville in 1911:

> I have a photo of that old school. It was a one-room school, one door for boys and another door for girls. I attended until I finished grade 7. It was an all-black school with black teachers. My teacher was Mr. Jemmot. He was old when he taught me. His son, Gordon, and his daughter, Melissa, also taught school......I also went to Seaview Church Sunday School. The deacons were running things, Deacon Edward Dixon and Deacon Arthur Dixon, Archie's father......I attended Sunday School at 10 a.m and services at 11 a.m. and 3 p.m. If we had a special day'......we had three services.

Another testimony comes from Ruth Johnson, born in Africville in 1919, who went on in later life to be appointed an indigenous community instructor, for the Nova Scotia Division of Adult Education, receiving numerous awards for outstanding community volunteer services, including the prestigious national Harry Jerome Award in 1987 in the category for outstanding community service and the Metro United Way Award in 1989 for the volunteer of the year.

> There were three stores in Africville, what we call penny shops. My mother inherited this store......My father worked on ships......Many of the men worked on boats......Some of the men worked on the CNR, some worked on the waterfront......And most of the people had good jobs......Most everybody lived in a two storey home, and I was born in a house where......there was a piano, and those homes [which] didn't have a piano always had an organ......So the life in Africville was good, a stable life......there wasn't anybody on social assistance in Africville in them days......It was good living in Africville. And we had a horse, and my father had a Model-T Ford......and we had a motorbike. It was lovely. You had to see it to believe it. [57]

Leo Carvery, born in Africville in 1916, had this to say:

> Living in Africville at that time was more like a dream. You were free to go as a kid, fishing, swimming, you name it. It was like a resort in the back of the yard. However, it was too good to last. The city had an eye on the place ever since the inhabitants took over. Life was very simple in Africville. You always had plenty to eat back in the depression times.[58]

These testimonies are recalled not to glorify the past but to give the facts. Media reports, evaluations by civic officials and administrators, policy makers and politicians, have all tended to present the negative side of Africville life since the opening years of the twentieth century, and even before. The settlement was labelled a ghetto, treated like a ghetto and removed because of the stigma that was permanently attached to it. Africville was treated like a miniature African colony under white colonial rule. As the African side of the story could only be properly told after colonial rule had come to an end, so the Africville side of the story can now be recorded, analysed and told free of fear, favour or self-interest.

160

Ruth Johnson, a former resident of Africville, is known for her community work. She was president of the Black Cultural Society, and winner of the Harry Jerome Award for distinguished community service.

One reason which had prompted the early residents to come to Africville was the economic prospects. These prospects were better in the capital city area than anywhere else in the province for obvious reasons, but these prospects were extremely limited for black Africvilleans. A white steamship agent in Halifax, one William Roche of Roche's Wharf, wrote to the mayor in 1906 asking that expressed good intentions to provide civic employment be carried out: "I beg to suggest that you manifest your interest in them, which you have often expressed, by instructing your Foreman of Works to employ the colored men when they offer to work; and to give them a preference over those who are not citizens, and who pay no taxes in Halifax." In another letter to the mayor on the same day and on the same subject, Roche stressed "the claims of the Colored men for a fair share of employment......that they be accorded fair treatment by all of them that are in authority......They are good citizens."[59]

In April, 1989 the mayor of the city of Halifax convened a public meeting in the North Branch library, Gottingen Street, in the north end of Halifax, where Africville relocatees were settled in the late sixties and early seventies, to review the situation of black people primarily in the area of civic employment. The mayor and his officials heard accounts which were similar to what William Roche was talking about in 1906. Not much had changed.

In spite of difficulties, the people of Africville did own land and houses which were of varying quality as the city learned in 1907 when it wanted to expropriate land in Africville for city use. The list of property owners is given here to give some idea of who lived in Africville, in those years: Thomas Brown, John T. Brown, Mrs. Rebecca Brown, John Brown, Walter Thomas, Alex Carvery, Edward Dixon, Mrs. Elizabeth Mantley, Miss Bertha Alexander, William Carvery, James Hamilton, Mrs. Esther Roan, Joseph Carvery, George Carvery and John T. Bulmer and wife. Mrs. Rebecca Brown and Alex Carvery had two pieces of land which would place them, with Thomas Brown and John T. Brown, among the top four assessed.[60]

The total value of the land and property assessed was just under nine thousand dollars which was not an insignificant sum for 1907. Given time, encouragement, financing and protection, the economic value as well as the social reputation of Africville would have grown in a positive direction. The misfortune for the residents was that the settlement was neglected by the civic authorities and officials. This neglect, coupled with unsatisfactory social influences during the period of World War I, contributed to a steady decline in social conditions. The residents and community leaders took stock of the situation and began to grapple with the issues that were contributing to the decline of the community. An example of their efforts is recalled here in some detail to show that they were responding positively to the challenges of the day: When the war ended, there was talk of reconstruction everywhere and Africvilleans requested that their situation be placed on the agenda as well. They petitioned the Halifax City Council for police protection in their neglected settlement in 1919. This petition throws light on existing conditions and circumstances.

The petition made the following points:

That a police officer seldom or never visits this district, except with a warrant or subpoena.

That conditions that now prevail here are worse than at any time heretofore.

That these lamentable conditions tend to turn the majority away from the good teachings which they have received.

That there is now an utter disregard of the Lord's Day by many residents.

That there are many persons, strangers in our midst, living openly in a state of debauchery, which must corrupt the minds of the youth, for we are more or less subject to our environment.

That there is nightly confusion, carousal and dissipation, which disturb the peaceful night.

That these carousals have been the centres for spreading infection through the village.

That we believe, if this disgraceful state of affairs continue, there will be some grave crime or crimes committed.

Having recited their problems, the petitioners pleaded for the omissions of the past to be rectified so that "the evil influences now at work may be greatly reduced, then shall we be better able to train the young in the way of good citizenship, and place the village on a better plane......"[61]

The recommendation of the Police Commission to City Council was a confirmation of the policy of ignoring the well being of Africville because of the stigma attached to a segregated black community: "That the residents of Africville district form their own Police Dept. and anyone they appoint to act as a policeman the Mayor would swear in as a Special Constable, as the City Dept. have no spare men to send such a distance. In the event of any serious trouble being reported the Chief is always in a position to send a squad to this district."[62]

The questions raised in these negotiations suggest that the segregated black communities of Nova Scotia were treated as outcasts as late as the first decades of the twentieth century. For whatever reasons, officialdom had not begun to integrate them into the broader society. The reasons advanced for the stand-offish positions taken were hardly rooted on solid grounds. In the case of the request for police services, was Africville all that distance away from City Hall? On the point of the Police Chief being able to send a squad to control any serious problem, the black communities were being reminded that they were the objects of crises management and not the subjects of an integrated society deserving of parity of treatment as taxpayers and as patriotic law-abiding citizens who, by the end of World War I in 1918, were part of the Nova Scotia landscape for almost three hundred years. During this period black communities were settled in some forty identifiable localities all over the province, held together by the church at the local level as well as the provincial level, producing leaders and followers, teachers, preachers and artisans, farmers and domestic entrepreneurs, labourers, taxpayers and consumers. In short, by 1918 when this chapter ends, the black communities were on the march towards finding their rightful place in Canadian society. By then, they had also provided the country and the international community with evidence of their presence and patriotism in the war effort as members of Canada's first and only segregated battalion to do service in World War I.

Before the story of this segregated battalion is told, the section on community growth will be concluded with an account of the achievements of two black Nova Scotians who emerged to become international figures in the period covered in this chapter. What John Perry, mentioned in earlier pages, was for the period before 1850, George Dixon and Sam Langford were for the period after 1850.

George Dixon, a member of one of the founding families of Africville, was born in that settlement on 29 July, 1870 when that settlement was barely thirty-years old. He worked as a photographer's apprentice in Halifax as a teenager and developed an interest in boxing through contact with boxers who came to the studio to have their pictures taken. Slight of build, some five feet three inches tall, a little over a hundred pounds in weight, this son of Africville moved in stages to become one of the world's greatest boxers of all

George Dixon, born in Africville, became a world boxing champion in the bantam and featherweight divisions.

times. He made his appearance in a Halifax gymnasium at the age of 16, had his first professional fight in Halifax at the age of 17, moved to Boston where he was nicknamed "Little Chocolate," won the world bantamweight title at the age of 20 and the world featherweight title at the age of 21. As Charles Saunders puts it: "At twenty-one years of age, Dixon was a dual champion. He was the most famous black man in the world, earning thousands of dollars for his ring appearances and spending the money as quickly as it came in. The black community idolized him, and he had many white friends as well. And he was in love with Kitty O'Rourke, the sister of his manager."[63] George Dixon's remarkable career took him to many parts of the globe, exposed him to the racial tensions and taunts more prevalent in his lifetime than today, pushed him to the frontiers paving the way for succeeding generations. He died in economic obscurity on 6 January, 1909 in New York City but has remained a boxing legend and an inspiration. He was elected to the Canadian Boxing Hall of Fame in 1956. In 1969 the George Dixon Memorial

Community Recreation Centre was opened on Gottingen Street not far from the Africville that produced this great man or the gymnasium in which he cultivated his skills or the photo studio where he earned his living. In 1988, black Nova Scotian playwright, George Boyd's play, "Shine Boy" further immortalised this great man who in his lifetime was looked upon and treated as a shoe-shine boy.

The other Nova Scotian black boxer of international fame was Sam Langford who was born in 1884 in the segregated black community settlement of Weymouth Falls. As in the case of George Dixon, Sam Langford left Nova Scotia at an early age for Boston. At the tender age of 14, young

Sam Langford, from Weymouth Falls, never won a boxing title, but is still considered one of the all-time greats.

Langford took on odd jobs in Boston and worked his way as a janitor in a club for boxers. At the age of 16, the very age when George Dixon made his fighting debut, Sam Langford had his first professional fight in Boston, winning in six rounds. Sam Langford was only three inches taller than the small-built George Dixon, but he gradually added weight to his meagre 135 pounds, making the scale at a modest 156 pounds in 1906 when he took on the Negro Heavyweight Champion of the world, Jack Johnson, who weighed in at 186 pounds. Langford lost after fifteen gruelling rounds but gained a moral victory after conceding so much in height and weight. Two years later, Jack Johnson won the heavyweight crown of the world and Sam Langford remained the number one contender who was never given a chance to fight for the crown since no champion agreed to fight him.

Between 1902 and 1923, Langford fought some 642 bouts. Although he was five foot, six inches in height, and his top weight was 162 pounds, Langford fought many heavyweight fighters and defeated most of them. Langford travelled around the world as uncrowned heavyweight champion, but was unable to get a title bout. In 1917, he lost the sight of his right eye. Woodman [his manager] urged him to give up boxing, but Langford refused to quit. He fought for seven more years until, in 1924, he became totally blind. Sam Langford fought at a time when Negro fighters battled not only their ring opponents, but prejudice as well, and he made a great contribution to the role of his race in the competitive sports world.[64]

What tributes of this kind miss is the simple fact that individuals like Sam Langford made their mark and earned their reputation not as members of any other race but the human race. Before his death in Cambridge, Massachusetts, on January 12, 1956, Sam Langford, the famous "Boston Tar Baby," was elected to the Boxing Hall of Fame of the prestigious *RING* magazine and was the first person ever to have been accorded that distinction without being the holder of a world championship crown. Sam Langford was indeed unique in the annals of boxing, a tribute to Weymouth Falls as well where his birthplace honours him through the constant reminder and the living monument in the form of the Sam Langford Community Centre.

Black Nova Scotians made their mark internationally in the squared ring and were followed not much later by their countrymen who answered the call of patriotic duty to serve their country on the battlefields of Europe during world war one, the subject matter of the next section of this chapter.

CANADA'S BLACK BATTALION: NO. 2 CONSTRUCTION

When the First World War broke out in Europe in August-September, 1914, most of the world was under the direct or indirect domination of European countries. Consequently, the colonies were drawn into what started off as a European conflict. Non-Europeans, including Africans and Asians, were recruited as combatants as well as non-combatants. In one colonial country, at least, there was a massive nationalist uprising to protest against the recruitment of local soldiers to do battle for a foreign cause. The country was the central African state of Nyasaland and the rising was led by a black religious leader, John Chilembwe, who returned home after receiving his education at the Lynchburg Theological Seminary in Virginia, U.S.A. Chilembwe died in the uprising in 1915 but his death made the point that patriotism required that one should make the supreme sacrifice in defence of the liberty and interests of one's own country. Unfortunately for John Chilembwe and those of his followers who thought like him, their struggle

Members of the No. 2 Construction Battalion, the only segregated black battalion in the history of the Canadian military.

was not against the Germans but against British colonial domination. Yet thousands of black Nyasalanders were recruited in the Kings African Rifles and did battle in overseas countries alongside Europeans, Americans and Asians.

In Canada, however, Canadian Blacks who volunteered their services were received with ambivalence in spite of the fact that their forbears had served in the defence of Ontario against American invaders in the War of 1812-14 and in the defence of the crown against the rebels of 1837. A few were signed on to accompany the Canadian troops to South Africa in 1899-1902. Reference has already been made to the military exploits of William Edward Hall.

While white English- and French-speaking Canadians were encouraged to join the army, black Canadians were only accepted in the few local regiments at the discretion of the commanding officers while many more were being turned away. Some individuals like Arthur Alexander in Buxton and a journalist, J.R.B. Whitney in Toronto, made strenuous efforts to seek official clarification on black participation in the effort. For over a year after the outbreak of the war, officials had no clear idea about what to do with the enquiries which were pouring in from coast to coast from prospective black volunteers. The formation of a separate black regiment was rejected by the Minister of Defence, while the commander of the 104th Overseas Battalion rejected nineteen black volunteers in Saint John, N.B. because he considered that it would be unfair to his fine white class of recruits to have to mingle with black troops. When one of the rejected recruits protested, the Militia Council, the highest military authority, upheld a ruling it had first issued on October 19, 1915 that black recruits were to be accepted in any battalion. Shortly afterwards, the commander of the 106th Overseas Battalion which was stationed in Halifax made his response to this ruling. Blacks should, of course, do their share and he was prepared to accept a few but the acceptance was both conditional and reluctant, a response that has been likened to a familiar white position towards blacks throughout the centuries of Canadian history: "Neither my men nor myself, would care to sleep alongside [Negroes], or to eat with them, especially in warm weather."[65] What would this commander have said had he shared a little of the terrain on that sultry hot day on 16 November, 1857 alongside the heroic black man, William Edward Hall, defending the white British Empire in its exploitation of its Asiatic holdings?

The ambivalence of the official position was further underlined when contradictory steps were taken simultaneously. The commander of the 106th Overseas Battalion asked the pastor of the Zion Baptist Church in Truro, the Rev. William Andrew White, to raise a separate black platoon. British Columbia affirmed that its colour line was more marked than was the case in eastern Canada and that it would settle for nothing more than a separate platoon. The Minister of Defence authorised J.R.B. Whitney, the founder of the *Toronto Canadian Observer*, to use his paper to recruit for a separate black unit—the terminology at the time was "coloured" rather than black. The Department of Militia and Defence issued a memorandum on December 22, 1915 while all these steps were afoot in varying degrees pronouncing that "The fiat has gone forth: there is to be no coloured line; coloured battalions are not to be raised; coloured men are to be allowed to enlist in any battalion of the C.E.F." [Canadian Expeditionary Force].[66] The proviso to this stipulation was that, since the last word rested with the local commanders, Blacks should be spared the humiliation of being placed where they were not welcome. The upshot was that no commander in Canada was prepared, in 1915, to accept a separate black platoon under his command and the matter had to be dropped. True to form, Canada came up with a compromise solution which was not without self-interest. Blacks would be recruited in a Construction Battalion and not in the Canadian Expeditionary Force. The basis for this decision was contained in a memorandum issued by Major-

General W.G. Gwatkin, Chief of General Staff on April 13, 1916, parts of which are recalled here to draw attention to the historical legacy of our times:

> Nothing is to be gained by blinking facts......The civilized negro is vain and imitative; in Canada he is not impelled to enlist by a high sense of duty; in the trenches he is not likely to make a good fighter; and the average white man will not associate with him in terms of equality......In France, in the firing line, there is no place for a black battalion, C.E.F. It would be eyed askance; it would crowd out a white battalion; and it would be difficult to reinforce.[67]

It was not that Blacks had themselves asked to be assigned to a segregated battalion. They had volunteered their services in response to the public announcements. Canada had found it difficult to come up with a quarter million recruits in 1915 and half a million in 1916. Blacks were responding as Canadians. After all, the services of their forbears had been used before in similar or worse circumstances. But in the eyes of white society who produced the policy makers, black Canadians made good labourers.

The No. 2 Construction Battalion was the name given to Canada's first and only segregated Black Battalion. It came into existence on July 5, 1916, almost two years after the commencement of hostilities. Its first headquarters was established at what is today the Market Wharf in the town of Pictou, Nova Scotia. (Negotiations were underway in 1989 between the Black Cultural Centre for Nova Scotia and the Town Council of Pictou, initiated by Mr. Calvin W. Ruck, the historian of this battalion, to declare this site a national monument in honour of the significance of the No. 2 Construction Battalion in the history of Nova Scotia and Canada.)

The Commanding Officer of this unit was Lieutenant-Colonel Daniel H. Sutherland, a railroad contractor from River John in Pictou County. All his fellow officers were white with the exception of the designated chaplain, Rev. W.A. White, the pastor of the Zion African Baptist Church in Truro who held the rank of Honorary Captain.

Two months later, on September 9, 1916, the headquarters was moved to Truro, Nova Scotia, which, unlike the town of Pictou which had no black residents in 1916, had a sizeable black population and it was felt that this factor would boost the recruitment of the desired number of a thousand. Though recruits were drawn in from coast to coast in Canada and included some 165 black Americans, the tally in early 1917 fell far short of this number. The various companies from different parts of Canada and the United States converged in Truro on March 17, 1917 when the No. 2 Construction Battalion was formerly constituted. Eleven days later, the battalion comprising 19 officers and 605 other ranks left Halifax by sea for Liverpool, England, on the first leg of their overseas service, en route to France where it was attached to the Canadian Forestry Corps, a labour unit confined to logging, milling and shipping duties. There were non-whites from other parts of the British Empire in France at the time doing non-combatant duties, but there were Blacks, too, from Africa and North America fighting in the trenches to save the world for democracy.

That there were serious racial overtones that debarred members of the Canadian family of non-white composition, the so-called "visible minorities," from making their contribution to the war effort in 1914-1918 is thoroughly confirmed in a recent study by James Walker.[68] While native Indians and Japanese Canadians were received with distrust and disdain by recruitment officers, it was only the Blacks who were ultimately granted the status of a separate existence. Their No. 2 Battalion followed the No. 1 Construction Battalion, an all-white Canadian battalion, which was none too happy with its proximity in title to an all-black battalion.

For the Nova Scotian Blacks, and indeed for all the members of the Number 2 Construction Battalion, the opportunity to serve and experience the lessons and trials of travel and duty, were valuable in character building. By association, family, friends and institutions had reason to share in the pride. The African United Baptist Association, for example, declared at its 1916 annual convention that "the African race was making history." It took pride in the fact that most of the volunteers in the battalion from Nova Scotia were members of the Association and that the chaplain was a senior minister of the Association. Rev. William Andrew White, about whom more will be said in the next chapter, was a respected member of the black community and the only black chaplain in the British Empire troops abroad. He was stationed with the Number 2 Construction Battalion near La Joux in the Jura region of France and carried out his chaplaincy duties here and in the smaller detachments of the battalion at Cartigny and Alencon. A man of his education, stature and bearing was unacceptable to the white units stationed at Jura and a white Protestant chaplain was brought in. Captain White kept a diary and made brief entries. From it we learn that on New Year's Day, 1918, he took the train from La Joux to Alencon where he met chaplain, Capt.

Reunion of World War One veterans of the No. 2 Construction Battalion at the Black Cultural Centre of Nova Scotia. Back row (l–r): Seymour Tyler, Sydney Jones, Isaac Phills, John Pannill; front row: William Carter, John Hamilton, Percy Richards, Fred Wilson.

Latimore. The day passed uneventfully and he did on that day what his diary indicates he did on other days: "Wrote Izie......" [his wife]. When one of his battalion members, J. Mansfield, died on 14 January, 1918 and was buried two days later, Capt. White made the following entry:

> It is nice to be dead and out of it—I used to think that I did not want to die but when work and worry get hold of you death is sweet.[69]

There was, of course, a lot to worry about especially in times of war. The men of the No. 2 Construction Battalion had, in addition, to put up with their second class status during the war and during the demobilization period, June–December, 1919 when they were the targets of anti-black demonstrations and insults in Liverpool, England and in Truro, Nova Scotia where they were attacked by whites because of the retention of their camp in Truro. After this, demobilization was hurried and all evidence of the camp that once housed them was carefully removed. For many Canadians, No. 2 Construction was best forgotten.

It took some years before the story and the tragedy of this battalion were resurrected for history and for posterity. In 1981 the Society for the

Protection and Preservation of Black Culture in Nova Scotia [the Black Cultural Society, in short] decided to honour the black veterans of World War I and to organize a reunion of the surviving veterans. The event was held in Halifax on November 12, 1982. Rev. Dr. W.P. Oliver, who was himself a chaplain to the black troops in Halifax in World War II, and who assumed the mantle of Rev. W.A. White at the Cornwallis Street African Baptist Church, paid his tribute to the black veterans of World War I in the following words:

> I do not know the exact number who paid the supreme sacrifice and who are numbered with the thousands of their comrades who now lie in Flanders Field. However, I am sure that the remaining group with us tonight, of that gallant and loyal six hundred, will remember them one by one and name by name. The veterans served with distinction, they and their Padre Captain White represented Canadian Blacks in a commendable manner.[70]

They were remembered also "one by one and name by name" when Calvin Ruck wrote his book entitled *Canada's Black Battalion No. 2 Construction, 1916-1920* which was published by the Black Cultural Centre for Nova Scotia in 1986.

In the concluding section of this narrative mention must be made of those black volunteers who enlisted in combat units during World War I. Their record on the battlefields of Europe certainly give the lie to the stereotype that was bandied about in 1914-1915 in official military circles in Canada that black soldiers were uncommitted or would be unreliable in the trenches. As already noted, some were recruited in the 106th Battalion, Nova Scotia Rifles, which also had its headquarters in Truro. Two notable members of a well-known Truro black family enlisted in the 106th Battalion: Sydney Morgan Jones, who was only fifteen-years-old and Jeremiah [Jerry] Jones. There were others, too, and in different battalions, too numerous to recall in this short narrative which will close with the contents of a letter addressed to the editor of a Truro newspaper during the war:

> All Nova Scotians, and especially those of us from Truro, were delighted when we heard that Fred Huntley had won distinction for bravery at the front. Word comes from those heroes, who are daily arriving in English hospitals, of numerous acts of bravery on the part of our boys

from home, many which should be rewarded with v.c.'s, but will never reach beyond the eyes of those who are now past recording such events. One of the humble citizens of Truro, always an honest, hard-working man was reported wounded several weeks ago. I last saw him in Bramshott in January before he had gone to France; had a few words with him; next heard he had been wounded and only today, from one of the lads in hospital, who was with him at the time did I hear the complete story of how Jerry Jones had captured a German machine gun, forced the crew to carry it back to our lines, and, depositing it at the feet of the C.O., said "Is this thing any good?" The report is that he has been recommended for a D.C.M. I hope it is true. All honour to this man, who is ready for the front again. May he live to return to Truro and receive the welcome he deserves.[71]

There is no record that Jeremiah [Jerry] Jones ever received the D.C.M. Given the climate of the time this is not surprising. However, the point was made: Nova Scotia Blacks did make a worthwhile contribution to the war struggle.

In the story of the black experience in Nova Scotia the period 1854-1918 is little known. Unlike the earlier years of the nineteenth century when events in the United States of America spilled over into Nova Scotia, the period which opened in 1854 marked the consolidation of black communities in different parts of the province and set a pattern of settlement which, except for slight shifts in population mobility responding to the job market, remained largely intact for the next one hundred years. In 1964, Dr. W.P. Oliver, Regional Representative in the Adult Education Division of the Nova Scotia Department of Education, listed 47 areas in the province in which members of the black population lived. These areas were largely settled in the period covered in this chapter. The black population in 1854 was in the region of 5,000 while in 1964 Dr. Oliver listed the population at 14,000.

The most significant institution in the black community in the period 1854-1918 was the African United Baptist Association. Those who were associated with this institution became the leaders and followers in the black community. The agenda for the Association became the agenda for the community. Under the aegis of the Association, the affiliated black Baptist churches provided for social cohesiveness through church activities while the Association looked to school education to provide social mobility and economic progress for Nova Scotia's black population.

While it is fair to say that the Association achieved considerable success and satisfaction in the work undertaken, it must also be recognized that many of its steps were tentative and limited by a number of factors such as poor finances, few educated leaders able to operate at the level required to counteract racial biases and prejudice in the bureaucracy and the political arena, and the continued reluctance on the part of the majority society to accept Blacks as fellow citizens with standard rights and obligations.

This reluctance was most noticeable in the policies relating to educational provisions for black children. Throughout this period segregated schools for blacks was the norm in Nova Scotia except in a few towns where small numbers of black children were accepted in public schools. The response from the leaders and parents in the Halifax city area was immediate and unequivocal: segregated schools in the city meant unequal standards and inferior education. In the rural black communities, segregated residential areas led to separate schools for whites and blacks. The debates in the legislature and the position taken by some white church leaders showed that a minority in the main society appreciated the obvious injustices. For as long as this vocal white minority existed, there was hope for better times. In the meantime, however, the black leadership of the day realized the need for self-help and local initiatives. The best example of these features were found in the thinking and planning for an industrial school and orphanage for black children, the forerunner of the Nova Scotia Home for Colored Children which, in 1921, found a permanent site and a durable organization ensuring its continuity. The groundwork laid up to 1918 was pioneering work with a vision and a determination.

Though few in numbers, this period produced leaders and thinkers who were a credit to Nova Scotia. If one adds men of adventure, valour and endurance, the list grows into an illustrious testimonial: Richard Preston, Peter McKerrow, James R. Johnston, William Edward Hall, George Dixon, Sam Langford, Clarence H. Johnston, James A.R. Kinney, Moses Puryear, Isaac Phills are but a few from a creditable list. Nor would one have to exclude black women from among the list of achievers even though the age in general relegated women to domestic roles in general throughout the world. Such pioneers among black women during this period as Sister S. Gray, Maude Sparks, Margaret Upshaw, Selina Williams Jefferson, Sara Middleton, Edith Samuel Sparks, Mary Anne Reid and Florence Ann

Williams, to name a few only, need to be remembered in the annals of the history of Nova Scotia's Blacks.

Individuals are remembered not for their own sake but because of their contribution to society as a whole. In the period covered in this chapter and, indeed, before the wider society labelled Blacks as a burden to the state, unable to integrate in the larger society, unable to contribute to development and change. There was a time, as the reader will discern in the first chapter, that legislators raised a unanimous call for Blacks to be returned to their ancestral continent. This was not carried out, could not be carried out given the reality of colonial and international politics, but the general drift in Nova Scotia and Canada was that this land was white persons' territory.

There were many illustrations of this drift but none better than the factors and circumstances that gave rise to the Number 2 Construction Battalion. Here was a situation in which black Nova Scotians and Canadians were denied the opportunity to serve their province and country in a life and death struggle as equals. Yet the World War was not fought in vain. Returning soldiers had had a glimpse of the other side of the vaunted western civilization. They would remember that in civilian life as the era of reconstructing a new world and social order began in 1918, the subject of the next chapter.

Rev. Adam S. Green, the white pastor of the Zion Baptist Church, Truro, anticipated this challenge in a lecture to the African United Baptist Association in 1904 entitled "The Future of the Canadian Negro." He ended with a poem, the last stanza of which was as follows:

Le Negre canadien, now up and be
The beat that in thee lies!
Readjust thyself! up, up, awake thee
And from thy stupor rise!
O strip thee for thy noblest race,
And stop not short of high First Place.

CHAPTER THREE

THE PERIOD 1918–1945

WAR AND ECONOMY

The opening years of the twentieth century set the stage for the social and economic patterns which influenced the lives of black Nova Scotians during the war years. The majority of the black population lived in a rural economy and less than 20% of this number lived in the Halifax–Dartmouth area. Farming, domestic industry, and a largely subsistence economy, were the mainstays of the black communities. Garden produce, whether directed to the Halifax market or to white residential streets all over the province through door-to-door sales, provided modest revenue. With the threat of food shortages looming large during the war years, emphasis was placed on what Ontario adopted as a policy of "a vegetable garden for every home." A local paper accused Nova Scotians of being indifferent: "With all the horrors of a world famine staring us in the face Nova Scotia is still sound asleep."[1]

There were few additional opportunities for blacks in general in Nova Scotia other than the sale of domestic produce, farm labour, and the occasional windfall when warships docked in Halifax harbour. Remittances from the few hundred black servicemen abroad added to the meagre resources but there had to be something put aside for the day the soldiers came home. As George Byard wrote to his mother from Bramshott, England: "Please let me know if you get my check every month. Save some for me when I get back, though it may be some time yet."[2]

One of the terrible disasters during the war was the Halifax Explosion of December 6, 1917 which claimed an estimated 2,000 lives, and left 9,000 injured and blinded. Six thousand were rendered homeless and the homes of some 25,000 persons were damaged. The explosion occurred in the north end of Halifax where most of the city's black residents lived. Miraculously, however, the only location in the north end to escape the ferocity of the explosion was Africville. Only one Africville resident was killed in the explosion. Newspaper reports and photographs, as well as personal accounts by black and white residents in the Metro area, testify to the humanitarian services rendered by survivors during this great tragedy which in terms of property losses alone exceeded some thirty million dollars.[3] This was a serious set-back to the Nova Scotia economy during the war years but, fortunately, through the international co-operation of friendly nations and the generous contributions of local governments and businesses, a like amount was raised to repair the damage. As Thomas H. Raddall, historian of Halifax, described it:

For months the people of the North End lived like cavemen, with black tarpaper in place of windows, with patched-up doors, with the heat of their stoves escaping through cracks and slashes in the walls and roofs. The Halifax Relief Commission imported labour as far away as Montreal, and all through the winter and spring four thousand men worked steadily to make homes weatherproof and to provide enough glass for a little blessed daylight.[4]

Part of this opportunity was shared by black labourers who were a small part of the 4,000 employed. The social and racial climate during the war years had brought no improvements in race relations. Blacks in Nova Scotia continued to stand at the end of the long line seeking employment opportunities. It did not matter whether one was educated, skilled, semi-skilled or unskilled, the result was the same: Blacks were employed if and when other candidates were unavailable or unwilling. Many Nova Scotia Blacks had emigrated to the southern United States where, during the period of reconstruction following the end of the civil war, new employment opportunities were opened up for black people at all levels of the economic ladder from humble labour to the learned professions, something which has never happened in Nova Scotia in quite the same way up to the present. One example of such an emigre was William Golar, who grew up in Beechville on the outskirts of Halifax, continued with his education in the United States and rose to the rank of Professor of Ancient Languages in Livingstone College, Salsbury, North Carolina in the closing years of the nineteenth century, rising to President of that institution in the early decades of the twentieth century. This was an exceptional but not isolated case. Eye-witness accounts testify to the hardships Blacks faced in those early years.

Peter McKerrow, who was mentioned in chapter 2, and who lived in Halifax until his death in 1906, has left us the following account which begins with a comparison between the opportunities in the United States with the lack of opportunities in Nova Scotia:

> Sad and sorry are we to say that is more than we can boast of here in Nova Scotia. Our young men as soon as they receive a common education must flee away to the United States [to], seek employment as did W.H. Gol[a]r......Very few ever receive a trade from the large employers, even in the factories, on account of race prejudices, which is a terrible barrier, and a direct insult to Almighty God. And still, some of these judicators of equal rights, after a fashion, will call the young men worthless, lazy, and good for nothing, when every avenue of trade is closed against them......

Peter McKerrow then went on to cite the case of young black mechanics from the West Indies who could only find employment in Halifax as menial labourers and who left shortly afterwards to seek better employment in the United States.[5]

There are other first-hand accounts describing how hard it was to get a job but a few examples will suffice. In the book entitled *Traditional Lifetime Stories. A Collection of Black Memories*, a number of such accounts appear. John Robert Pannill, who was born in Yarmouth in 1898, served in the Merchant Marine for two years during World War I and worked for Samuel Cunard driving a horse drawn coal cart and delivering coal from door to door. John Pannill, who is alive and well in Halifax as these lines are being written in July, 1989, was a remarkable man, self-assured, confident and capable even in his youth. Surrounded by racial discrimination and by gross denials, he went headlong into challenging situations, knowing he was responsible and reliable. His life story is a good example of how one can and should confront prejudice and respond with strength that comes from recognizing one's self-worth. The work he did for Samuel Cunard in 1917 was hard and extended over long hours for which he was paid seven dollars a week. For six months he did his work faithfully and efficiently but consulted the newspaper advertisements every night. One day he saw an opening and addressed his employer candidly:

> I told him I wasn't driving no more coal for $7 a week. I'm going to get another job with Imperial Oil. The boss said that they don't hire colored fellas. Well, I said, that's you saying that and so I left and went to the company branch of Imperial Oil. I arrived and on the door it stated 'Ring and Walk In.' I rang but didn't walk in, just waited. So, when someone came to the door, they asked why did I wait. I stated that since your company is large and prosperous, and a branch of Standard Oil Company, I felt that I may be interrupting something. He discussed with me things like could I read, write and count. After saying, yes sir, to all that, he asked if I knew the city. Yes, sir, was the answer. So he said, all right. I made $7 a week with Cunards and started off with Imperial Oil for $18 a week......[6]

John Pannill knew what the problems were but he was determined to overcome them. Just prior to his employment by Samuel Cunard, he had suffered the humiliation of being locked up for a week by the immigration authorities in his hometown of Halifax, while in the service of the Merchant Marine, on suspicion of being a Spanish stowaway. He seemed to have taken all these adventures in his stride. In 1919, John Robert Pannill entered the service of the Canadian National Railways as a sleeping car porter and remained in this service for 43 years until his retirement in October, 1962.

It is important to recall the story of John Pannill to show that Blacks were responding courageously to the challenges of the day. While he and his contemporaries would all agree that racial discrimination existed everywhere in Canada, and nowhere more than in Nova Scotia, they could not fight this situation only by emigrating to the United States. They had to do something about it at home as well. Even if opportunities were few and far between, it was important for members of the black community to improve themselves so as to inspire others and to educate the wider society. One early enterprising effort was made by Alexander Parris who came to Sydney with the Barbadian immigrants at the opening of this century. A shoemaker by trade in his home country, he worked initially as a labourer in the steel plant for five years before opening his own shoe repair shop on Tupper Street.

Until the mid-1970s, blacks were employed as railway sleeping car porters, and carried out these tasks effectively and with dignity.

He extended his business in stages to a candy store, a grocery store and an apartment building for rent. And, as a talented musician who played at least six instruments, he gave music lessons to young boys and girls in the total community.[7]

While individual and family advancement was important, it had little meaning and no place outside the parameters of the black community itself. This was the only structure that mattered when individuals and families went about their daily chores. At the end of the day, it was the community structure and its institutions that provided endorsement, advice, support and comfort since these desirable and necessary features were not forthcoming from the political system and the majority society that controlled this system. While other ethnic groups in Nova Scotia, whether Acadian, Scot, English, Irish, German or Dutch, could at least look to the political system and the majority society, of which they were a functional and visible part, for acceptance and help, Blacks had to look mainly to themselves and their institutions for survival. The remaining sections of this chapter will look at black initiatives and institutions in the context of community growth.

COMMUNITY INITIATIVES AND LABOUR HISTORY

The growth of church-related activities, the development of small-scale business enterprises, and the employment of increasing numbers of Blacks in the service of the Canadian National Railways will constitute the main features of this section in the period beginning with the end of the first world war and closing with the end of the second world war [1918-1945].

The opening of this period coincided with the 65th session of the African United Baptist Association which was held in Halifax in September, 1918. The affiliated black Baptist churches numbered 21 at this time. One church in Moose River closed down shortly after the formation of the Association in 1854 through lack of members and the church in New Glasgow had not yet become affiliated. A total of 22 black Baptist churches existed in Nova Scotia by 1904. No additions were made after this date while one was demolished in 1969 with the relocation of Africville, leaving 21 churches in all since 1969. It is worth recalling excerpts from the opening speeches to the Association in 1918 by the Lieutenant-Governor of Nova Scotia, MacCallum Grant, and the Mayor of Halifax, A.C. Hawkins, to analyse them in the light of the existing realities facing the black people of Nova Scotia. The Lieutenant-Governor praised the Association for uplifting the Blacks socially, spiritually, and morally. "The best man I ever met in my life was a godly man belonging to the Baptist faith. My parting message to you is, may we all try to live better lives so when we are done with the things of this earth we may leave behind us names that will be revered and remembered." The Mayor said: "Among the colored population of Halifax are some of my best friends. Canada is a country of great opportunity for the colored man. It all depends upon the man himself as to what position he finds himself placed. Ancient history proves the capabilities of the [black] race."

Given the reality of what was happening to black people everywhere in Canada in 1918, and having particular regard to what had happened to them in Nova Scotia and Halifax over the centuries, it is remarkable that men of high office could be so insensitive to the real life experiences and expectations of their fellow beings. The secretary of the Association, James A.R. Kinney, who spoke at the same convention on "The Progress of the Colored Race for Fifty Years" had other realities in his mind. His background was indicative of his priorities. Born in Yarmouth in 1878, Kinney was in 1897 the first black graduate of the Maritime Business College in Halifax. For the next 26 years he worked as advertising manager for the Halifax firm of

William Stairs, Son and Morrow. The fact that he served as a faithful member of the Association, as clerk from 1916 to 1921 and as treasurer from 1939 until his death in 1940, and was a founder and leading figure in the establishment of the Nova Scotia Home for Colored Children, is a confirmation of the community context in which black leaders and followers worked and served during the period covered in this chapter.

Kinney's address began with a catalogue of achievements of black Americans since the Civil War starting with economic progress, moving to educational progress and on to religious progress. If, by his choice of presentation, Kinney was laying down what was for him the appropriate order of priorities for black Nova Scotians, he was drawing attention to a strategy for progress which, unfortunately for black Nova Scotians, was reversed from the beginning: religious progress came first, educational progress came next and economic progress came last.

Kinney restricted his subject area to American Blacks. Their numbers were significantly larger than their counterparts in Nova Scotia but the relative advancement over the years was staggering. To take one example only from each category the following picture emerges: In 1866, there were 2,100 businesses conducted by American Blacks while the figure for 1917 was 45,000. While there were 600 black teachers in all schools in 1866, the figure rose to 36,900 in 1917. From 700 black churches in 1866, the number increased to 42,000 in 1917. He listed the outstanding firms and factories and the brilliant students, scientists and prize winners. Kinney even quoted in detail an excerpt from a pledge card issued by the Dean of the College of Liberal Arts of Harvard University, saying that the pledge was "worthy of our youth in the Province of Nova Scotia." The youth that Kinney had in mind

The First Congress of Colored Women in Canada was held in Halifax in 1920.

in his address of 1918 was, of course, the black youth. It is recalled here for the reader to compare this message of 1918 with its reality and relevance for 1989:

> I will never bring disgrace upon my race by any unworthy deed or dishonorable act. I will live a clean, decent, manly life, and will ever respect and defend the virtue and honor of womanhood. I will uphold and obey the just laws of my country and of the community in which I live, and will encourage others to do likewise. I will not allow prejudice, injustice, insult or outrage to cower my spirit or sour my soul, but will ever preserve the inner freedom of honor and conscience. I will not allow myself to be overcome of evil, but will strive to overcome evil by good. I will endeavour to develop and exert the best powers within me for my personal improvement, and will strive unceasingly to quicken the sense of racial duty and responsibility. I will in all these ways aim to uplift my race, so that to everyone bound to it by ties of blood, it shall become a bond of ennoblement, and not a byword of reproach.[8]

Kinney's address is a remarkable document, not only for 1918. If this was the kind of intellectual spread that was being laid out by the annual convention of the African United Baptist Association, it boded well for the twentieth century. While the minutes of the Association's 65th session do not give information on Nova Scotia parallels relating to the issues raised in Kinney's address, the resolutions adopted give some idea of the agenda for the ensuing years. Prior to listing the resolutions, the officers of the Association called for unity and resolution in the black community, for good leadership to provide practical solutions to pressing problems. This was a call that was repeated in one form or other at every Association annual meeting throughout the twentieth century. Unity, dedication and leadership became synonymous with an annual refrain. Was it because the message had to be reinforced by repetition or was it because these qualities were hard to come by in a community whose struggle for survival was an uphill one all the way?

The 1918 resolutions give some idea of the tasks ahead for the church and community: it was recognized that since women were the mainstay of the community, every local church should organize the Ladies Auxiliary and where this was not possible a number of local interested women should be co-opted to carry out the work of the Ladies Auxiliary under the supervision of the elected President of the Ladies Auxiliary of the African United Baptist Association. Mention has already been made in chapter 2 that the first Ladies Auxiliary of the Association was established in 1917 with Mrs. Maude Sparks as first president. The second resolution referred to financial support for the Home for Colored Children in order to make it a reality after the first building was destroyed in the north end of Halifax in the explosion of 1917. This objective would only be realized in 1921. The third undertaking was to build a Home for the aged. Two resolutions referred to funds to support pastors in the smaller churches as well as to provide more liberal salaries to enable pastors to do their work free of financial stress—always a difficult challenge for a poor community. One of the resolutions called for the Association to be incorporated "with powers to hold property in trust, and assist in the upbuilding of the Baptist cause in a material way." This was an implied business proposition which a person like James A.R. Kinney would see as a useful means to promote church ends.

The later history of the Association will show that, up to 1989, the Association has no landed property of its own nor a building of its own from where its operations are carried out. The final resolution in 1918 was an enigmatic one containing two unrelated objectives or concerns listed together:

As the colored people's main source of uplift is the Church, we being without strong organizations, other races have to foster and care for us. And whereas our status in the future will be the result of our strength as a race, we urgently recommend......that earnest endeavour should be made to have all communities that have colored Churches made eligible to send delegates to sit and discuss with us the various phases of race uplift......It should also be made known to these outside Churches that they are eligible for membership by complying with the rules.

Why the Association would need the services of "other races to foster and care" for it in 1918 is unclear, while it is understandable why it would like all the black Baptist churches to be affiliated with it. In 1918, the 2nd Baptist Church in New Glasgow was not affiliated to the Association. This matter was rectified in 1947.

While 22 churches existed throughout the province to spearhead community progress, it was clear that their existence alone would do little without the initiatives and the dedication of the women members. While it is only in the past decade or so that the historical and contemporary role of women has begun to be recognized and respected, women throughout the world have made a tremendous contribution to global progress since time immemorial. In Africa, for example, the role of women was clearly defined in both matrilineal and, patrilineal societies. Where both matriarchal and patriarchal political systems existed in juxtaposition, African women were treated with respect and recognized for their roles and contribution. Where peaceful agrarian societies were disrupted by slave raids and slave trades, it was the women who bore the great burden of rearing, nurturing and holding the family together in distressful circumstances. When African women were transported as human chattel through the trans-Atlantic trade to the Caribbean and the Americas, more was required of their courage and resilience. The literature on this, particularly in the United States, has already reached rich proportions. Nova Scotia is coming along slowly but surely.

Sylvia Hamilton of Halifax, one-time journalist, Assistant Nova Scotia Regional Director, Secretary of State, on leave of absence with the National Film Board as of November 1989, has provided a brief overview of the contribution of black women in Nova Scotia in an article significantly entitled "Our Mothers Grand and Great: Black Women in Nova Scotia." Beginning with the tragic and unsung heroines of the slave period, Sylvia Hamilton moves to the Loyalist era of Catherine Abernathy, school teacher, Phillis George, pastor's wife, Rose Fortune, policewoman and baggage and transport service in Annapolis Royal, the Maroon mistresses of 1796-1800 and on to the twentieth century personalities mentioned in this chapter and the following chapter. The author points out that much more remains to be done: "As research and exploration into the lives of Black women in Nova Scotia continues, a fuller view, one with dimension and perspective, will emerge. We will then know where to erect our monument. Now there are only signposts pointing the way."[9] In the meantime, Sylvia Hamilton, has provided a monument herself in the National Film Board production of "Black Mother Black Daughter," a thirty-minute film on black Nova Scotians which she co-directed with Claire Prieto, of Jamaican descent. This film had its premiere at the World Trade and Convention Centre, Halifax, before one of the largest crowds that ever assembled at this venue, on April 18, 1989.

There are others, too, such as the poetess, Maxine Tynes, who says it in verse. Her first book of poems, *Borrowed Beauty*, won the award of People's Poet of Canada in 1988. As teacher, journalist and member of the Board of

Governors of Dalhousie University, Maxine Tynes, is pre-eminently placed to document the signposts and plan for the monuments as envisioned by Sylvia Hamilton. In the early 1980s, Carolyn E. Fowler wrote short biographies on four Nova Scotian personalities: Edith Clayton, Portia White, Corinne Sparks and Dr. Carrie M. Best, based on personal interviews and secondary sources. These studies have not been published to date as the researcher left Nova Scotia to take up a Federal appointment in Ottawa in 1988. Such research is, of course, important to future investigators both in the results achieved and by the example set.

From the above accounts one can see why the African United Baptist Association appealed to the women to organize further. Whether the members had any knowledge of the historical roles played by such persons as Lydia Jackson (who fled on foot from Lunenburg to Halifax to appeal to John Clarkson in 1791 for release from her employer who had abused her physically, calling for redress through the judicial system and for an opportunity to go to freedom in Sierra Leone) or Mrs. William Deer (wife of the owner of the Stag Hotel in Preston who had actually run that business in the mid-1850s) or the black women who were prominent vendors at the Cheapside Market on Halifax's waterfront since the early decades of the nineteenth century, did not matter since contemporary examples were abundant. It is to these examples that we shall now turn to trace some community initiatives.

The task entrusted to the women in 1918 was such that in the following year a full-time salaried organizer was selected. Mrs. Margaret Upshaw held this position until her death in 1922. In less than four years, funds were collected for the projected Home for Colored Children, women's activities were organized in all the churches and the groundwork was laid for the First Congress of Coloured Women in Canada to be held in Halifax in 1920. The fact that Nova Scotia was selected for this national event in 1920 was a tribute to the organizational ability and reputation of the Ladies Auxiliary of the African United Baptist Association.

The annual conventions of the Ladies Auxiliary in the succeeding years, coupled with the work of the branches in the local churches, contributed to community growth in many ways. Since the women who spearheaded the activities were spouses of church leaders, school teachers, market vendors, domestic servants, market gardeners, basket weavers and producers of domestic goods, housewives and parents, and owners of small businesses, they were involved actively in every facet of community life. In many ways they set the pace and gave the lead even in a male-dominated society which was so characteristic of the twentieth century.

One other feature of church-related community initiative was in the sphere of youth activities. The credit for taking the lead in this field belongs to James R. Johnston, already mentioned in chapter 2, who, in 1898, began his almost seventeen-year pioneering work for black youth in Nova Scotia as Superintendent of the Sunday School in Halifax and as President and Organizer of the Baptist Young People's Union (B.Y.P.U.). Johnston's preoccupation with the need for urgent educational advancement for black youth has been noted earlier. According to Pearleen Oliver, some of the churches had already begun to organize the youth as early as 1890 and that youth delegates were being accredited to the Association annual meetings since 1896. This record is a commendable one and its value is reflected in the fact that many of the youth who made headway, in spite of the many handicaps prevalent at the time, were products of this environment and initiative. In 1937, the local nature of youth organization was raised to become part of the Association's structure when Rev. William Pearly Oliver, the new pastor of the Cornwallis Street Baptist Church, then a young man of 25, was asked to head the B.Y.P.U. of the Association, a responsibility which he held as Supervisor till 1942.[10] Rev. H.D. Thomas held this position from 1942 till 1945 when the first woman to hold this position, Mrs. Pearleen Oliver, assumed the position for the next three years. Her experience and work held her in good stead when, in 1976, the African United Baptist Association honoured her with the position of Moderator, the first woman to hold that office since the Association was formed in 1854. Twelve years later, in 1988, Mrs. Carolyn Thomas of East Preston followed in those distinguished footsteps as Moderator.

The contribution of the men to church and community initiatives was equally important. In a period when the church was the bedrock upon which the community was founded, the church was expected to be all things to all its members. Until provincially-based black secular organizations were founded in Nova Scotia from 1945 onwards, it was the African United Baptist Association which represented both spiritual and secular interests. To that extent, the pastors were synonymous with leaders. In the literature and folklore of the black community, the pastors occupy a venerated position. In the concluding chapter where concerns for the 1990s and beyond are analysed, the roles of church leadership will be considered further, but for the period of this chapter [1918-1945] the contribution to community development of such church leaders as Rev. W.A. White, Rev. A.A. Wyse, Rev. A.W. Thompson, Rev. M.L. Anderson, Rev. W.N. States and Rev. W.P. Oliver was uniformly well received and well regarded. Two of them served as chaplains during the two world wars. Further biographical details on some of them will be given later in the section dealing with inter-war personalities.

Just as the pastors were helped by the Ladies Auxiliary of their churches and the Moderator of the A.U.B.A. was helped by the Ladies Auxiliary of the Association, pastors were given assistance by the male counterparts at both levels by the deacons and the Laymen's Council respectively. It took much longer for men's church-related community organizations to be formed. Women not only organized earlier but provided more active participants throughout the twentieth century covered in this study. And it was a woman who initiated the first meeting at a local level to organize men to add their weight to further community development. This lady was Muriel V. States, a remarkable twentieth-century personality whose work will be featured in greater detail in the section on inter-war personalities.

The meeting in question took place at Hammonds Plains on October 29, 1929 and resulted in the formation of the Men's Progressive Club of Hammonds Plains. The relationship between the church and this secular organization was obvious: the convenor of the meeting was the official organizer of the Ladies Auxiliary of the A.U.B.A., and the main speaker was the Rev. A.W. Thompson. In the following nine years, only three other venues could speak of similar men's organizations: New Glasgow in 1930; Windsor Plains in 1936 and Halifax in 1938. Whatever it was that accelerated the growth of men's organizations during the war years, the black Baptist church historian, Pearleen Oliver states: "Perhaps it was the call of war during the years 1939-45 that served also to rally the men of our Association to service within their churches; for it was during these years that the Laymen's Council took root and men's groups were organized in almost every church within the Association."[11]

The fact that the Ladies Auxiliary of the A.U.B.A. was formed in 1917 and the Laymen's Council of A.U.B.A. was formed in 1944 raises obvious questions of gender difference in the participation of Nova Scotia's Blacks in church and church-related community activities. If an important stimulus in 1944 was the war, there was a war waging in 1917 as well. Savanah E. Williams, who was authorized to research the history of the African United Baptist Association in the late 1970s, puts it in these words: "Numerically and financially, the Ladies' Auxiliary is the strength and backbone of the Association. During various years, the Auxiliary has raised more money than the total receipts of the Association......it appears that the women's organization has been more productive than the Laymen's Council."[12]

Whatever the strength and numbers of these gender organizations, the constituency served was the same. The cooperative efforts of women and men made the ultimate progress possible. Seen in this light, the formation of the Laymen's Council in 1944 was a further milestone in community initiatives, adding to the previous outlets that men had as clergy, deacons and elders. The first President was James A. Ross Kinney, the son of J.A.R. Kinney mentioned in various places in this chapter, who was born on December 3, 1910 and who died in tragic circumstances in the Bedford Basin on December 8, 1980. Both the Kinneys served the church, the A.U.B.A. and the Nova Scotia Home for Colored Children for many years and with great devotion and are fondly remembered in the annals of community work in Nova Scotia. They rank among the many family members of different generations who have carried the torch high and well for the community which nurtured them and which they in turn served. Nova Scotia's black community is well endowed with such family achievements, a matter of local and provincial pride.

The other office-bearers of the first Laymen's Council were equally distinguished members of the black community: William Robinson Johnston, the first Secretary, was an active member of the Cornwallis Street Baptist Church; Allan W. Evans, church deacon, East Preston, Richard S. Symonds, deacon, Hammonds Plains, and Howard Lawrence, deacon, New Glasgow, were vice-presidents; Russell Christmas, businessman from Digby, was the assistant secretary, while the two committee members were Clarence Harvey Johnston, deacon at Cornwallis Street Baptist Church, and Edgar Johnson, deacon at the Cherrybrook Church. All these personalities held positions of responsibility in their respective communities which they served with distinction for many years. The service they rendered is reflected in the positions they occupied. For example, Ross Kinney later became the treasurer and founding member of the George Washington Carver Credit Union which received its charter on 17 July, 1950, as well as Moderator of the A.U.B.A., and Superintendent of the Nova Scotia Home for Colored Children. He promoted the economic, educational and religious advancement of the black community as his father had highlighted in his address to the A.U.B.A. annual meeting in 1918 referred to in the earlier pages. A.W. Evans was a successful farmer and served for thirty years as Halifax County Councillor from 1930. Russell Christmas [living in 1989] ran a taxi business in Digby while Howard Lawrence [also still living in 1989] ran a trucking company in New Glasgow. They were the new men in the new age that was in the making. As custodians of the old order entrusted to them by church and society, they attempted to merge the old with the new. If the house of God had an important place for the young, the laity and the committed, the community at large had good reason to expect that its worldly needs would be well promoted.

As one of the earliest founding peoples of Nova Scotia, the black population did not enjoy the status of a charter group as did the earliest founding peoples of European descent. They needed help in order to participate fully in the opportunities available. The fishing, forestry and farming industries were not open to black participation. The civil service had no room for persons of colour not trained or educated sufficiently. Training, education and work experience were difficult to come by. Besides selling labour at a discount, blacks had to fend for themselves in small ways. Of the three phases identified by Clairmont and Wien in the history of the Blacks in Nova Scotia, the period covered in this chapter fell into their description of the second phase: "It appears useful to think of Nova Scotian development and black–white relations in terms of three phases. The first phase, referred to as *Establishing The Patterns*, covers the time-period from settlement to the founding of the African Baptist Association in 1854. The second phase, colloquially labelled *Hanging In There*, deals with the period from 1854 to the establishment of the Nova Scotia Association for the Advancement of Coloured People [N.S.A.A.C.P.] in 1945; and finally there is the contemporary period which we treat under the rubric *Making Changes*."[13]

For now it was a question of "hanging in there." Some examples will illustrate the point of modest but meaningful endeavours. Florence Diggs operated her grocery store in East Preston for 43 years. The Marsman brothers owned and operated the largest cooperage in Hammonds Plains with their own mill fully equipped to turn out barrels and dry fish packages, selling between 3-6 truck loads of barrels weekly in Halifax, with other black entrepreneurs responding seasonally to supply the demands in the valley for barrels during the apple season. Sydney Jones, formerly of Truro, later deacon of the Cornwallis Street Baptist Church, opened the Wilberforce Barber Shop on Gerrish Street in Halifax.[14] Russell Paris' grocery store in New Glasgow was an early black initiative. In Halifax, George Roach owned and operated a restaurant at the corner of Gerrish and Gottingen assisted by his wife, the former Josephine Webber from Mt. Denison. This restaurant was for years a favourite eating place known particularly for the excellent pies prepared by Josephine Roach. John Desmond, who was born in Tracadie in 1905, came to Halifax in 1928 and began working for a construction company. He lost the use of one eye while working in 1930 and two years later opened a barber shop on Gottingen on what, in 1989, is the parking lot opposite the North Branch Library. There were a number of black barbers plying their trade—notably John Desmond, four years younger than Sydney Jones. Jones first took to this trade after being demobilized at the end of

World War I and became the chief barber at the Camp Hill Hospital in Halifax. We have already noted that Sydney Jones opened the Wilberforce Barber Shop on Gerrish Street in 1929. These barbers, Desmond and Jones, came closer when Sydney Jones married the sister of John Desmond. Soon the barbers joined business bonds as well when they combined their resources in a single business on Gottingen Street.

Jack and Viola Desmond, owners of Viola's Hairdressing and Jack's Barber Shop at 445 Gottingen Street in Halifax.

John Desmond was the only registered black barber in Nova Scotia. Still buoyant in spirit and sharp in memory, Jack Desmond, as he likes to be called, shows visitors, in 1989, the framed certificate, the barber's chair and the picture of his deceased wife, the famous Halifax beautician, whose place in Nova Scotia's history is assured through the infamous Viola Desmond case of racial discrimination in 1946—an incident treated in greater detail in a later section. Both husband and wife operated their respective businesses in different sections of the same building, an excellent example of early black economic initiatives.

This remarkable couple started their respective businesses in 1932 and 1937 calling the firm "Viola's Hairdressing & Jack's Barber Shop" and the location was designated 445 Gottingen Street. Viola Desmond died in 1965.[15]

Both the former barbers, John Desmond and Sydney Jones, 84 years and 88 years in 1989, are articulate, active, deeply religious and respected. They represent the earlier generation of black entrepreneurs who had their own formula for "hanging in," deeply steeped in the church tradition of individual morality and community service, accepting the pitfalls of life but working hard to overcome them. Jack Desmond's generation would agree when he says: "Things have improved......since the days when Viola was thrown in jail, but prejudice will always exist. You've got to know how to handle it......Take it to the Lord with a prayer."[16] A later generation would entreat Jack Desmond to add: take it to the political arena; take it to human rights; take it to the law courts. The good Lord has enough on His hands.

While more black businesses opened in the period after 1945, a few more examples will be added to the above information to show that serious efforts were being made during the period covered in this chapter to improve the quality of life as well as the resources of the black community. One of the areas of limited opportunity was in the small-scale construction industry. Alex Jackson, born in Truro, moved to Halifax to try his hand as a building and concrete contractor in the 1930s. As a member of the Wilberforce Oddfellows Lodge which drew its membership from the black community and which applied itself to individual and group advancement, Alex Jackson was able to provide employment for members of his community, as indeed did all the other enterprises run by black entrepreneurs.

The point must be made that these were small business ventures, often little more than family initiatives. For their time, they were very important: bank loans were hard to come by; affirmative action from authorities was non-existent; the kinds of support available and encouraged in the 1980s were foreign to the period 1918-1945. In this context, the small businesses assume greater importance. Perhaps the most common business was the small grocery store of which some mention has already been made. There were others: Dorthea Jones operated one at 185 Creighton Street which had been started years before by her mother and which remained in the family. Sarah Brown ran a similar business on the same street and drew customers from near and far for her famous homemade taffy apples. Mary Alberta Gray was the second generation to run a convenience store on Cornwallis Street. When the Halifax explosion of 1917 destroyed the store, Mary Gray, an accomplished seamstress, ran a dress-making business out of her house until her death in 1949; Beresford Augustus Husbands, of whom more will be said later, was involved in businesses in a bigger way. He owned a real estate company on Duke Street and ran a store on Gottingen Street where the present Metropolitan store stands. Alexander Thomas operated a shoe repair store in Creighton Street while holding a full-time job at the Halifax Dockyards. The Thomas Furrier business at the corner of Barrington and Sackville was one of the largest of its kind in Nova Scotia.

In the Preston area, mention has been made of the Stag Hotel and the Diggs family store in this period. In addition, mention must be made of the family seasonal businesses such as making Christmas wreaths and picking mayflowers and blueberries which were sold at street corners and from door-to-door in the Halifax–Dartmouth area. Most of this back-breaking, laborious work kept the home fires burning and put bread on the table. Women grew old and the domestic businesses declined as succeeding generations raised their expectations and refused in increasing numbers to follow in the time-hallowed footsteps of their forbears. Quite understandably, the later generations wanted to move out of the "hanging-in" syndrome.

Basket-weaving in the black community was associated with the Preston area from the very early days of the Preston settlement in the nineteenth century. It, too, declined in production with the passing years. Had it not been for the high-profile, ingenious craft work of a remarkable Prestonian on the contemporary scene, Mrs. Edith Clayton, a legend in her time, who belongs properly to the period after 1945 which brought her national and international acclaim, little would have been known or remembered about this remarkable craft work in the black community. Indeed Edith Clayton, as she herself noted in the autobiography on which she was working in early 1989—and which the present author has had the privilege to read in draft—was only carrying on with a tradition which has come down the family line for many, many generations.

The isolated and neglected black community of Africville had its complement of small but viable businesses ranging from piggeries to grocery stores. Edith Macdonald Brown was the proprietress of what was called the "Handy Store," today modernized to read "Convenience Store." This was located on 1805 Barrington Street. This store was first opened by her uncle in 1846 and was the first black business in Africville. Edith Macdonald married William Brown of Dartmouth and continued to run the store until 1952, four years before her death, while raising her family of four daughters. Here was a fine example of a family business which remained in the family from 1846 to 1952.

A second store in Africville was owned by Ida Carvery and was called the "Penny Shop." Other such "Penny Shops" were owned by Mrs. Hester Sparks and by Mr. and Mrs. Albert Sparks. The former earned both popularity as well as notoriety for the homemade root and spruce beer which was sold at the competitive price of ten cents a bottle.[17]

What all the above information tells us about features of the black community efforts to raise itself is a confirmation of the initiatives of the time. If people wanted to make it in life, they had to do so on the basis of their own strength and resolve. The historical evidence which would be used later to reach conclusions on the basis of all the facts available, would have to take note of the incipient development in the period 1918-1945 and compare it with the period 1945-1989 to ask a number of pertinent questions, such as: Was the momentum maintained? What part did personalities play? Was the direction of the church maintained? What part did national politics play? What part did international politics play? Were there discernible changes in such matters as education and race relations?

One feature in the black community was clear. Significant small steps were taken or were being planned to move forward to a better plane. When one looks at the provincial picture at a point in time in the last quarter of 1929, one feels the force of a society on the move. In Weymouth Falls, a small community, black people were owning homes and property, farming and lumbering, with the Pioneer and Progressive Club providing secular and cultural activities and the Mount Beulah Baptist Church and the St. Matthew Church of England providing spiritual strength to the black community. Two halls were erected for social and public affairs. In Glace Bay, the new Liberty Hall was nearing completion and white and black families continued to reach out to each other for the good of all, a characteristic in a mining town which provides a good lesson to all in race relations. Many things were on the move in Sydney, Nova Scotia. St. Phillip's African Orthodox Church was well and active. Lawyer F. Allan Hamilton, B.A., LL.B. was practising at 205 Charlotte Street, while a number of black businesses were making headway. Ruck and Arthur were in the furniture moving and general trucking business while R. Best, custom tailor, George Ruck, plastering, Thomas Straker, grocer and second-hand furniture were other business people. In Halifax, Portia White, about whom more will be written later, was hard at her studies in business at the Halifax County Academy while Mrs. Morris V. Davis, who was the first and only black person to graduate in piano and voice from the Halifax Ladies College and Conservatory of Music in 1916-17 before the institution split its two-sided specialities, returned to the Halifax Conservatory of Music to further her studies in piano [her son, George Davis, would later, in 1948, be the second local-born black to graduate in law from Dalhousie University]. In New Glasgow, the 79 black families, mainly represented in spheres of occupation as mine workers, factory workers, with a sprinkling of truckmen, had succeeded in paying for the fine church built and were close to settling the cost of the parsonage. Two of the townspersons who would later go down in Nova Scotia black history as distinguished personalities, Carrie Best and her son, Calbert, had just left the town to attend a Christian Workers Conference in Quebec.[18]

The black community in Nova Scotia was striving as were other communities. Individuals, institutions, businesses, and professionals were becoming part of the Nova Scotia landscape. Most of them were located in areas where black community settlements were prominent. Patrons and clients were drawn from among community members in the main for, while many Nova Scotians have been brought up to believe that historically such things as segregation, exploitation and racial discrimination did not exist in this province, the truth points in the other direction. For Nova Scotia's black population, progress meant looking inwardly first and only then from a position of inward strength to move forward to greater participation and performance in the wider society. For this to happen, leadership of a secular kind was needed. Black church leaders in the period before 1945 were beginning to acquire university education but university graduates in general in the local-born sector of the community numbered three only before the 1930s ran out: Stanley Clyke of Truro, William P. Oliver of Wolfville and Gordon T. Jemmot of Halifax.

The professional Blacks operating in this period were immigrants from the West Indies. In a country made up of immigrants, the distinction was really not necessary since these professionals contributed their services as individuals of substance rather than as new immigrants. Nova Scotia's black history has a chequered place for such personalities from the West Indies as Dr. A. Calder, one-time President of the Medical Association of Cape Breton, Dr. F.B. Holder, who lived and practised on Maynard Street in Halifax, Dr. Waddell, whose office was in Brunswick Street, where Hope Cottage stands in 1989, and who later moved to Quinpool Road. Mention has already been made of lawyer Hamilton of Sydney, Nova Scotia.

One early West Indian immigrant couple had the distinction of seeing two of their children, both born in Halifax, both educated in Halifax, move on in life—one to become a medical doctor and the other a dental surgeon. Ernest Marshall graduated from the Dalhousie Medical School and moved to Toronto where he opened his practice. He was joined by his sister who became a dentist and worked in Toronto. Their parents remained in Halifax.

The professional contribution as well as the qualifications of these West Indian black immigrants served to raise the profile of the black community in Nova Scotia. Their background, too, was one of racial discrimination and exploitation in their ancestral homes—wherever these were at any time. Most, if not all, came to Nova Scotia not as privileged and prosperous citizenry but as adventurous, determined and proud people in search of a better life for themselves and their children. They and their children after them pioneered an interesting path which has been well served ever since. Through their example, then and now, they have established an undeniable claim to respect and recognition, not because of their colour or origins but through their achievements. Through their education, their work and their vision of a progressive society, they have shown that a racist society can be penetrated and challenged and reformed. To that extent, they have been, and continue to be, excellent role models.

If one's origins, then, were an unimportant accident of history, the contribution of Blacks in Nova Scotia to the development of the community and the province could be considered without the drawing of distinctions. Before the Nova Scotia Association for the Advancement of Coloured People came into existence in 1945, secular organizations which appeared in various black communities, in the form of progressive clubs with various designations, were in fact offshoots of the church. Two particular organizations were different in scope. Their membership and mandate foreshadowed the era of "making changes" which is associated with the period after 1945.

The first of these was the Halifax Colored Citizens Improvement League founded in 1932. Its President from 1932 until his death in Halifax on June 19, 1968 was Beresford Augustus Husbands, mentioned in earlier pages as a businessman. The period covered by Husbands' chairmanship was an important one provincially, nationally and internationally, covering the Depression, the rise of Nazism, World War II, and the civil rights movement in the United States and its entry on the Nova Scotia scene, foreshadowing the first steps leading up to the formation of the Black United Front. Indeed, B.A. Husbands died just six months before the most significant "Black Family Meeting" in the history of Nova Scotia, discussed in later pages.

Halifax Colored Citizens Improvement League Emancipation Day gathering on August 1, 1967. At far left is B. A. Husbands, who was president of the league from 1932 to 1968.

Under Husbands' presidency, the League became involved in the politics of change in a way not pursued by Nova Scotia's black population before. B.A. Husbands was pre-eminently placed to provide leadership in a situation which was new to many of his constituents. He had been a black employee with a Halifax white merchant. He was a sizeable real estate owner. He was an importer who ran a wholesale and retail store. His network cut across narrow social, economic, cultural, political and national boundaries. He could indeed be labelled the father of incipient black politics in Nova Scotia. One can only conjecture on what this man's contribution might have been to the dynamic politics of 1969 and beyond. But he was already 85 in 1968 and his life had run its course.

The work of the League was quite significant. Public meetings were called to sensitize the black community on the need to close ranks and unite so that political representation could be made to the authorities on such issues as education, housing, recreational facilities, a cultural hall and opening the nursing profession to Blacks. These meetings were held regularly in such venues as the Gerrish Street Hall and the African Methodist Episcopal Church Hall at the corner of Falkland and Gottingen—both of which no longer exist in 1989, having been demolished years ago. Indeed, one of the long-term projects which the League had considered was the need for a permanent hall to serve the black community. It had gone so far as to identify a site adjoining the present Armoury, on Cunard Street. It was concerned with amenities and organization to promote cultural, educational, sporting and political activities. To that end the League built outdoor rinks, constructed playgrounds, ran educational and fitness classes, took children on tours, organized summer camps for underprivileged children and sponsored a hockey team. For the period beginning in 1932, such activities were both innovative and forward-looking. While it is always incomplete to credit a single person, it is fair to say that the leadership provided by B.A. Husbands had much to do with the achievements of the League. Especially in the period before 1938 when no other black secular leader appeared on the scene and when there was no other black secular organization with the profile that the League had, the League and its president were seen as synonymous— as a sort of one-person show.

One public meeting was convened in 1944 to protest the denigration of black people in the story of "Black Sambo" in the grade II reader then in use. Pearleen Oliver addressed this meeting and recommended that action should be taken to remove it from the schools. B.A. Husbands took up the issue on behalf of the League and wrote to the premier of the province:

> The story holds the colored race up to ridicule and our League asks it to be eliminated and instead the true history of our race from the days of slavery be taught so that better understanding be promoted. You should also tell the stories of our great men and the contributions we as a race have made to culture. We are a people striving for our democratic rights, to overcome prejudice and triumph over intolerance. Will you help us?[19]

Forty-five years later, almost to the day since this protest meeting was held in Gerrish Hall, Halifax, on January 26, 1944, a racial incident erupted between white and black students at Cole Harbour District High School, in Halifax County, on January 10, 1989. The whole of 1989 was spent talking about the very issues B.A. Husbands had raised 45 years previously. What was new? What had gone wrong with both the white and the black community that had failed Nova Scotia in this regard? There is a salutary lesson here for political activists, community leaders, parents and teachers who would be inclined to believe that the credit for breaking new ground belonged to 1989.

In 1937, the League took up the matter of sponsoring the Halifax North Cultural and Recreation Youth Centre and B.A. Husbands was at the forefront once again, making representations for such a Centre to the Halifax City Council in the dual capacity of president of the League as well as president of the Colored Men's Conservative Social and Athletic Club. He did not live to see the opening of the George Dixon Community Recreation Centre in 1969 but the north end of Halifax had at last got what the League had striven for since 1932.

There is no question that the League, its programme, its leaders and followers, deserve a special place in the run-up to the era of the politics of change. An assessment of the League and its personalities and programs will draw attention to many factors. White and Blacks were shadow boxing to feel each other out. Blacks and Blacks were also shadow boxing to determine who should lead, who belonged and who didn't belong, who went to which church and who did not, who dealt with Whites and who dealt with Blacks. Such shadow boxing was, of course, not limited to that period or

Halifax Colored Citizens Improvement League parade float, 1966. Left to right: Debra Brown (Young), Lyn White (McCurdy), Carmella Talbot.

Youth who went on to hold prominent positions. Back row (fourth from left, to right): Frank Boyd, Blair Lopes, Gregory States, Louis Gannon, Carson Jackson; front row (centre): B. A. Husbands.

that organization. Husbands would have found, like other leaders before and after him, that leadership could be a lonely and painful experience. Not many would understand why this black man who was born in Barbados in 1883 and who emigrated to Canada at the turn of the century, who was working hard for internal improvements in the capital city of Nova Scotia, should be in correspondence with Eleanor Roosevelt, Pope John xxiii, British Prime Minister Ramsay Macdonald and John F. Kennedy, or why those black individuals throughout the British Empire who were awarded the Order of the British Empire—as B.A. Husbands was—were heroes at the time but collaborators at another, time in history. Yet a legacy that has validity in the annals of black history in Nova Scotia, associated with the life and times of Beresford Augustus Husbands, OBE, was that a small minority of Blacks in an overwhelming majority of Whites should take their place with confidence and be prepared to interact, to employ as well as be employed and to give as well as take. B.A. Husbands did not have the pulpit to deliver his message but, then, he was not limited by the pulpit, feeling equally comfortable at St. Paul's Anglican Church, the African Methodist Episcopal

Church, and the Cornwallis Street Baptist Church. He was once employed by a white merchant and during his term as an independent businessman and real estate owner, he employed both Blacks and Whites. He and the League worked hard to see that Blacks were admitted to the nursing profession, a battle later taken up by the Nova Scotia Association for the Advancement of Coloured People. When Gwendolen Barton and Ruth Bailey became the first black nurses in Nova Scotia, the credit for the opportunity belonged to the efforts of both organizations.

At a time when this had not been achieved, B.A. Husbands was once admitted to the Victoria General Hospital where he was attended by all white nurses. Edith Gray, the secretary of the League when it was founded, was requested to bring flowers for each of the nurses. When she demurred, B.A. Husbands made a point which was part of the legacy of the man: "I am a black man here. I will pave the way for the next black man who will come after me."[20] There were many ways like this incident in which the League paved the way for subsequent developments.

Contemporaneous with the work of the League, and in many ways covering the same ground, the Colored Education Centre was formed in 1938 by a group of some twenty concerned Metro residents under the chairmanship of Dr. F.B. Holder, a medical doctor from British Guiana. Whether the

organizations led by Husbands and Holder, both powerful black leaders operating in the same field and serving the same constituency, acted in concert or competition did not matter as much as results did. Interviews with individuals who lived at the time, who attended the meetings called by these leaders and their organizations, and who had a feel for the standing of these movements in the black community, testify that rivalries and self-interest did exist at the time—as indeed at any other time. They are agreed that Dr. Holder and his Centre did valuable work, that Dr. Holder kept abreast of what was happening in the United States and placed these issues before the public in Halifax on such matters as education, employment, and current affairs.[21]

B. A. Husbands gave strong leadership in educational, athletic, and community affairs. He also had real estate holdings, was an importer, and ran a wholesale and retail store.

Public support for the work of the Colored Education Centre in the years following 1938 increased to a considerable extent, especially with the outbreak of war with its consequences for youth and servicemen. The broad aim of the Colored Education Centre included these objectives: "To do everything possible for the benefit of the growing generation, also to help our boys who return from the war into getting good positions."[22]

Seven years later, the Colored Education Centre became the Nova Scotia Association for the Advancement for Colored People. The merger is described in the following words: "Approximately 500 or more people are backing this organization. We should be able to draw up a constitution that will be well received by all our Colored people, first in the city of Halifax, and eventually spread throughout the province."[23] This decision was taken at a public meeting on January 7, 1945 at which a constitution committee was formed and instructed to consider re-naming the Colored Education Centre. Two weeks later, on January 28, the constitution and the new name were both adopted.

The Nova Scotia Association for the Advancement of Colored People was incorporated by statute on 29 March, 1945 in the name of the following founding members: Arnold F. Smith, Richard S. Symonds, William Carter, Bernice A. Williams, Carl W. Oliver, Walter Johnson, Pearleen Oliver, William P. Oliver and Ernest Grosse, all of Halifax.

The first chairman was Arnold F. Smith. His assumption of office marked the beginning of a new era in the politics of change in Nova Scotia. The work of the Association from 1945 to 1989 will be considered in the next chapter. For now, two features will be recalled, the aims and objects as well as the endorsement received from contemporary black institutions. The four main objectives of the N.S.A.A.C.P. were "to improve and further the interests of the colored people of the province, to provide an organization to encourage and promote a spirit of fraternity among its members, to co-operate with governmental and private agencies for the promotion of the interests and welfare of the province or any community therein, wherein colored people are resident, and particularly in reference to colored people, to improve the educational opportunities of colored youth and to raise the standard of living of the colored people of the province or any community therein." Reduced to practical terms, these objectives related to education, employment, housing and human relations.[24]

The endorsement issue draws attention to the support from the church, the servicemen and the fraternity in which is implicit a strategy to draw upon

Rangers baseball team, c. 1940. Back row (l–r): J. Springer, G. Jemmot, W. Izzard, H. Bruce, E. Nickerson, D. Dawson, W. S. Skeir, A. McCallum; front row: I. Spear, C. Davis, W. Skeir, G. White, C. Smith, L. Gannon, W. S. Skeir, R. Smith (seated).

the resources from sectors of the community which had a broad-based membership. The three black organizations which supported this enterprise were the Cornwallis Street United Baptist Church whose pastor at the time was Rev. W.P. Oliver, The Royal Canadian Legion which, in 1938, created the William Hall V.C. Branch 57, and The Independent Order of Oddfellows Manchester Unity whose membership included the leading personalities of the day. There was a recognition at the time that "the Black church, by itself, could not do the job that needed to be done."[25]

This was a positive recognition on the part of the new church leadership. Rev. W.P. Oliver assumed the pastorship of the Cornwallis Street Baptist Church at age 25 in 1937. He had spent his earlier years in the white setting in Wolfville and could not be expected to lead in Halifax without reaching out as he did to the N.S.A.A.C.P. Whatever could be argued for the role of secular organizations at the time—and there was a lot crying out to be done—the church, its teachings, its fellowship as well as its leadership were still held in high esteem and would continue to be so held in the black com-

.

munity. While the community was prepared to give support to such organizations as the Halifax Colored Citizens Improvement League, the Colored Education Centre and later the Nova Scotia Association for the Advancement of Colored People, it was not prepared to do so at the expense of the church. For the Olivers to be brought in as founding members of the N.S.A.A.C.P. was a useful combination of the spiritual and secular interests of the community.

There is no question that there was quality material in the black community in the 1930s and the 1940s either harnessed or waiting to be harnessed to advance community initiatives and forward-looking objectives. Some examples have already been given for the entire province. In addition to these examples, there was a unique organization in Halifax called the Criterion Club which was founded in 1936. It was a social club for Blacks, drawing together the who's who of the Metro area at the time. Viewed in some circles as an elitist club it was certainly reflective of the strengths that the community could draw upon from various walks of life. It gives the lie to an enduring stereotype that Blacks belonged to a rag-tag community. One 1942 picture taken at a Criterion Club meeting at Gerrish Street Hall featured the pastor of the Cornwallis Street Baptist Church, a number of leading employees in the Canadian National Railways drawn from Nova Scotia, a

Criterion Club Meeting at Gerrish Street Hall, 1942.

leading printer, a famous early school teacher, the future first President and first Secretary of the N.S.A.A.C.P., and a senior deacon of the Cornwallis Street Baptist Church (identified in the accompanying photograph). A gathering of such a representative group was an index of resources available. Succeeding generations have good cause to draw comfort and inspiration from the Criterion Club.

The final subject in this section is an extension of community initiatives in this period through participating in employment opportunities available to Blacks in the Canadian National Railways. Though an aspect of labour history, this feature was also an aspect of community history in the sense that almost every able-bodied male black person in Nova Scotia not otherwise employed, and in search of employment, participated in or was touched in some direct way by this employment category. It was, and remained for long, *a rite de passage*, which provided male Blacks either with a starting point or a permanent place in the working world.

From the 1880s to the mid-1950s, Blacks in Canada were employed as railroad sleeping car porters, the only category in the railroad service open to them, even though a forerunner in this service, the Grand Trunk Railway, employed Blacks as cooks and waiters in its sleeping cars. In 1926 the Grand Trunk Railway was taken over by the Canadian National Railways and black employees in the dining car service of the G.T.R. were rapidly replaced by Whites with the exception of a few cooks. While the western Canada service provided by the Canadian Pacific Railways actively recruited black Americans as porters well into the 1950s, the eastern service provided by the Canadian National Railways responded positively to the demands of the Order of Sleeping Car Porters [which was admitted to the Canadian Brotherhood of Railway Employees and Other Transport Workers (C.B.R.E. & O.T.W.) in 1919 with separate local units for Whites and Blacks] that Blacks from within Canada should be given preference.

Separate black locals of the C.B.R.E. & O.T.W. were set up in Halifax, Montreal, Toronto and Winnipeg in 1919 made up of black sleeping car porters, an arrangement which continued to separate white and black employees into better-paid and lower-paid categories based on racial lines [conductors, dining car cooks and stewards being open to Whites and sleeping car porters open to Blacks] until 1957 in the western service and 1964 in the eastern service. As one writer puts it: "When the amalgamation of the locals took effect in 1964, everyone, white and black, was amazed and stunned. Most have never expected it to happen. The white workers had been opposed because they feared loss of their positions; as many porters had greater seniority than they did. There were some problems at first, with white train crews who did not want to work with, or under, black sleeping car conductors or dining car stewards. Also some were convinced that the black man would not be able to do the job......"[26]

The truth is that black men not only did the job but did it well. One could begin with the personal testimony of a fine black gentleman from Halifax who is mentioned in earlier pages, John Robert Pannill, who worked for C.N.R. for 43 years:

> It wasn't easy for a black man to get work but I got a job with CN as a porter on a train. I worked there from 1918-1962, that's 43 years. I received my pension. In that time I travelled and had a choice to go with different jobs, but I stayed on as porter. That company treated me like Royal(ty). Today it's VIA Rail. I travelled all over Canada, met some of the greatest businessmen and women in the world. We had to serve these people, like the Prince of Wales, on a special car. Mr. John Labatt of Labatt's Ale, was kidnapped, but after a short time he was found and rescued and transported back home. So, whenever he travelled afterwards, it was in secret. On one trip Mr. Labatt was going to the West Indies. I had the privilege of tending him. No one knew, the Government, the R.C.M.P., chose me to see to Labatt from Halifax to Montreal. I took care of him the whole distance, met and talked to him. I talked to J.K. Ross, of Ross Rifles, a great supplier of guns in those war times. I had the privilege to go to Mr. Ross' house with a friend, Mr. Thornton whose father was President of Montreal Trans. Company, Sir Henry Thornton, Sir James Dunn [the Dalhousie Sir James Dunn Theatre is named after him]. I took care of Premier (sic) Bennett and his daughter (sic), Mildred, when they travelled from Ottawa to New Brunswick. His daughter (sic) would always leave me a gift of flowers for my wife. I talked to Mr. Borden of Borden Milk and Prime Minister Mackenzie King, the Silver King, H.J. Kelly, President of Dominion Steel and Coal Company, Lieutenant Governor......Mr. Grant and Son; Mr. Brookfield of Brookfield Milk and Judge Fiedland. I received an invitation to visit Prime Minister Borden.[27]

John Pannill may not have had all the names, relationships and titles right in his later recollections but he was one of many Nova Scotia Blacks who conducted themselves with dignity in this service and who were given responsibilities beyond the calls of duty or race.

Among the earlier personalities in C.N.R. service in Nova Scotia were many members of the Criterion Club mentioned earlier: Tom Macdonald, Harry Bowles, William Prevoe, George Grant, Morris Earle, Arnold Smith, George Jones and Booker Roach, some of whom climbed the ladder to hold such positions as conductor, supervisor and instructor. In turn, they were responsible for training and guiding others who joined the service in later years.

When a fuller history of this remarkable labour movement and experience is told, there will be room for many more up to 1989 and beyond, though numbers are dwindling as we get closer to the present for a variety of reasons which include increasing reductions in passenger rail services, requirements for bilingual services and other aspects of higher qualifications as salary incentives continue to be more attractive than they once were when black labour was exploited in the days of a less-caring society. Nova Scotia Blacks who once worked in this service have become pastors, civil servants, authors, community workers and businessmen who through their earning and learning have put a lot back into Nova Scotia. As personal testimonies become available, the human side will show that the service exposed Nova Scotia Blacks to the politics of trade union movements, to the events leading up to the formation of the first national industrial union in Canada in 1908—the Canadian Brotherhood of Railway Employees, (C.B.R.E.) to the efforts of white workers like A.R. Mosher of Halifax—the first president of the C.B.R.E.—who spoke up for racial equality at a time when such support was hard to come by, to the efforts of black workers like Lee Williams, chairman of the Winnipeg black local of the C.B.R.E., whose determined leadership contributed to the ending of job discrimination in the C.N.R. service from coast to coast in 1964.

Besides the senior black Nova Scotia employees in the C.N.R. service mentioned in conjunction with the Criterion Club above, there were others who, in different ways, contributed to the development of the black community and by extension to progress in Nova Scotia. Drawing upon the list of persons recruited in railway service from 1936 to 1945 in Nova Scotia, we find many who went on over the years to occupy senior positions when job discrimination ended and, upon retiring, went on to other occupations or became involved in community organizations: C.B. States, R.F. Fowler, C.G. Lawrence, J.E. Brindley, D.F. Bauld, L.F. Brown, S.A. Brothers, A.R. Kelley,

E.A. Skinner, C.R. Wyse, W.H. Williams, from the Halifax–Dartmouth Metro area; L.T. Izeard from Amherst; and C.M. Chase, J.S. Clyke and R.C. Tynes, from Truro. The list after 1945 is even longer.

The progress made by Nova Scotia Blacks in the service of the Canadian National Railways from 1919 to 1964, from the days of segregated black sleeping car porters to the days of black–white integrated service in 1964 in both the sleeping and dining car departments, included conductors, illustrated the gradual progress made by Blacks in Canadian society over these years in all sectors. This progress was not without its ups and downs. Rivalry between the races continued to exist.

Opportunities for employment continued to be few and far between. Many positions continued to be seasonal for a few months in the year. There was always the chance factor, that favourable providential tide, that provided an opening and subsequent opportunities. Take the case of Coulter B. States, son of the well-known Rev. Wellington States and Muriel V. States who joined the service in 1936, beginning with a chance meeting with S.J. Fullerton, then Superintendent of the Sleeping and Dining Room Department of C.N.R. in Halifax at a scout camp at Miller's Lake in Halifax County, when boy scout Coulter States was asked by the camp director to row the superintendent through the many coves on a sight-seeing trip. The casual conversation led to an invitation which culminated in a job offer. Coulter States never looked back. Beginning with four months work in a year for a few years until an all-year-round permanent position was obtained, he learned the ropes aided by fellow Nova Scotians, Booker Roache, William Prevoe and Herb Gray. He worked his way up from sleeping car porter to buffet porter to porter-in-charge to porter instructor, to service instructor and was later assigned to Special Trains duty on three Royal Trains, a duty which kept him on a Royal Train for a month at a time, found him in group photographs with royalty, receiving autographed copies. In a society in which Blacks were at the bottom in Canada's multicultural mosaic, such opportunities were, of course, welcomed by the beneficiaries who deemed the recognition of their services to reflect confidence in their ability. As Coulter States puts it: "We got along well. Blacks accepted the fact that a place was given to them. This was our job and we did it. Later we wanted to be waiters and conductors, too. After years of negotiation, we got these jobs."[28]

THE NOVA SCOTIA HOME FOR COLORED CHILDREN

The background to the formation of this institution is reviewed in chapter I where the period up to 1918 is covered. In summary, the following constitute the important developments. The need for an institution to care for neglected or orphaned black children was raised in church and community circles as early as 1900. The first formal step was taken in 1908 when a proposal was received from James R. Johnston. In 1914, Rev. Moses Puryear convened a public meeting on the issue and presented the matter to the annual convention of the A.U.B.A. in 1915 when the project setting up the Nova Scotia Home for Colored Children was incorporated by provincial statute and a board of trustees of ten members, three of whom were black persons, was set up. A public appeal was launched by the board of trustees in October, 1917 for financial support. A building belonging to the Halifax Industrial School on Quinpool Road was procured to accommodate the project in 1917 and the sum of $1,500 dollars was identified for renovating and equipping the proposed Home, of which sum $500 was donated by the City of Halifax, $100 by Stairs, Son and Morrow for whom J.A.R. Kinney, a key person behind the Home, worked and $25 dollars from a black businessman

Nova Scotia Home for Colored Children

named George Roache. A matron by the name of Julia Jackson was recruited in the same year from Philadelphia in the United States. The matron assumed office in November, 1917 but the building was destroyed in the Halifax explosion of December 6, 1917. This marked the end of the first phase of the history of the Nova Scotia Home for Colored Children.

The need for a Home was such that the matter was kept alive by the trustees, by the churches, by the Ladies Auxiliary and by the African United Baptist Association after the explosion. The matron returned to her home in Philadelphia and Nova Scotians mobilized their resources to get a new site for what was in fact the only institution of its kind in Nova Scotia and Canada. This work was promoted by both black and white citizens. Given the resources available to black people alone during this period, it was reasonable to enlist the support of the total society. Indeed, the strongest supporter of the project was H.G. Bauld, the first chairman of the board, who served it with unflinching devotion for many years (1921-1948) until he was succeeded by another white Nova Scotian, Dr. Melville Cummings, who in turn served the Home for a total of thirty years, eighteen of them as president (1948-1966). In an interview with Mrs. Muriel States who joined the Home in 1931 as Supervisor, she commented on the dedication of H.G. Bauld who was president until 1948: "I was surprised that he was so interested in the Home. The Whites did not have a good feeling for us. I believe he has a son, Stanley, still living in Halifax. Mr. Bauld would come out day after day to see how things were going."[29]

Of the first ten trustees, Rev. Moses Puryear left Halifax shortly after the explosion, leaving H.G. Bauld, Judge E.H. Blois, C. Strickland, R.H. Murray, G.R. Hart, C. Blackadar, John Murphy, J.A.R. Kinney and Thomas P. Johnson to keep the project alive.

This section will trace aspects of the history of the home from 1918 to 1945.

Planning, fund-raising and searching for a new site occupied the whole of the intervening period since the Halifax Explosion in 1917 until the trustees learned from Rev. A.A. Wyse, pastor of the Preston–Cherrybrook churches, in February, 1919 that a 211-acre site known as the Mckenzie property, located in Westphal, Halifax County, was available for purchase. Through funds made available by the Government of Nova Scotia the property was purchased.[30] The next challenge was to erect a building, a challenge which the Ladies Auxiliary and the A.U.B.A. had anticipated ever since the Home was incorporated in 1915.

J.A.R. Kinney, Sr., was placed in charge of fund raising. As the advertising manager for the firm of Stairs, Son and Morrow, then located in Lower Sackville, and himself a graduate of the Halifax Business School, Clerk of the A.U.B.A. from 1916 to 1921 and again from 1929 to 1939, Treasurer of the A.U.B.A. from 1939 to 1940, Kinney was remarkably well placed to spearhead the fund-raising drive. Dr. W.P. Oliver, a perceptive observer, contributor, and member of the black community, whose life spanned the period 1912-1989, noted Kinney's role as follows: "Mr. Jas. A.R. Kinney became Secretary-Treasurer of the institution and was probably the guiding force of the entire undertaking. He was one of the most highly trained Black citizens of the time......His exceptional ability as an organizer and fund-raiser, with the support of leading citizens in the Halifax community as members of the Board of Directors, resulted in the Nova Scotia Home for Coloured Children being officially opened on June 6, 1921."[31]

Ten months before the official opening, the following report was presented to the annual convention of the A.U.B.A.:

We are exceedingly pleased to bring to the attention of the Association that the beautiful building which is to house the N.S. Orphan and Neglected Children is now under construction, some $40,000 having been raised. At the present time the Building is all boarded in and being shingled, and from the plans it can be seen that it will be one of the beauty spots of the Preston Road when it is completed. $1000 guaranteed by the Association will be due on the 15th inst [September 15, 1920]......We would urge that a definite policy be taken to supply funds for this Home to the amount of $2000 yearly from the several communities of Nova Scotia; because if we fail to render the assistance necessary, it is quite likely that a situation will be created which would be quite unpleasant to each and everyone of us who holds a deep measure of pride for Institutions for racial betterments. It is a Home of great possibilities to the Race, and from it can emerge those fitted for training which will enable them to pursue higher educational branches, and lay a foundation for Leadership of the Race. If we fail in this means of support, we will lose out in the great essentials of racial opportunity which the Government and our friends have seen fit to provide.[32]

This is an important contemporary analysis that draws attention to the higher objectives anticipated from the work of the Home. The development of black racial pride in an institution set up to effect improvements for Blacks, provision of basic training to lay the foundations for further education by black residents leading up to the emergence of black leaders, vindicating the confidence vested in the black community by the Nova Scotia Government as well as other Nova Scotians that their help initially given to get the project off the ground was not given in vain, and, finally, a call to A.U.B.A. to make a firm policy commitment to donate the sum of $2000 annually towards the costs of running the Home. It is against these higher objectives that the achievements, the departures, as well as the failures should be measured in future years.

One of the first documents produced by the Home takes the story of the Home further to fill the gap between the report presented to the A.U.B.A. on September 4-7, 1920 and the actual historic first year. This document bears the caption: "On March 11, 1922, We Were One Year Old—Just a Crawling Infant." It goes on to say:

The Nova Scotia Home for Colored Children was opened in an informal way on March 11, 1921 by Mrs. Martha G. Harris, R.N., of New York City, she, however, returned to her home in June, last, and was succeeded by the present Matron, Mrs. Sadie Steen, R.N. Since the opening 20 children have been received, and three discharged, leaving 17 little ones to receive care and attention. Notwithstanding this short space of time splendid progress has been made with the equipment, and little bodies have been built up with nourishing food, and minds and hands have received their first training for future usefulness......Much is yet to be done, however, the unfinished portion of the Building must be completed, the grounds laid out, farm operations extended, a teaching staff competent in all branches......must be engaged......

Reports after 1931 have listed March 4 as the date when the Home opened its doors informally in 1921. However, the first anniversary report gives the date as March 11 as does the tenth anniversary report. March 11 would appear to be correct.

The Home was officially opened on June 6, 1921, an important date in the annals of Nova Scotia's black history because a need which had been identified by the black community itself to provide care, comfort, shelter, education and life skills for orphans and neglected children, as early as 1900, had become a reality twenty-one years later. It was the first undertaking of this magnitude which was a truly community effort supported by all sectors of Nova Scotian society, black and white, rich and poor, different levels of government, by churches of different denominations and by prominent individuals whose support and association earned for the Home more than a provincial reputation. It became nationally known as an important symbol of Nova Scotia's history and society.

The first president of the Board of Directors, Henry G. Bauld, mentioned earlier, served in this capacity from 1921 till his death in 1948. Before that, he was associated with the project in its initial stages of planning, discussed in chapter I and chapter II since the first public meeting held in 1914, and as chairman of the board of trustees since the Home was incorporated in 1915. This public service by a white Nova Scotian from 1914 to 1948 in an institution which was initially set up to serve black children only stands out in the history of the Nova Scotia Home for Colored Children. His successor to this office in 1948 was Dr. Melville Cumming whose service was comparably meritorious. He was Director from 1936 to 1948 and President from 1948 until his retirement in 1966 at the age of 90 years, after which he served as Honorary President until his death in 1969. Both these personalities gave almost identical years to the cause and both have been remembered through the naming of sections of the Home buildings: H.G. Bauld School facing Highway No.7, directly opposite the Black Cultural Centre for Nova Scotia, and the Melville Cumming Annex, the new wing added to the Home in 1960.

The first black person to be appointed President of the Board of Directors of the Home, Rev. Donald E. Fairfax, assumed office in 1974. In a report prepared and presented five years later, Rev. Fairfax touched upon highlights from which the following excerpts have been taken to capture the sentiments of a distinguished member of the black community and first black President of the Home. After mentioning the reasons for the Home, as reviewed in the first chapter, he traced the landmarks in its early history:

Aside from housing the children in the beautiful new home, a farm was also operated. Many of the young girls living in the Home learned very meticulously the fine art of house keeping. They were taught practically every aspect in the art and craft of home making. One must remember, at this particular period throughout Nova Scotia, black people were mainly servants and so a young lady leaving the home usually found her first job as a domestic servant. Very often these fine ladies, who indeed were of the finest type, soon married and began a home of their own. The young boys at the Home during this period assisted with the work on the farm and in those days, of course, wood was used......It was not until the late 50s when things began to change at the Home. By this, I mean the two-room school was outdated and children moved out into the community to obtain a better education. However, this was the beginning of a change for which the institution was not really prepared since it had enjoyed a very close environment......33 ·

As a review of the history of the Horne in the period covered in this chapter [1918-1945], the above excerpt draws attention to the following features: education, the farm, life skills training and that a pattern was pursued throughout the period and well into the fifties when discernible changes occurred [which will be treated in the next chapter].

Children of school-going age were admitted to the school section and placed in charge of a teacher. Among the teachers in the early years of the Home, the following names appear: Gladys Walcott and the later world-famous Portia White. All subjects from grade 1 to 9 were taught—reading, language, writing, history, geography, arithmetic, drawing, nature, elementary hygiene and physical culture. The school was subject to inspection and standards as for any other provincial school with the salary of the teacher being provided by the province.

The training of the girls was entrusted to the matron. The first three holders of this office were Martha G. Harris of New York City for a year, Sadie Steen, also from the States whose stay was also short, followed by Elizabeth A. Fowler, a Nova Scotian, who was in office a few years after the opening and remained well after the second decade was reached. Domestic work, sewing, cooking, domestic science were part of the training for the girls.

The farm was started for a variety of economic, social and educational objectives. Of the 211 acres (85.39 hectares), mostly woodland, 20 acres (8 hectares) were available for cultivation within the first ten years which opened with promise: "We specialize in raising Peas, and a year or two ago we were able to send over 1000 quarts (940 litres) to Market. Chickens are raised by the hundreds, and marketed, also a fair quantity of eggs. We also have a few Grade Guernsey Cows which form the nucleus of a fine herd. These supply the Milk for home use. Last year [1928] besides what was used in the Home, we marketed 1000 bushels of Root Crop, potatoes, turnips, beets, parsnips, carrots, etc. This work provided fine training for the Boys and Girls, in weeding and other light work."[34]

But this report, as well as subsequent reports, anticipated difficult times ahead for the farming operations unless more land was put under cultivation, more funds were available, and more pasture and feed for the stock. Why farming eventually failed in the later period of the history of the Home remains unclear. Perhaps the changing character of society and the new features relating to numbers, foster homes, and educational institutions in the fifties were contributory factors. Whatever came later, the earlier years were well served by farming, especially reinforced by the excellent qualifications held by Dr. Melville Cumming: "As an internationally respected Agriculturalist he introduced modern methods to the Home farm operations, made it feed all the children with some left over for a profit, until times changed and farming was profitable for no one."[35]

This 1969 explanation, though beyond the time-frame of this chapter, is important for an understanding of the changing complexities. It further compounds the causes of the decline and belongs more appropriately to the next chapter.

The Home admitted one hundred children in its first decade with the annual average standing at 37. When Mrs. Muriel States joined the Home as Supervisor in 1931, the number stood at 58, with ages ranging from 5-20, some were orphans, some neglected and some born out of wedlock. The fact of incorporation permitted the institution to receive children from anywhere in Canada. Its story traced in this section up to 1945 is a uniformly successful story from its Directors to the administrators, the tutors and the resident boys and girls. The words of the institution's first black president sum up the early years aptly:

Many will remember that the Home was the finest of any institution in the Province of Nova Scotia, and needless to say, the Dominion of Canada. The long-time Matron of the Home, the late Mrs. Elizabeth Fowler, spent the greater part of her life in this great work of the institution. She hired dedicated women from various parts of Nova Scotia and mainly those who loved children and were prepared in every possible way to meet their needs......During the Depression years, there were times when the members of the Staff had to be told they would have to wait for their money. Very often they were compensated with produce from the farm until such time as there was enough money to pay them......Some of the outstanding highlights of the Home have been the musical training of the children. At one time there was a string orchestra of some 25 to 30 children who oft times performed for many Service clubs and church groups and, of course, there were those who had very fine singing voices.[36]

An institution which could boast of having had the internationally-renowned singer, Portia White, as a teacher in 1931 and another renowned singer of Nova Scotia, Donald Fairfax, as a teacher in 1952 was fortunate indeed. A who's who of everyone connected with the Nova Scotia Home for Colored Children, from the days of incorporation in 1915 to the present, would certainly be one this province and its people would receive with pride and pleasure.

EMERGENCE OF NOTABLE PERSONALITIES

The names of many black Nova Scotians, as well as white Nova Scotians who contributed to the history of Nova Scotia's black population, have been mentioned in various sections in this chapter as well as the earlier chapters. In the period 1918-1945, many church leaders and workers as well as school teachers earned a prominent place in Nova Scotia for their services to their community and province. Living and working in an environment which still provided for segregated communities, segregated schools, segregated military battalion, segregated seating in cinemas, the black people of Nova Scotia in the period covered in this chapter, whether local-born or foreign-born, moved ahead, in spite of handicaps and against many odds, in all walks of life as church dignitaries, professionals, small business operators, teachers, artisans, farmers, soldiers, market gardeners, domestic workers and humble labourers. Many of them carried their work well into the period after 1945 and, some indeed, up to 1989 when this book ends. It is not possible to do more than select a few examples here and leave the diligent reader to search out, and include, others.

In addition to the many personalities already mentioned, three notable personalities, selected in order of date of birth, made significant contributions in many ways before and during the period covered in this chapter. They are William Andrew White [1874-1936], Wellington Naey States [1877-1927] and James A.R. Kinney [1878-1940], already mentioned in earlier

pages—three remarkable men who deserve a special place for their contribution to the development of the black society in Nova Scotia in the twentieth century. Of the three, the first-named was born outside Nova Scotia.

William White was born at King and Queen Court in Old Dominion,
Virginia, U.S.A. After his early school education in the schools of the state
of Virginia and night school in Baltimore, he entered Wayland Seminary in
Washington where his potential was recognized by a Baptist missionary,
Helena Blackadar, a Nova Scotian, who was responsible for introducing him
to Acadia University, Wolfville, Nova Scotia, which he entered in 1899 at the
age of 25. Four years later, in 1903, he obtained the Bachelor of Arts degree,
and was perhaps the first black graduate of Acadia and in Nova Scotia to
attain this level of education.

Following his ordination to the Baptist ministry in 1903, Rev. White was
engaged by the Baptist Home Mission Board to do missionary work in New
Glasgow where he organized the Second Baptist Church, a new church,
with the help of the existing First Baptist Church, New Glasgow, the
Cornwallis Street Baptist Church, Halifax, and the Zion Baptist Church,
Truro; the pastors of all three being placed on the council of the new
church. For the newly-ordained young pastor this was an auspicious beginning. After two years of service to the new church, Rev. White accepted a
call to the Zion Baptist Church, Truro, in 1905 and served this church with
devotion for 12 years. The local press produced a lengthy report on the
installation service, saying: "Mr. White's response made a most favorable
impression upon all present, and judging by the good speech which he
made Zion Church will not suffer for edifying pulpit matter."

Indeed, Rev. White's education, personality and dedication edified an
audience that extended far beyond the corridors of the Zion Baptist Church
and the geographical boundaries of Truro to the service of the African
United Baptist Association, the national and international military service
and, finally, to the service of the mother church, the Cornwallis Street Baptist
Church, before his work was done.

Rev. White served the A.U.B.A. as Clerk from 1915-16 and 1922-29 and
as Moderator from 1929-30 and 1930-31. As Moderator, with an intimate
sense of the churches and the black community of Nova Scotia, after some
thirty years of experience, his message in 1929 calling for unity and for
action, has special significance: "It is our hope that we are at the beginning
of a new era of prosperity in the churches, and among our people as a
whole. If this is to become a reality, there are some things which must be

borne in mind by all members and adherents of the Association. First, we would lay stress on the necessity for united efforts on the part of all those who would see the work progress. The selection of a group of officers, however capable they may be, is not sufficient to accomplish the task before us. Every individual must hold himself in readiness to do his bit for the advancement of all. Then there must be faith in the task we have assigned ourselves......"[37]

These words have a relevance for the many churches as well as the many organizations which serve the black community sixty years later, in 1989.

On February 1, 1917 William White was appointed Chaplain to the Canadian Militia and commissioned to the service with the rank of Honorary Captain, He was the only black man to serve in this capacity with the British Empire forces during World War I, a subject which has been covered in chapter two. When the Zion Church gave him a touching farewell, his reply was characteristic of the goals he set for himself: "......he felt he should be doing all he could to help in this great war emergency and he thought his duty now was with the noble soldiers of No. 2 Construction Battalion......"

After demobilization in 1919, he was called to the Cornwallis Street Baptist Church which he served until his death on September 9, 1936.

On May 28, 1936, three months before his death, Rev. White was awarded an honorary doctorate by Acadia University, an occasion which attracted favourable responses throughout the province. A typical comment, beginning with the last ten years of his life, reads as follows:

For ten years Dr. White has been the efficient secretary of the Halifax and Dartmouth Ministerial Association and has the affectionate regard of the clergymen of that organization. As a speaker, and preacher, the genial Doctor ranks high. He has a melodious voice with the pleasing accent of the old South. His sense of humour is well developed, and among the preachers of the city few, if indeed any, are more popular with the masses as a Radio preacher. Dr. White is a cultured Christian gentleman, of force and character. He has accomplished a fine work among his people at the Cornwallis Street Baptist Church, and his new honor from Acadia is certainly richly deserved. Halifax has a fairly large colored population; orderly, law-abiding citizens, and it is good to see one of their number receiving merited distinction at the hands of one of our Universities.[38]

An excellent sportsman and athlete, scholar, preacher, teacher, singer, radio producer, administrator, patriot, public servant and humanist, parent and family man, Dr. the Reverend William Andrew White, was one of Nova Scotia's finest personalities of this century. The funeral address delivered by Dr. E.S. Mason was published and is a document of tremendous depth, content and quality.[39] A fitting tribute to this great man would be to recall his own poem written in the trenches of France and entered in his diary on January 12, 1918.

Little Things
Space is but a little thing
That God takes like a ball
To toss up for a moment's flight
And laugh to see it fall.

Love is but a little thing
It is a tossed-up ball
Yet it embraces life and hope
The world and God and all.[40]

Dr. White's place in Nova Scotia history is assured in its own right as well as through the work over the years by his wife, Izie White of Truro, later Mrs. C.H. Johnston, now deceased, and by his children who distinguished themselves in various professions and through meritorious services to church and society.

The second notable personality, a contemporary of Rev. W.A. White, and whose careers covered common ground, was Wellington States who was born in Wolfville, N.S. on November 1,1877. When he was three his mother died and when he was nine his father died. At this tender age, he was taken in by his white maternal grandparents at Kingsport, a situation which was sadly fraught with racial tensions. Five years later, at age fourteen, young Wellington took to the seas, reminiscent of his famous predecessor in such adventure, William Edward Hall, with a modest school education behind him and a promising talent in carpentry. The rest was up to the hard school of learning while working. His sea travels are not documented and the little-known threads of these early years are picked up again on his return to Nova Scotia and his new residence at the home of his paternal grandparents at Mount Denson. In this friendly and supportive environment,

Wellington States was led to the Christian fold, encouraged to further his education with a view to entering the Christian ministry—a field invariably pointed out to every male black student of promise at the time and for years to come.

This resolute young man, his hard years behind him, responded with determination and enrolled at the Horton Academy at Acadia to prepare for the ministry. In 1898 he obtained a licence to preach from the Cornwallis Street Baptist Church, Halifax, and accepted a position to serve the Baptist churches in Granville Ferry and Inglewood in Bridgetown, finally receiving his ordination by the Rev. G. Coulter White [Rev. States chose the name Coulter for his only son who was born in 1914] at the Inglewood Church in 1899, the very year that William White entered Acadia University as a student. Wellington States' ordination preceded that of White's by four years.

This marked the beginning of 28 year's service to church and society in Nova Scotia until his untimely death at the age of 50 on May 3, 1927. Besides the places mentioned above, he served in Delaps Cove, Hammonds Plains, Beech Hill, Cobequid Road, Falmouth, New Glasgow and Victoria Road, Dartmouth. Thirteen years in New Glasgow at the Second Baptist Church [1906-1919] and eight years at the Victoria Road Baptist Church [1919-1927] represented the two places that ranked foremost in time.

This friendly pastor, of frail health throughout his life, left his imprint in Nova Scotia in the ways open and available to him. Military service was not possible on health grounds but his contribution in other ways were significant. He was the first field missionary of the A.U.B.A. He pioneered an important service by taking his portable organ from church to church. The beautiful church and parsonage of the Second Baptist Church in New Glasgow owe much to his carpentry skills as well as to his devoted services over a thirteen-year period. The observation in a local newspaper when Rev. Wellington States died on May 3, 1927 referred to other achievements: "......he was a most practical man of varied activities with high executive ability—by trade he was a carpenter, and there is hardly a colored church in Nova Scotia that has not felt his hand as a builder. He built churches at New Glasgow, Hammonds Plains, Granville Ferry and Delaps Cove, besides repairing and remodelling the ones at Acaciaville, Tracadie, Sunnyville, Kentville, Beechville, Africville, Cherrybrook and Dartmouth—a man who made such gigantic sacrifices in physical strength that at the early age of fifty years the sun of his life has set."[41]

Like Rev. White, the place for Rev. Wellington States in Nova Scotia's history and society is assured through his own work and through the contemporary and succeeding work of a dear public-spirited wife and three children who went on to become professionals and instructors.[42]

The third personality, whose life and work brought him in close contact with the other two mentioned earlier, was James Alexander Ross Kinney, described most eloquently by Baptist Church historian, Pearleen Oliver, as "Perhaps the most outstanding layman ever to enter our work."[43]

References have already been made in earlier pages to his birth in Yarmouth, his graduation from the Maritime Business College in Halifax, his foundation work for, as well as later managerial duties at, the Nova Scotia Home for Colored Children, and his services to the African United Baptist Association as Clerk and Treasurer. What is particularly significant about this man, his philosophy and his objectives, was his vision beyond the view from the pulpit to the more distant vistas of the world of economic strength which was necessary for the black person to rise in stature, dignity and self-worth. This is not to say that his two contemporaries mentioned in this section were unmindful of economic concerns, but to acknowledge that the leadership of the church had not placed economics and politics high on the agenda at this time. When Pearleen Oliver speaks of Kinney's vision in such words as "his goal always stood a little beyond the people and in their struggle to reach it" and "He could not, and would not, do God's work with pennies,"[44] the conclusion is obvious that Kinney's plans encompassed more than morality and that the church leadership would have to come to grips with the expanding horizon and the rising expectations sooner or later. Some of Kinney's speeches foreshadowed the position to be taken later by the next generation of church leaders.

In his 1918 address to the A.U.B.A., Jas. A.R. Kinney, referred to United States president Woodrow Wilson's remarks on local issues and local priorities in the United States and made his own observations on them. Kinney cited the following remarks made by Wilson:

There is a personage nearer home that we must be prepared to lose, Mr. Sambo, the darktown Coon. He is no more. Gradually there has appeared in his place a stern young man, trained and alert, musket in hand. His forefathers were Africans, but he is loyal, intensely loyal to the Flag, and the world has found no more determined fighting man."

To the above remarks made by Wilson, Kinney added his own assessment of the place of the black person in the war and what was expected once the war was over, the continuation of united action and the application of the eternal law of social justice for all. Kinney said that:

> White, black and red, are now going 'over the top' in a splendid union of patriotism and loyalty which inculcates its own lesson. There is also a degree of generosity mingled with the devotion, for the red man looks back to wrongs unredressed, and the black man cannot yet be said to have entered fully into the heritage of the square deal which the nations are pledged to give to all their citizens. Yet the men of both races have flung aside their grievances to share whole-heartedly in a struggle which is to remake the world for all races. If this be a pledge, as it certainly is, that we may count on the unfaltering allegiance of Black men and Red men for all time to come, it should ensure to both a rightful place in that wider democracy and ampler justice which are to be ushered in after the war—an acknowledgment of Heaven's eternal Law, the Fatherhood of God, and the Brotherhood of Man.[45]

Kinney was breaking new ground talking about the common plight of Blacks and native Indians, of future co-operation between them, of such virtues as "wider democracy and ampler justice." Observers of the 1989 scene in Nova Scotia—71 years later—have had occasion to recall the same issues in the wake of the Donald Marshall, Jr. inquiry into the criminal justice system in Nova Scotia. It would be some decades after 1918 that such matters would be placed on the agenda for action. Kinney was stimulating the black community to consider such matters.

When he took over the running of the Nova Scotia Home for Colored Children from 1921 to 1940, he accepted the assignment as a challenge to him to translate precept into practice and to tackle the global issue of social, educational, economic and cultural progress of the black community. In a personal interview granted to the author in 1977, Muriel V. States, who worked with Kinney, described him as a great church worker, a wonderful man, one who conducted himself in strictly business terms, one who was a "no-nonsense man." "With Mr. Kinney, you had to walk a straight line; he was very strict. We had to be on our toes and so it was with the children. They were his life." Muriel States spoke of his work at Stairs, Son and Morrow, first in Sackville and later at Strawberry Hill, in Halifax, where it is still located in 1989. Though he was afflicted with arthritis and walked with a limp, he maintained a busy schedule and even used his two-flats residence at 36 King's Place, at the corner of May and Agricola in Halifax, for much of the work of the Home, church and community.

Kinney's 1930 address to the A.U.B.A. was entitled "Racial Identity and the work of the African United Baptist Association." Given the fact that the secular organizations formed in 1932, 1938 and 1945, reviewed in earlier pages of this chapter, were not in existence in 1930, the title and the content show that Kinney was anxious that the existing church platform should be put to good use. In his address, he traced the origins of man in Africa, the place of African references and incidents in the Christian scriptures, the contribution of the Egyptians to civilization, the rise of western civilization and its association with the spread of Christianity: "And when the White race came into its ascendancy,......I cannot but feel that the great responsibility of humaneness and helpfulness is laid on their shoulders......they have seen the TRUE LIGHT while other races saw but the glimmer, and should they fail mankind must fail......But the Black Man has done his part......"

Kinney traced black immigration, settlement and experiences in Nova Scotia, presenting these in an imagery which was at once highly original and most perceptive for that time:

With traits of character and mannerisms so much different from the other settlers, they must have been greatly misunderstood—prejudice was rife, and for many years every door of opportunity opened to them reminded one of that old cartoon of the Boxer rebellion—the open door of China—that bristled with bayonets, which must be faced by anyone who dare enter......Many that came from the United States were tradesmen—carpenters, blacksmiths, stone-masons, coopers, etc., and even to this day some of these trades are carried on—but they were looked upon as scab labour, a position which could not be bettered as Trade Unions would not admit them to membership, so they could do little more than job around......The thoughts I wish to advance are, with climatic conditions altogether different, with no knowledge of procedure, with no money, with no education, no sympathy, little patience and helpfulness, how could they quickly acquire an equal status with the dominant race? Yet their brains were just as fertile, as is clearly proved by their quick response to encouragement.[46]

James Alexander Ross Kinney spoke from personal experience and observations. His life spanned the period 1878-1940, a crucial period of settlement and consolidation. His speeches and testimonies constitute important primary sources for Nova Scotia's black history. His lasting memorial in Nova Scotia is, of course, the Nova Scotia Home for Colored Children, but his place in history is assured through his manifold contributions and through the later work of an only son, mentioned in this chapter, who succeeded his father as Treasurer of the A.U.B.A. in 1941 and went on to become the first President of the Laymen's Council in 1944, as referred to in an earlier section. J.A.R. Kinney died on November 6, 1940.

As for women personalities whose main work was either begun, completed, or ongoing, in the period 1918-1945, various names have come up contextually in chapter two and in the earlier pages of the present chapter, including such as Selina [Williams] Jefferson, Madeline [Francis] Symonds, Melissa Jemmot, Margaret Upshaw, Florence Diggs, Viola Desmond, Portia White and Muriel States, to name a few. Some of these names will come up again in the next chapter on the period after 1945.

In the concluding part of the present section, reference will be made to some of the first black women teachers whose careers coincided with the period 1918-1945 in whole or part. The point must be made again that the women were most versatile and that almost everyone made contributions, directly or indirectly, to every facet of family, group, community and provincial activity.

One of the earliest and best-known woman teachers in the black community in this century was Martha Jones of Truro whose students have birthdates going back to the nineteenth century. One of them is Gertrude Smith who was born in East Preston in 1898; another was Mabel Saunders who was born in Newport, Hants County, in 1900, while the third is Belle Langford-Barnes who was born in Weymouth Falls in 1901. Martha Jones taught all three in different localities—East Preston, Three Mile Plains and Weymouth Falls. The words of the last-named person speak for all three, and many others: "The greatest teacher was Martha Jones. She was from Truro. She was a big, tall woman, had strong African features and was a very good teacher. She was a good ball player and when she spoke we obeyed. She dressed and acted like a lady, was well educated and highly respected."[47]

Black teachers were only permitted to teach in the segregated black schools. The pioneers were themselves possessed of modest education.

Mention has already been made that the first person from the black community to graduate from the then Provincial Normal College in Truro, Madeline Symonds, did so in 1928 and went to teach at Upper Hammonds Plains until 1964. One of her remarkable achievements was the setting up of a committee in 1945 to raise funds for a new school. Raising the sum of $1750 at that time was no small feat. With additional funds from the Halifax County Council and plans donated by a community worker named Carl Oliver, the project was successfully completed in 1946. Madeline Symonds also taught adult classes from 1946-1951. Her son, Rev. Calvin Symonds, is presently the pastor at the Zion Baptist Church in Truro.[48]

Teaching often ran in the family. One good example for this period and later is that of the family of Jessie Hawkins who lived in Greenland, near Bear River, not far from either Annapolis Royal or Digby, from the mid-nineteenth century onwards. Her daughter, Florence, came all the way to East Preston as a young lady around 1912-13 to teach school. Here she met and married Deacon Allan Wesley Evans, mentioned again in the next chapter for his work as a county councillor, but died in 1918 at the tender age of 29.

Other members of the Hawkins family to teach school in this period were Eva Blanche [Hill] David also of Bear River who began her teaching career in North Preston in 1935, then moved to Lucasville, where she continued to teach until her death in 1962 and Georgina Elizabeth [Hill] Harper who also hailed from Bear River and who began her teaching career in Conway, the black community on the periphery of the town of Digby, in 1931. After spending five years in her first post, she moved to take up short-term positions in Hammonds Plains, Cherrybrook and Lake Loon before obtaining a post in East Preston where Georgina Harper taught school for 22 years. In a remarkable teaching career which spanned 32 years in total, this lady from the rural village of Bear River moved from school to school, improving her qualifications as well as expertise over the years, graduating from the Nova Scotia Teachers' College in 1958—at the age of 47—teaching all ages and grades from one to nine, later teaching evening classes to help adults upgrade their qualifications. This impressive variety in a long career is the kind of quality contribution that exemplifies the work of the black teachers in the period covered in this chapter. Often starting off themselves with grades 10-12 education, they moved to distant outposts in search of the elusive opportunity in the wooden, unheated, one-room school with sparse furniture, poor amenities, uncertain enrolment, in the very midst of unequal education fraught with racial discrimination and prejudice. The lot of the

black teacher was certainly easier in the years after 1945 but those who prepared for and began their careers before 1945 ranked among the pioneers
to whom much is owed by the succeeding generations.

There are other pioneers, too, whose careers ran deep into both periods
1918-1945 and 1945-1989 and whose intellect, determination and drive
proved Jas. A.R. Kinney right when he said those prophetic words in 1930,
previously mentioned, and recalled here to introduce the emergent personalities in the teaching profession in this period whose work would only be
completed in the next: names such as Edith Cromwell, Florence Bauld, Doris
Evans, Marion Skinner, Gertrude Tynes and Marie Hamilton as examples in
an incomplete list: "......how could they quickly acquire an equal status with
the dominant race? Yet their brains were just as fertile, as is clearly proved
by their quick response to encouragement."

Their response to whatever encouragement will constitute part of the
subject matter for the next chapter dealing with the period 1945-1989.[49]

The period 1918-1945 is characterized by self-help efforts on the part of the
black community throughout the province. There was an absence of the
overt and aggressive posture of the dominant society in the previous two
periods aimed at unsettling and undermining the black population of the
province. Conversely, there was no positive efforts on the part of the dominant society to alleviate by deliberate design the continued state of unequal
opportunities for the black population.

Jobs continued to be scarce and black labour continued to stand at the
periphery even when the outbreak of World War I tended to diminish the
white labour force through the recruitment and conscription process. There
were always the poor in the majority community who were given preference, aided and abetted by the trade unions which denied black artisans
training or admission.

Led by the driving force of religious conviction and moral certitude, the
youth and adults, both male and female, rallied to the call and example of
parents and preachers to organize themselves into various sectors of activity in a way that never existed before. The result was that before the period
had run its course, there were many new structures, mandates, constitutions,
office-bearers, meetings and activities to serve the black community.

The period also saw the fruits of the upsurge of patriotic fervour which
had taken so many years to impress itself upon the military establishment

that Canadian Blacks were as patriotically disposed to defend their country in times of war as any other Canadians. World War I veterans (Black and White) came back to a society no better than they had left it. Most Blacks picked up their lives as barbers and construction workers and, in increasing numbers, became inducted in the new labour force as sleeping car porters.

While religious organizations, patriotic fervour generated by two world wars, sleeping car porterage, community organizations, and small businesses were all on the upswing, social and secular organizations made their appearance. They produced leaders and followers for new ventures including the Nova Scotia Home for Colored Children, the Halifax Colored Citizens Improvement League, the Criterion Club, the Colored Education Centre, and the Nova Scotia Association for the Advancement of Coloured People. All these made their appearance in this period and, in the case of the first and last-named organizations, braced themselves to serve the black community well beyond 1945.

The period also saw the emergence of notable personalities in the black community whose life and work exemplified the best in a community so riddled with discrimination which continued to prevent its members to do more than to "hang in," which they did with a courage and conviction that left their mark even on the detractors. One co-operative effort between Whites and Blacks surfaced and endured in the case of the Home for Colored Children. While it created new friendships, it left an unanswered question for the future regarding the paternalism underlying the display of public-spirited support and Christian charity.

The period saw the exit of the nineteenth-century born church leaders, leaving the field open to the next generation leaders and followers whose individual and collective world view would be shaped by the new order born in the wake of the Atlantic Charter, the United Nations, the Universal Declaration of Human Rights, the Civil Rights movement, Canadian Multiculturalism, and the Canadian Charter of Rights and Freedoms.

The period 1945-1989 was one for making changes. Whether these would be for better or for worse as far as the black population of Nova Scotia was concerned, only time would tell.

CHAPTER FOUR

THE PERIOD 1945–1989

POST-WAR EXPECTATIONS AND MILITARY PERFORMANCES

When the Colored Education Centre was founded in Halifax in 1938, the war clouds were thickening over Europe. This Centre, as stated in the previous chapter, lasted for seven years, most of which were the war years. Founded in peace time, its later years were mainly occupied by issues arising out of the war in Europe. The plight of the many Nova Scotian Blacks who were recruited to the armed forces featured importantly in the concerns of the black community and of the black institutions of the time, both spiritual and secular. The Second World War added to the existing challenges which assumed grave proportions for a number of reasons. The racial climate in Nova Scotia had not improved in spite of the patriotic fervour which gained ground as the Second World War proceeded in intensity.

Take the case of Roy Wellington States, a member of a famous Nova Scotian family who, at the age of 20, applied for enlistment in the Canadian Armed Forces. He was told that the war "was, a white man's war" and there was no place for him. This was the standard response in the first year or two to other black aspirants but the racial bar to recruitment came down reluctantly, either because recruits in general were in short supply or the emerging war-time philosophy, such as that embodied in the Atlantic Charter of 1941, spoke of a better world order based on respect and regard for individual human and political rights.

Many more Blacks joined the armed forces in World War Two as soon as the racial barriers which prevented the recruitment of black soldiers came

228

down than was the case in World War One when such barriers were very rigid. Many saw active service in the European theatre of war and on the high seas; many died and equally many returned to civilian life with very little to look forward to. But their expectations had been stimulated on the field of battle and in the gossip in clubs, trenches and trucks. Naturally, they, and many others, expected to be given special treatment on return as the heroes of the land. In the annals of Nova Scotia's black history many veterans of World War Two will be remembered for their patriotism, for what they achieved in civilian life and also for the tragedy that befell so many who failed to make it in civilian life because of frustrations, disappointments, failure to adjust to peace-time discipline and to the rigours of keeping a job. A large proportion of the tragic cases were among those veterans who chose to stay on in the familiar, though depressed environment, of Nova Scotia. Many of the more successful ones made progress by moving to other provinces.

Many names come up of those who survived the war and those who died either overseas or shortly after their return: Bunny Carvery, Leo Carvery, Primrose Hamilton, Gerald Jackson, Peter Tab, William Grant, Royal Jones, Ernie and Bud Reddick—father and son—Hubert Upshaw, Clarence Saunders, Norman Desmond, Jack Tynes, Victor Jones, Leslie Farmer, Murray Warrington, Ricky Anderson, Bobby Downie and Harold Farmer.[1]

Roy Wellington States was twenty-years old when the Second World War broke out in 1939. This native of New Glasgow turned up to enlist immediately, as previously mentioned, but was turned away with the standard response to black applicants in 1939-1940: it was a "white man's war." But Wellington States persisted and was accepted in 1940 and went on to remain in the Canadian Armed Forces for 25 years. His war years, as well as the years following, presented many challenges to this enterprising man who moved to Montreal in 1953 where he rendered distinguished service to the Royal Canadian Legion, the British Commonwealth Ex-Servicemen's League and the National Black Coalition of Canada which he served as Executive Secretary for three years while also being a columnist for *The Black Voice* in Montreal.[2] The war made a deep impression on Roy Wellington States and he never lost interest in national and international politics throughout his life.

The exposure to the world community, which was striving to further the cause of peace and democracy, opened new prospects and new horizons. Some veterans went with the favourable tide and never looked back. One of them was Alan Bundy of Dartmouth who joined the Royal Canadian Air Force and became the first black Canadian pilot. There were other black Dartmouthians, too, who, served in various sections and capacities and whose names are inscribed in a roll of honour in the Victoria Road Baptist Church.[3]

The close community of Cape Breton where people generally had fewer economic opportunities, and where people had to work hard to keep the few jobs that were available, produced a number of recruits who enlisted, performed creditably, and re-entered civilian life with a fresh determination to succeed. Many brothers joined up: Winston and Lionel Ruck, William and George Nurse, Egbert and Lionel Best, Golbuorne and Charlie Sheppard, Arnold and Billy Campbell, Clyde and Dawson Hoyte, Evelyn and Kenneth Braithwaite. There were single members, too, whose war years were a boost to their determination to continue to succeed as parents, as entrepreneurs, as sports personalities, employees, employers and church and community activists: Thomas Miller, Oscar Seale, Vernol Braithwaite, William Lucas, Mickey Jones, Seibert Innis, Wesley Roett, Lemuel Skeete, Cecil Parris, Harold Kirton, Charles Dorant, Charles Pyle, Louis Blackman, Sam Estwick, Billy Talbot, Bob Talbot, Clarence Lashley and Wilfred Streete.[4]

The list of black veterans of World War Two is by no means exhaustive. There are many more who are not mentioned here. Those mentioned are intended to show examples of black Nova Scotians who responded to the call of duty in spite of the unequal treatment accorded to them on racial grounds. The reluctant reception was, of course, an improvement on World War One. Some of them re-entered civilian life as failures while others went on to improve their lives, encouraged by the lessons learned as a result of meeting people from different parts of the world. If there was a lesson in this war-time experience and environment, it was that the perceived superiority of western civilization was not without its blemishes, and that persons of colour from the colonized parts of the British empire were not necessarily inferior or backward.

The influence and impact of the war years did not begin and end with the war but lived on for many generations. As Captain [Rtd] George Borden, who joined the Royal Canadian Air Force in 1953 and rose to the rank of Lieutenant in 1967 and Captain in 1970, describes this development:

Between 1939-45 many Blacks lined the ranks of Canada's contribution to defeat Hitler. Most healthy black males served in the European theatre and at sea, a number of whom made the ultimate sacrifice. They are the grandfathers and the great-grandfathers of today's black communities in Nova Scotia. After a brief lull in military recruitment between 1945-48, the call went out for a 'peace-time force.' Commencing in the early 50s, every young black Nova Scotian with sufficient education to pass the entry tests joined one of the three branches of the Canadian military in hopes of finding steady employment, a saleable trade, and escape from what seemed to be 'dead-end street.' Today [late 1980s] many of these early entrants are retiring at the end of long, successful and rewarding careers. They have served their country well in war-time Korea and peace-time Egypt, Cyprus, Europe and many other uneasy parts of the eastern world in what has become known as peace-keeping.[5]

George Borden has lived the experience he describes. Coming from the conservative climate of New Glasgow where the racial divide was wide and long, he knows what trampling 'dead-end streets' meant for young, unemployed black youth. The opportunity to join the armed forces meant character-building, education, economic advancement, community development, leadership training and nation building. While it is true that quite a number of demobilized veterans of World War Two wasted their lives in succeeding years, perhaps lacking the confidence and self-esteem which comes from a good grounding in education and a stable family environment, there is a greater number of those who must rank among the successful, though the term must always be relative to the opportunities available to disadvantaged black persons in Canadian society.

A few examples of a biographical nature will surely inspire students and teachers, scholars and researchers, as well as curious readers to explore further and develop more case studies. One such person was Oscar Seale, born in Sydney, Cape Breton, on June 16, 1920, and who worked in the Steel Plant before enlisting in 1941. He reached the rank of sergeant while overseas. After being demobilized at the end of the war, he returned to the Steel Plant but also operated a taxi business for the next ten years, making good use of the modest stipend awarded to all veterans to re-enter civilian life. After this, he was employed as an inspector in the Motor Carrier Division of the Department of Highways. A talented athlete and baseball player, Oscar Seale is a popular figure on the Cape Breton landscape.

Another such figure was Thomas Miller who enlisted in 1943 and was sent to New Glasgow from his home in Sydney for his basic military training. He soon moved into the rank of instructor and was selected to go to Aldershot, a military base in England, to continue as an instructor. He was demobilized in 1947 with the rank of Warrant Officer and returned to take up his former job at the Steel Plant until his retirement in 1982 as General Foreman Supervisor. Thomas Miller's contribution to society was strengthened by his war experience and by his post-war expectations of himself and the society he lived in and served. While working in the Steel Plant, he joined the Whitney Pier Air Cadets in 1953, rose to the rank of Squadron Leader and was instrumental in the formation of the first female squadron in Sydney, while the Whitney Pier Squadron of which he was a member was acclaimed during his years of leadership as the best in Canada. He served the squadron faithfully for 14 years. Thomas Miller's service progressed when he was elected alderman of the Sydney City Council which he adorned for 17 credible years. His election earned him the distinction of being the first black alderman in Eastern Canada, another important landmark for Cape Breton. In his life and work Thomas Miller was the embodiment of those qualities of the black person in Nova Scotia directed to raise standards of performance to levels that were not generally credited to black folk. Born in Halifax, Nova Scotia, on August 12, 1917, Thomas Miller had an average school education, a distinguished military service, long and loyal factory service, was a devout family man and parent, public servant, community leader, gave civic service and was a Club and Restaurant owner. He died on January 20, 1987.[6]

While opportunities for advancement in the workplace continued to be limited, the military, like the sports world, offered better prospects. Individuals like Chief Warrant Officers John Madison and Raymond Lawrence, Warrant Officers John Bowden and Angus Paris, and Sergeant Cricklow were awarded Military Medals in appreciation of their contributions. A singularly distinctive place belongs to Major Marguerite [Peggy] Downes, born in Dartmouth, Nova Scotia, whose brother, Leo Brown, saw service in World War Two and is one of those mentioned in the Dartmouth roll of honour referred to above. Major Downes has had a distinguished career to 1989 with promise of more ahead. In 1956, she moved to Toronto from Nova Scotia in search of better prospects, wrote and passed the Ontario Civil Service Examination with a 100% mark, did private studies to obtain nursing qualifications, joined the Royal Canadian Army Service Corps in 1957, became Deputy Commanding Officer of the Canadian Forces

Communications Reserve Unit at Toronto's Fort York Armoury and A.D.C. to the Lieutenant-Governor of Ontario. In 1988, Major Downes was awarded the Order of Military Medal, a rare honour for a remarkable woman of humble Nova Scotian black origins. Extremely talented in voice and music as well, Peggy Downes founded the Voices of Joy Choir in 1978. In September, 1989, the Black Cultural Centre for Nova Scotia honoured this distinguished Nova Scotian by inviting her to deliver the prestigious Sixth Anniversary Lecture and included with this invitation a request that the Voices of Joy Choir, made up predominantly of former Nova Scotians, perform at the anniversary function under the direction of their founder and Choir Director, Major Marguerite A. Downes, OMM, CD, ADC.

Major Marguerite (Peggy) Downes, from Dartmouth, was awarded the Order of Military Medal in 1988.

While Peggy Downes and her brother Leo Brown [who died in 1989] are but one Nova Scotian black military family, there are others, too, where influences have passed down the family line, in the same generation as well as more than one generation. Some examples have already been cited. Other examples, drawn at random include such family names as the Bordens, the Crawfords, the Desmonds, the Jacksons and the Toussaints.

Post-war Nova Scotia for the black population was like the post-war situation in the depressed parts of the world for disadvantaged populations. The end of the war marked the beginning of a new era of heightened expectations: the end to colonialism and exploitation, better living conditions with more jobs and better housing, harmonious race relations based on mutual respect for the dignity and worth of the human person and the equal rights of men and women and of nations large and small. It was a time of hope which was nourished upon the promises that were embodied in such international declarations as the Atlantic Charter, the Charter of the United Nations and the Universal Declaration of Human Rights. If Hon. Captain William Pearly Oliver, Black Baptist clergyman and Chaplain to the black troops in Halifax during the Second World War, counselled the dejected and the forlorn who arrived for spiritual and social guidance on the virtues of faith, hope and charity, he realized, as he said so often, that the road ahead was rough and that the black person had to raise himself by his own boot-strap.

The returning soldiers brought their own messages and worked on their own agendas. After 1945, things could never be the same again, whatever the problems, whatever the obstacles. The post-1945 period, in the words of sociologists Clairmont and Magill, was one of *making changes*. The soldiers and the civilians all made changes of one kind or other and it is these changes that have given the period 1945-1989 a distinctive character.

BLACK SOCIETY AND ECONOMY

The middle years of this period are graphically described by a knowledge-able insider whose perspective was sharpened through his insights as a teacher, a member of the Nova Scotia Human Rights Commission, as presi-dent of the Nova Scotia Association for the Advancement of Coloured People and later as a lawyer:

> The general condition of the negro, in the Maritimes today, (1968) may be described accurately as *depressed*. His community is usually an impoverished ghetto with dilapidated housing, unpaved roads and only minimal public services, even if it may be located within the boundaries of a city or town. The children of this ghetto community, who usually attend segregated schools, are potential school dropouts, while the adults, because of a lack of education or training, remain unemployed or underemployed for the greater part of the year. The urban ghetto is further exploited by slum landlords, storekeepers and investors who make profits on small investments, regardless of the human misery caused, all within the purlieu of the law. Within the con-claves of poverty tensions fester, frustrations mount and implode as crime of violence and race riots.[7]

H.A.J. "Gus" Wedderburn was drawing attention to a downward trend in a society in which politicians preached of better times and better things. In the black community in the 1930s, 1940s and 1950s, there were indications of limited opportunities in trades which provided jobs for coopers, black-smiths, basket and broom makers. The major industries in the province employed black labourers in what has been described as "the heaviest and

Rev. Dr. William Pearly Oliver (1912–1989) was a clergyman, educator, and activist who made a significant contribution to advancing the black cause in Nova Scotia.

lowest paid jobs" in agriculture, mining, lumbering, steel and the railway and shipping industries.[8]

Rev. W.P. Oliver, who must rank as the most informed and knowledgeable black commentator on the situation of the black population in Nova Scotia from the time he entered public life in 1936 to his death on May 26, 1989, made the following observation in an address to the Canadian Humanities Council in June, 1949, on how black people in Nova Scotia were making a living, placing his remarks in the broader context of local-born blacks and others—a distinction which has already been referred to in earlier pages and which will come up again:

The following represents the various trades and occupations in which there is at least one member of the [black] race, in most cases they are unable to support themselves wholly from this trade, nor in most cases are they members of the Union representing their trade. I shall list twenty-two: carpenters, painters, plasterers, electricians, bricklayers, auto mechanics, cement finishers, sign painters, chimney sweeps, blacksmith, shoemaker, barber, tailor, printer, hairdresser, cooper, interior decorator, cook, acetylene welding, tin-smith and roofer. Prior to the last war, girls were limited to teaching school or domestic work; during the war many were employed as stenographers, while the nursing field was opened when two girls graduated in 1949 as registered nurses. One Negro boy has taken the course in pharmacy at Dalhousie University and is serving very capably in a Halifax drug store, two other young men are employed as office clerks in government departments, several others are employed in the Postal service. Attempts at business are limited to barber shops, beauty parlors, business, trucking, shoe-making, a newspaper and one co-operative store."[9]

The facts presented by Rev. Oliver showed that members of Nova Scotia's black population were eking out a living in the late 1940s, as many others were, in the lower rungs of the occupational scale. Except for the two nurses, a few teachers and a pharmacist, they were conspicuous by their absence in the professions. There were black persons of African descent in the professions but Rev. Oliver places them in a separate category: "In the professional field there are two doctors, two lawyers, all of whom came directly from the West Indies, received their education here and remained here to practise, which indicates that they are not truly products of the local culture. The same might be said of the two nurses; although the barrier was removed by the efforts of the slave descendants, it was children of West Indian parentage who took advantage of it. I point out this fact because it has been so evident throughout the history of our people in Nova Scotia and the United States and raises a question that cannot be opened in this paper; yet it is evident that the answer to the difference between the West Indian Negro and the Nova Scotian Negro in cultural development would reveal much that would help us to understand our local problem. The professional field is completed with six ordained ministers and two or three dozen teachers, either active or retired."[10]

Rev. Oliver raised an issue in 1949 which is still alive in Nova Scotia in 1989, two generations later. The professions are still weighted heavily in favour of black individuals who do not claim descent from Black Loyalist or Black Refugee origins but who also claim descent from slave ancestors, and whose forebears were brought up in colonial situations outside Canada which also discriminated against their forebears, the colonized peoples. In the 1940s life for colonized West Indians was little different from that for black Nova Scotians. Thus, if West Indian blacks could succeed, so could Nova Scotian-born blacks. Some examples illustrate this. In Nova Scotia, James R. Johnston had completed a law degree at Dalhousie University as early as 1898 while three black Nova Scotians, mentioned in earlier pages, completed university degrees in the 1930s. George Davis, born in Halifax, completed his law degree at Dalhousie University in 1948. The answers to the vexing question raised by Rev. Oliver on what factors help or hinder progress might well lie beyond cultural differences and countries of origin.

Fifteen years later, in 1964, Rev. Dr. Oliver surveyed the black community, this time as Regional Representative, Adult Education Division, Nova Scotia Department of Education. He found that in the city of Halifax, with a black population of 1,300, the main avenues for employment were the railways, armed forces, seasonal construction and the federal public and provincial civil services, that while many of the black women worked as charwomen in private homes and institutions, an increasing number of younger women were employed as clerks, teachers, nurses, nurses' aids, stenographers and laboratory technicians, that educational facilities were integrated and 13 black students were in High School and 3 in Vocational High. That year, 3 girls graduated as nurses, 3 as nursing assistants and 2 obtained university degrees. In the city of Dartmouth, with a black population of 500, the city was one of the principal employers, taking black employees in what Oliver describes as "unusual positions, without giving an explanation. He describes the community of Cherrybrook [700] as "one of the more aggressive communities" with a few self-employed gardeners, hog growers and wood vendors while many of the men worked for the cities, National Defence and private contractors and women in domestic labour.

As for the largest black community, North Preston [1,800], the survey notes that most of the men worked at unskilled seasonal labour and did not have the educational background to do maintenance and janitorial work for the provincial civil service. The women did domestic work while there were very few in this large community who were self-employed people. The problems for this community seemed to be compounded by the fact that teachers could not be recruited in sufficient numbers and that pupils had to wait a year or two beyond the legal age of 5 for admission to school. The second largest black settlement, East Preston, with a population of 1,200, was described as a small farming community "with probably the highest percentage of self-employed of any of the other Negro communities."[11]

The examples given in the large black settlements suggest a pattern for the rest of the province with minor variations influenced by local factors such as masonry work in Lucasville, lumbering and cooperage in Hammonds Plains, factory work in Bridgetown, lumbering in Weymouth Falls, industrial and mining employment in New Glasgow. In all, 47 communities were surveyed and the provincial black population, according to Dr. Oliver's survey, stood at 14,000 in 1964. The survey identified small numbers of high school graduates and very few university graduates, leading the author to the conclusion that poor educational standards had much to do with the type of jobs which were available to the black labour force in general. Significantly, this is what Dr. Oliver wrote about Sydney, Cape Breton:

The residents [black population, 800] are mostly of West Indian origin, coming to Cape Breton about 70 years ago. With an Anglican background they attend the local churches and schools and have a high academic standing. One family alone, has produced a medical doctor, a chemist, a psychologist, a household economic teacher and a stenographer. Another Negro has been very successful in Politics. A Negro doctor is a Commissioner on the Hospital Board.[12]

There were other surveys, too, pointing to conclusions that were similar. In the language of the day, the terms "Negro" and "coloured" were commonly used. These terms have been retained in this book in direct quotations only.

In the period after 1945, the plight of minorities all over the world attracted attention. Surveys everywhere pointed to serious concerns which had important consequences for minorities as well as majorities. Kurt Lewin, a social scientist, wrote in 1948: "In recent years we have started to realize that so-called minority problems are in fact majority problems, that the Negro problem is the problem of the white, that the Jewish problem is the problem of the non-Jew, and so on. It is also true of course that inter-group relations cannot be solved without altering certain aspects of conduct and sentiment of the minority group. One of the most severe obstacles in the way of improvement seems to be the notorious lack of confidence and self-esteem of most minority groups......"[13]

This observation is crucial to a proper understanding of the black experience in Nova Scotia. There is an accountability factor on both sides. Both Whites and Blacks have a case to make and a case to answer.

Between 1959-1961 the Institute of Public Affairs, Dalhousie University, conducted a survey of 248 black families in mid-city Halifax, in effect the historic north end, with a population of 1227, and 82 black families in Africville, with a population of 248. The survey found that Blacks earned less than the mean city income; that Blacks were unemployed for many more weeks than the average for all unemployed; that Blacks were concentrated far more in manual and menial jobs, and that Blacks were unrepresented in the professions. The explanation offered for this situation found racial prejudice on the part of white employers, while fear of being rebuffed or rejected led disadvantaged black employees to accept the lowest positions. Blacks were further disadvantaged in income by the large number of single mothers accepting part-time work as well as a number of young black men doing part-time work as sleeping car porters in the hope of getting full-time jobs later. Poor education was also found to be a factor against the black employees but this was offset by the findings of a companion survey which showed that there was "an increasing trend among the coloured men to remain in school longer than was evident in former years. The more education a coloured man has, the better chance he has of obtaining training in the professional, clerical and skilled trades......"

There was a salutary comment in the above remarks that holds good even for today: The opportunities for Whites and Blacks may not be the same, either in the quality of education received or in parity of treatment given, to equally qualified candidates for a job, but "it does mean that increased education usually does furnish by itself increased advantages to its holder. The opportunities of whites and Negroes may be arrayed along different scales, but in both cases the person with the more education tends to do better than others of his own race."[14]

This study was published in 1962 and the comments and conclusions must be seen in the context of that time. The provision of "different scales" is unacceptable in the context of 1989.

There was another salutary conclusion that was reached in this Institute of Public Affairs survey published in 1962. Since it is being recalled here twenty-seven years later, it deserved serious attention and analysis. The question at issue is whether education by itself can raise the socio-economic level of the community or whether it needs to be reinforced by other factors and circumstances. The following excerpt from this survey is meant for parents and politicians, teachers and policy makers who would dare to ask why the situation in Halifax (and, by extension, elsewhere in the province) has not improved all that much from the 1960s:

> If this is true (i.e. depressed condition of Blacks), it is probably unrealistic to expect the Negro population to pull itself up by its own educational bootstraps. Without further education, it is true, the future of Halifax Negroes is bleak indeed; but without improved living conditions and what these imply (broader employment opportunities, high income, better housing, a feeling that education is of some use, a more intellectual environment) the probability of Negro receptivity to increased education is very slim. Even though Negroes are almost certainly, in some aptitudinal sense, as intelligent as whites in general, they are far less likely to be capable of receiving the advantages of education. Like the poorer white children in the city, Halifax Negro students appear likely to repeat the limitations and disabilities of their parents. Only improvement in Negro employment and living conditions, largely supported as it must be by resources from outside this

group, can bring about a situation in which further education can profitably be assimilated, and the self-defeating circle of lower-class deficiencies in educability be broken.[15]

A year later, Rev. W.P. Oliver raised four questions before an assembly of representatives of thirty-two nations meeting at the Coady International Institute on the occasion of Human Rights Day, December 10, 1963 relating to the life of Blacks in Nova Scotia:

1. Why are they almost compelled to remain on reservations?
2. Why are problems in housing instead of improving, becoming worse?
3. Why are they limited to certain jobs?
4. Why have they not been assimilated into the life of this province?

These questions were asked in the context of the reception accorded to other immigrants of varied ethnic backgrounds who "arrived at the Halifax piers with carpet bag in hand and in a few years they and their children were able to scale the ladders of social acceptance and material substance."[16]

Though Oliver admitted that the picture was bleak on all fronts: education, housing, employment and inter-group acceptance, there were new indicators on the horizon which pointed to new directions, new philosophies and new strategies. In this analysis he was reflecting on what was happening in 1963 in Africa and North America while Nova Scotia was limping behind. The politicization of the masses had not yet begun in Nova Scotia and he used the occasion to show the new strategies being put in place:

The Negro community has not functioned in accordance with the democratic processes. For generations he has depended upon benefactors or so-called champions of his cause. It is our objective as adult educators to train the masses in the techniques of group action within a democratic society. This is being done through community development associations, where group planning, discussion, negotiation and action are the prime concern. A taste of group achievement will dispel fears and frustration and liberate them from the paralyzing grip of the so-called Negro supporters.[17]

240

While Oliver was speaking of local community development associations, the scale of the contemporary political process in Africa and the United States seeking new political dispensations for peoples of Africa and of African descent was, of course, larger in scope than could ever be contemplated for Nova Scotia on purely numerical grounds. However, community development through adult education deserves further attention.

The Nova Scotia Department of Education was the first official agency in Nova Scotia to note the fact that the black population of Nova Scotia lagged behind the rest of the population in education, income, employment and cultural development. It attempted to improve this situation through its Adult Education Division set up in 1946. The programs of this Division were described variously to help groups of people solve the problems of community livelihood through short courses and through existing organizations such as Home and School Associations, farm organizations, labour and church groups. The target communities were those in rural or semi-rural areas where ten or more residents could make a request for classes to be set up. To involve the black community, the Division began to work closely with the Nova Scotia Association for the Advancement of Colored People which devoted its main focus on adult education between 1945-1963. The thrust was community planning through adult education.[18]

The first two classes were set up in Hammonds Plains and the Preston area in 1946-47 where literacy and self-help activities were introduced. In Hammonds Plains woodlot cultivation was begun with the planting of 500 trees while in Preston high-bush blueberries cultivation was started under the supervision of the Dominion Experimental Farm in Kentville. Within three years, classes were begun in 16 communities on nutrition, housing, gardening, health and community recreation. A project relating to surveying lands and recording deeds, both crucial to economic development, was started in the Preston and Cherrybrook areas in 1950-51 but was discontinued shortly afterwards through lack of community interest. A later effort in this direction will be discussed below.

In subsequent years, more classes were offered in new fields like leatherwork, sewing, and singing while new projects included the cutting and selling of timber in Lincolnville, erecting new schools at Weymouth Falls and Cherrybrook between 1950-1952, the building of the George Washington Carver Centre in East Preston, inspired by the Rev. J.D.N. Macdonald, which opened on July 2, 1956, the provision of rural mail delivery in Cherrybrook, housing surveys of Maynard and Creighton Streets, scholarships for teachers to attend Summer School, the first conference of black teachers and leaders in Halifax in 1948 and the introduction of short courses each year since 1951 in the black community settlements of East Preston, Hammonds Plains, Beechville, Cherrybrook and New Road (North Preston).

The work of the Adult Education Division in the black communities of Nova Scotia was indeed positive and impressive. The irony was that this good work was happening after Blacks had been living in this province for over two hundred years.

In 1954 the program of the division was reviewed by Dr. William Cooper of Hampton Institute, U.S.A. Dr. Cooper paid particular attention to the situation in New Road where there was a chronic shortage of teachers, and where some 100 or more younger children had had no classes for several years. As a result of Dr. Cooper's survey and recommendations, public, government and private financial support was received for the building of a teacherage (model home for teachers) and in September, 1956 the services of a trained teacher and community worker (Mr. Frissel W. Jones, of Virginia) were obtained through the Division. [19]

In the years following, the work begun by the Adult Education Division was carried forward by the Nova Scotia Association for the Advancement of Coloured People through community councils, credit unions and Home and School Associations. Once a measure of training was given and leadership skills were cultivated and encouraged, the next phase was to provide avenues and outlets for economic advancement. The formation of various Ratepayers' Associations and the co-operative housing project at Beechville were two examples of the changing emphasis from adult education to economic progress through self-help projects but also through improved employment opportunities as individuals upgraded their skills and their educational capacities to cope with broader-based jobs. But stumbling blocks remained and the province passed the Fair Employment Practices Act in 1955 to remove discrimination based on race, religion, colour or national origin in employment as well as in trade union membership. Four years later, the Fair Accommodations Practices Act was introduced to remove discrimination on similar grounds in such public places as hotels, barber shops, taverns and pool rooms. Blacks, Micmacs and other so-called "visible minority" immigrants were the main target groups who were to be protected by the laws of 1955 and 1959.

Clearly, given the above context, the road ahead for Nova Scotia's black population was fraught with many difficulties. Individuals, the church, the various organizations which became the N.S.A.A.C.P., the Adult Education Division, had all given help in one form or other to combat racial discrimination and to promote the interests of the black population. Their efforts were not without modest successes but more needed to be done, both through legislative means and through more aggressive community organizations.

On the matter of using the law as an instrument to prohibit anti-social conduct, Professor W.A. MacKay, the Dean of Law at Dalhousie University, made certain observations at a human rights conference in 1967, the very year the Nova Scotia Human Rights Commission was set up. He was to serve for many years as Chairman of the Commission before becoming Ombudsman of Nova Scotia and then Judge of the Federal Court of Canada. Professor MacKay's 1967 comments were:

> ......legislation to combat discrimination is generally considered a shield, a protective device, against anti-social conduct. Yet legislation in the twentieth century has come to be accepted as having a much wider role than merely prohibiting, on threat of punishment, certain kinds of conduct. It is now accepted as a device for actively promoting social goals, a positive instrument, a sword if you will.[20]

The landmarks in this process of legislative protection as well as promotion were the Interdepartmental Committee on Human Rights set up by the provincial government in 1962 to provide equality of opportunity for all Nova Scotians. Through the work of this Committee—a considerable extension of the work begun by the Adult Education Division—studies and surveys were carried out, legislation was introduced to support the acquisition of land clarification titles, structures were introduced to provide support for education for black children as well as employment opportunities for members of the black population for, as Professor MacKay said, such measures "are most important for unless there is assurance of equal opportunities, discrimination may never be overcome......"[21]

While Professor Mackay looked at what the law could do to protect as well as promote human rights, Dr. W.P. Oliver stressed the role of education at the same conference, and recalled what was already in place for black students. An exploratory fund of $25,000 was set up by the province to provide emergency assistance, promotional awards, achievement awards, special assistance for students seeking post-high school and university training.

Besides this provincial fund, there were other sources of help available through the endeavours of local committees struck by members of the black population, through bursaries awarded to deserving black students by such organizations as the N.S.A.A.C.P., the I.O.D.E., Rotary and Kiwanis Clubs, and the A.U.B.A. There were other aspects of assistance provided to black children and school students, such as pre-school programmes, tutoring services and special days like the Teen-Guidance Conference organized for some 150 black high school youth by the Council of Christians and Jews. Dr. Oliver also referred to the steps being taken by the Department of Education to scrutinize the material used in school texts so as to remove embarrassing and derogatory references to Blacks and other minorities.

It is important to recall these developments of the 1960s for a number of reasons. The problem areas identified in the 1960s and the remedial measures put in place represented forward thinking, planning and implementation. Had these progressive steps been maintained and built upon, the next generation would have had reason to look back with appreciation and gratitude. Some things went wrong in the next twenty years since the situation in the 1980s suggests that, insofar as black youth and society are concerned, the position is no better in general than the 1960s. When the 1980s are reviewed later, a picture will emerge showing that the Education Department is working on reviewing material for bias and stereotypes, that while a minority of black youth are moving upwards in education, employment and social status, the majority are still in the opposite categories of poor education, serious unemployment and on the bottom rungs of Canada's vertical mosaic. The black family, the black church and the black society in general are similarly under the focus to ascertain why an upward mobility was not maintained for a greater number over the span of an entire generation.

The following personal experience described by Dr. Oliver in 1967 has an ironic relevance for 1989:

......not so long ago I was in a room with a Grade X student when all of a sudden I heard a loud shout of triumph and he showed me a photograph in his Science book, illustrating a laboratory scene. Why the shout? Because never before had he, nor I, ever seen the picture of a negro in a school textbook. It was good for him to see this illustration. It is also of educational value to the other members of the class. The picture spelled out the fact that vocations and professions are not based on the color of a skin.[22]

As a descendant of Black Refugee ancestors from the United States, and as a student of science himself before his specialization in theology at Acadia University, Dr. Oliver could have shared with this startled student a long list of famous black inventors and scientists in the United States, George Washington Carver (1864-1943)—an agricultural scientist whose researches in peanut and soybean products revolutionized the economy of the southern United States; Benjamin Banneker (1731-1806)—a mathematician who is credited with having invented what was probably the first clock in America, whose knowledge of astronomy enabled him to predict the solar eclipse of 1789 and who was the first black person to prepare and publish an almanac with scientific data such as tide tables and eclipses and was one of six surveyors who helped to do the town planning for the American national capital, Washington, D.C.; Charles Drew (1904-1950)—a medical doctor who developed a technique of separating and preserving blood in the form of plasma, a Professor of Pathology who was invited in 1940 to set up the first blood bank in England; and Lewis Howard Latimer (1848-1928)—an inventor, engineer and draftsman who was employed by Alexander Graham Bell to make the patent drawings for the first telephone and who went on to become the chief draftsman for the world famous General Electric and Westinghouse companies.[23]

The list could go on but the necessary digression is intended to make the point that black inventors and scientists have been around for a long time in North America and that books researched and published in North America have no excuse to exclude deserving and renowned North Americans.

In January, 1969 a major two-day workshop was organized at Saint Francis Xavier University on the theme "Teach-In Report: The Black Man in Nova Scotia." The purpose of the workshop was to provide a platform for black people to discuss their problems and to inform students of a pressing social problem in Nova Scotia. The timing was propitious as events over the preceding months, some of which will be treated in greater detail later in this chapter, had provided the black community, the leaders, the media and the general public, with a reason to pay the occasional attention to a minority issue, especially one which dealt with the plight of Black or native Nova Scotians—the usual attractions for sensational and dramatic media attention.

Some of the events which preceded the 1969 workshop included an all-black family meeting in Halifax in late November, 1968, a Nova Scotia Human Rights Conference in Halifax on December 6-7, 1968, and the preparatory work by a seven-member interim committee leading up to the inauguration of the Black United Front of Nova Scotia. Many of the speakers and participants at this workshop in 1969—and all the issues raised, the problems identified, the strategies proposed for effecting changes—could well be transposed to the Nova Scotia scene of 1989. Not much has changed in twenty years. The following excerpts from the 1969 statements bear examination in 1989:

......I suggest to you that part of the problem may be that the things that we offer and the things that we talk about are not relevant to the black people. You know the hierarchy of human need—food and shelter, then the matter of security and safety. And then we get into the matter of the social need of all human beings to be accepted and then we go a bit further into the ego needs—self-esteem, and then the high pinnacle of creativeness, the opportunity to contribute. I suggest to you that the matter of food and shelter is not the crying need for black people. They want to be themselves. They want to be able to create, and they want to be able to determine their own destiny. This, to me, is the issue, the right to self-identity.[24]

The question of self-identity, argued in 1969, before 1969, and repeated in 1989, poses a serious challenge, primarily to members of the black community and secondarily to society at large. If individuals and groups strive for self-determination it becomes a matter of self-effort and if self-effort is consciously or unconsciously blocked by the conduct of the larger society, it becomes a matter beyond the control of individuals and groups. The question of the hierarchy of human needs, as articulated by Dr. W.P. Oliver, win always exist but it should not be allowed by the larger society to exist as a roadblock to the progress of a people—if this is in fact the case.

Another excerpt from the 1969 workshop addressed the very question of the institutionalized behaviour of the larger society which makes up the power and the system:

The first thing I want to deal with is, what is the role of the white person in my liberation struggle......If someone wants to help you, should they go to the person who is being beat and talk to them? That don't make no sense. Go to whoever's beating me. Talk to him. Get him off my back. In other words, a white person has no business going into the black community to try to talk to us and organize us. Go talk to

the racist society out there. Look in the mirror and deal with yourself.
You cannot help me by trying to explain to me what my problem is. I
know. I know my problem is racism, capitalism, imperialism and colonialism. I know that. I may be one of the brothers who doesn't know
the exact words but I know that when I go for a job, I've got to be
twice as good. I know that when I go for a house, that the man is
going to say: 'I'm sorry, gee, this place has just been taken, and maybe,
uh, um, look, I'll give you the name of this guy down the street. He's
got some places.' That's racism......[25]

There was much more along the same lines discussed and debated at the
Saint Francis Xavier workshop of 1969. Most of the active participants are
still active and articulate as this chapter closes in 1989 although Dr. Oliver,
as mentioned earlier, died in May, 1989. The chairman of the conference,
Gordon Earle, then Executive Secretary of the Nova Scotia Human Rights
Commission, later Deputy Ombudsman of Nova Scotia, is now the
Ombudsman of Manitoba and maintains contact with his native province
through occasional lecture visits when his insightful comments and first-
hand knowledge draw attention to the chronic persistence of age-old problems. Burnley Jones continues to be a knowledgeable and articulate voice
whose passion never ceases to command attention but because it has been
repeated with such frequency and consistency it tends to be taken for granted. His present platform, the Afro-Canadian Caucus of Nova Scotia, newly-
formed in 1989, is a new medium and opportunity to keep the Burnley
(Rocky) Jones call for revolutionary change alive.

While it is important to consider what happened, workshops and conferences where ideas were exchanged and strategies were inspired, an understanding of the forces that influenced black society and economy in the period following the end of World War Two is strengthened by an analysis of
what was actually happening to bring about changes. One such development was the Transition Year Program at Dalhousie University for Nova
Scotian Blacks and Micmacs, known popularly as T.Y.P. The genesis was in
the work done by a planning group drawn from Dalhousie University students and members of the Afro-Canadian Liberation Movement in 1969
whose initial focus was to develop black studies. A curriculum was devised
to help black Nova Scotians, and later Micmacs, who did not have the academic qualifications or the financial means, to gain entry into Dalhousie
University through the T.Y.P. The first students entered in 1970, ranging in

ages from 17-24, with academic levels from Grade 5 to high school. Fourteen of the first 23 students were admitted into the university main stream in 1971, on the basis of what was acknowledged in the first Director's Report for 1970-71 as "a second chance" for these students to enter university studies since the normal direct entry would have been impossible because of their poor high school credentials in mainly non-academic courses.

In the first seven years, 119 students entered T.Y.P., of whom 14% had graduated and 37% were still at Dalhousie; a withdrawal rate of 81% was registered either in the T.Y.P. year or in the first year of regular university studies; and, while more men than women entered T.Y.P., more women actually graduated.

In the first ten years of its existence some changes were instituted, mainly with respect to raising the minimum entry requirements to Grade XI, to administration, and to the curriculum, which included Black History and Culture, Micmac History and Culture, English and Mathematics: Students are given free tuition, room and board, books, and a small allowance. [26]

The success rate in this program in its first decade was not high but it did provide the "second chance" to those who would not have had it otherwise. But since so few graduated, and a tradition was in danger of being established that Blacks and Micmacs could only, or should only, enter because of the category of candidates lining up for "a second chance," there was also the real danger of a "ghetto" perception which branded its beneficiaries as inferior students, the program was rightly reviewed from time to time between 1976 and 1989. While it should always be argued that disadvantaged Nova Scotians should be given every help and consideration to overcome their disadvantages, special provisions should not be an excuse to ignore the root causes of disadvantage. Temporary measures can easily become permanent by habit and by benign neglect.

If there is a picture that emerges in an analysis of black society and economy in the period 1969 to 1989, for example, it is that very few progressive changes have taken place in the twenty-year period. This conclusion is not only based on the observations of a few of the more prominent public figures whose statements and speeches have made headlines or found their way in newspapers, magazines and books. There is a groundswell of new and emergent members of the black community whose voices joined the echo a decade ago, and still newer voices who are beginning to be heard on the contemporary scene of 1989.

248

In 1979, Cynthia M. Thomas addressed the subject of black youth and education, giving a refreshing analysis from the perspective of a youth. She acknowledged that black youth have come a step forward from the past but questioned the value and quality of the education imparted: negative self-images, name-calling, unresponsive curriculum, problems faced by students moving from segregated schools to integrated schools, subtle and overt acts of racism in classrooms with predominant white students, the malady of dead-end programs resulting from placing black students in general streams as well as the different criteria used by different school boards for carrying out this detrimental exercise, the lack of strong black organizations the black youth can count upon. The analysis closed with an equally refreshing suggestion for a course of action:

> The answer to the educational problem of black youth is in the hands of the black youth, the black community and, in large part, the educational system as it exists. We, as black youth, must recognize the problems and injustices that have been thrown into our faces throughout history. We must formulate possible solutions to have our interests and values attained. Once these are formulated, we must find resources to work through and get the majority of the population to support the methods and the ideas set. The final step, once the organization of black youth has a firm grip, is to plunge forward by presenting the whole case to the administrative educational system and demand immediate action. We are important and we have ability. However, we should first deal with a problem we can solve and thereby gain the strength, confidence, and experience needed to carry out greater feats.[27]

Here was an analysis and a line of action formulated ten years before the unfortunate events at Cole Harbour District High School in January, 1989 which gave rise to the formation of the Parent and Student Association of Preston and to demands for a public enquiry into racism in the schools of Nova Scotia. The Graham Royal Commission Report of March 1971 had itself made perceptive allusions and recommendations to remedy shortcomings in the Nova Scotia schools system. Thus, what is being articulated in 1989 is nothing new. The fact that it is not new is greater cause for concern that there is an apathy and an indifference that needs to be replaced by positive action and conviction in the interest of all Nova Scotians.

There must surely be tremendous scope for positive action given the will and the determination. Cherry Paris of the Nova Scotia Human Rights Commission has for long been a positive role model for social change and a member of the black community who has recognized that one "of the greatest flaws in the record of human relations in the northern half of the western hemisphere has been our inability to deal judiciously with the issue of relations between the races......the one greatest blight on the society that has developed in this part of the world."[28] One institution in Nova Scotia, traced by Cherry Paris, is the very institution she works for, the Nova Scotia Human Rights Commission, founded in 1967, and entrusted with the mandate of carrying out the terms of the Human Rights Act of 1969 which prohibits discrimination against any person on the grounds of race, religion, colour, creed, ethnic or national origin, physical or mental disability, and sex in such matters as employment, accommodation, services and facilities. While the services of the Human Rights Commission are available to all Nova Scotians, its historical links with the plight of the most disadvantaged Nova Scotians brought it close to the concerns of the black community. Thus, as Cherry Paris pointed out in observations made as early as 1979, its promotion of textbook analyses for bias and stereotypes, formation of human rights affirmative action committees, setting up of a joint committee with the Nova Scotia Department of Education on Human Rights and Education, rank among its main accomplishments in working towards alleviating some of the difficulties faced by black Nova Scotians.

While institutions like the Nova Scotia Human Rights Commission can provide redress against cases of blatant racial discrimination, they cannot enforce affirmative action and employment equity proposals unless and until the legislation governing such cases calls for mandatory compliance or contract compliance which will make employers more receptive to employing minority persons. It is precisely in the area of employment that members of the black population are hardest hit, a point that has become the common denominator in any analysis of black society and economy throughout the many centuries. To take two final observations to end this section, the first made in 1979 and the second made in 1987, the obvious conclusions of depressed employment opportunities are reinforced.

Eleanor Dorrington, formerly of the Black United Front, drew attention to the low wages, the hard work and the long distances travelled by black domestic workers in the Halifax–Dartmouth metropolitan area. These black women who served the industrial sector as chambermaids and cleaners and also had the added burden of no job security and no union protection. Where such security and protection did exist, few openings were available. Black males who found employment at one time as free lance gardeners, handymen or heavy cleaners for individuals and institutions, or as railroad porters, survived irregular hours, insecurity, low pay and menial and back-breaking chores, only to find themselves rendered redundant with the competition from national and multinational companies. Similarly, while black railroad porters, once the vaunted favourites when pay was low, promotion was impossible, and hands were few and scarce, now found competition from whites, who were chosen for their vaunted bilinguality, but were in fact encouraged to start at the bottom for that was the route to becoming a conductor and better. It was no wonder, then, that no new black sleeping car porters have been recruited since 1979, after a virtual century of loyal service. Construction labourers and freight handlers faced a similar plight in the declining economy of the late 1970s. The picture that Eleanor Dorrington saw at the time was a bleak one:

> Given these depressing circumstances, one must ask if blacks have any hope for employment. What types of jobs are available in the metro-politan area? Recognizing that jobs are advertised in many places, a survey of newspaper want-ads over the past year indicates that most advertised positions are for skilled tradesmen, technicians, profession-als or sales persons with experience to get these jobs. Unless some major changes occur in education and training, a large number of blacks will remain unemployable and be a drain on the resources of our society.[29]

For most of the decade since these comments were made at a Black Studies Conference in Halifax, the employment position for the black population has hardly improved. While it is true that short-term programs have continued to be funded for recipients of social welfare grants and mature persons re-entering the job market, by the Canada Employment and Immigration Commission, and that the projects funded have been run by a number of black organizations, these have tended to be short-term, dead-end ventures, leaving the general situation and the affected persons no better than before. The years 1988-89, however, have seen an upsurge of community, individual, institutional as well as political initiatives at various levels whose effectiveness will only be properly evaluated in the course of the next decade. The good thing for now is that they are being put in place to respond to the bleak picture described above. While these most recent initiatives will be discussed later, it is important to recognize that black individuals and black organizations have themselves done much to help themselves. This holds true for the period after 1945 as it does for the period before 1945, for the eighteenth century as for the twentieth century. They have not always succeeded—and that is another matter—but they have always tried—and that is a matter that deserves the utmost commendation lest it be argued, in the unhappy phraseology of the contemporary Canadian scene, that they were "the authors of their own misfortune."

One recent study commissioned and published by the Black Cultural Centre for Nova Scotia traces the history and society of the largest aggregation of black people in Nova Scotia in the geographical complex comprising North and East Preston, Cherrybrook and Lake Loon from 1784—when the first land grants were surveyed for allocation—to 1987. It is a people's history, one which traces the interrelationship in the economy and society of such issues as land tenure, the church, domestic industries, education, credit unions, market forces and local organizations. It is an account of a people's struggle for development, the title chosen for the book, placed in the context of Nova Scotia and Canada, a context which is absolutely fundamental for a proper and rational analysis of the interplay of the different factors and forces. The following excerpt from the study illustrates some of the factors and forces at work:

> Like other non-European communities throughout Canada, the Preston communities were able to develop alternative economic opportunities as producers of potatoes and vegetables which allowed them to come into contact with the market economy. Self-employment allowed members of these communities to raise families and to build a community-based support system. At some times, when opportunities were available, both self-employment and indentured labour were practised. The black communities in Preston Township supplemented their income by raising hogs and by woodcutting, both for family use and for trading. The hogs were used to break the land and their manure was used for fertilizer. Woodcutting played an important part in the life of the communities. It provided shelter and fuel to cook with and to heat their homes during the long winter season. Some of the communities still practise hog farming. Traditional subsistence farming declined

while indentured labour as domestic workers, and woodcutting continued,......until the first two decades of the twentieth century......A number of factors contributed to the change from a farming economy to one based on wage earning. The most important factor was that the economy of the Province of Nova Scotia as a whole was becoming gradually integrated into the metropole center of the Canadian economy, particularly the Golden Triangle of Ontario. Second, the linkage between the producers' communities and the commercial centre declined in Nova Scotia. Third, the hinterland communities, particularly those communities dependent on long distance trade for the sale of forest products, coal and fish, began to decline. Members of these communities moved within and outside the province in search of employment. Fourth, Dartmouth and Halifax, which had become the urban centers of the province, wholly depended on the service industry. The peripheral communities close to Dartmouth and Halifax were the first to benefit from the growing urban economy......The more the urbanization of these cities increased, however, the less likely it became for the Blacks to obtain decent jobs within the urban economy. Unions and employers resisted hiring Blacks in favour of Europeans whether they were locally born or immigrant. Some Blacks were forced to leave their communities in search of decent jobs in the provinces of Quebec and Ontario......[30]

This is the kind of contextual analysis that is both meaningful and instructive. It throws light upon the historical past as well as the contemporary present; and it challenges society as a whole to respond as well as to be accountable. If the future is to be better, the present must be prepared to be less defensive, and more receptive to the reality and the lessons of the past.

THE AFRICVILLE SAGA

One of the best known topics in the twentieth-century history of the black experience in Nova Scotia is the story of Africville. This is not to say that the details are well known but that the message conveyed and the lessons extracted provide scope for lively discussions and debates within and outside the black communities, in Nova Scotia as well as in other parts of Canada.

In Chapters I and II of this study, brief references are made to the origins and early years of this historic settlement within the town and, later, city limits of Halifax, Nova Scotia's capital. The fifteen-odd acres (6 hectares) of land, adjoining and in close proximity to the Bedford Basin, which constituted the settlement, were acquired first by Whites and were sold to Blacks much later. The land which the original black purchasers, William Arnold and William Brown, acquired in January, 1848, was purchased by a white man in 1818 from the original owner who had obtained the land before 1818.[31]

What started out as a promising rural settlement in the mid-nineteenth century soon found itself challenged within the span of half a century by the forces of industrialization. The population of Halifax grew from 21,000 to 47,000 between 1851 and 1911. New industries looked towards the Bedford Basin area for sites and these included an oil plant storage complex, a bone mill fertilizer factory, a cotton factory, a rolling mill and nail factory, as well as two slaughter houses, a tar factory, leather tanning and stone-crushing industries. On adjoining vacant city property, Rockhead Prison was built in 1853, a hundred yards from Africville. Night soil disposal pits started in 1858. An Infectious Diseases Hospital was erected in the 1870s and a little more than a mile away the city dumped its garbage. In 1905, a Trachoma Eye Hospital was built near Rockhead Prison.[32]

The Seaview African United Baptist Church was the heart and soul of the Africville community.

254

The black settlement of Africville was beleaguered from its very inception, surrounded by factories and filth and kept in isolation. This unpleasant circumstance was compounded by the demands from the Nova Scotia Railway Company for portions of Africville land for the construction of new tracks as well as for the demolition of existing buildings to make way for these tracks. Thus, the beginnings of the relocation of Africville go back to as early as 1855 when the Board of Railway Commissioners reported that "Difficulties have arisen during the past year, in adjusting the damages due to parties whose land has been taken by the Commissioners. None of the parties had been paid......cases of hardship have already occurred."[33]

What is worse is that the city officials had already made up their minds that it was Africville, by whatever designation it was referred to, that was to bear the brunt of accommodating factories, industries and dumps that were rejected by other neighbourhoods, a point which was vociferously recalled at a mammoth public meeting at St. Stephen's School in the north end of Halifax—not far from where Africville once stood—in early 1989 when a proposal to locate a gypsum plant in the area was unanimously rejected by the residents. But this time, there were no black residents in Africville whose case would be taken up by concerned citizens. In 1989, the mayor and city council heeded public opinion to keep the residential area free of industrial pollution and nuisance while in 1915 the emphasis was expressed in these words: "The Africville portion of Campbell Road will always be an industrial district and it is desirable that industrial operations should be assisted in any way that is not prejudicial to the interests of the public; in fact, we may be obliged in the future to consider the interest of the industry first."[34]

In 1915, racial discrimination and racial bigotry were common features of Canadian life from coast to coast, as they were in other parts of the British Commonwealth (so-called since 1926): South Africa, Australia, Great Britain and New Zealand as well as in the many colonies under British rule. The British Secretary of State for the Colonies in the early years of the twentieth century made the point which was the beacon guiding British rulers everywhere: "I believe that the British race is the greatest of governing races the world has ever seen......I say that it is indeed a craven and poor spirited creature who despairs of the future of the British race."[35]

The point of this comment is that the ruling ideology in Nova Scotia, as elsewhere throughout the British Commonwealth, was rooted in the tradition of racial superiority of the Anglo-Celtic race and that in this context the black settlement and black settlers of Africville had no prospect for relief or growth. As the white British population increased in Halifax so did the threat to the survival of Africville. In 1945, the City of Halifax considered a proposal for the removal of the settlement of Africville. Two years later it was designated industrial land. Yet it was always a residential area and residents of any area are expected to be consulted or informed when matters concerning their future are debated by government. It was only in 1947, when seven Africville homes were destroyed by fire and the question of basic civic amenities such as water and sewerage services emerged in the discussions that consultations began. Africvilleans were determined to stay on and to work in concert with the city to develop their residential area while the city for its part remained indecisive to the extent of borrowing funds to provide water and sewerage services but never in fact installing them. In 1961, Halifax City Council unilaterally took the firm decision to demolish the residential settlement and relocate the residents. From that point the story of Africville is a story of two solitudes—one trying to save the settlement and the other determined to raze the settlement. Fortunately for posterity, the fuller story, the intimate story, the people's story was finally told and known when the many sides to the 1989 project, "Africville. A Spirit That Lives On" unfolded between October and November, 1989 with a major exhibition and a conference, reinforced by publications scheduled to appear in 1989 and 1990.[36] The exhibition is scheduled to circulate nationally from August 1990 to December 1992, after which it will be permanently housed in the Black Cultural Centre for Nova Scotia.

Within the short space of a decade (1960-70) the fate of Africville was sealed, the settlement was demolished and the residents were relocated in the south end of Gottingen Street. The great design in the town planning for the Africville site was to turn the place into a beehive of industrial complexes as part of the urban renewal plan for the city of Halifax, including an expressway which would link with the city of Dartmouth through the construction of a new bridge. While the city of Halifax proceeded with its plans for demolition, compensation and resettlement, the people of Africville and their supporters and sympathisers mobilized their own resources.

In this unfortunate human drama, the city of Halifax had a headstart, not only in its financial base but because it was in possession of a report prepared by Dr. Gordon Stephenson, Professor of Town and Regional Planning, University of Toronto, as early as 1956. The people's organization was activated by the visit to Halifax in 1961 by Alan Borovoy, a lawyer and human rights activist from Toronto through whose persuasion a body of nine persons, four from Africville, and the remainder drawn from both black and white communities, formed the Halifax Human Rights Advisory Committee under the chairmanship of H.A.J. (Gus) Wedderburn, an organization which endured from 1962-1967. Many meetings were held over this period but most of them were poorly attended. Alan Borovoy's visit to Halifax received national attention when an article appeared in *Maclean's Magazine* in 1962 entitled "The Counterattack on Diehard Racism" but, in the end, it was a matter that rested squarely on the shoulders of the residents of Africville themselves. Their supporters and sympathisers outside Africville were peripheral to the protest or opposition. A few Africville residents like Mrs. Emma Steed, a member of the Human Rights Advisory Committee and Deacon Ralph Jones were uncompromising in their opposition, but a greater number remained confused and unsure. The non-Africville members of the Advisory Committee were more convinced that a firm stand had to be taken. For them, the issue was a political one of greater dimension than a single issue in which the political conservatism of the Nova Scotia and Canadian black population took second place to the more vigorous political agitation carried out in the south.

Appearing on national television, Gus Wedderburn said: "Our people are lethargic, maybe even afraid. I don't see the possibility of a march on Ottawa, or sit-ins, or even white violence," while Rev. Charles Coleman, pastor of the Cornwallis Street Baptist Church at the time said: "There is a lethargy, almost a hopelessness, about our people. They are just becoming aware of the fact that they are not just colored people; they are Negroes of African descent."[37]

There was little comfort or immediacy in such observations for an isolated, exploited black community of some 80 families comprising some 400 persons at the height of the relocation in the late 1960s who "have always maintained that they do not want to move. The only thing they ask is that they should receive what is rightfully theirs, namely, fresh water, a sewage system, paved streets and sidewalks, a school, to have the dump removed, and all the other tax-resulting privileges that other Haligonians enjoy."[38]

It was a losing battle from the inception: Africville was too close for comfort. From start to finish it was only a matter of time that railway expansion, industrial expansion, urban renewal and rejuvenation, would all be heaped up in a mountain of argument that would be presented by the political authorities, the business community and by the social structure—all of which were controlled by and representative of the dominant society—asking in one way or other that the Africville settlement be closed down. The black community in general and Africvilleans in particular could not be blamed for reaching the obvious conclusion that in general it was the white community that made up this sector, that if Africville had been a white settlement, such as the container pier section of the south end of Halifax bordering on Point Pleasant Park, the stages would have been different and the affected residents would have received more care, compassion and respect.[39] Africvilleans saw the issue as a race issue and not a class issue.

In rapid stages, landmarks and personalities left their mark for history: the school which had served the community for almost a century closed down in 1952, leaving precious memories of teachers who had rendered faithful services over the years—names such as Gordon Jemmot, senior and junior, Clyde Jemmot, Clarice Jemmot, Portia White, Laylia Grant, Verna Davis and others. The post office, the church, the penny stores, the piggeries and the poultry, the horses and the harvests, the Africville Ladies Softball Club which had performed all over the province over the years, the famous George Dixon whose name adorns the pages of boxing, the tribute that the world-famous heavy-weight boxing champion, Joe Louis, paid to the settlement when he chose to visit it on a trip to Halifax and to spend a night there at the height of his fame and fortune, all belie the public perception of the dominant society that the black settlement of Africville deserved what it got as the best deal possible at the time.

The black settlement of Africville was demolished during the 1960s, and its residents relocated to the south end of Gottingen Street in Halifax.

But Africvilleans and their descendants have another version to present. Even before the 1989 Africville project referred to previously, they have continued consistently to give their side of the story. One of these earlier group presentations was made at the Halifax Northend Public Library on September 13, 1986 which was attended by such notable residents as Matilda Newman, Aletha Mantley, Elsie Desmond, Jessica Kane, Ruth Johnson, Laura Howe, Wilhelmina Byers, Mrs. Roland Howe, Daniel Izzard, Brenda Steed Ross, Linda Mantley and Stanley and Alice Carvery. Some of their testimonies appear in published form.[40] Two of the final developments linked with the saga of Africville will bring this section to an end: the last Africvillean to leave and the birth and work of the Africville Genealogy Society.

The last person to leave the settlement, on January 2, 1970, was Aaron "Pa" Carvery, then 72 years old. While the 80 other families and some 400 persons were moved between 1964 and 1967, Aaron Carvery held out. He owned four lots with a house on each lot until the later years when he owned only three houses. A fifth lot had been expropriated in 1967. As an owner of considerable property he had good reason to hold out for the best price for his property, which, in his estimate, was $35,000 in 1966. City Council countered with an offer of $12,000 which was subsequently raised to $14,387.76, and accepted under threat of expropriation. The last acts in this drama were described in a local daily in the following words: "An incident which upset Pa terribly, occurred at city hall about two weeks ago. Relating what happened, he said, 'They sent for me and when I got there I was taken into someone's office. There was [were] five or six persons in the room plus a suitcase full of money all tied up neatly in bundles......The suitcase was open and stuck under my nose so as to tempt me and try to pay me off right there and then......I didn't like that at all......it hurt me......I told them you guys think you're smart......well, you're not smart enough......when they finally paid me it was by cheque and they came to my house to do business.' "[41]

Aaron Carvery's last Africville home was demolished on January 6, 1970, after all other Africville houses were already demolished, and with it the old chapter of the Africville saga closed. What lived on were the memories and the legacy. The memories included the indignity inflicted by the city authorities when they chose to move out the residents and their belongings in garbage trucks, an experience not lost on young impressionable minds. As the children and the youth of the sixties grew older in their new residence in Uniacke Square in the north end of Halifax, some five kilometres from their old settlement, looked at photographs, were reminded by elders of the painful experience of losing their homes, compared notes on preserving the memories of ancestral times, a few of them took practical steps to form an organization. The result was the formation of the Africville Genealogy Society in 1982. One of the founders described this development as follows: "To me and many more like myself, as a former resident of Africville, the loss of our community will always affect us. To assuage this feeling of loss, Brenda Steed Ross, Linda Mantley and Debbie Dixon Jones founded the Africville Genealogy Society. The aim is to bring our people together through annual picnics, five-year reunions, involvement with the youth and recognition benefits......Africville is gone as a community but will never be forgotten."[42]

The lessons of Africville will surely be remembered in many ways. One way was the influence it had on the residents of North Preston, East Preston, Cherry Brook, Lake Loon and Lake Major who joined hands between 1977 and 1981 to protect their interests in a situation where the city of Dartmouth, the province of Nova Scotia and the residents of the area worked out a mutually acceptable solution to protect other interests in a watershed area: "The memory of what had happened to the people of Africville, the suspicions of the activities of the City of Dartmouth as it sought to protect its

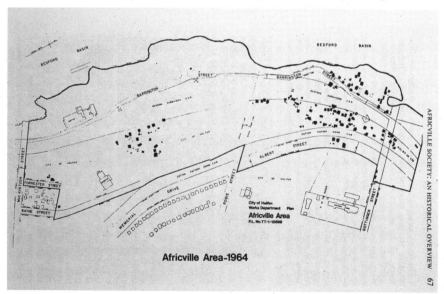

Map of the Africville area.

water supply, and the fear of losing what they had, created the conditions for mass opposition to the attempt to enforce the building bylaw on the watershed."[43]

In the meantime, the much-vaunted industrial development argument for the demolition of Africville never happened. In its place, the Seaview Memorial Park was officially opened on June 23, 1985. The park comprises 25 acres (10 hectares). The original Africville settlement comprised 15 acres (6 hectares) of land. It is no wonder, then, that the Africville Genealogy Society and its supporters cry out for restitution to the former residents and their descendants of the lands that still lie vacant—a cry that will be difficult to satisfy today.

The legacy, however, will continue to be recalled every time disadvantaged residents contemplate the worst that could happen to their homes, as was the case with the residents of Mulgrave Park in the north end of Halifax, half-way between the old settlement of Africville and the relocation area of Africvilleans in Uniacke Square. A daily newspaper carried the following account: "The President of the Mulgrave Park tenants' committee looks at the decayed housing project that is home to 841 people and sees the spectre of Africville" and goes on to cite this official's words: "My fear is that Africville is just down the road......We live with that memory. And the power of the middle class and their need for location to build houses. I would very much hate to see Mulgrave Park continue to deteriorate......another ten years of neglect and officials could call themselves progressive by moving people out of broken-down blocks."[44]

Emergence of New Organizations, Challenges and Responses

The two organizations which carried the burden of representing the interests and aspirations of the black population on a provincial scale between 1945 and 1968 were the African United Baptist Association and the Nova Scotia Association for the Advancement of Coloured People. While the A.U.B.A. was ever vigilant in addressing both spiritual and secular concerns of its constituents, this valuable work was carried out unobtrusively through the churches and their various committees but rarely caught the public limelight through media interest or endorsement. Its existence and its work were both taken for granted as pillars of strength.

One of A.U.B.A.'s notable branches was the Baptist Young People's

Union about whose origins and early work some reference has been made in earlier sections. The annual meeting of the provincial B.Y.P.U. held in New Glasgow in July, 1947 provides some illustration of the quality of individuals produced by this union and the part played by the officers and membership in the history of black Nova Scotians. At that meeting Noel Johnston was elected president for a two-year term. In the years since this individual has made a notable contribution in many ways. He was the first black industrial arts teacher, a treasurer of A.U.B.A. and the Cornwallis Street Baptist Church for many years, a prominent member of the Laymen's Council, a founder and chairman of the George Washington Carver Credit Union, a director of the Black Cultural Society and a member and official of numerous other bodies, serving both the black community and Nova Scotia in general. The son of Clarence Harvey Johnston, who died on 30 November, 1973, after a lifetime of service to the black community, Noel Johnston followed in his father's footsteps in the church, in the Order of Oddfellows and Equity Lodge and in serving the public—traits for which the B.Y.P.U. could claim considerable credit. This example, as well as a few more recalled here, associated with the New Glasgow meeting of 1947 underline and confirm the contribution of the black church in Nova Scotia to character building and to meritorious service to the whole province and the total population.

Other elected office bearers went on to carry out their respective responsibilities with equal credit and have earned a place in local and provincial levels: Beatrice Viola Johnson of Preston, Shirley Morgan of Windsor Plains, Lalia Smith of Halifax, Bradford Barton of Acaciaville, Donald Skeir of Halifax, Carl Evans of Preston and June Williams of New Glasgow. Licentiate Donald Fairfax, himself a young man and a product of B.Y.P.U., addressed the meeting and asked that old and outmoded traditions be abandoned in favour of progressive ideas: "Unless we......realize the seriousness of the times, we shall have to start all over again. We have the tools but we must be educated as to how to use them."

The church and its senior membership have continued to stress the same message over the years. It needs as much reinforcement to keep going in 1989 as it did in 1947 and as it will no doubt need in 2047—the point being that new actors and spectators will continue to appear on the scene, times will change, new challenges and circumstances will emerge, and new experiences will instruct the wisdom of the day. In 1989, Noel Johnston, now retired from school teaching, is still active in numerous organizations, Rev. Donald Fairfax is still active as pastor of the Victoria Road Baptist Church in

Dartmouth, Rev. Donald Skeir is pastor of the three churches in the Preston and Cherry Brook areas and Bradford Barton is the senior black school principal in Nova Scotia at the C.P. Allan High School in Bedford. They will no doubt echo in 1989 the words of Donald Fairfax of 1947 and in the process recognize what B.Y.P.U. did for them and will do for present and succeeding generations.

When the definitive history of the African United Baptist Association is written, there will be fuller mention of the role played by the moderators, the membership, the clergy, the committees and auxiliaries, the councils and the conventions. A book of considerable size will be needed to cover the ground from 1853-54 to 1989. Teachers and students as well as the public at large will easily obtain information from the churches and the pastors in the meantime. The annual minutes of the A.U.B.A. contain useful statistical information. At the time of the compilation of this book, the A.U.B.A. does not have a central office or building of its own. The most logical repository for this purpose would be the Cornwallis Street Baptist Church—the mother church—founded by Richard Preston, founder of A.U.B.A.

Over the years, the minutes of the A.U.B.A. carried reports from the Committee on Education, recalled here because of the stress placed on education and how education could be the great cure for societal ills. In 1948, the report stated that the indifference on the part of parents and children to higher education was fast disappearing and that though the number of high school students was still small, the number was growing. The 1951 report spoke of improvements in school buildings and equipment, a lack of black teachers for domestic science and industrial arts and, with pride, of two black university graduates from Acadia University. The 1952 report went even further to document considerable progress in the church family as more and more young people came forward to further their education and assume responsibilities. Both Donald Skeir and Donald Fairfax were ordained ministers in 1951, the report went on, and thus was begun a long and distinguished service to Nova Scotia by two distinguished sons who were joined in 1952 by Willard Clayton. All three rendered pastoral as well as educational services extending well into the next four decades. All three Baptist ministers were active in their respective churches in the Preston area, Dartmouth and Hammonds Plains as this chapter was being compiled in October, 1989.

In 1952, two other names surfaced as emerging aspirants for service in the ministry: Arthur Kelsie and Peter Paris, both of whom went on in succeeding years to complete their university studies and receive ordination. But neither Rev. Kelsie nor Rev. Paris was able to secure pastoral positions to serve the black Baptist Church in Nova Scotia. The remarkable thing is that this did not hold them back. After completing the B.A. degree at Acadia, Arthur Kelsie went to McMaster University in Hamilton to complete the requirements for the B.Ed. degree, took teacher training at the Ontario College of Education, went to teach in Ghana, West Africa from 1963 to 1965, ministered for a while at the First Baptist Church in Toronto, returned to his native province to take up an appointment with postal authorities and provided supply preaching in fifteen different churches—a remarkable and trend-setting achievement for the young man from Middle Sackville who could have sat back and waited for an opening to come up and in the mean-time blame the province, the economy, the church and the community for his woes.

The case of Peter J. Paris of New Glasgow is even more remarkable. In 1989, the Elmer G. Homrighausen Professor of Christian Social Ethics at Princeton Theological Seminary in the United States, Peter Paris has an aca-demic record second to none in the annals of Christian education in Nova Scotia. Holder of the B.A. and B.D. degrees from Acadia University and the M.A. and Ph.D. degrees from the University of Chicago, Peter Paris was ordained minister by the A.U.B.A. of the Atlantic Baptist Convention in 1959, taught at various universities in the United States, travelled widely in Africa, North America and Europe. In 1988, he was invited to deliver the Fifth Anniversary Lecture by the Black Cultural Centre for Nova Scotia; in 1989, McGill University conferred on him an honorary doctorate and Mount Saint Vincent University invited him to deliver the prestigious Seton Lecture in October, 1989.

Both Arthur Kelsie and Peter Paris are an embodiment of what black youth can and did achieve in the complex and much criticized Nova Scotian context which weighed heavily against black advancement. While it cannot be denied that obstacles existed—and will continue to exist—there is no substitute for hard work and determination. The balance sheet of black achievers in Nova Scotia has room for illustrious entries in various walks of life and neither the present generation nor the future generation can afford to bow its head in shame when presented with a list of names, at random, of such distinguished Nova Scotians as Edith Clayton (who died on the very day these lines were being written on October 7, 1989), William Pearly and Pearleen Oliver, Judge Corrine Sparks, Major Peggy Downes, Dr. Carrie M.

Best and her son, Calbert Best, Dr. Marie Hamilton and her daughter, Sylvia Hamilton, the teachers, lawyers, doctors, musicians, boxers, politicians, civil and public service people, community leaders, church leaders, business people, politicians, too numerous to mention by name in this narrative. This point is mentioned for the strong message it contains: make the loud and proper noises whenever necessary but fight the good battle by personal example and earnest endeavour, like Arthur Kelsie, Peter Paris and their kind did in the past and continue to do so in the present.

The absence of vacancies in the black churches in Nova Scotia to accommodate new recruits like Arthur Kelsie and Peter Paris pointed to the limitations facing the black churches and the communities they served: finances were extremely limited while the membership hardly warranted expansion of personnel and services. In the midst of this dilemma, a further problem developed as individuals and communities began to scatter in search of better economic opportunities. One committee of A.U.B.A. which looked at this situation and reported on it was the Rural and Urban Life Committee which was organized in 1950 to foster and co-ordinate programmes of a social nature which were relevant to the living standards of the communities served by A.U.B.A. The areas covered by this committee were education, housing, human rights, human relations and employment. In 1950, except for the Nova Scotia Association for the Advancement of Coloured People, there was no other black organization which covered the areas mentioned. When the Rural and Urban Life Committee was set up, the reasons were many. The A.U.B.A. had the responsibility as the most highly organized body in the black community to look at the social problems faced by this community in a concerted way and to provide moral leadership in matters of social change. This was an extremely challenging mandate which could well be likened to the secular wing of the church. Between 1950 and 1989, this committee was led by two powerful personalities who were dedicated public figures: Rev. Dr. William Pearly Oliver, previously mentioned in various pages, and Wayne Adams, broadcaster, affirmative action officer, businessman and county councillor. A study of the work and deliberations of the Rural and Urban Life Committee from 1950 to 1989 would produce a socio-economic picture of considerable importance, especially for the period before 1969 when a number of other organizations began to appear on the Nova Scotia scene to take up areas of specialization. In this brief overview of the work of the Committee only a few examples will be given.

In 1967, the Committee looked at the significance of the break-up of

Africville for the black church and the black community and stated in part: "The Church is a social institution and exists because of the communities. When communities disintegrate and are broken up, the church disappears......The question arises, does the church keep the community together or does the community keep the church together......?[45]

This was a question that Dr. Oliver and his fellow church leaders have had to grapple with for generations. The Rural and Urban Life Committee lamented the fact that the black community in the urban areas failed to organize themselves to develop their land. Dr. Oliver noted that in 1967 black residents in Halifax County comprised some 6000 of the population and owned hundreds of hectares of land within 25 kilometres of the cities of Halifax and Dartmouth. His view was that industrial and housing development would not take place until the community organized itself into concerted action: "All that is needed is credit and services. These could only be obtained if you are willing to organize and move as a group, not as individuals It is the Negro, as a group, that is denied housing not the individual exception. He gets by, but Negroes as a group are still unwanted."[46]

Dr. Oliver was speaking from personal experience of community development in the Beechville community through the Beechville Education and Community Development Association which was incorporated by provincial statute in 1967. One of its major undertakings was co-operative housing. By 1971, 26 out of 40 families living in Beechville were housed in new homes. This was the kind of effort that was suggested by the Rural and Urban Life Committee in the rural areas while it also gave attention to what was happening in the city areas by showing a film entitled "Conflict in Kwatcha House," following which the Committee held a meeting with the Mayor of the city of Halifax. The result of this meeting was the formation of the Mayor's Committee on the Employment of Negro Youth in 1968. A Human Rights code pamphlet was printed by the city to be placed in every business establishment while the City Council passed a resolution supporting adherence to the Nova Scotia Human Rights legislation prohibiting racial discrimination in areas of employment and accommodation. Indeed, the Rural and Urban Life Committee went as far as organizing a Human Rights Day on June 23, 1968 in co-operation with the Moderator of the African United Baptist Association.

Thus we see that as early as 1968, the City Council of Halifax was already expressing good intentions and commitments that were heard and made all over again in 1989. In 1968 the A.U.B.A., through its various committees, like the Rural and Urban Life Committee, was actively engaged in proposing and implementing schemes to raise the social and economic status of the black community while recognizing that the time had come for "a strong non-partisan undenominational Negro organization......so structured that it can plan programs based on a knowledge of the expressive needs of the people......"[47]

By 1968, the scale and complexity of black history and society had certainly reached the point when a provincial secular black organization was needed to complement the work of the black church and its various committees but not to replace them. The A.U.B.A., its churches and their committees have continued to function effectively and productively. Many provincial bodies have come into being since 1968—and we shall turn to them shortly—but none has challenged the primacy and the prominence of the religious institutions of the black community which have survived difficult times over three centuries.

In the opening sentence in this section reference was made to two province-wide organizations which represented black interests in Nova Scotia in the period 1945 to 1968: one was the A.U.B.A. while the other was the Nova Scotia Association for the Advancement of Coloured People whose establishment is mentioned in chapter three.

As at the time when this study ends in 1989, the N.S.A.A.C.P. will have been in existence continuously for 44 years. In the period up to 1968 its most valuable work was done in the areas of education, housing, employment and human rights as these issues related to the black population of Nova Scotia. After 1968, when a number of secular black organizations came into being, the N.S.A.A.C.P. has used its limited resources and its small membership to concentrate on awarding scholarships to deserving black students. An excellent example of its work in this regard can be gleaned from the Report of the Education Committee for the period March, 1988 to March, 1989 compiled by chairman, Calvin Ruck: 67 applications were received, 52 were successful and the total funds dispersed amounted to $15,711.

During its 44-year history to date, the N.S.A.A.C.P. has had six presidents: A.F. Smith (1945-47); R.S. Symonds (1947-50); Charles Wilson (1950-52); J. Wm. Carter (1952-54); Charles Wilson (for another term from 1954 to 1959); George Davis (1959-1963) and H.A.J. (Gus) Wedderburn (1963 to date).

A year after the Association was formed it gained prominence for its support to Viola Desmond, a Halifax Beautician, who was arrested on November 8, 1946 in the Roseland Theatre, New Glasgow, for sitting on a

Rev. William P. Oliver and deacons of the Cornwallis Street Baptist Church, mid-1940s. Back row (l-r): Donald E. Fairfax, Richard Symonds, Vernon Upshaw, Clarence H. Johnston, Thomas Gray; front row: Harriett Johnson (clerk), Rev. William P. Oliver, Pearleen Oliver, Mrs. Vernon Upshaw.

downstairs seat instead of the balcony seat to which Blacks were relegated on the basis of racially-segregated seating arrangements. Viola Desmond was thrown in jail for twelve hours for this offence and was charged the following day for attempting to defraud the federal government of one cent in amusement tax on the basis that the amusement tax for an upstairs seat was two cents and a downstairs seat was three cents even though the only ticket that Viola Desmond—a black person— could have bought in the cinema was one for an upstairs seat. She was sentenced to a fine of $20 plus costs or thirty days in prison. She paid the fine. The Association did appeal the decision but lost on a legal technicality though the learned judge agreed that the real motive in the case against Viola Desmond was "a surreptitious endeavour to enforce a Jim Crow rule by misuse of a Public Statute."[48]

The charter members of N.S.A.A.C.P. played a prominent part in the Viola Desmond case by convening public meetings and raising funds to defray the legal costs. They were: Arnold P. Smith, Richard Symonds, William Carter, Bernice Williams, Carl Oliver, Walter Johnson, William and Pearleen Oliver and Ernest Grosse. *The Clarion* newspaper, the second black newspaper in Nova Scotia which was founded July 26, 1946, used its columns to publicize this case and draw attention to the racial bigotry which was so rampant in Nova Scotia at the time in general and in New Glasgow, the home of its editor, Carrie M. Best, in particular.[49] The newspaper carried the judgement handed down by Justice W.L. Hall when he dismissed the application submitted by the Association for a "writ of certiorari" (an order for a Provincial Supreme Court to quash the decision of a lower court) by saying that "Had the matter reached the court by some other method than 'certiorari' there might have been an opportunity to right the wrong done this unfortunate woman."[50]

The Association and the black community knew that the wrong done to Viola Desmond was but one example in a long list of discriminatory practices from which Blacks suffered. In a teach-in on racial discrimination held at the Dartmouth High School in February, 1967, the chairman of the membership committee of the Association, Calvin Ruck, who has devoted more than a quarter century to various causes aimed at eradicating racial discrimination in Nova Scotia, pointed out that housing and employment were major areas in which Blacks felt the force of racial discrimination. Calvin Ruck has documented his experiences in various publications and speeches from 1968 when he was appointed to the position of social development worker for the Preston area.[51] He came to Halifax from his native Sydney, Cape Breton, in 1945—the very year the N.S.A.A.C.P. was founded—joined it in 1952, served for many years as chairman of the membership committee and then chairman of the scholarship committee, which position he currently holds in 1989.

The N.S.A.A.C.P., through speeches, conferences, press statements, and representations to government authorities, sought relief for Blacks in areas of housing and employment. As a result of the facts and figures that it produced, a strong case was made for the promotion of human rights in Nova Scotia through the creation of a Human Rights Commission with, a full-time provincial director. Through the efforts of this Association, the Nova Scotia Human Rights Federation was formed in December, 1966 under the chairmanship of Justice Gordon S. Cowan. Among the officers elected was H.A.J. Wedderburn, the president of N.S.A.A.C.P. The Nova Scotia Human Rights Federation was a private body whose advent in 1966 contributed to the steps taken by the Nova Scotia government to establish the Nova Scotia Human Rights Commission in 1967. The lobby of the N.S.A.A.C.P. in these developments was unmistakable. Indeed, it was at a meeting of N.S.A.A.C.P. that Hugh Macleod, the director of labour standards for the province of Nova Scotia, announced the imminent establishment of the Human Rights Commission.

The N.S.A.A.C.P. continued to press for more and better things for the black community. On October 25, 1968, Wedderburn led a delegation of six members of the N.S.A.A.C.P. and met with Premier G.I. Smith and Housing Minister James Harding for three hours discussing housing, education, employment and human rights as these issues affected Nova Scotia's black population. The delegation was drawn from a cross-section of the black population who could speak to the various issues affecting them: H.A.J. Wedderburn was a Halifax School principal at the time; Wilhemina Williams was a Windsor school teacher; Vernon Johnson was a Dartmouth High School student; Delmore "Buddy" Daye was a staff member of Neighbourhood Centre in Halifax; Carrie Best was a New Glasgow resident with considerable experience in media and community and Donald Oliver, Halifax lawyer and legal adviser to the N.S.A.A.C.P., a powerful and informed delegation whose agenda in 1968 was as forward-looking as anything that has gone forth since. The delegation requested that the administration of the Human Rights Act be transferred to the Human Rights Commission, domestics be included in the Minimum Wage Act, prohibited housing discrimination be extended to four or fewer units, more black history and literature in the school curriculum, and that books in elementary grades to be integrated to have more relevance for black children. Given the climate of the civil rights movement in the United States and the recent visit to Halifax of representatives of Stokeley Carmichael's Black Panthers, the delegation reminded the government of the increasing militancy of the youth and called upon the government to accept the responsibility for leadership to effect social change.[52]

Two months later, Premier G.I. Smith, addressing the Nova Scotia Human Rights Federation Conference, showed that the case presented by the N.S.A.A.C.P. delegation had not been forgotten: "If the disgrace of racial discrimination is to be completely purged, it won't be a triumph of government alone......It will be a triumph of leadership in the field of human rights in every Nova Scotia community......leadership by men and women responsive to the call of fundamental human justice."[53]

By 1969, the most prominent and public years of the Nova Scotia Association for the Advancement of Coloured People were virtually over though the organization has continued to exist. In 1945, the Association inherited the mantle of Dr. F.B. Holder's Colored Education Centre and became the province's first black secular organization. It became the training ground for contemporary as well as future leaders of the black community, including among its stalwarts such names as H.A.J. Wedderburn, W.P. Oliver, Calvin Ruck, Donald Oliver, Richard Symonds, Bernice Williams, Wayne Adams, Gertrude Tynes, Sandra Paris, Gerald Tynes, Sydney M. Jones, George Davis and J.E. Brindley—to name a few only. Whether in this volume or in other accounts of the black history and society of Nova Scotia, these names, as well as many other members and officials of the Association not mentioned here, feature prominently. In this respect, it was not only the work but the training and experience provided by the Association that must be counted among its most durable services.

As for its work beyond the training of leaders, the 44-year period may be highlighted by the following notable achievements. It organized the Africville relocation protest and protection. It made representations for the establishment of the Nova Scotia Human Rights Commission with empowering and effective legislation to combat racial discrimination. It established a scholarship fund to award bursaries. It made representations on behalf of aggrieved members of the black community suffering disadvantage and discrimination from whatever quarter, ranging from high-handed police to bigoted landlords. It provided support and co-operation since 1968 for the formation of such black organizations as the Black United Front, the Black Educators Association, the Black Cultural Society and the Black Cultural Centre—organizations which in one way or other took over the one-time global issues affecting the black population of Nova Scotia which had invariably ended up on the agenda of the Nova Scotia Association for the Advancement of Coloured People which responded as a dutiful custodian of black interests.

THE POLITICS OF THE 1960s AND THE EMERGENCE OF NEW ORGANIZATIONS

The early 1960s was a time of great ferment in the world. Colonialism was dead or dying; depressed and oppressed parts of the world were rebuilding, replanning, rethinking, new agendas were being planned and presented by continents and sub-continents which had been previously dominated by foreign European powers. Conspicuous among the emerging giants was the continent of Africa where 20 countries regained their independence in a single year in 1960, establishing a record for such a feat in modern history. Given this context, descendants of the African continent now living mainly in North America, South America and the Caribbean, could not remain unaffected, especially because they continued to be depressed and oppressed.

How North American Blacks were affected is best captured in the words of Dr. Martin Luther King, Jr.:

The American Negro saw, in the land from which he had been snatched and thrown into slavery, a great pageant of political progress. He realized that just thirty years ago there were only three independent nations in the whole of Africa. He knew that by 1963 more than thirty-four African nations had risen from colonial bondage. The negro saw black statesmen voting on vital issues in the United Nations—and knew that in many cities of his own land he was not permitted to take that significant step to the ballot box. He saw black kings and potentates ruling from palaces—and knew he had been condemned to move from small ghettoes to larger ones. Witnessing the drama of Negro progress elsewhere in the world......it was natural that by 1963 Negroes would rise with resolution and demand a share of governing power, and living conditions measured by American standards rather than by the standards of colonial impoverishment.[54]

While there was nothing comparable to the urgency and militancy of the United States situation in Nova Scotia, the problems in the black community were acute and the politics of discontent and protest was gaining ground. For a capital city, Halifax was a poor example of justice, care and compassion for the black population which had contributed in many ways to the growth of the capital city since its establishment in 1749. Wages and salaries for Blacks were the second lowest of all capital cities in 1960. Unemployment of Blacks was twice as much as whites. More black females than males were employed while black females earned a figure of $800 annually on average. Housing conditions in the crowded areas of Creighton and Maynard streets were legendary and continued to be a blot on the city's reputation. (In 1966, H.A.J. Wedderburn presented a proposal for the development and revitalization of the Creighton-Maynard Street area in which he argued that "although the cost of the total program may appear high, it should be remembered that the cost of poverty itself [in terms of welfare assistance and the unemployed, or indigent, when added to the cost of maintaining penal institutions] is even more exorbitant.") Of the 135 families living in this complex in 1960, the majority had inadequate housing in which they had to share the facilities. The educational achievements were at a low level with some six percent of the students completing high school while of the thirty Blacks who had acquired university degrees between 1960 and 1964, nearly all had left to take up employment elsewhere.

Between 1945 and 1970 the saga of Africville—the unfortunate relocation, the indifference of officialdom, the callousness with which the deed was done through the deployment of garbage trucks to transport people's treasured worldly possessions and the recourse to luring the obstinate by packing a bag with dollar bills—these and much more were adequate reasons for the appearance in 1969 of a number of organizations earmarked to serve the black population of Nova Scotia solely or primarily. The two organizations which fall into the former category are the Black United Front and the Black Educators Association while the institution alluded to in the latter category is the Nova Scotia Human Rights Commission, actually established in 1967 but only invested with empowerment and effectiveness through the passing of the Nova Scotia Human Rights Act in 1969.[55]

THE BLACK UNITED FRONT OF NOVA SCOTIA

The events which took place in Halifax, Nova Scotia, between November, 1968 and August, 1969 which resulted in the formation of this organization were set in motion by external factors which called for urgent and decisive local responses.

The opening round was a visit to Halifax by Stokeley Carmichael, the leader of the Black Panther movement in the United States. The Black Panthers subscribed to political change through the use of Black Power, a more militant approach than the civil rights movement associated with the leadership of the late Dr. Martin Luther King, Jr. who was assassinated on April 4, 1968.

As a perceptive commentator put it, a great many people were upset with the visit—and for different reasons. The comment referred to makes for interesting reading:

A great many people are upset about Stokeley Carmichael's visit to Halifax last month. As far as I'm concerned, if they're upset enough to do something about some of the conditions here, then Stokeley Carmichael ought to visit Halifax every weekend. I must admit that I'm upset too. I'm upset about the things that Stokeley Carmichael must have seen while here: bad housing; lack of recreation space; disinterested (sic) educators; young Negroes looking for work and a future to no avail; welfare institutions that perpetuate poverty; Negroes who lack information about their rights, and a human rights commission that has no teeth, no director and no meaning. This is the reality that we have to face. These things do exist in Halifax. They exist for both Black and White. But they are driven home with much more force for the black community......In the past, I have noticed the media throughout Canada have always referred to Halifax's "Black Problem." Let me now once and for all make something very clear. We do not have a black problem. We have a white problem. [56]

The fact that Stokeley Carmichael was the leader of the Student Non-Violence Co-ordination Committee in the United States was not sufficient comfort for those who felt uneasy about his trip and that of his fellow members of the Black Panthers, T.D. Pawley and Wardell Smith (also referred to as George Sams) who were invited to address a meeting of the N.S.A.A.C.P. The fact that the Black Panthers stayed with Burnley "Rocky" Jones, an articulate, charismatic Haligonian who caught the spirit of the youth movement for social justice in the 1960s (and continues to articulate and interpret this spirit in his more mature years in the late 1980s) was even less comfort to those who feared that a political storm was imminent in the calm Atlantic waters of Nova Scotia. There were three identifiable responses aptly summarized by the veteran black leader, Dr. W.P. Oliver:

Delmore "Buddy" Daye was a founding director of the Black United Front, a former Canadian boxing champion, and served as sergeant-at-arms for the Nova Scotia Legislature.

1. Whites became afraid, thinking it would mean violence and burning. They advised their black friends not to talk to the Panthers. Schools, churches and halls were subsequently closed to them. (Whites) The Police alerted.

2. Many Blacks suffered humiliation when they realized that their

social problems had attracted national publicity. Their pride was badly damaged.

3. Then there were the Blacks who felt the Panthers should be heard.[57]

A local newspaper described the atmosphere in the following words: "The appearance on the scene of the Black Power advocate Stokeley Carmichael last October, followed by representatives of the Black Panther group in the United States, indicated that the militant group was on the increase. The presence of these well-known militants caused precipitable jitters throughout the province, jitters which indicated a guilty conscience on the part of the Whites. If they had treated black people properly they would have had no cause for alarm; indeed the U.S. militants would not even have bothered to come to Halifax."[58]

But there was no reversing of the events underway. The Black Panthers were in town in November, 1968 to address a meeting of the only province-wide secular organization serving the black community at the time, the N.S.A.A.C.P., whose membership was open to Whites and Blacks. Pawley suggested that the mixed audience would inhibit the Blacks present and that it would be a good idea to hold a "black family meeting"—a proposal which met with the predictable mixed response, especially from Whites and older members of the black population at the meeting. Despite any misgivings the black family meeting was held at the Halifax Regional Library where some 400 members of the black population deliberated behind closed doors at what was described as the largest meeting of its kind held anywhere in Canada.

This Halifax meeting of black Nova Scotians held in the last week of November, 1968 marked the birth of the Black United Front of Nova Scotia under an Interim Committee chaired by the Rev. Dr. William Pearly Oliver. The other members of this seven-member Interim Committee, all drawn from the Halifax–Dartmouth metro area, were Burnley "Rocky" Jones, Edith Gray, Ross Kinney, Keith Prevost, H.A.J. Wedderburn, Councillor Arnold Johnson and Churchill Smith—all well-known in the black community, and all associated in one way or other with the N.S.A.A.C.P. or the A.U.B.A.

In an interview published shortly after the Interim Committee came into being, the chairman, Dr. Oliver, likened the new organization to an umbrella for the black family, an organization that would create unity through consensus, a kind of co-ordinating and catalystic body, "one of anti-violence, in favour of a new firmness, dignity, aggressiveness, even militance......wanting action in the immediate future."[59]

This catalogue of expectations was long and impressive. Since the turn of events that brought B.U.F. into existence happened so quickly, there was really no groundwork laid. While it was firmly decided that this was to be a black organization it was less firmly agreed whether the organization was to follow the path of radicalism which had found expression in, for example, the black students' protest against a university professor's alleged racial prejudice at Sir George Williams University for a whole year between February, 1968 and February 11, 1969. This was when black students set fire to the computer centre to prevent the police from gaining access to the faculty lounge and other offices occupied by the students. Subsequent government response to B.U.F. would show that the fact that one of the members of the newly-established Interim Committee had addressed a student rally at Sir George Williams University on February 4, 1969 was not lost on the highest levels of Canadian Government.[60]

Two months after coming into existence, the Interim Committee prepared and submitted a brief to the Secretary of State (Gerald Pelletier) and the Minister of Manpower and Immigration (Allan MacEachern). The case was made for the Black United Front to be a co-ordinating body for the existing black organizations in Nova Scotia, to supplement their activities but not to duplicate or replace any of the activities. B.U.F. would serve all the black communities in the province. It would strive to present a united voice for Nova Scotia's black population through the means of a "Black Consensus." It would promote and assist programmes relating to Afro-history and culture, businesses, drama, recreation, conferences, education, housing, employment and any other issues affecting the black population.

The brief which was presented in Ottawa on January 20, 1969 by three members of the Interim Committee, William Oliver, Gus Wedderburn and Keith Prevost, argued that:

Black people now for the first time in the history of the Nova Scotia Negro have collectively realized that their frustration emerges from the subtleties of racism and discrimination by the whites. They realize that they cannot fight the intangible thing called 'discrimination' without some power to control it. It is hoped that the Black United Front would be the tool that would assist in the developing of sufficient power to overcome the monotony of anxiety, frustration, poverty and depression caused by overt and insidious discrimination.

It is hard to see, from historical hindsight, how B.U.F. expected to achieve these most laudable goals given the fact that the leadership as well as the constituency serving it were virtually identical to the longer existing African United Baptist Association or the Nova Scotia Association for the Advancement of Coloured People which were in fact already doing the same things that B.U.F. had put on its agenda. In earlier pages and chapters references to racism and discriminatory practices were alluded to long before B.U.F. came into existence. Given this context, a heavy burden was placed on B.U.F. to do what its predecessors were supposedly unable to do.

In its brief of January 20, 1969, B.U.F. set out how it would do things differently by positing the following goals for itself: to achieve a black consensus in all matters involving black people in Nova Scotia, achievement of economic power, development of improved self-image, development of black leadership, the researching and documenting of problem areas, the development of consumer power and political power, the provision of opportunities for black people to analyze and define their own problems and to suggest their own solutions. The last goal stated was "co-operation and more Federal assistance."

On the point of federal assistance, a further brief, prepared by four members (William Oliver, Gus Wedderburn, Jules Oliver and Jesse Dillard) was presented to the federal government in March, 1969, seeking a grant of $100,000 for the first year of the program mainly for the appointment of an executive director, four field workers and for an extensive study of the black environment. There were necessary expenses involved in setting up the administrative structure, which was both complex and ambitious, including a council, a board of directors, and an administrative staff comprising the core staff and the projects staff. The chairman explained the structure and the immediate staffing in the following words: "This isn't a crash program. The flash in the pan programs of the past is why black people are in their present position."[61]

The federal government responded speedily and for a number of reasons of its own and in the process unwittingly set off a barrage of criticism against itself and B.U.F., thus beginning a chapter of unevenness which has, unhappily, visited this important organization in its twenty-year history to 1989. The Federal Minister of Health, John Munro, visited the Preston area in Halifax County on June 6, 1969, by-passing the county authorities, and said he was "shocked at the deplorable conditions that existed there." This was followed shortly afterwards by an announcement by the same minister that a grant of $100,000 to B.U.F. had been approved by the federal government. Two county councillors representing the area responded angrily. Councillor Arnold Johnson of North Preston said: "Mr. Munro was quoted in the local paper as saying the federal grant would help B.U.F. 'raise hell' by becoming a pressure group. B.U.F. didn't deny that they were a hell raising organization. It's my request to Dr. Oliver and his little hell raising group to stay the hell out of Preston." Dr. Oliver regretted that the Preston area had been drawn into the picture as a focal point of the federal government's interest. He made it clear that B.U.F. would be concerned with the community development of every black settlement in the province. This incident marked an unfortunate beginning.[62]

Eight years later, in 1977, a cabinet document was obtained and a disclosure made of the imperatives that influenced the government response at the time to the formation of B.U.F. A memorandum to Cabinet from the Cabinet Committee on Social Policy and Cultural Affairs, dated June 16, 1968, read in part as follows: "There was a possibility of violence in the black community of Nova Scotia and as possible disruption of the Canadian Games this summer by black militants. A grant now might alleviate this situation. Absence of support might enable black militants to take over from the moderates now in charge of the Black United Front......"[63]

On 15 August, 1969, a further announcement was made by the Minister of Health and Welfare that B.U.F. would receive a federal grant of $470,000 over the next five years from that ministry while the Secretary of State announced that an additional amount of $45,000 would come from that source over the next three years. Thus, with assured funding for a number of years, the Black United Front of Nova Scotia came into existence on a permanent basis in August, 1969.

With the advent of B.U.F. many new factors appeared on the Nova Scotia scene. For the first time in the history of Nova Scotia's black population a black organization could speak of funding in the region of half million dollars. For the first time a complex and challenging structure which included a council, a board, and a staff representing the entire province had come into being. Given the circumstances of its birth, its scope, its structure, its funding and the personalities involved, it was normal to expect both division and criticism from within the ranks of the black community as well as from outside. In the centre of both the fury and the fanfare was the steadfast figure of Rev. Dr. William Pearly Oliver whose name was destined to be associated with many major black organizations and institutions in Nova Scotia including the N.S.A.A.C.P., B.U.F., the Black Cultural Society and the Black Cultural Centre.

Dr. Oliver's biographer has reviewed the early difficulties faced by B.U F. as well as the early criticism. The fact that some of the founding members left the organization suggest that the black community was not altogether pleased with the new developments. What an "umbrella" organization was supposed to do when the very idea had been criticized before as taking away from existing organizational activities and programmes presented problems to B.U.F. throughout its twenty-year existence to 1989. Dr. Oliver had himself reported to A.U.B.A. as follows in 1968: "Another concern has been the tendency to create 'umbrella organizations' that are inclined to take over the programs carried on by existing organizations. This type of activity when initiated without consultation with residents......actually discredits their activities and weakens their leadership structure." Now it was being argued that B.U.F. would in fact enhance activities and strengthen leadership. Given the mixed reception that heralded the birth of B.U.F., it was an added disadvantage that the first Executive Director appointed was Jules Oliver, a well-qualified and able young man but who was the son of the Chairman of the Interim Committee who was looked upon by many as the power behind the throne.[64] A public meeting was held on September 6, 1969, attended by the 40 representatives from black communities in Nova Scotia who made up the Council and who adopted the following resolution: "We, the black people of Nova Scotia, are united in our aim to achieve full equality for all our people......(and) by this we mean, social, economic, and political. We support the Black United Front which will be the public organ of our people."

The first Board of Directors elected were the following 18 persons: W.P. Oliver (Halifax), Carrie Best (New Glasgow), Donald Oliver (Halifax), Carlyle Warner (Halifax), H.A.J. Wedderburn (Halifax), Sandra Paris (Yarmouth), Eldridge Brindley (East Preston), Neville Gibson (Sydney), P.A. Best (Yarmouth), Murray Warrington (Halifax), Jess Dillard (Halifax), Jules Oliver (Halifax), Delmore "Buddy" Daye (Halifax), Clyde Bishop (Cherry Brook), Anna Hunter (Amherst), Dorothy Marsman (Truro), Edith Cromwell (Bridgetown) and Howard Phee (Antigonish).[65]

Thus the largest black organization in Nova Scotia was now on its way. The path chosen was the middle path between the Black Panther movement in the United States and the Afro-Canadian Liberation Movement, which was started in Nova Scotia by supporters of the Panther movement. As Buddy Daye, community worker in the Neighbourhood Centre in Halifax, and a director of B.U.F. put it: "What you have is a lot of people suddenly realizing there are three ways to get something. First you ask for it, then you beg for it, and if that doesn't work, you take it."[66] How much of each of these approaches B.U.F. would take in the future, only time would tell.

In the first decade of its existence, B.U.F. moved into many worthy endeavours. It gave support to initiatives such as Blacks United for More Money, a welfare rights group concentrating on welfare and medical needs. It lent its good offices to serve as a liaison between welfare recipients and the welfare office. It started a newspaper called GRASP which got its name from the following key words: Growth—Readiness—Advancement—Self-determination—People (GRASP), signaling these attributes for itself as it moved towards providing its constituents with an avenue to voice their concerns. Unfortunately, GRASP did not survive the first decade.

B.U.F. also provided technical assistance to individuals and groups who applied for Initiative Program (LIP). It obtained a LIP grant for itself for a Health Workers Project which looked at the prevention of physical and mental health problems. The various LIP projects generated some 150 jobs in the black communities and led to the distribution of over a quarter million dollars among the black communities. B.U.F. could also claim some credit for the formulation of the plan in conjunction with the Continuing Education Division of the Nova Scotia Department of Education to build a black cultural centre. The Black Horizon television programme as well as the Black Horizon newsletter, and black cultural festivals, were other notable activities. It also submitted briefs on various occasions and thus took upon itself the role of articulating the black voice of Nova Scotia.

Its endeavours failed to dispel the criticisms which were expressed in 1968-1969 that B.U.F. had come along too soon, too hastily, too boldly, too unsurely and was too dependent on federal financial support. The Nova Scotia Black Students' Association for Higher Learning wrote to the Halifax 4th Estate in June, 1975 that "The Black United Front and the Human Rights Commission seem to be doing nothing to ensure that our people get a fair share in the social structure." When a member of the black community picketed outside the B.U.F. offices in 1977, it was symbolic of a disenchantment that was growing. It was in this climate that information on cabinet papers were made public. While a 1969 memorandum, referred to already, stated why it was urgent and imperative to fund B.U.F. to prevent it from falling into the hands of radical youth, a 1977 update showed how the continuation of that policy had secured the desired results for government:

> In 1975 the B.U.F. dispersed hundreds of thousands of dollars in government programming. The organization has been transformed from a potentially militant movement which might challenge the social structure which keeps N.S. Blacks at the bottom of society into part of the welfare state. B.U.F. now housed in one of Halifax's more exclusive office buildings serves as a buffer between militant Blacks and the State, a dispenser of patronage, in that time honoured Maritime tradition, and an avenue of advancement for the more opportunistic Blacks in the province. The existence of B.U.F. begins to dictate the nature of black politics in Nova Scotia for it is B.U.F. who have the offices, the newspaper and the government funds; and it is to B.U.F. that the media and the white establishment turn for "a black viewpoint." When John Munroe and Gerard Pelletier supported the funding of B.U.F. because they believed "that the leadership of the Black United Front represents the conservative and moderate elements within the Black community of N.S." they acted wisely. B.U.F. has served them well.[67]

When any organization is funded for the wrong reasons it cannot be held altogether to blame for conducting itself differently. Because so much was expected from B.U.F., it had to come up with quality performance and inspiring leadership. Its much-vaunted democratic structure from the grass roots upwards called for dedicated and informed citizenry who would understand as well as uphold democratic principles and practices personally and professionally.

As it entered into the second decade, B.U.F. became involved in research into the demography of Blacks in Nova Scotia and in co-operative ventures with other organizations which came into existence to look closely at specific issues and concerns. Between 1969 and 1989, a whole host of black organizations appeared on the scene. They were: the Black Educators Association, the Black Cultural Society, the Black Business Consortium, the Watershed Association Development Enterprise, the Black Cultural Centre, the Black Professional Women's Group, the Congress of Black Women, local chapter, the Association of Black Social Workers and the Afro-Canadian Caucus of Nova Scotia. As they appeared on the Nova Scotia scene, the role of B.U.F. became less central. The umbrella concept never really had a chance from the outset. There was a fleeting opportunity in 1985-86 when talks were underway to merge the Black United Front and the Black Cultural Centre to form a new body under a new name such as the Centre for Black Development. The proposal was defeated because of the opposition that came from B.U.F. The merger would have meant that B.U.F. would move its offices into the Black Cultural Centre in Cherry Brook but that both organizations would have continued to maintain their separate mandates.[68]

The merger talks in 1986 found the Nova Scotia black community deeply troubled and deeply divided. Besides the breakdown of the merger talks, the Black United Front lost its Executive Director, Richard Joseph, who resigned his position in great disappointment, saying that "the Black United Front has lost the will and the desire to serve the interest and needs of Black Nova Scotians. The major responsibility for this lies with the Council. However, I feel that the black community as a whole must share the blame. Black Nova Scotians have lost the will to take hold of their destinies and march into the future, but would rather wallow in the injustices of the past and die in the present." While the thrust of his disappointment was the Council itself, the entire community was drawn into his picture because of the structure of B.U.F.

Winston Ruck, former secretary of the Sydney Steelworkers Union and director of the Black United Front of Nova Scotia.

However hard the disappointment and the criticism, the present and the future could not afford to ignore his indictment of the leadership: "Since July, 1985, when this Council came into existence, there has been no direction, no decision making of consequence and not a single policy or proposal put forward. Indeed, more time has been spent at meetings discussing hotel accommodations rather than planning ways of dealing with the tremendous problems facing our community."

Between 1986 and 1988, the B.U.F. Council appointed and dismissed two executive directors as well as other staff members. The organization went through yet another period of crisis which reminded older members of the community and the public of other times in its twenty-year history when the organization faced difficulties of management, credibility and performance. In 1989, a new enthusiasm and a new direction were heralded under the banner of "A New Beginning" which was marked by the appointment of Winston Ruck (whose term of office turned out to be short-lived owing to poor health), retired trade unionist, one-time director and chairman of B.U.F. With this man of maturity, moderation and good commonsense at the helm, the new beginning may yet be the culmination of the hopes and expectations that were felt and expressed in 1968-69.

In the twenty-year period since 1969, the following have served as executive directors of B.U.F.: Jules Oliver, Hamid Rasheed, Richard Joseph, Gerald Taylor, Yvonne Atwell and Winston Ruck, with Captain George Borden as Interim Director between Rasheed and Joseph. The Black United Front has its offices in 1989 on Gottingen Street, Halifax.[69]

THE BLACK EDUCATORS ASSOCIATION

One of the most remarkable and enduring features in the history of the black population in Nova Scotia is the contribution of black teachers to the noble calling of their profession and also to the development of Nova Scotia's society in general. These women and men, whether in Granville, Acaciaville, Beechville or Africville, wherever in the province, in remote and ramshackle quarters in general, survived the odds and emerged as dedicated and deserving citizens. They served not only the black society but when circumstances permitted it they reached out and served the entire society.

In earlier chapters, reference has been made to the education system and legislation in Nova Scotia as well as to the part played by black teachers in the period up to 1945. Here the story will be taken forward to the present day. This will incorporate the work of the B.E.A. as formed in 1969.

To recapitulate the legislative framework within which education for black children was provided, segregated schools for Blacks legislated for in 1884 were re-affirmed in 1918 and continued until 1954 when the law was struck from the statute book. However, de facto segregated schools continued to exist. In 1964, there were some six segregated schools. In 1972, the school in Lincolnville was still a black school while the Nelson Wynder School in North Preston continues to be such a school to this day (1989). In 1987, in the all-black community of North Preston, the Nelson Wynder School had the following composition: of the eight full-time teachers, there was an equal number of white and black teachers; of the five special teachers, three were white. Given the fact that the proportion of black teachers in the schools in Nova Scotia is abysmally small, the composition of the Nelson Wynder School in North Preston in 1987, in an all-black community, is surprisingly disadvantageous to the black teachers since there is no good reason why a majority of black teachers should not be employed in an all-black school.

When a comprehensive book appears to document the lives and times of black teachers in Nova Scotia in the twentieth century, there will have to be room for over 150 teachers who, to 1989 alone, have left their mark on the educational landscape of this province. A few random samples will be reviewed in this section.

Edith (Mitchell) Cromwell began her teaching career with a permissive licence in 1939 at the Inglewood School, Bridgetown, until 1944—covered in chapter 3—and resumed her career in 1955 as Principal of the Sam Langford School in Weymouth Falls for one year before entering the Provincial Normal College in Truro (which black students were not allowed to attend in terms of the 1918 Education Act) for the 1956-57 academic year. Upon graduating in 1957, Edith Cromwell taught at C.F.B. Greenwood for the next twenty years before retiring in 1977. Edith Cromwell has continued to serve education and society since 1977 as a community worker, resource person on black history, member of the Annapolis District School Board and a past president of B.U.F.

Three other teachers who, like Edith Cromwell, held principalships in earlier years were Hattie Ash, Doris Ida (Clements) Evans and Irene Reddick. Hattie Ash obtained her early education in the Guysborough Academy and then at the Girls High School in Boston, Mass., began her teaching career with positions at Upper Big Tracadie and Sunnyville before assuming the principalship at the Mary Cornish Elementary School for five years in Lincolnville. Hattie Ash retired after giving more than 35 years service and continues to be active in church and community.

Doris (Clements) Evans has had a remarkably active career in school, community and society and continues to render service in 1989 with considerable enthusiasm. She began her teaching career at the age of 19 after completing the teachers' course at the Provincial Normal College in 1946, whereupon she had a choice of teaching at Hammonds Plains or East Preston at a time when black teachers could only teach in black segregated schools. Her first posting was to the newly-opened Partridge River School in East Preston in September, 1946 where she taught for twenty years, six of them as Principal. In 1970, Doris Evans moved to the integrated Ross Road School from where she retired in 1985—after 35 years of creditable service. Doris Evans remains active in public life as a director of the Black Cultural Society, Literacy Nova Scotia and as a member and official of numerous organizations. This gracious lady from the backwoods of Gibson Woods has become a regular feature of Canada's emergent open society for all citizens but counsels that much work remains to be done to counter the racial prejudice she experienced while growing up and even in her adult years as a school teacher at Ross Road School.

Irene Reddick was the Principal of the New Road School in North Preston for twenty years after which she transferred as a resource teacher at the Humber Park Elementary School. As a founding member of the Black Professional Women's Group, Irene Reddick has continued to be in touch with the church and her professional society.

Three teachers whose careers took them to Beechville at different times were Marion (Prevost) Skinner, Marie (Waldron) Hamilton and Lalia (Smith) Grant. Marion Skinner taught in Conway for a few months in 1943 and at New Road School from 1943 to 1945 after which she came to Beechville for two years. After a stint of four years as a field worker organizing church-related community activities she returned to teaching in schools in Beechville and Halifax, retiring in 1985 with 39 years teaching in all. Marie Hamilton received an honorary doctorate degree, the second woman in the black community to 1989 to be so honoured—the first being Carrie Best—in 1985 after fifteen years of teaching in the black communities of North Preston, Hammonds Plains, Beechville and Cherry Brook. Dr. Marie Hamilton has received the highest honour in the land for dedicated community service, the Order of Canada. Of the three teachers mentioned in this paragraph, Lalia Grant taught for the longest period—a total of 43 years, 35 of them in Halifax. She graduated from the Provincial Normal College in 1935 and, besides Halifax, taught in Digby and Beechville.

Among the teachers whose careers began in the mid-forties were Elsa Evelyn (Reddick) Barton who taught for a period of 35 years in East Preston, Cherry Brook, Upper Big Tracadie, Conway and Weymouth Falls before retiring in 1978; Patricia (States) Riley who retired in 1975 after 35 years service in Hammonds Plains, Cherry Brook/Lake Loon, North and East Preston, the Nova Scotia Home for Colored Children and Camp Petewawa in Ontario; Gertrude Evelyn (Phils) Tynes who taught Home Economics for 35 years in eleven schools throughout the province, ending her interesting career at

Cole Harbour District High School in 1985; Elizabeth Isabelle Smith from Weymouth Falls also taught Home Economics and, after twelve years of this service, recalled what a challenge, and also what excitement, it was to carry equipment in a station wagon, provided by the school board, from school to school.

Five teachers who had rendered valuable services to the community and the province were honoured in 1987 by the Black Educators Association. The oldest of them, Madeline Symonds, the first black teacher to graduate from the Provincial Normal College in 1928, is mentioned in chapter three. The remaining four are all in well-earned retirement in 1989 as this chapter reaches its conclusion. As mentioned earlier in a general comment on black teachers, these four continue to bring credit to the province and the profession by their continued contribution to the voluntary sector in particular and to society in general. Rev. Dr. Willard Clayton is not only a highly qualified and much-respected clergyman, ministering of late at Hammonds Plains and Beechville, but one who could look back on many years as a senior school administrator at Cole Harbour District High School, Graham Creighton High School and Weymouth Consolidated High School, having retired from school teaching in 1986. Delbert Hodges came to Nova Scotia in September, 1948 after teaching for six months in an all white community in New Brunswick in that year. He obtained a teaching position in East Preston and remained there for 38 years. He was also Principal of Lake Loon School for several years. Noel H. Johnston was the first black teacher—and the only black teacher to date—to graduate in Industrial Arts and became the Industrial Arts Instructor for Halifax County, and also Instructor for Adult Vocational Education in Dartmouth before being promoted to Head Instructor in Halifax. The last in the list of the 1987 honorees, Roland Lorne White is a well-known Nova Scotia and Canadian personality, the son of Rev. Dr. William Andrew White, referred to in early pages, and the brother of Portia White. The holder of a string of university degrees—Bachelor of Arts, Bachelor of Education, Master of Physical Education, Master of School Administration, Lorne White was a successful school teacher and vice principal who retired after 35 years of teaching, 13 years of which were spent as vice-principal of Bloomfield School in Halifax. This veteran teacher who sat on such high bodies as the Nova Scotia Appeals Board and the Canadian Council on Multiculturalism and performed on radio and television in a way no other teacher in Nova Scotia did during his years, retired in 1986 without having been accorded what many of his peers and well-wishers felt was

Rev. Donald Skeir is honoured by his peers, Doug Skinner and Johnny Saunders, November 1960.

his well-earned reward—a school principalship in the province he served so faithfully and so selflessly.

One famous black Nova Scotian who became a teacher by chance, has provided a personal testimony which tells of a concerned citizen who responded to the call of public service in the 1960s in North Preston where it was so difficult to get teachers. What started off as temporary help, led to 24 years of teaching and a teaching diploma with which to do it. The Reverend Donald D. Skeir retired from teaching in 1986 for health reasons. He has left us this moving testimony to a noble profession:

> I had come to admire the teaching profession and those involved in it, especially upon learning of the sacrifices and dedication of those teachers in the past. The status and benefits of teachers today is a vast improvement over the pioneers. I felt it a privilege to be involved in this badly-needed effort to improve the communities and to serve as a role model for young Blacks......Teaching is a living experience in that every day is a new day. It is really wonderful to see the sparkle and

wonderment in the faces of the children......I enjoyed the loving affection children had for their teachers, regardless of race......I can truthfully say I enjoyed my years in teaching. It certainly supplemented my total career as a pastor and community, leader. I only hope I did some good, though little it may have been.[70]

Like his fellow pastors, Willard Clayton, referred to previously, and Donald Fairfax, one-time school principal in North Preston and teacher at the Nova Scotia Home for Colored Children, Donald Skeir has left his imprint on the Nova Scotia educational scene.

Another testimony comes from Deacon Churchill Stewart Smith, a respected member of the black community, one-time Moderator of the African United Baptist Association, whose two teacher-sisters, Elizabeth Smith and Florence Bauld are mentioned in sections of this chapter, tried his hand as a part-time teacher in North Preston in 1955-56 but chose to build upon his previous business college education which led after decades of serious endeavours to the position of Staff Officer, Civilian Training Administration at Maritime Command Headquarters, HMC Dockyard, Halifax, in 1986. The fact that this native-born Haligonian from Bear River made it in what is understood to be a hard field for Blacks, must itself be a confirmation of the plea that many have made before and many continue to make today: Don't blame it all on racism and unfair practices—however much they exist. Do something to overcome them as Churchill Stewart Smith did. His testimony has a salutary message for young people:

The need for a good education and formal training was not seen as a necessity 30 years ago as there was employment available for those with very little training or education. However, my parents and sisters encouraged me......to get a good education and stay in school so I might get a good job when I leave school. I am glad I listened to their good advice and obtained a high school education and continued my education beyond high school, otherwise I would not be where I am today. It is more important today to obtain a good education and a trade or training in a specialized field. A high school education is not good enough today because one could graduate from high school and still not be qualified for any particular job. With the advance age of machines and high technology, such as the use of computers, specialized skills are a must.[70]

It was surely thinking of this kind and beyond in the heady and challenging days of 1969 that led people like the first president of the Diogenes
Teachers' Study Club, Delbert Hodges, and another active member of the
club, H.A.J. Wedderburn, both of whom were connected with the East
Preston School—Hodges since 1948 and Wedderburn as Supervising
Principal from 1957 to 1961, to extend the philosophic discussions of the
Diogenes Club to reflect on the reality of the challenges confronting black
teachers in the education system. Gus Wedderburn was particularly well
qualified with B.A., B.Ed., and M.A. degrees added to his senior standing as
a Supervising Principal, followed by five years as Science and Mathematics
teacher at the Bloomfield Junior High School, Halifax from 1961 to 1967, one
year as Vice-Principal at the same school, culminating as Principal of the
Ardmore Special School in Halifax from 1968 to 1971, to give leadership to
black teachers. As President of the Nova Scotia Association for the
Advancement of Coloured People since 1963 and Chairman of the Africville
Relocation Committee and as Co-Founder and Chairman of the Nova Scotia
Civil Liberties Association, Wedderburn's interest in the well-being of the
black community was well founded since the late 1950s when he came to

**H. A. J. "Gus" Wedderburn was president of the Nova Scotia Association for the
Advancement of Coloured People and co-founder of the Nova Scotia Civil
Liberties Association.**

the Maritimes from his native Jamaica. Another active member of this Club was a lady who went on in future years to acquire a formidable string of degrees, Donna Lee Byard Sealey, B.A., B.Ed., M.A., who was the first black teacher from Truro to graduate from the Normal College which was located in her home town.

Beginning with the meetings of the Diogenes Club, a Negro Education Committee was set up in 1969 to investigate the quality of education for black students in Nova Scotia. Two years later, the Black Educators Association of Nova Scotia was formed out of the Negro Education Committee. The chairman during these foundation years was H.A.J. Wedderburn (1969-1972), who left the teaching profession to take up the practice of law in 1973. The chairmanship of B.E.A. from 1972 to 1989 was held by five persons: Rev. Dr. Anna Hunter (1972-74), Brad Barton (1974-1978 and 1983-1987), Gerald Clarke (1978-1980), Patricia Barton (1981-1982) and Sheila Cole (1987-1989).

As can be expected from a professional organization committed to advancing the quality of education as well as access to equal opportunities for black Nova Scotians and other minorities, the scope of the activities of the Black Educators Association is very wide indeed. It reaches out to parents and students through workshops and conferences. It works on common areas of mutual interest with other black organizations, the Nova Scotia Department of Education, the Multicultural Education Council of Nova Scotia, the Nova Scotia Human Rights Commission and the Nova Scotia Teachers Union, to name a few organizations and institutions.

In its twenty-year history to 1989, B.E.A. has made a considerable impact on the Nova Scotia scene. The success registered by its leaders and members through their professional, public and community roles adds to the credit of the Association. The profile of Brad Barton is a case in point. Having served as chairman of B.E.A. for 8 years, his achievements have brought credit to the profession, the province, the Association and the international community. Hailing from Acaciaville in rural Nova Scotia, Brad Barton graduated from Digby High School, began his teaching career in North Preston, went to Teachers College and became a Physical Education teacher at Bedford Junior High School before becoming a department head at Sir John A. Macdonald High School. The upward journey had begun and this modest young man made good in rapid strides: vice-principal, then principal of Graham Creighton Junior High, principal of Bell Park Academic Centre and in 1988 principal of the C.P. Allan High School in Bedford—the

290

Bradford Barton, prominent teacher, principal, and administrator was awarded the Order of Canada in 2000.

first black teacher in Nova Scotia's history to hold this rank in the teaching profession. He has also made considerable strides as an international referee and official at the Pan-American Games and the Olympics in the sport of volleyball which is so close to his heart.

There are other black teachers waiting in the wings to walk in Brad Barton's footsteps. While this happens, the Black Educators Association continues to grow in strength and scope. In 1984, Angela Cromwell was appointed Secretary/Information Officer. In August, 1988, Gerald Clarke, one-time president of B.E.A. was appointed the first Executive Director of the organization on secondment by the Department of Education from the Halifax City District School Board with a two-fold mandate, to help raise the overall level of educational achievement within the black community by working with students, parents, teachers, school, and school systems and to survey the provincial school systems so as to locate black students within the educational system.

The introduction of this office to be filled on an annual basis is a significant one. For the first time in the province, a senior black teacher and member of B.E.A., Gerald Clarke, was able to give undivided attention to the needs of black students. The first holder of the office of Executive Director has impeccable qualifications: B.Sc., B.Ed., M.Ed. He began his teaching career in the Richmond School in Halifax in 1966, became vice-principal at Westmount in 1973, acting vice principal at Halifax West High School in 1982-84 after which he became vice-principal at Fairview Junior High. On completion of his year as Executive Director of B.E.A., Gerald Clarke was appointed acting principal of Clayton Park Junior High School. His stocks are indeed rising.

The second Executive Director, appointed in August, 1989, was Robert Thomas Upshaw, a graduate of Acadia University, who was seconded from

Graham Creighton Junior High School where he has taught Social Studies, Health and Physical Education for eight years. He brings to this position much energy and enthusiasm. As one of the younger members of the teaching profession, his youthful enthusiasm and commitment will serve the Association well. The seriousness of purpose of the Black Educators Association is well established. What it needs to do as the years go by is to consolidate its work and respond effectively to the current situation. As the Executive Director's report dated April 15, 1989 put it: "As a significant black organization, the B.E.A. must make every effort to increase the level and spirit of co-operation to the development of heightened awareness [of] and sensitivity to issues facing society as a whole."

The day must surely come when B.E.A. will have no need to represent a parochial cause, when the education system and every other system in Nova Scotia will provide equally and justly for all Nova Scotians. Until then, it has an important function to perform.

On September 23, 1989, B.E.A. celebrated its 20th anniversary and honoured four retired teachers: Florence (Smith) Bauld, Rev. Donald Douglas Skeir, Dr. Marie Hamilton and Nazir Rizvi. Of this list, Florence Bauld started her teaching career in Weymouth Falls and moved to Lucasville before taking up a position at the Partridge River School for twenty years. A graduate of the Normal College and Saint Mary's University, this accomplished teacher also obtained an Education Diploma in Music. She spent the last thirteen years of her teaching life at the Nelson Wynder and Allan W. Evans schools from 1975 until her retirement in 1988.

Dr. Marie Hamilton, mentioned previously in this chapter, taught in the predominantly black communities of North Preston, Hammonds Plains, Beechville and Cherry Brook for 15 years. Upon retiring, Dr. Hamilton began work with the Early Childhood Education program training local women to run pre-school programs. Her education work included tutoring adults in the literacy program at the North Branch Library, Halifax.

The third teacher honoured in 1989 was the Rev. Donald Skeir, also previously mentioned in this chapter. Rev. Skeir taught for 24 years in three schools, North Preston Elementary School, Sir Robert Borden Junior High School and the Bell Park Academic Centre.

The fourth teacher honoured was Nazir Rizvi whose teaching career in Nova Scotia, like Rev. Skeir's, extended over a period of 24 years since 1964. He taught in Middleton, N.S., then moved to Graham Creighton High School in 1966 and finally to the Cole Harbour District High School.

In honouring the retired teachers, the Association was carrying out a time-honoured tradition of remembering the past for the sake of the present and the future. With very few new teachers being recruited, most of the black teachers in service are, in 1989, in their early or middle years with only a very few within striking distance of retirement. Whatever the numbers in the profession, the B.E.A. will continue to be challenged and kept busy. Its new constitution provides for greater participation from the general society who can join the Association through anyone of its expanded categories of membership: regular, associate and membership-at-large and also through service on a advisory board. The Association's first volume of Beneath the Clouds of the Promised Land: The Survival of Nova Scotia's Blacks, 1600-1800 appeared several years ago. With the appearance of the second volume in the form of this book, a significant project has been completed.

As it moves beyond the 20th anniversary, the Association can rightly define its own position, as it did in the concluding paragraph of its anniversary brochure:

> The Black Educators Association has become a formidable force in the development and implementation of educational policies and programs in this province. It has survived a twenty-year struggle against the complacencies and ineptitude of a system, often content to maintain the status quo, to stand proudly as a grass roots organization with a dream. This 20th Anniversary celebration marks not an end, but a beginning. This struggle will not be over until every black child is able to maximize his potential in the schools of Nova Scotia. There will be new challenges and new directions for the current sixty members of the Black Educators Association, but their dedication will not go unrewarded. The B.E.A. has come of age."[71]

When taking stock of its twenty-year history, B.E.A. acknowledged the support it received over the years from the Department of the Secretary of State, the Nova Scotia Department of Education and the Nova Scotia Human Rights Commission. Dr. George William Frederick McCurdy, who joined the Nova Scotia Human Rights Commission in 1971, and Dr. Paul Anthony Johnstone, who was appointed Co-ordinator of Ethnic Services for the Nova Scotia Department of Education in 1974, were among the earliest supporters of B.E.A. Both received most honourable mention in the 20th Anniversary booklet of the Black Educators Association, together with a third distinguished Nova Scotian, Dr. William Pearly Oliver, previously mentioned in various pages of this chapter. All three, who have passed on, have left an important influence on the B.E.A., its work and its members. Their legacy to education, human rights and the church is an important part of contemporary black history and culture in Nova Scotia.

THE SOCIETY FOR THE PROTECTION AND PRESERVATION OF BLACK CULTURE IN NOVA SCOTIA (THE BLACK CULTURAL SOCIETY)

This Society was incorporated by an Act of the Nova Scotia Legislature on May 19, 1977 with the main objective of raising funds to build a cultural centre to serve primarily but not exclusively the black population of Nova Scotia.

When the matter of a cultural centre was first raised, the parties involved were the Continuing Education Program of the Nova Scotia Department of Education and the Executive of the Black United Front. The link between these two parties was Dr. W.P. Oliver who, in 1972, was a Regional Representative in the Adult Education Division where he had been employed for almost a decade. His other link role came from his influential position in the Black United Front, which he had served as Interim Chair from November 1968 to September 1969 after which he retained his position as director with the added status of an elder regarded as the Board's Honorary Chairman. In consultation with the two parties, Dr. Oliver prepared a proposal for a Cultural Education Centre to be sponsored by B.U.F. since it had province wide representation and by the Continuing Education Program since it had been involved in educational programs in the black communities since 1949. In making his case, Dr. Oliver argued as follows:

> What I have endeavoured to say is that the problem of cultural awareness, self-identity and self-esteem represent formidable problem areas for the black minority. They are so formidable that a limited few are able to overcome its repressiveness. Unless calculated efforts are directed toward these problem areas, the result will be a locking in of expediency forms of behavior, completely unrelated to and inconsistent with the value system of the majority society. One means to remedy and overcome cultural awareness within any minority group is the provision of an adequate facility where they can be exposed to their

own culture and at the same time share their culture with other cultural groups. Both functions must be performed concurrently.[72]

The proposal was favourably received by both the Education Department and the B.U.F. executive who viewed this development as the logical third phase in the progress of the black community since 1945: phase one being the N.S.A.A.C.P., phase two being B.U.F., and phase three the Black Cultural Education Centre.

The proposal also received a favourable response from the provincial government which hosted a luncheon meeting for invited members of the black community on October 26, 1974 to discuss the matter further. At this meeting Donald Oliver, a black lawyer who had been practising since 1965 after a distinguished academic performance in high school, university and law school, was invited to chair a committee which would convene a provincial meeting of black representatives to put the machinery in motion to erect a

A Steering Committee of eleven members was formed to carry out this important assignment. All of these committee members deserve special mention in the more recent history of Nova Scotia's black population. Some of them had been involved in different ways in the development of the earlier stages mentioned above: Donald Oliver, Rev. P.A. Best, Geraldine Browning, Arthur Criss (now Hamid Rasheed), Edith Cromwell, Rev. Donald Skeir, Neville Gibson, Rev. Dr. W.P. Oliver, Ken Pinto, H.A.J. Wedderburn and Joan Browne. The committee divided itself into various sub-committees to deal with liaison with government, artifact finding, site development, community relations, architectural design and planning and fund raising. It held a number of local and regional meetings throughout Nova Scotia preparatory to the convening of the Black Cultural Conference in May, 1976. It was at this crucial and historic meeting that the delegates agreed to erect the Black Cultural Centre "as a portrayal of the sum total of the attainments and activities of the black people of Nova Scotia" on a site to be obtained through negotiations with the Nova Scotia Home for Colored Children in Westphal, Halifax County.

The rest happened very quickly and effectively. The Act of Incorporation of the Society for the Protection and Preservation of Black Culture in Nova Scotia was passed a year later. The first meeting of the foundation Board of Directors (then referred to as the Executive Committee) was held on 15 August, 1977. The first Directors and office-bearers were as follows: J.C.

Mack, D.H. Oliver, K. Pinto, Alice Croft and Joan Browne (Halifax); D.E. Fairfax and H.A.J. Wedderburn (Dartmouth); P.A. Best (Yarmouth); W. Ruck and N. Gibson (Sydney); Hazel Johnson (Annapolis County); W.P. Oliver (Lucasville); Geraldine Browning (Kings County); Carrie Best (Pictou County); Jeanette Brown and W. Bryant (Colchester County); Pat Skinner and L. Clarke (Antigonish County); D.D. Skeir, Carolyn Thomas and Joyce Ross (Preston); Elsie Elms (Guysborough County); Anna Hunter and J. Davidson (Cumberland County) and R. Gibson (Queens and Shelburne Counties).

The first President was Donald Oliver. In its 12-year history to date (1989) the Society has been served by the following persons in succession as presidents: H.A.J. Wedderburn, Geraldine Browning, Ruth Johnson and Alma Johnston. The Act of Incorporation, which is in fact the constitution of the Society, provided for 27 members drawn from all over the province with one representative from A.U.B.A. This representative has usually been the Moderator. The Act provided for an Honorary President in the person of Dr. W.P. Oliver. With his death on 26 May, 1989, this position has ended.

With the coming into being of this society, which is commonly known by its short title, the Black Cultural Society, the hoped-for joint structure conceived and publicized in the original proposal of 1972, was abandoned in favour of an independent structure. What led to this has never been made public. There are two possible explanations: disenchantment with the strength and image of B.U.F. or rejection by B.U.F. itself which by now had had an independent existence for almost eight years. The organizational chart in the 1972 proposal placed the Board of Directors of B.U.F. at the top. Under it came the Executive Director of B.U.F. and the Board of Directors of the Black Cultural Centre. The Cultural Centre came under its own board with a co-ordinator at the head of its own staff. The overall control of the cultural centre would be vested in B.U.F. In this scheme there was no place for the Black Cultural Society as the parent body running the Black Cultural Centre. What all this suggests is that the umbrella concept, the much-vaunted call for one black voice, a united people chartering a common programme, never really got off the ground and, in 1989, remains an elusive dream. When Africa, and much of the present Third World, was under foreign domination, their new nationalists, filled with the euphoria of the coming glory one day, preached the virtue of continental or regional unity. When the day of glory arrived, separate flags were raised and separate, fragmented, and often woefully weak, countries came into being and have perpetuated their separateness. Perhaps this is what happened when organizations proliferated in Nova Scotia. When an opportunity came to reverse the trend in 1986, leaders and pace-setters were not ready or willing. It should no longer be thought possible since the post-1969 organizations have defined specific agendas for themselves.

The agenda for the Black Cultural Society was one such specific agenda: the building of a cultural centre. In 1979, Sharon Ross was appointed Project Co-ordinator with the task of raising funds from all levels of government, business firms, groups and individuals. In the end, $1.2 million was raised. The official sod-turning ceremony was held on April 24, 1982 and within the remarkably short time of seventeen months, the task was completed and the Black Cultural Centre was officially opened on 17 September, 1983 at a function graced by the presence of the federal Minister of State, Gerald A. Regan and the then premier of the province of Nova Scotia, John M. Buchanan.

The word "Education" was dropped in the name given to this remarkably impressive building—the only one of its kind in the whole of Canada owned and run by a black community organization and located in the very heart of one of Canada's oldest black settlements. The Black Cultural Centre for Nova Scotia houses a museum, an auditorium, a reference library and office space.

Official opening of the Black Cultural Centre for Nova Scotia, September 17, 1983. Left to right: Rev. Dr. William P. Oliver, Hon. John M. Buchanan (premier of Nova Scotia), H. A. J. Wedderburn (president), Hon. Gerald A. Regan (federal minister of state).

Rev. J. C. Mack, Ruth Johnson, and Rev. Donald Skeir at the unveiling of a plaque dedicated to Dr. William P. Oliver in 1989.

In the six years of its existence since 1983, the Centre has proceeded gradually but purposefully to implement the objectives which represent the raison d'etre for its existence, to create an awareness of the black identity, the black heritage and the black experience within the black communities, to create a confident and healthy self-concept among Blacks, to disseminate knowledge and understanding of these factors and features among the broader Canadian community, to cultivate a spirit of harmony and mutual respect upon which will be founded a meaningful society of equal partners in a multicultural setting.

The Black Cultural Centre is a place of pride for all Nova Scotians and Canadians who are strengthened by the knowledge so graphically presented in pictures, paintings, artifacts, books, exhibits, slides and videotapes of the contribution of great and ordinary men and women who graced the provincial, national and international stage and brought glory to Nova Scotia and human kind including William Hall, V.C., Portia White, Sam Langford, Richard Preston, George Dixon, William Pearly Oliver, Edith Clayton, Mum Suze, Wellington States, and many, many others, dead and living, young and old, urban and rural, well-known or little-known. It includes exhibits on the community, the church, the military, the sporting personalities. The publications of the Black Cultural Centre include the five Anniversary Lectures given by James Walker, Gilbert Scott, Pamela Appelt, Peter Paris and Marguerite (Peggy) Downes and books by Calvin Ruck, Colin Thomson, Mohamed Abucar, Raymond Parker, George Borden, John Grant and Charles Saunders.[73]

It is not possible to list the many concerts, conferences, workshops and public lectures organized by the Centre during its first six years. Thousands of students and adults from all over Nova Scotia and Canada and indeed other parts of the world have visited the Centre. It is now listed in tourist brochures in this country and in the United States. Its doors, its services and its membership are open to everyone. The financial support it has received from the federal government for projects and the provincial government for operations have been used with care to promote the Centre's activities under the able and committed guidance of its Board of Directors and a small core staff, one of whom, Maxine Brooks, has been with the Centre since its inception and who, since August, 1989, headed the Centre Staff on an interim basis. The Centre's first curator, Henry Bishop, is still active. The present project officer is Anne V. Johnson while the other core members in 1989 are Ramona Hill, Richard Sparks and Elroy Howe. The Centre's first Executive Director was Frank Boyd, Jr. The second Executive Director, Wayne Adams, served for some fifteen months on secondment from the civil service between 1985 and 1986 while the third incumbent of this office is the author of this volume, Bridglal Pachai, who began his service as program director in April, 1985 and succeeded Wayne Adams in 1986. In August 1989, Dr. Pachai was invited by the government of Nova Scotia to assume the directorship of the Nova Scotia Human Rights Commission following the death of Dr. P. Anthony Johnstone on July 30, 1989.

The Centre's involvement in 1989 with the Africville project already mentioned is but one example of the co-operative ventures it engages in with black organizations, other organizations and institutions, including universities and schools. At a time when the call for more black history and more information in general about black society and culture is being sounded in various places and in various forms, the Black Cultural Society and the Black Cultural Centre have important functions to perform in carrying out their mandate.

OTHER ORGANIZATIONS

A number of organizations have come into being to promote the economic development of the black communities and individuals since the 1950s. They have met with varying degrees of success to date for a number of reasons. The economic base of Nova Scotia's black population has been weak because of historical factors and circumstances connected with slavery, segregated settlements, poor employment opportunities, racial discrimination and prejudice, limited communal markets, lack of access to capital, absence of family traditions of successful business, absence of government contracts and so on. But efforts have been made and continue to be made to develop business skills and to undertake innovative ventures on relatively modest scales.

The George Washington Carver Credit Union, inaugurated on July 17, 1950, through the initiatives of three leading members of the Dartmouth–Preston communities: Councillor A.W. Evans, J.A. Ross Kinney, Superintendant of the Nova Scotia Home for Colored Children and Coulter B. States, senior employee with the Canadian National Railways, is still in existence in 1989. While the Credit Union operated as such unions do to encourage savings and to grant loans, this Credit Union was also concerned with recreational facilities to promote social, cultural and sporting events. Over the years, its membership and capital increased modestly under the stewardship of its president for many years, Noel H. Johnston of East Preston whose residence holds the offices of the Credit Union in 1989.

The Black Business Consortium whose founding Memorandum of Agreement was signed on November 24, 1981 under the chairmanship of David Hill, published a directory of black businesses in the province, makes representations to government on behalf of its membership, holds meetings and provides a structural framework for its organization. Its principal aims and objectives are to promote the formation, growth and development of profitable minority-owned businesses and to preserve and protect existing minority firms. It strives to promote an environment that is conducive to the growth and development of black business. It attempts to gain access to domestic and international markets. It strives to obtain capital from public and private sources. These endeavours require imaginative and responsible leadership so that proper representations can be made, confidence cultivated and co-operation among members engendered. With over one million small businesses operating in Canada in 1989, the majority in the hands of immigrant Canadians, the competition in this field is extremely keen. However, the black community in Nova Scotia has a particularly strong and relevant reason to press on towards economic advancement which is a good cultivator of self-esteem and a strong answer and deterrent to racial prejudice. In a survey conducted by the Black Cultural Centre in 1985-86, over fifty black businesses were identified in the province. If this figure is accurate, the economic position in this regard is quite bleak and much catching-up needs to be done urgently.

The North Preston Ratepayers' Association is an example of a community organization whose mandate is wide and all inclusive. The Association was founded in the late 1940s by Councillor Allan W. Evans to serve both North Preston and Cherry Brook. After an existence in this form for three years, the North Preston Association branched on its own under the direction of such local personalities as Clarence Johnson, Peter Downey, Bernard Cain, Joseph Smith and Arnold Johnson. The Association came into being to promote the socio-economic life of the community by acting as the mouthpiece of the community. Over the years, it looked into the various sides of community development: housing, water, sewage and employment. North Preston is the largest black community in Nova Scotia. In the middle years of this century the media presented a negative image of this community which in actual fact has fought long and hard to improve itself on the basis of family businesses, self-help projects and agricultural initiatives. When Edna Staebler wrote an article in *Maclean's Magazine* of May 12, 1956, she was constrained to record the testimony of more knowledgeable people who admired the fortitude of the residents of North Preston:

> I went to the government buildings to study the county and provincial records of New Road and to talk to the men who'd compiled them. They told me the settlement has been called the most depressed area in Canada. Until not long ago, its people lived on what they could find on the barrens to eat or to sell. They cut wood, they picked berries, they fished. A trip into town took them all day; they started at dawn in an open cart drawn by an ox and the women would sit at the Halifax market with Mayflowers, tea berries, Christmas wreathes, while their men peddled bean poles, twig brooms and tubs they had made.

Here was a story of the struggle for survival that the media and public commentators often missed. This was the community that started its volunteer fire department, its Medical Child Care Society, its Senior Citizen's Organization, the Anne V. Johnson I.O.D.E. chapter, the North Preston Girl Guides, North Preston Brownies and so on in an effort to raise quality and standards. In 1989, North Preston can no longer be described as one of the most depressed areas of Canada.

THE BLACK PROFESSIONAL WOMEN'S GROUP

This group was organized in 1969 by a few teachers to honour some of their number for successfully completing a course of study. Its interests soon extended to seek improvements in the working conditions of teachers and also to assist teachers to improve their qualifications. Its scope and membership soon expanded to include black professional women from all sectors of employment. Its founding members and office-bearers of 1969 were all teachers—most of them mentioned in other contexts in this chapter—Alma Johnston, Florence Bauld, Doris Evans, Lalia Grant and Patricia Riley, and its executive in 1989 are still mainly teachers, both practising and retired.

At its 20th Anniversary Recognition Dinner, the Group honoured Florence Bauld, its first vice-President, Dr. Carrie Best, founder of the *Clarion* and author of *That Lonesome Road*, Edith Cromwell, referred to elsewhere in this chapter, Connie Glasgow-James, the first black teacher from East Preston to obtain a Master's degree in Education in 1980, Ruth Johnson, then President of the Black Cultural Society, winner of numerous awards for over four decades of volunteer work and third Nova Scotian to win the prestigious Harry Jerome National Award

Edith (Drummond) Clayton (1920-1989) became internationally famous for her handcrafted baskets. She was awarded a Silver Jubilee Medal by Queen Elizabeth in 1977, and was honoured by the Black Hall of Fame and the Black Professional Women's Association. In 1986, she represented the province at Expo in Vancouver.

(after Carrie Best and Calvin Ruck), Alma Johnston, founding President of the Group, teacher at the time for 28 years and holder of a Master's degree in Education, Guidance Counsellor and community worker for some 35 years, Pearleen Oliver, black historian and author, first female Moderator of the A.U.B.A., volunteer church worker for 53 years, holder of numerous church offices and one of the founders of N.S.A.A.C.P., Sharon Ross, Senior Human Resources Officer of the Public Service Commission, graduate in Business Administration of Mount Saint Vincent University, inducted in the Black Wall of Fame in 1982, and recipient of numerous public awards, Anne Simmonds, graduate of Saint Mary's University, working for a Master's degree in Social Work, first female university graduate from North Preston and a vice-president of the Black Cultural Society, Donna Smith, graduate in Nursing Practice of McMaster University, the only holder of this qualification in Nova Scotia, Co-ordinator of the Child Development Clinic at the Children's Hospital in Halifax, lecturer in the department of Pediatrics, Dalhousie University, recipient of the Y.W.C.A. special recognition award, 1989, Corrine Sparks, first black female Family Court Judge in Nova Scotia and Canada, appointed on March 25, 1987, after eight years of legal practice, Maxine Tynes, poet, writer and teacher, graduate of Dalhousie University, member of the Board of Governors of that university, winner of numerous awards for her poetry, including the Peoples' Poetry Award for her book of poems entitled *Borrowed Beauty*.

Dr. Carrie Best, journalist, editor, and founder of the *Clarion*, was honoured by the Black Professional Women's Group at their twentieth anniversary recognition dinner.

Citing the honorees during the twentieth anniversary celebrations of the Black Professional Women's Group provides a good opportunity to acknowledge the progress made by black women in the professional field in Nova Scotia. The number is rapidly growing. There are many more in

Nova Scotia who are climbing the ladder and making a mark in society. Their story cannot be told in this volume because of the constraints of space but it will be told in due course and should be the subjects of local, thematic and biographical studies and researches: Carolyn Thomas, Betty Thomas, the sisters Delvina and Kim Bernard, mother and daughter, Joan Jones and Tracy Jones, Cherry Paris, Valerie Miller, Jean Whalen, Dolly Williams, Nina Adams,

Pearleen Oliver in the robing room, Saint Mary's University, October 28, 1990, prior to receiving an honourary doctorate. The author, Dr. Bridglal Pachai, presented her for the degree.

Josephine and Anne Johnson, mother and daughter, Sylvia Wedderburn, Lynette Mensah, Clotilda Yakimchuk, Ada Fells, Yvonne Atwell and Joyce Ross—to mention a very few not included already in this volume.

THE EAST PRESTON LIONS CLUB

This most valuable and energetic club was granted its charter on June 25, 1977 through the vision and foresight of James E. Brindley who was installed the first King Lion. When James Brindley died in 1982, the Club decided to set up the J.E. Brindley Scholarship Award. The first award was made in 1986 to Charlene Sparks of Cherry Brook–Lake Loon for a three-year period to study science at Dalhousie University. The second award was made in 1989 to Lillian Downey of North Preston. These scholarships represent one aspect of the many projects that are supported by this service club which is ably assisted and complemented by the East Preston Lioness Club which was inaugurated on November 8, 1980 under the stewardship of Queen Lioness Carolyn Thomas.

In the case of both the Lions and the Lioness Clubs of East Preston many able and devoted persons have been at the helm or in the committees to raise funds for numerous deserving causes and to lend support to kindred organizations not necessarily restricted to the black communities. This example of public spiritedness shows that members of the black communities of Nova Scotia as well as their organizations have made the effort to serve common society causes, such as hospitals and the Red Cross as Nova Scotians and Canadians.

Three organizations will bring this section as well as the chapter to an end, two relatively new and one in existence since 1915. The first of these is *Congress of Black Women in Canada, Local Chapter*. The idea for a national body to provide a forum for black women originated with Kay Livingstone in Toronto in 1972 and became a reality in 1977 after a series of meetings in various cities including Halifax in 1976. But it was only a decade later that the Halifax Dartmouth Local Chapter became active. Since then various workshops were organized to deal with political, social and economic issues. Research projects have begun to document the achievements of black women as well as to analyze the influence of racism on Nova Scotia black women. Here is an organization like the Association of Black Social Workers which can concentrate on aspects of the black experience not particularly covered in the work of other organizations. The ninth national congress of the Congress of Black Women in Canada was held in Halifax in May, 1989 under the co-chair of two Nova Scotians, Lynette Mensah and Dolly Williams.

The most recent addition to the family of black organizations in Nova Scotia is the *Afro-Canadian Caucus of Nova Scotia* formed on March 18, 1989 by former members of the Black United Front who argued that B.U.F. had lost its focus and effectiveness. The Caucus chair is Yvonne Atwell one-time President of the B.U.F. Council and later its Executive Director. The Caucus vice-chair is Burnley (Rocky) Jones who has been involved in Nova Scotia politics for over twenty years. The Caucus has announced that it will take a strong stand against racism. As reported in the Dartmouth weekly, Burnley Jones has said: "I won't be satisfied unless a full inquiry is launched into racism in our school system. We tend to patch up situations rather than look deeply at them."[73] In this respect, the Caucus took the same position as expressed by the Parent and Student Association of Preston through its chair, Evangeline Cain-Grant, and its response to the racial conflict at the Cole Harbour District High School in January, 1989 between white and black students.

The earlier history of the *Nova Scotia Home for Colored Children* up to 1945 is traced in chapter three though references are made to the later period when the Home was under the Presidency of the first black person to hold that office in 1974. In this concluding section on the Home a brief overview will be provided to bring the story up to date in 1989. It is understood that the Home is presently engaged in compiling its own history. That finished and comprehensive product will be a useful addition to information and knowledge on the Home.

With the retirement from the position of president of the Board of Dr. Cumming in 1966, the time was fast approaching when members of the black community would wish to direct the destinies of this time hallowed institution which had come into existence during the second decade of the twentieth century. Besides J.A.R. Kinney, Sr., who died in 1940 and who virtually ran the Home from its official opening in 1921, the policy directives came mainly from white leadership. While this was not necessarily detrimental to the institution, the post-war years since 1945 had seen the emergence of black organizations, greater black participation and black determination of the directions that were best for the affected people.

Directions changed after 1945. The farming which had been carried out on the 14 acres (5.6 hectares) of arable land was discontinued in 1946. The Henry G. Bauld School, which had been an important feature of the Home, closed in 1969 and the resident children were enrolled in three different public schools. In that year there were 38 children in residence as of March 31 but the number in residence was drastically reduced half a year later. One contributory factor was the introduction of the foster-home program which was based on the premise that children were better off in foster homes than in institutions. The Home itself became one such foster home on the basis of funding received from government sources at the rate of $3.50 per child per day in accordance with the Canada Assistance Plan. This did not result in any increase in the number of residents at the Home. In actual fact the decline continued as the Children's Aid Society placed more children in private foster homes. The success of such placements was questionable since very few black families were economically able to accept the children.

The management and staff of the Home grappled with the challenges presented as best they could. The following picture presented in the annual report to A.U.B.A. in August 1970 by the Matron, Mary Paris, of New Glasgow—sister of Dr. Peter Paris and Cherry Paris mentioned in earlier pages—is a contemporary report of vital significance:

I think most of you know by now that I only report factual statements, whether they be pleasing or not to the hearer, is not my intention to present a rosy picture that all is well when this is contrary to the facts. I believe that you are all aware of the internal upheaval that has been prevalent at the home for the past six months. I do not intend to go into detail re this except to say that as a result of all trials and tribulations that we had to endure we can be thankful to God for a time of hope. For the first time in 49 years of the Home's history, we have now a majority representation of Black directors (9) in decision making roles. We have five committees with all chairmen black. Friends, June 24th, 1970 will go down in my book as a day to be remembered. I know much has been written and voiced in the past months about the Home both pro and con, and maybe for the first time in the Home's history people have dared to speak independently and found that they possessed the ability to stand up and be counted with a clear and firm position on all issues which affect our lives and the lives of our children. The Home has had a proud history, and because of that fact I feel we have been justified in our actions. And to all of you here today I implore you to be concerned about the well-being of our black children, our family relationships, the future of these children lie in your hands.

This was a powerful statement marking the opening of a new chapter in the history and the fortunes of the Home. As it moved towards celebrating its golden anniversary on 6 June, 1971, the Home could indeed acknowledge the force of the winds of change which left in their wake more black representation on the Board of Directors, a successful financial campaign and appropriate and substantial salary increases for the staff, all of which were proudly presented by the acting matron, Portia Provo, to A.U.B.A. in August, 1971. What had not changed was the small number of children (18) in the care of the Home. A resolution moved by Rev. D.D. Skeir called upon the A.U.B.A. and its affiliates to petition the provincial government, Children's Aid Societies and agencies to support the admission of more black children since black children were not receiving proper attention and care in foster homes. The resolution stated that there were many more children throughout the province who should be placed in the Home but were in foster homes.

More should be said in summary of significant events that took place in the Home's golden anniversary year, 1971, during which the president of the Board of Directors was Alice K. Croft and the treasurer was Rev. D.D. Skeir.

On a sad note, the matron for 19 years, Mary Paris, died on November 7, 1971, after having given extremely loyal and faithful service. The commemoration of the fiftieth anniversary provided an opportunity to reflect on the recent changes and situation. The farm and the school no longer operated. The number of children at the Home was reduced considerably. The annual radio broadcast for the previous two years was absent. The success recorded by a former resident of the Home, Wayne Kelsie, in obtaining the LL.B. degree from Dalhousie University was noted with pleasure. In presenting her annual report to the A.U.B.A., the president, Alice Croft, asked the most crucial questions of the day: "Are we accomplishing the purpose for which the Home was originally intended? Or are we just drifting along?"

These were questions that would have to be asked over and over again up to the present. No institution can dwell on the past without adapting to changing times and changing circumstances. The reluctance to change or to innovate while being tied to tradition can be more than frustrating in the formulation of policy for development and change. Alice Croft recognized the changing scene which would in time provide the challenges for the growing black leadership when she presented the annual report to A.U.B.A. in August, 1972. "In the Province of Nova Scotia" she wrote "there are at least 500 Black children in need of foster home or institutional care. The Nova Scotia Home has all the facilities to be of great assistance to the children of the Black race as well as any of the White race needing care and it grieves the members of the Board when we only have so very few receiving care at the Home. It is gratifying however that we now have 29 children at the Home whereas about a year ago there was a period when we had less than twelve children."

The following year, the Home sought more funding, the Board decided on experimenting with the practice of setting up Group Homes on the property on a trial basis, and convened a meeting with three major black organizations and the Human Rights Commission to work out more co-operative exchanges. The fact that the 1973 report to A.U B.A. by the last white president of the Board of Directors of the Home in her final year of office could include favourable mention of many public-spirited persons was reassuring for the future of the Home: Rev. Donald Skeir, Dr. W.P. Oliver, J. Eldridge Brindley, Churchill Smith and Dr. John Savage, medical practitioner working for the upliftment of the black community in particular. That very year a new executive director, Robert Butler, was hired with the mandate of converting the Home from an orphanage to a child development residential centre. The focus of the Board was directed to four areas: finance, facilities, programmes and personnel. A new constitution was drawn up. Plans were drawn up for the construction of new residential facilities, one of which was earmarked to open in Halifax and be located near the professional centres. The Home was incorporated in terms of the Children's Aid Society and emphasis was placed on parenting-related responsibilities on the part of the staff as well as on structured activities of a recreational and character-building nature.

Thus was begun a new era in the history of the Nova Scotia Home for Colored Children in 1974 under the leadership of the first black president of the board of directors, Rev. D.E. Fairfax, working with a majority of fellow black directors and a newly-appointed white executive director, together charting a new and responsive course for the future. This era would see the vacating of the old Home building and the occupation of two new buildings in 1978. There is no record available to the author on the outcome of the projected third facility in Halifax. This era would take us to the present in 1989 and would see a succession of presidents drawn from the black community between 1974 and 1989, beginning with a three-year term for the first: Rev. D.E. Fairfax, Wayne Kelsie, Gertrude Tynes, James Francois and Bryan Darrell, with Wilfred Jackson holding the post once held by Robert Butler.

The annual reports presented to the A.U.B.A. conventions in the 1980s to the present show an interesting spread of cultural, educational and social events. The utilization of student and community resources to write the history of the Home deserves support. Current consideration is being given to the renovation and use of the old building which deserves to be classified as a historic property. The creation of a multi-purpose centre in the old building is being actively pursued in the on-going planning. While it has been decided to retain the corporate name of the institution, the Board of Directors has given consideration to name buildings and programmes after personalities who have graced the institution in the historical past: Kinney, Fowler, Paris, Bauld and Cumming—all of whom are mentioned in this study. Included in this worthy and deserving exercise was the dedication of the Rev. D.E. Fairfax Chapel in 1985.

With its current involvement in family and child care programmes and activities, the Home is moving confidently into the 1990s. To move forward is to move progressively. It is fitting to close this section with the words of the president in 1987, James Francois, in his report to A.U.B.A.: "Throughout its history the Home has reflected the changes in society. The closure of large orphanages, the establishment of the Children's Services Act, the shifts in education, the humaneness of the community, the new Young Offenders Act......have all impacted on the N.S. Home for Colored Children, and have been instrumental in the movement of this Home to its newer facilities, and its service to a smaller population." It is this service factor which will determine the future fortunes of this landmark historic institution.

POLITICS AND POLITICIANS

As of 1989, no Nova Scotia Black has been elected to provincial or federal legislatures. Since 1945, a small number have contested provincial seats in Sydney, Halifax and Annapolis Royal. A number have over the years taken keen interest in politics as members as well as in administrative positions in all provincial and federal political parties. Perhaps the most prominent of them is Donald H. Oliver, Q.C. who has been active in political affairs with the Progressive Conservative Party for over 30 years, completing a term as National Vice-President Atlantic Region and as Vice-President of the party.

Donald H. Oliver, a prominent politician with the Progressive Conservative Party, was appointed to the Canadian Senate in 1990.

It is in municipal politics that black Nova Scotians have made the greatest contribution since the opening years of this century. While it would be natural to expect that training and experience gained at this level would lead to participation at the higher levels, this has not been so since all the municipal politicians who have been successful at that level lacked the independent and strong economic base to move higher.

It was in Halifax County that the first black municipal politicians were elected to represent the strong black settlement areas of Preston. The first councillor to be elected was Thomas Johnson whose term of office began in the closing decades of the nineteenth century. He served till 1903. He was succeeded by Councillor John Thomas whose term of office ran from 1903 to 1906. The third councillor was George Diggs who served for 22 years from 1906 to 1928. Councillor John Colley was the fourth councillor who served a single term from 1928 to 1930 when he was succeeded by Councillor Allan W. Evans whose term of office from 1930 to 1960 has remained the longest term served by any incumbent from the Preston area. His position as a successful farmer and a prominent church leader in the Laymen's Council kept him in the public limelight for many decades. Evans was succeeded by William B. Thomas (1960-1964). Councillor Arnold Johnson served for four terms from 1964 to 1976 and was succeeded by the only white councillor to serve the Preston area, Patrick Lachance (1976 to 1979), following which the present incumbent, Wayne Adams was elected to office and is presently (1989) serving his fourth term.

These nine councillors, with one exception, were members of the black community who went into office and served alongside their white counterparts when opportunities for blacks were limited and their standing in society was harmed by the general hostility towards Blacks as a people. The environment changed over the years but each of the eight councillors who served Preston during this century has done so competently and courageously. The standing in 1989 of the immediate past black councillor, Arnold Johnson, attests to this fact: President of the Watershed Association Development Enterprise (W.A.D.E.) which was incorporated in 1984, Arnold Johnson has brought to WADE the experience and knowledge he gained during his years as councillor. In his Council years he pushed for community development, building by-laws, fire protection, upgrading of housing and construction of roads. In his present position as president of WADE he is able to steer the younger staff members like the hard-working Executive Director, Wayne Desmond, to sharpen the focus and performance of WADE in such areas as housing, land clarification titles, utilization of land for development, pollution and water and sewage.

Similarly, Wayne Adams, who was born in Halifax, moved to his present home in Lake Echo which is located in the District 8 which he has represented energetically since 1979, has continued to be involved in numerous community organizations. A former media man, and civil servant, Adams was voted in 1975 as one of Nova Scotia's five outstanding men. In 1989, he has resumed part of his former media work while pursuing his independent business.

Moving from Halifax County to Halifax City, one identifies Graham Downey who first ran for council in 1971 and was successful in 1974. He has continued to serve as alderman since then, completing 15 years in 1989.

Alderman Downey has worked for the Canadian Broadcasting Corporation for 21 years. Alderman Downey's challenges in the northend of Halifax which he serves are tremendous given the housing, employment and economic issues of the area. He has also served a term as deputy mayor.

In the hinterland of Nova Scotia, blacks have served in municipal politics in Amherst, New Glasgow and Annapolis Royal. In Amherst, Councillor Donald Paris was elected to office in 1976 and continues to serve in 1989. Employed as a machinist, Councillor Paris is an active member of the Lions Club in his area. In New Glasgow, Councillor Francis Joseph Dorrington was first elected to council in 1976, like his Amherst counterpart. He has served on numerous bodies since then, including the local school board from which he was elected to serve as a director of the Nova Scotia School Board Association. Councillor Dorrington has served a term as deputy mayor and a few months as acting Mayor.

Councillor Daurene Lewis was first elected to the Annapolis Royal town council in 1979. Two years later Councillor Lewis was elected deputy-mayor which office she served ably for two years. In December, 1984 she was elected mayor of Annapolis Royal, the first black mayor in all of Canada. A descendent of the first black policewoman in Canada, Rose Fortune, of Black Loyalist stock, Daurene Lewis followed in the traditions of independent business and hard work which ran in the family and opened her own crafts business called Studio Wefan where this pioneer worked full-time as a designer and weaver. In 1988, Mayor Lewis won the Liberal Party nomination in her area but was narrowly defeated in the subsequent provincial election. But Mayor Lewis has made her mark and there can be no turning back from further success for this remarkable Nova Scotian.

Finally, in the Cape Breton area the names Thomas E. Miller and Eddie Parris come up in the context of municipal politics. Thomas Miller, mentioned in an earlier section on the military, was the first black man in Eastern Canada to be elected alderman when he won a seat on the Sydney City Council in 1955. He held this seat for seventeen years up to 1972. A distinguished military man, Alderman Miller worked for many years for Sydney Steel. He died on January 21, 1988.

The second black Cape Bretoner to serve on the Sydney City Council was the genial musician, Eddie Parris, who was first elected in 1975. Eddie Parris has worked for Sydney Steel since 1962. He lost his seat in 1988 but will surely attempt a comeback some day.

The men and women mentioned in this brief overview of black politicians have pioneered a path and pointed a direction. If the black community is to accelerate its march towards progress and a confirmed and recognized place in mainstream society, political participation is absolutely vital, as voters, organizers and contestants. When Carolann Wright, the black woman from Beechville, Nova Scotia, ran for the office of mayor of Canada's largest city in 1988 on a shoestring campaign budget of $6000, she was given no serious chance. Carolann won 25,000 votes in Toronto and ran a respectable third. Nothing is impossible.

Given the small percentage of black voters in Nova Scotia and the scattered areas of residence, no black candidate can hope to run for elective office and win without the strong support of the majority. The development of political consciousness and strategies for participation should include the will for total immersion into Nova Scotia politics and the will to participate fully in Nova Scotia life.

In November 1989, for the first time in the history of the United States, a black mayor was elected in New York City and a black governor was elected in the state of Virginia. Their historic victories did not come from minority voters but from majority voters. More black and other minority Nova Scotians should emulate the examples of black politicians like the late Alderman Thomas Miller of Sydney and Mayor Daurene Lewis of Annapolis Royal and play active roles in the political process. While it is true that such participation will be costly in terms of money, time and anguish, it cannot be put off indefinitely.

A survey of a people's history and society covering a span of some two hundred years raises the obvious questions of successes and failures, of problems and prospects, of the present and the future. Observers and analysts, teachers and students, pastors, professionals, politicians and pugilists will all raise questions of their own. Some will turn to the pages of this book to seek answers and explanations and will surely realize that no single book will provide all the answers and explanations. Some will be challenged to find answers and explanations elsewhere, whether from their own particular reservoirs of information or from external sources best known to them. Some may be tempted to pick up from where this study ends. All that can be assumed at this stage is that this book presents an opportunity for reflection.

If any one single generalization can be permitted to exemplify the history of the black people of Nova Scotia from 1800 to 1989, it must surely be their unrelenting search for the best way to use every opportunity that came their way. This search has not been an easy one whether in the church, in education, in business, in politics or even in the social sphere. The important thing is that the attempts were made—and continue to be made. So, if readers were to reflect on why so many organizations have come and gone in the black communities over the centuries, they might be constrained to remember the search for opportunities by a people determined to do well by their religious faith and by their sense of family. Every now and then this religious faith and sense of family have risen and fallen as barometers do—leaving in the wake of the rise and fall fresh and urgent problems for the custodians of faith and family.

Another generalization that cannot be ignored is the existence and vitality of the community. There have been many identifiable black settlements in the history of Nova Scotia, beginning with the dominant ones of Shelburne–Birchtown, Digby–Brindley Town, Guysborough–Tracadie and Halifax–Dartmouth–Preston creations. From the few dominant, to the many scattered and rural, the black communities of Nova Scotia must all be regarded and respected for their contribution to Nova Scotia. When one looks at the black renaissance in the arts in Nova Scotia, this sense of community origins, often in humble and remote settings, but always spurred on by friend and family, stands out as clearly as the quality and confidence of the individuals themselves: the inimitable Walter Borden, Nova Scotia's outstanding professional black actor; the quiet and cultured George Boyd, playwright and newscaster, whose production of *Shine Boy* in 1988 prompted this modest man to say: "One of the reasons 1 wrote *Shine Boy* was the lack of recognition of Dixon in the larger community. People drive by the George Dixon Centre every day, and don't know anything about the man it's named for. It seems Nova Scotians don't want to honour people who make contributions in fields other than the navy and politics." [74]

This is changing; honours have indeed come and will continue to come: George Boyd and the production team and actors in *Shine Boy* including Walter Borden, Lucky Campbell and Leonard Kane of Nova Scotia's black communities, were honoured at various functions, one of which was held at the Black Cultural Centre—an event George Boyd was later to acknowledge as the best tribute he could hope for—one from his own community."

To continue the black renaissance in arts, representatives can be drawn from all over Nova Scotia: from Lincolnville comes Lucky Campbell, mentioned above, born in Glace Bay, a versatile song writer, musician, playwright who is quietly making the country and city rounds, writing, singing and acting. His achievements and philosophy are worth recording: "I know I am through with ordinary jobs. I may never be famous or rich but I know I can make a living as a performer. My favourite original song is *We can be*. We can be whatever we want to be. The major factor is to determine what it is we want to be. I have tried a bit of a lot of things and I now know I want to be involved in theatre and music."[75]

Theatre and music have been well served in the black renaissance. Theatre in this context is synonymous with the name of Walter Borden who grew up in New Glasgow in a family of 18 children. (His father died in October, 1989). He began his theatre appearances at the Neptune in the 1970s and since then has travelled successfully in North America and Europe. His stunning and awe-inspiring performances in such plays as *Can't Stop Now—Saints Have Trod, God's Trombones and Tightrope Time* have earned him many awards and accolades, including a recent award entitled the 1989 Outstanding Theatre Achievement Award by the Nova Scotia Drama League. The nomination by the Black Cultural Centre read in part: "He has pioneered a difficult path, expressing the black experience through his acting and his plays. He has inspired a whole generation. As an artist, he stands without peer in this field and has never hesitated at an opportunity to give something back to his community." As an artist, Walter Borden transcends the artificial boundaries of race and colour: "When we're talking about art, I'm sometimes most reticent to use words like black and white."[76]

In the field of music, Nova Scotia's black community has produced an enormous array of talent: Portia White and other members of the White family, including Lorne White and his immediate family, Donald Fairfax, Suzanne Herbert, the Gospel Heirs, Four the Moment, the Sonlight, Faith Nolan and Lionel Williams, both of whom now work successfully out of Toronto, Charles "Bucky" Adams, Ernest Symonds, Anne Johnson, Ernest and Bernice Flint, Marguerite "Peggy" Downes, Florence Bauld, Pearleen Oliver, Carolyn Thomas, Eddie Parris, Raymond Parker—the list could go on and on. In each of the 40-odd settlement areas in which black residents live in sizeable numbers, one can produce a long list of accomplished and deserving musicians. This volume cannot find place for them all, nor can it find the space to provide biographical sketches, except for a few random notes.

Both the Gospel Heirs and Four the Moment came into existence in 1982, both were invited to perform at Expo '86 in Vancouver and both have received numerous awards over the years. On the contemporary scene, Nova Scotia's best known classical singer is Donald Edward Fairfax, pastor of the Victoria Road Baptist Church in Dartmouth who graduated from the Halifax Conservatory of Music in 1953 while, historically, the famous Portia White, who died on 13 February, 1968, remains the legend she was during her short life time. Born in Truro in 1910 in the well-known family of Rev. W.A. White, Portia White left her mark on the provincial, national and international scene. The following account written a few years ago pays tribute to her greatness and her contribution: "In 1940 Portia was studying at the Halifax Conservatory of Music. The phrase 'black is beautiful' had not yet been coined but could have been inspired by her stunning physical presence and distinctive appeal. It was more than the schoolmistress manner she had learned in the classroom, for Halifax had discovered the emerging Portia White, beautiful as Aida and courtly as only a black ambassadress can be in a white society......Halifax embraced Portia: the Ladies' Musical Club decided to help her with her training; the provincial government created a trust for her musical education; she sang in numerous halls for groups that had never before invited a Black, or a Micmac."[77]

Portia White (1910-1968), a Nova Scotian contralto who climbed to international fame as a singer.

Portia White broke new ground and left behind a legacy of hope for members of Nova Scotia's black population who, for whatever reason, might be driven to give up in despair. Portia White was not born into greatness or have greatness thrust upon her. She toiled long and hard for all that she achieved. The reader will recall that Portia White's growing up years were as challenging as they would have been for any contemporary black person: she taught school at Africville and at the Nova Scotia Home for Colored Children, saved what she could to advance her education and her talents, and proved her ability and determination through successful performance. Only then did the world around her sit up and take note. That is a legacy and a lesson for all Nova Scotians.

What was done for Portia White and what Portia White did in return is a good example of positive race relations which carries a strong message for the contemporary scene as efforts are being made to find common ground.

In another aspect of black renaissance in the arts, the work of contemporary writers deserves mention. The field of journalism has been exceptionally well served by a number of individuals from New Glasgow. Foremost in this field is Dr. Carrie M. Best who was the editor of the *Clarion* which started as a church bulletin in July, 1946 and grew into a national newspaper, *The Negro Citizen*, in 1949. It ceased publication in 1956. Dr. Best has described her work as a journalist and in other fields in her autobiography, *That Lonesome Road*, which was published in 1977 and is being updated in 1989. Aleta Williams worked for 18 years with *The New Glasgow Evening News* before retiring in 1989. Born in Halifax and educated at Joseph Howe and Bloomfield schools and the Maritime Business Academy, Aleta Johnston, as she then was, moved to New Glasgow after her marriage and made her contribution to her family, her community and to journalism.

Calbert James Best was perhaps the first black Nova Scotian to obtain a Diploma in Journalism from Kings University College, Halifax, after completing the B.A. degree in 1948. The son of Albert Best and Carrie Mae Prevoe Best, mentioned above as the founding editor of the *Clarion*, Calbert Best was a regular columnist in his mother's paper. In subsequent years Calbert Best rose through the ranks of the Public Service Alliance and in August, 1985 was appointed Canadian High Commissioner in Trinidad and Tobago, completing his assignment in August, 1988.

It was interest in writing in general that has produced a number of black Nova Scotians to continue to make a contribution to the black renaissance in arts: Maxine Tynes, George Boyd, George Borden, Raymond Parker and George Clarke, among others. Maxine Tynes, mentioned earlier in these pages, teaches Canadian literature at the Cole Harbour District High School, has written over a thousand poems, produced books of poetry and is working on others, has been included in a number of anthologies, and is in constant demand to do readings in public. George Boyd deserves one other mention to what has already appeared above and that is his appointment in June, 1989 to do the morning sports broadcast for C.B.C.'s Newsworld. In the previous month, Boyd won an Atlantic Journalism Award.

George Borden has been writing poetry and newspaper columns for many years, including his long years in the military. His first book of poems entitled *Canaan Odyssey*, published by the Black Cultural Centre in 1988, tells of the black experience in North America. Currently Literacy Facilitator for the Department of Higher Education and Job Training, George Borden is well placed to share his literary talents with a wider community.

Raymond Parker is a good example of a writer who persisted in writing in spite of a modest education and the absence of a helpful environment. He wrote the scripts for his novel, which was published by the Black Cultural Centre under the title *Beyond the Dark Horizon*, in Annapolis Royal and is now working on a companion volume in the quiet and remote setting of Lequille. Not far from there, in Digby, another black writer, Grace May Lawrence, has been writing pieces of poetry for decades, publishing in modest anthologies, and in the process has inspired a son and a granddaughter to do likewise. Their combined effort has produced a book of poems, *To The Third Power*, of which the moving spirit and senior citizen, Grace Lawrence, can be justly proud. (The co-authors are Daniel Vincent Lawrence and Correena Zenee Lawrence.) Another proud senior citizen is Viola Parsons of Cobequid Road whose book, *My Grandmother's Days*, was published in 1988.

The last writer to be considered in this section is George Elliott Clarke whose first book of poems entitled *Saltwater Spirituals and Deeper Blues* was published in 1983. Clarke has been a regular columnist in Nova Scotia for many years. For the past three years he has worked as an assistant to Dr. Howard McCurdy, M.P. but has continued with his studies, graduating with a Master's degree in English from Dalhousie University in October, 1989.

Another aspect of the vitality of the black communities of Nova Scotia is to be found in the outstanding personalities produced in sports. Anne V. Johnson, a graduate in physical education and theatre, presently (1989) Program Officer at the Black Cultural Centre, has compiled a study on black boxers in Nova Scotia. This study has been taken forward and expanded by Charles Saunders in a book published by the Black Cultural Centre and Lancelot Press in 1990 under the title *Sweat and Soul*. This title is significant. For too long it was a common stereotype which attributed physical prowess and success to black persons as a race, to whom it was said success in this field came easily. What has been discounted in this assessment was the drive and the discipline which combined to bring success. Charles Saunders' book provides an intelligent framework and presents an interesting interpretation.

Nova Scotia has produced many distinguished boxers. On October 1, 1988, a Black Boxers Reunion and Remembrance Night was observed in Halifax, chaired by Delmore "Buddy" Daye, one among this number. The booklet produced on this occasion tells the story—which cannot be told here—in capsule form of who the greats were, where they hailed from, what they achieved and why they are remembered and saluted. Names such as Sam Langford, George Dixon, Tiger Warrington, Jesse Elroy Mitchell, Ricky Anderson, Dexter Connors, Delmore Buddy Daye, Dave Downey, Ozzie Farrell, Cecil Gray, Clyde Gray, Roy Hamilton, Poole Izzard, Jojo Jackson, Donnie Johnson, Leroy Jones, Leroy Lawrence, Sherrie Lawrence, Archie Lee, George Munro, Keith Paris, Percy Paris, Joe Pyle, Allison Sparks, Arnold Sparks, Len Sparks, Lawrence States, Bryan Gibson and Raymond Downey— all from different parts of Nova Scotia—are included. When Kirk Johnson, the 17-year-old Prince Andrew High School student in Dartmouth returned to Halifax on March 20, 1989 after winning the World Junior Heavyweight Boxing Championship in Puerto Rico, it was a reminder that old traditions are in safe young hands. Lest it be concluded that it is only in physical endeavours, such as in boxing, that generations of black Nova Scotians of early settler descent have left their mark, it should be noted that many firsts have been recorded in other fields as well: consider Dr. Harris Barton, M.D., of Halifax, Drs. Cameron Brothers and Carl Lewis, Dental Surgeons, Murray Miller of Digby, first architect, and Sinclair Williams, first black policeman in Dartmouth in 1968, and Layton Johnston, of Cherry Brook, first black police-man in Halifax in 1967 after serving for two years in Toronto.

A third generalization that may be permitted in this closing chapter is the prevalence and prominence of the issue of racism in Nova Scotia and what this practice has done and is doing in the lives of black Nova Scotians. There is no shortage of short and long studies that give chapter and verse to under-line the fact that racism has existed in the past, does exist in the present and that black people are among its greatest victims. What to do about it has divided both the black community as well as the dominant community. Some members in both groups have called persistently for immediate revo-lutionary methods to effect improvements, such as the introduction of leg-islative measures, introduction of mandatory contract compliance measures to promote employment opportunities, and the introduction of judicial enquiries to determine the causes and extent of racism in the Nova Scotia school system, for example the vocal and vigorous call by the Parent and Student Association of Preston (PSAP) since the Cole Harbour racial inci-dents erupted in January, 1989.

While the vocal minority remains unassuaged, enquiries and reports, some old and some more recent, confirm the malady and propose remedi-al measures. An example of an older enquiry of a broader nature is the

Graham Commission on Education, Public Services and Provincial–Municipal Relations whose recommendations in 1971 pointed to inequalities in the school system and referred to the impact of these inequalities on the black population. It called for more black teachers, for race-relations education for all teachers, for a review of the curriculum to introduce more black history and so on. On page 12 of Chapter 52, the Graham Commission stated: "We have been made vividly aware of how black students feel that their race and culture simply do not appear in the conventional school programme and that they are left without models, symbols and achievements with which to identify themselves. The implementation of our recommendations would result in putting blacks in the school programme; in ending forever the ignorance and general lack of awareness of their presence, of their contribution, and of their legitimate expectations; in recognition and respect of their rights; and in an end to discrimination and prejudice against them in the schools." How much of these recommendations have filtered down in the 18 years to 1989 is difficult to establish. The surface appearances and the fact that similar things are still being called for in 1989 would suggest that very little has actually happened.

Among the new enquiries and reports, the study commissioned by Ron Macdonald, M.P. on racism in the metro area, released in September, 1989 was a

Sugar Ray Downey displays the bronze medal he won at the Seoul Olympics in 1988.

Halifax Police Department hired its first racially visible officer, Constable Layton Johnston, in 1967.

further reaffirmation of an old fact to which was added a qualification that racial inequalities existed not because the masses were overtly racist but because too many people remained silent about injustices. This latter feature could be a new discovery for the politicians but the cry that the silent majority are to be held culpable for their silence has been sounded before. In this context, it has also been stated many times before now that the notion that there is a black problem should be replaced by the reality that there is a white problem, by whatever phraseology this problem can be stated to exist.

The other recent report dated September 21, 1989, entitled *Breaking Barriers: Report of the Task Force on Access for Black and Native People* was commissioned by Dalhousie University. The report recalled the submission by Mrs. Eleanor Elms, retired black school teacher in Digby, who said: "Discrimination will likely always be here but like dusting a lamp in a hurry—you just dust around it." The report picked up this point on page 154:

> Dalhousie University should lead the way in not only dusting the lamp of discrimination but also in setting new standards of cleanliness. It is hoped that this lead will be followed by the Nova Scotian and Federal governments and other social institutions, in a genuine effort to cleanse our society by reducing and ultimately eliminating barriers that deny full access to Nova Scotia's Black and Aboriginal Peoples.

Dalhousie University has pointed the way for now: the Transition Year Program will continue and the Law School will provide special access for its two target groups.

In the meantime, the Halifax County–Bedford District School Board has set up special committees to effect changes to the system that led to the outbreak of racial friction at Cole Harbour in January, 1989; the P.S.A.P., mentioned above, challenged the courts for allegedly violating the provisions of the Charter of Rights and Freedoms in charging certain black students allegedly involved in the disturbances. The decisions of the court were unfavourable.

Another landmark report was issued in January, 1990. This is the Donald Marshall, Jr. Inquiry report which, while analyzing the criminal justice system in Nova Scotia, refers to the racial situation in the province.

While all this goes on, crucial questions remain that must be wrestled with. To the south of us where there are some 30 million blacks, representing some 15% of the population of the United States, Blacks have made much headway as politicians, business persons and professionals, but not as a people. A special report of Newsweek of March 7, 1988, devoted to the theme "Black and White: How Integrated is America?" came to a dismal conclusion: "Twenty years after the murder of Martin Luther King, blacks have gained a fragile new middle class and a troubled 'underclass' while the civil rights movement itself has fallen into a neglect that hurts everyone."

In Canada, the black population as a whole stands in the region of 300,000 or roughly 2% of the population. As a minority group, it comes behind the Chinese and the Indo–Pakistani. In Nova Scotia, the black population, including recent immigrants, is in the region of some 20,000 (census figures are considerably lower while provincial figures are somewhat higher, depending on the source) which gives it the same percentage as the national average. Since over half the black population resides in the Halifax–Dartmouth metro area and in Halifax County, the concentration is a crucial determinant of needs.

There can be no question that in this crucial concentrated area, the existence of talent, professionals, entrepreneurs and ambition is more than adequate to respond positively to opportunities to work in partnership with the dominant society to find a place as an equal member and not as an appendage. The question is how to find a modus operandi that will break new ground so that the talents of, for example, Sylvia Hamilton in film-making, and Jessica Bowden in modeling and body-building and as a business proprietor running Ebony Chanelle Coiffure in Barrington Place, or Iona Crawley's ground-breaking Management and Consulting Services, will grow to cultivate, sustain and expand the economic base so crucial for black advancement. In the provincial civil service as well as in the federal public service, Nova Scotian Blacks continue to hold positions with distinction, in the province as well as outside. While it is not possible to list them all, it is important for the younger generation to know that sound education and a disciplined approach will enable them to join such illustrious predecessors as Calbert Best, Jules Oliver, Calvin Ruck, Eugene Williams, Matthew and Carolyn Thomas, Carolyn Fowler, Sharon Ross and Blair Lopes who, in 1989, holds the significant position of Atlantic Regional Director of the Public Service Commission of Canada. There is a powerful base of lawyers whose role it would be to continue to enhance the image and assume senior positions of power and decision-making: George Davis, Donald Oliver, Judge Corrine Sparks, Wayne Kelsie, Ken Crawford, Andres Fanning, Doug Ruck,

Valerie Miller, Jean Whalen, Gus Wedderburn, Cas Williams, Anthony Ross, Davies Bagambiire and Paul Walker. The medical and related fields have through their respective specialities presented a model of excellence that must be seen, felt and emulated: Dr. V. Audain, Ophthalmology, Dr. A. Bodurtha, General Surgery (Oncology), Dr. D. Haase, Internal Medicine, Dr. R. Holness, Neurosurgery, Dr. E. Ross, General Practice, Dr. O. Ikejiani, Pathology, Dr. Dennis Payne, General and Vascular Thoracic Surgery and Dr. George Sewell, Optometrist.

While this reservoir of individual talents will continue to adorn the landscape, they will serve to inspire future generations to follow in their footsteps. While this happens, the many black organizations could mobilize their internal resources to respond positively to fresh and anticipated challenges so that more books will be published, more land clarification titles will be obtained, more businesses opened, more teachers appointed and promoted, more social, economic and political progress registered and more students will complete high school and university education. While old-type family meetings should continue, should not thought be given to new-type family meetings where the family will be determined not only by race or colour but by culture as well.

Should this not be the new agenda for the twenty-first century for the black population of Nova Scotia? There must surely be something exciting, daring and new to write about in a volume of the people's history for the year 2000 and beyond. If that good state is attainable, then this volume which tells the story from 1800 to November 5, 1989 will not have been put together and presented in vain.

This section covers some two hundred years of a people's history and can only hope to have covered some aspects of this history. Much more could have been said and much more could have been included. There are limitations to every endeavour; this volume is no exception. However, one clear conclusion remains: Nova Scotia's black population has always made, and continues to make, a valuable contribution to the history and culture of this province and of this country.

CHAPTER FIVE

THE PERIOD 1990-2006

Future researchers and writers will remember 1990 for a number of publications which added to the literary output by black Nova Scotian writers. Charles Saunders, an avid researcher on boxing, produced *Sweat and Soul: The Saga of Black Boxers from the Halifax Forum to Caesar's Palace*. The Black Cultural Centre added to its impressive publications with *Traditional Lifetime Stories, Volume II and Three Nova Scotia Black Churches*. Three noted poets brought out new publications: Maxine Tynes with *Woman Talking Woman*, David Woods with *Native Song*, and George Elliott Clarke with *Whylah Falls*.

The Oliver family, already well known in Nova Scotia before 1990, produced two notable achievements during 1990. Dr. Pearleen A. Oliver received an honorary doctorate from Saint Mary's University, while Senator Donald H. Oliver, Q.C., was appointed to his new position in Ottawa.

The Black Cultural Centre and the Black United Front had a number of staff changes in 1990. Wayne Adams left his business venture to return to the position of Executive Director of the Black Cultural Centre. The Black United Front continued its process of renewal and restructuring with Reverend Ogueri Ohanaka taking over as Executive Director from Winston Ruck, who retired on health grounds.

In the educational sector, the aftermath of the Cole Harbour incidents of January 1989 continued to surface in public debates and in court trials. Two significant developments related to education for the black community occurred. The Halifax County–Bedford District School Board carried out public hearings and worked on a new policy. A new position, Supervisor of Race Relations, Cross-Cultural Understanding and Human Rights, was created by the school board. A prominent educator, Janis Jones Darrell, was appointed to the position.

EDUCATION

Nova Scotia's black communities have, since early historical times, invested their resources and hopes in educational advancement as a foundation for progress. The schoolyard brawl between white and black students on the premises of Cole Harbour District High School on January 9, 1989, was a tremendous catalyst for the changes that marked the difference between what happened before 1989 and what happened after 1989.

Evangeline Cain-Grant co-founded the Parents–Students Association of Preston. She graduated from Dalhousie Law School in 1993, and was the first African Canadian woman to start a law firm in Nova Scotia.

Integration of black and white students, who lived primarily in segregated communities, began in earnest in 1964. In practice, this meant that while local black schools were being closed down, black students were being bused into predominantly white schools. The parents of black students filed a class action suit with the Nova Scotia Human Rights Commission in 1975. The corrective terms of the settlement reached by the school board dragged on ineffectually for years while underlying discontent continued. Following January 9, 1989, the Parents-Students Association of Preston was formed, and it called for a judicial enquiry. Chairperson Evangeline Cain-Grant said: "It is our thesis that racism is deeply embedded in the educational system in Nova Scotia." The MLA for Cole Harbour countered with the remark: "There is no problem with racism in the educational system—it simply doesn't exist." Black parents, students and communities disagreed strongly.

While the government refused to set up a judicial enquiry, this did not prevent other steps from being taken. These steps could be classified as damage control rather than a belated overhaul of a system in urgent need of a new direction. The school board administering Cole Harbour District High School set up committees to study human relations at this school and throughout its jurisdiction. They focused on human rights, race relations, and cross-cultural understanding. The issues were serious and urgent. VanRoy Tobitt, one of six black vice-principals or principals at the time in Nova Scotia, summarized the situation candidly: "Nothing has been done to alter the way teachers are taught to teach, so we have culturally deficient teachers teaching culturally different kids."

Years before the racial brawls at Cole Harbour High, individuals and groups, educators and pastors, and organizations large and small called for changes, reforms, and restructuring. The efforts of the Black Educators Association, the Cultural Awareness Youth Group, the African Canadian Education Project and the Black Learners Advisory Committee (formed in the aftermath of Cole Harbour) cannot be forgotten. By 1990-91, the situation had reached a breaking point. When racial disturbances erupted at a downtown Halifax nightclub on July 19, 1991, three levels of government stepped in; an Advisory Group on Race Relations was set up under the joint leadership of Carolyn Thomas (Province of Nova Scotia Human Rights Commission) and John Dennison (Race Relations Advisor to the Federal Minister of Multiculturalism and Citizenship). Besides Carolyn Thomas, members of the committee drawn from the Nova Scotia black community were: Archy Beals, Ken Hudson, Alma Johnston, Allister Johnson, Janis Jones-Darrell, Rev. Ogueri Ohanaka, Dolly Williams and Cecil Wright. Mildred Royer represented the city of Halifax.

This advisory committee worked speedily and 94 recommendations appeared in its report dated September 1, 1991. There were 19 recommendations on education, 19 on employment-economic development, 14 on black community participation and access to services, 21 on policing, justice and human rights, 12 on black community development, 3 on communications/media, and 6 on tourism and culture.

As of the end of 2006, some had been implemented, some were still being worked upon and some had been set aside—but they remain on record as a formidable checklist.

Here we are concerned with the main outcome of the recommendations on education. These were widely supported (with suggestions for improvements and implementation) by the Black Educators Association. The Black Learners Advisory Committee on Education, with the assurance of a longer life and blessed with a formidable membership, set to work with speed, thoroughness and vision. Motivated by Delmore "Buddy" Daye, a visionary with an established reputation, who was newly appointed as the first Black to hold the position of sergeant-at-arms in the provincial legislature. Daye had the ear of the minister of education and the society at large. The chair was Castor Williams—a lawyer who was appointed to the Bench in February 1996. Other members were key players: Brad Barton, Rev. Dr. Willard Clayton, Melinda Daye, Alma Johnston, Sheila Lucas-Cole, Rev. Ogueri Ohanaka, Hamid Rasheed, Carolyn Thomas, Jonathan Smith and Olusegun Odusanya.

Past members of the Black Learners Advisory Committee, formed after the confrontation between white and black students at Cole Harbour District High School in 1989.
Back row (l to r): Dr. Patrick Kakembo, Sheila Lucas-Cole, Brad Barton, Alma Johnston; middle row: Carolyn Thomas, Hon. Castor Williams, Robert Upshaw, Melinda Daye; front row: Jonathan Smith, Rev. Willard Clayton, Deacon Olesegun Odusanya; not pictured: Rev. Ogueri Ohanaka, Hamid Rasheed, Rev. Dr. Donald Skeir, Winston Ruck, Delmore "Buddy" Daye.

In December 1994, three volumes of the *BLAC Report on Education: Redressing Inequality—Empowering Black Learners* were presented to the provincial minister of education. A team of researchers and consultants, led by Robert Upshaw, program coordinator, and Dr. Patrick Kakembo, research director, produced a document that remains the most comprehensive to date, not only on education but on all aspects of the black population's concerns and aspirations.

Here, only two key recommendations will be touched upon: first, that the Black Learners Advisory Committee be elevated to a Council on African

Canadian Education with a mandate to function as a monitoring body, and secondly, that
the minister of education establish a branch in
the department to deal with African Canadian
Education, as a member of senior management. The government accepted both recommendations. The Council on African Canadian
Education (CACE) was set up in January 1996,
followed by the African Canadian Services
Division a month later.

The tenth anniversary of the release of the
BLAC report was celebrated in December
2004, and the same anniversary for CACE and
the African Canadian Services Division was
reached in January-February 2006. The
ground covered by both, as well as projec-
tions for the future, will not be dealt with
here. Excellent information is available in the
"Report of the BLAC Implementation Review
Committee" (2003) and the journals, called
Ahennwa—the African throne, produced by CACE
since 2000. At the Dawson Lecture given on
March 26, 1997, at the closing of the Nova
Scotia Teachers College in Truro on the topic
"Education in Nova Scotia: The African Nova
Scotian Experience," contained the following
words with reference to the initiatives of 1996:

Robert G. "Ted" Upshaw,
born in Windsor, Nova
Scotia, became the first black
commissioned officer in the
RCMP. In 2004, he attained
the rank of superintendent
in charge of North East
Nova District of H-division.

> The success of the provisions for the edu-
> cational upliftment of one of the charter
> peoples of Nova Scotia will, no doubt, be
> closely followed by the First Nations.......It
> will be watched, too, for lessons to be
> learned, by the increasing number of other
> minorities in the province.

As of 2006, both the African Canadian
Services Division and CACE were fulfilling

Delvina Bernard was
the first executive director
of the Council on African–
Canadian Education.

328

their original mandate as well as responding to current challenges and opportunities. It is clear to both supporters and detractors that a parallel system cannot last forever. The true measure of progress will only be seen

Sylvia Parris, an educator from Guysborough County, was recognized by the Simon Wiesenthal Centre for Holocaust Studies for her efforts to advance race relations and equity within the province of Nova Scotia.

when barriers are replaced by equal opportunities for all—this is the desirable goal for both sides. In the meantime, partnerships are necessary for building blocks to be put in place, such as the one between the education faculty at Mount Saint Vincent University and the CACE to start a master of education programme on Africentric leadership in September 2006. In the words of Brad Barton, retired school principal and supervisor: "The partnership with the Mount is a tremendous move forward because it will legitimize our efforts with an already established post-secondary institution."

BUSINESS DEVELOPMENT

The Africentric leadership and management concept is "to explore and uncover......African-centred creativity." The Black Business Initiative Society turns its own creativity into something concrete with its impressive motto. The words used in the motto—"Strength, Security, Prosperity, Togetherness"— have symbolized the faith and aspirations of the black population for centuries.

The Black Business Initiative (BBI) came into being as a result of an announcement on May 24, 1995, by the federal and Nova Scotia governments supporting the development of businesses and job opportunities for African Nova Scotians. A grant of $5 million over a five-year period set BBI going. The official opening took place on October 25, 1996 at Pier 22 in Halifax. The keynote speaker was Grace White, President of Canjam Trading, a remarkably successful business that started in 1989 as a dried fish company, and which was trading internationally in 1996. Since that memorable beginning, six components of this initiative have grown: business skills development, strategic planning and sector roundtables, youth entrepreneurship training, business financing: loans and equity, and business communications. In its first ten years, BBI has made an impressive start in all

Hector Jacques was the first chairperson of the Black Business Initiative's board of directors. He co-founded Jacques Whitford Group, Ltd., ranked one of the fifty best-managed private companies in Canada in 1994.

Cassandra Dorrington, a certified accountant and human resource professional, has been honoured for her community service, and has chaired the Black Business Initiative.

Rustum Southwell became executive director of the Black Business Initiative in 1996. He helped introduce the Black Business Summit, and the periodical *Black to Business*.

sectors of its mandate, providing just under two hundred loans totaling $2 million, and supporting 44 community development projects worth over $190,000. Its high-powered summits over the years have brought together delegates from all over Canada and the United States.

BBI is already looking ahead to build on its successes—to create economic independence for individuals, increase business development, education and training, build partnerships and linkages with the broader community, and create, as well as improve, access to the public and private sectors. Its periodicals are an excellent record of black entrepreneurs who run small, medium, and large businesses, while its comprehensive 2006 directory does what it sets out to do: "Help Black Business Succeed." In the words of Rustum Southwell, CEO: "Our journey over these 10 years has been challenging yet very rewarding. For me, the key to our continued success is our unwavering commitment to our Task Force values and principles."

]

THE BLACK BAPTIST CHURCH

In the period before 1990, much was written about building churches, pioneering pastors and church personalities, and of the long and virtually unbroken existence of the African United Baptist Association and its committees since 1853. In the 1990s, the time had come to celebrate historic milestones. These were often accompanied by publications, such as *Song of the Spirit* by Pearleen Oliver, which marked the 150th anniversary of the Beechville United Baptist Church, and *Reflections* by Carolyn Thomas, which marked the same milestone for the East Preston United Baptist Church. Many more anniversaries have been, or will be, celebrated in the twenty-first century. One example is the celebration of the 160th anniversary of the Emmanuel Baptist Church in Upper Hammonds Plains on August 29, 2005, when a group of about 600 people, including the congregation and well-wishers, met in an expanded building and a new sanctuary. The churches' parent body, African United Baptist Association of Nova Scotia, marked its own 150th anniversary in 2003.

In the annual reports of AUBA from 1999 to 2006 a picture of continuity and efficiency emerges. It meets in different locations each August, and receives reports from its various committees, including: the executive, finance, licensing, evangelism, education, scholarship, hospital visitor, social action, music, historical, and planning. Its three lay groups, the Women's Institute, Baptist Youth Fellowship, and Laymen's Council, also give reports. The internal highlights of its affiliated churches, numbering 20 in 2006, are presented in the form of summaries of activities.

True to its reputation as one of the main pillars of the provincial black population, AUBA responds to the challenges and opportunities of the day. An institution which celebrated 153 years of service in 2006 is understandably faced with concerns that need attention. In its 2006 report, some of these challenges were identified as churches without pastors, rural church ministries, challenges and struggles facing youth ministries, and low participation levels in several metro churches and districts. But the healthy pool of trained personnel, and the number training to assume positions of responsibility, is encouraging.

In an article in the *Mail Star*, November 14, 1996, Joan Jones commented on the report and action plans by the Women's Institute of AUBA on domestic violence: "The church has always played a leadership role in all black communities, and was a leading supporter of the women conducting the research for this report."

Women have served the black churches and AUBA well. To 2006, there had been four female moderators: Althea Pearleen Oliver (1976-78); Carolyn G. Thomas (1988-92); Doreen Paris (2002-04) and Reverend Tracey Grosse (2006–). The Rev. Tracey Rebecca Grosse of Cherry Brook was ordained on November 23, 1996, and holds the distinction of being the first ordained female moderator of AUBA.

While men have historically held dominant positions in the long history of the black churches and AUBA, the contemporary picture of ordained female pastors of AUBA is impressive: Rev. Rhonda Britton (New Glasgow); Rev. Pauline Coffin (Guysborough); Rev. Maxine Gough (Dartmouth); Rev. Tracey Grosse (Cherry Brook); Rev. Dr. Elizabeth Legassie (Bridgetown); Rev. Sherrolyn Riley (Dartmouth); Rev. Alfreda Smith (North Preston). Pastor Jennifer Riley was ordained on December 2, 2006.

Joan Jones, former columnist, has written about issues such as the Women's Institute of the African United Baptist Association's action plan on domestic violence.

In these hands the future is assured, but the future will certainly hold new and emerging challenges, too. In the words of the moderator in 2006:

Reverend Tracey Grosse of Cherry Brook became the first ordained female moderator of the African United Baptist Association in 2006.

The Black Church has always been a vital part of our black communities and their development. While I do not see this role changing, I do feel we must be prepared to do some things better and make some necessary changes. For example, the Black Church in Nova Scotia must be better equipped to address the changing needs of our youth, as well as family breakdown, education, the black male, the various forms of abuse and violence, addictions, HIV and AIDS, health, and the list goes on.

The vision of the Rev. Tracey Grosse embraces these challenges: "My personal vision for the AUBA, as its current Moderator, is to see our churches become healthier and stronger spiritually, numerically and financially. I want to see our churches become better equipped to meet the needs of a diverse community."

COMMUNITY HIGHLIGHTS

From 1990 to 2006, community achievements outside of education, black business, and the black church (which have already been mentioned) may be seen in significant publications, at conferences, through individual achievements, political and immigration profiles and developments, as well as in an overview of the fortunes and directions of provincial organizations.

Gertrude Tynes and Doris Evans, both retired teachers, co-wrote *Telling the Truth–Reflections: Segregated Schools of Nova Scotia* in 1995.

Seven books by Nova Scotia female writers have added considerably to our understanding and appreciation of the black community: *Bear River Untapped Roots: Moving Upward* by Florence Bauld (1997), who taught school for 35 years in Digby and Halifax County, received the Dartmouth Memorable Women Award, and was one of the founders of the Black Professional Women's Group of Nova Scotia; *Telling the Truth–Reflections: Segregated Schools of Nova Scotia* (1995) by Gertrude Tynes and Doris Evans, both long-serving teachers who wrote of their experiences and those of their peers and their predecessors; and *Invisible Shadows: A Black Woman's Life in Nova Scotia* (2002) by Verna Thomas, with a foreword by George Elliott Clarke. Thomas's words on the concluding page of the book sound like a clarion call that resonates deep:

"How long do we plan to stand in the same spot, looking back at the chains of slavery, the master's whip and dreaming of the pain they inflicted upon our race. Let's take our share of blame for what we have done to each other and get on with doing something for our community to accomplish our present and future needs. Let's not remain at the border between the work of progress and the world of decay."

Carol Aylward, the first black Nova Scotian to obtain a master's degree in law from Dalhousie University, wrote the book *Canadian Critical Race Theory* (1999). The fifth book, entitled *Fighting for Change: Black Social Workers in Nova Scotia* (2006), was compiled by female writers and edited by Wanda Thomas Bernard. This is an excellent resource book describing vital aspects of the black experience from an Africentric point of view. The book explains the concept and practice in some detail. "The history of the Association of Black Social Workers in Halifax since 1979" by Candace Bernard Roker is most valuable for an understanding of evolving challenges and opportunities in the social sphere in Nova Scotia. Dr. Wanda Thomas Bernard, director of

Christie Cromwell Simmonds wrote *The Colours of My Memories* at age seventy-one.

the Maritime School of Social Work at Dalhousie University, and her team of social workers use their learning and lived experiences to acknowledge, analyze, and respond to societal issues and challenges in the book and in their professional work. The sixth book in this impressive list of black female writers is Donna Byard Sealey's *Colored Zion: The History of Zion United Baptist Church and the Black Community of Truro, Nova Scotia* (2000). The seventh book, *The Colours of My Memories* (2006), was the first and last book written by Christie Cromwell Simmonds at age 71, and published after her death on April 29, 2005. Described by George Elliott Clarke in his review column on December 17, 2006 as a "pleasant book......chock full of rich descriptions......a banquet of images," this remarkable book of a remarkable family is a true testimony to the spirit of survival, of siblings helping siblings in an orphaned family of ten in rural Nova Scotia:

In all of my seventy-one years I have never been able to figure that one out. I should think we needed an increase of money instead of a decrease (i.e. from 25 dollars to 15 dollars). Ten orphans needed more help not less......Mamma's brother was appointed as guardian over us.

And so, there we were, all ten of us living on our little farm, which-was not a farm now but just a house, a big empty barn and lots of land.

Ricky Anderson, former Canadian welterweight champion and member of the Nova Scotia Sport Hall of Fame and Canadian Boxing Hall of Fame, wrote *Win in the Arena of Life* **in 2003.**

Other writers also made significant contributions during the period under discussion. Ricky Anderson's book, *Win in the Arena of Life: Living a Life You Love Is Worth Fighting For* (2003) is, like Wanda Thomas Bernard's book, aggressive in title and wonderfully comprehensive in scope. Ricky Anderson has been part of the provincial and national boxing scene since 1975, and continued to serve the sport in 2006. A former Canadian welterweight champion, Ricky Anderson was inducted to the Canadian Boxing Hall of Fame and the Nova Scotia Sport Hall of Fame. James Marcus Johnston wrote a book on his famous relative, entitled *James Robinson Johnston: The Life, Death and Legacy of Nova Scotia's First Black Lawyer* (2005).

In another area of service to the province and country, Corporal Craig Marshall Smith wrote a valuable book called *"You had better be white by six a.m.": The African-Canadian Experience in the Royal Canadian Mounted Police* (2006). Corporal Smith gives valuable insights into the difficulties faced by Nova Scotian blacks trying to enlist in the RCMP in the 1940s, including distinguished personalities like Leslie Bryan, Alfred Coward and Lorne White (who later went on to become an educator and vocalist of marked distinction). In chapter five of the book, Smith has written a tantalizing caption: "Towards Inclusion?" In 2006, in a force of 16,000, there were "approximately 200 Black members serving in the Force. While this number is encouraging, it indicates that there is much room for progress."

One Nova Scotian black author whose writings and output demonstrate great progress is George Elliott Clarke, recipient of the Governor General's Award for poetry and the Pierre Elliott Trudeau Fellowship. Clarke's first novel, *George and Rue* (2005), made the long list for the 2007 IMPAC Dublin Literary Award for first novels. This remarkable output by Clarke and the other authors mentioned in the period 1990-2006 represents a marked growth in the Nova Scotia literary scene.

On the political landscape, Wayne Adams moved from municipal politics to provincial politics in 1993 when he was elected to the Nova Scotia Legislative Assembly in the newly created Preston riding. He was appointed to Premier John Savage's cabinet in the same year, becoming the first black incumbent. Yvonne Thomas Atwell was elected in this riding in 1998, and was the first black female in the provincial legislature. Both Adams and Atwell held their seats for one term. In June 2006, Percy Paris was elected to the legislature in the riding of Waverley-Fall River-Beaverbank—a riding that is significantly different from the Preston riding held by Wayne Adams and Yvonne Atwell. In his first speech on June 30, 2006, Percy Paris drew attention to many things, including his election experience:

Corporal Craig Marshall Smith's many contributions to the community include acting as diversity policing analyst for the RCMP, writing an African Canadian educational resource guide, serving as president of the Black Hockey and Sports Hall of Fame, and acting as a member of the African Canadian Advisory Committee to the Nova Scotia Community College.

One of the things I realized in this election which reaffirmed that racism is alive and well in the Province of Nova Scotia......I didn't win the election on the votes from the people of African descent. I could probably count on one hand the number of African-Nova Scotians that live in the entire riding. But I can tell you this, during the course of the campaign, our campaign telephones, the calls we got that weren't

George Elliott Clarke won the 2001 Governor General's Award for Poetry.

Henderson Paris, elected to the New Glasgow town council in 2004, founded the town's annual Run Against Racism.

so complimentary. The anonymous messages we received, how a black person could run in a riding such as this with so much wealth, so much to offer......But I had good people around me. I was supported by good people."

These are surely words that coming generations of Nova Scotian society will take to heart.

The year 2006 produced two significant social and political milestones that honoured the Nova Scotia black contribution to the province: the late Delmore "Buddy" Daye, who died in 1995, had a street named after him in Halifax on a portion of Gerrish Street, near Gottingen. As mentioned in earlier pages of this book, Daye's manifold contributions to the community, professional positions held, and titles achieved in the sport of boxing transcend race and colour.

The other significant event was the swearing-in of the Honourable Mayann Francis as the province's first black lieutenant-governor on September 7, 2006. Her remarks: "I am a black woman......I crossed over many barriers to get to where I am today," bear testimony to a long list of notable positions she held before reaching this pinnacle, including director and CEO of the Nova Scotia Human Rights Commission (1999-2006), first female ombudsman in Nova Scotia (2000-03), former assistant deputy minister, Ontario Women's Directorate and first employment equity officer at Dalhousie University.

At the federal level, three well-known Nova Scotians entered politics during this period: Donald H. Oliver was appointed to the Senate on September 7, 1990, and Calvin Ruck assumed the same position on October 19, 2004. Gordon Earle was elected Member of Parliament for Halifax West in 1997, after serving in the province as deputy minister of housing and consumer affairs.

Besides the books published, and developments in politics, education, and business, the black community's profile continued to be highlighted in other fields. *Canadian Idol* runner-up Gary Beals of Cherry Brook added to his laurels with several awards from the African Nova Scotian Music Association in January 2005, including best new artist. The works and performances of David Woods, artist, poet, playwright, storyteller, actor, and founder of the Cultural Awareness Youth Group, kept the Nova Scotia black experience alive in various forms throughout the 1990s, and up to 2006 in his role at the Art Gallery of Nova Scotia. The Africville story, reunions, books and films throughout this same period kept the Africville Genealogy Society active and prominent. Sod was turned on the proposed new church site, with Martin Luther King III and actor Anthony Sherwood among the special guests). The film *Remember Africville* (produced and directed by Shelagh Mackenzie), the book *The Spirit of Africville* (which includes contributions from Donald Clairmont, Stephen Kimber, Bridglal Pachai and Charles Saunders), the exhibition "Africville: a Spirit That Lives On" and "Africville: A Lingering Legacy of Mixed Messages" (postscript in

Norman Paris was first elected to New Glasgow's town council in 1997, and served as deputy mayor.

Percy Paris was elected to the Nova Scotia Legislative Assembly in 2006, and was director of Dalhousie University's Diversity Initiative from 2000 to 2006.

Mayann Francis became the province's first black lieutenant-governor in 2006.

Gary Beals, *Canadian Idol* runner-up, won the African Nova Scotian Music Association's best new artist award in 2005.

Historic Black Nova Scotia by Bridglal Pachai and Henry Bishop, 2006) were produced during this period.

Joe Sealy, a descendant of Africville who left with his parents for Montreal as a child and now resides in Toronto, returned to visit when he was seventeen. He was inspired. When his father, Joseph Maurice Sealy, died in 1992, Joe Sealy wrote a musical piece called "Africville," later part of the album *Dual Vision*. Another album, *Africville Suite* followed in 1996, and the heroic—and tragic—story of Africville became part of music for posterity. That same year the well-known group Four The Moment produced their third album in fifteen years of performing locally, nationally, and internationally. The highly acclaimed North Preston group, the Gospel Heirs celebrated its 20th anniversary with two albums produced and another in preparation. Though these musical groups no longer exist in their former designations, their music and reputations remain in high regard.

Two organizations deserve inclusion for their focused contributions to important features of the black experience: the James Robinson Johnston Chair in Black Canadian Studies at Dalhousie University, and the Black Loyalist Heritage Society. Professor David Divine, the incumbent chair in 2006, who succeeded Dr. Esmeralda Thornhill of the Dalhousie Law Faculty, convened a highly successful conference titled "Multiple Lenses: Voices from the Diaspora Located in Canada," in Halifax in October 2005. This conference brought together academics, politicians, administrators and activists connected or contributing to the black experience, locally and nationally. The Black Loyalist Heritage Society was formed in 1991 and acquired its present name in 1999. Spearheaded by Elizabeth Cromwell in its early years, its membership and management have grown considerably under a distinguished board of directors. The society convened a conference in August 2005, called The Mugomeh Conference (*Mugomeh* is a Sierra Leone language word for "let's get together/let's meet") with a view to preparing a provincial strategy for the African Nova Scotian community.

There have been many previous attempts by organizations to work on strategies for provincial unity and direction for development, notably by the Black United Front and the Black Cultural Society, both mentioned in earlier sections of this book. The former ceased to exist in 1996.

On January 30, 1996, *The Mail Star* published an article under the heading "Black United Front remains in limbo," in which one paragraph read as follows: "throughout its 27-year existence BUF made headlines, some say unfairly, for board resignations, unlawful dismissal lawsuits, accusations of fiscal mismanagement and internal debates over priorities." On the priorities issue, the article reported the immediate past-president's words "that some blacks in rural areas complain that high-profile advocacy issues in the Halifax area get more attention from BUF than the day-to-day needs of people in outlying communities."

An accumulation of factors, some mentioned above, led to BUF's demise in spite of efforts to save it. The regional offices located in Shelburne, Lincolnville, Windsor, Amherst, and Sydney were shut down due to lack of funds in 1994. A government-appointed task force of twelve well-known members of the black community, chaired by Geraldine Browning and Clotilda Yakimchuk, presented a fresh set of recommendations to the government on October 8, 1996, but failed to get a reprieve. By year's end, BUF ceased to exist.

Meanwhile the Black Cultural Society has gone on since 1977 with few changes to its board of directors under the leadership of eight presidents

Joe Sealy wrote an album called *Africville Suite* in 1996.

Everett Cromwell, brother of Christie Cromwell Simmonds, is a founding member of the Black Loyalist Heritage Society. Everett was the only black member of the Second Division during World War Two.

Dr. Vincent Audain, an ophthalmologist originally from St. Kitts and Nevis, was president of the Medical Society of Nova Scotia in 1988–89. Dr. Audain was awarded the Dr. John Savage Memorial Award for his outstanding humanitarian contribution to international health in 2003.

Herman Ssebazza, a retired airworthiness engineer, immigrated to Nova Scotia from Africa in 1994. He contributed significantly to the African Canadian Immigrant Action Research Project, was named president of the Ugandan Canadian National Association, and is a founding member of the African Diaspora Association of the Maritimes.

from 1977 to 2006: Donald H. Oliver (1977-80); Hobartson Augustus (Gus) James Wedderburn (1980-85); Geraldine Browning (1985-87); Ruth Johnson (1987-89); Alma Johnston (1989-91); Anne Simmons (1991-93); Betty Thomas (1993-94) and Brian Johnston (1994-). In 2006, the society held strategic action planning sessions, and the final report was presented by Wayn Hamilton, chief executive officer for the Office of African Nova Scotian Affairs. Notable in the report was the emphasis on a business strategy plan: "Without such a plan, no cultural heritage institution can be sustainable, no matter how compelling its mission or treasured its collections."

The Office of African Nova Scotian Affairs was set up in 2003 "to act as a broker to other government agencies and the community" and "to serve as an advocate for cross-cultural understanding and a conduit to assist Nova Scotians of African descent in reaching their full potential." To date it has forged a partnership with the African Diaspora Association of the Maritimes with a view to adding the voices and concerns of individuals from the Caribbean and Africa to the voices of the indigenous black population. This is a response to the reality of changing demographics.

In the long history of the Nova Scotia black experience over the centuries, the contribution of members of the African diaspora (those not born in Nova Scotia), has been recorded, most recently in the book *Historic Black Nova Scotia* (2006). Distinguished professionals from the Caribbean have made their mark, such as world-renowned neurosurgeon, Dr. Renn Holness from Jamaica, who began working in Halifax in 1987 as a professor and neurosurgeon. There are others, too, like Dr. Vincent Audain, distinguished ophthalmologist, originally from St. Kitts and Nevis, who has worked in Nova Scotia for more than four decades, and among other positions held, was president of the Medical Society of Nova Scotia (1988-89).

In the early 1990s, the Halifax Police Department increased its efforts to recruit racially visible officers. Don MacLean (seen here in the Gambia, West Africa in 2006) became the highest ranking African Nova Scotian in the department's history when he was promoted to staff sergeant in 2005.

Representatives from Africa, too, have made and continue to make valuable contributions. Dr. Patrick Kakembo, second director of the African Services Division in the Department of Education, headed the research team that produced the BLAC Report mentioned in earlier pages, and was instrumental in putting together the African Canadian Immigrant Action Research Project aimed at integrating and uplifting newer members of the African diaspora. Two notable members of this group deserve mention: Herman Kizito Ssebazza, retired Airworthiness Engineer and Dr. Abdullah K. Kirumira, President and CEO of BioMedica Diagnostics Inc.

Thus, as 2006 draws to a close, one sees that the story of the Nova Scotia black experience is growing in leaps and bounds, marked by variety and growth, new visions, and voices from within and without. Well-wishers from the United States have come on board, notably the Fosty brothers, George and Darril. They are the authors of *Black Ice: The Lost History of the Colored Hockey League of the Maritimes* and co-founders of the New York-based Society of North American Hockey Historians and Researchers, which includes board members from Nova Scotia as well. The Fosty brothers organized the inaugural induction ceremony to the Black Hockey and Sports Hall of Fame of 50 individuals in Dartmouth, Nova Scotia, in August 2006. Their work continues in many ways, including donating many boxes of relevant information to the Black Cultural Centre, and compiling comprehensive lists of former black hockey players and administrators. New information is also emerging on the sporting activities of such well-known black personalities as James Robinson Johnston and James A.R. Kinney. Darril Fosty is working on a new book on George Dixon.

Nova Scotia's black community is growing in scope and vitality, with a changing demography, and new enthusiasm from many quarters. As Joan Jones, perceptive columnist, wrote in the *Mail Star* on February 22, 1996: "One need only be in Nova Scotia a short time before recognizing how vital heritage, and ancestry and traditions are......our past must be unearthed, honoured and shared."

APPENDIX

DOCUMENTARY SOURCES: PETITION ON EDUCATION, 1845*

To the Honourable, the Members of the Provincial Parliament of Nova Scotia, now in general assembly convened, the Petition of the undersigned, persons of color residing in the vicinity of Windsor, humbly sheweth,

That there are connected with your Petitioners, and residing within the circuit of a few miles, eighteen families of colored people, containing between fifty and sixty children under sixteen years of age, who have never enjoyed the advantages of common school instruction. The soil upon which your Petitioners are located, is of so poor and barren a quality, that with the most enlightened and diligent cultivation it would afford but the most scanty subsistence, and, under existing circumstances, they would not be able to contribute, except to the most trifling extent, towards the support of an efficient school. Since your Petitioners were first liberated and brought to this Province by the British Government, one whole generation has grown up in ignorance and another is solidly advancing, without any prospect unless prompt and effectual aid be immediately afforded them of improving upon their predecessors in their intellectual and moral condition, Your Petitioners would gratefully acknowledge all past favors, derived both from publick and private beneficence, and they beg to state for the information of your Honourable House, that through the exertions of benevolent individuals, a neat and commodious school house has lately been completed in a central and convenient part of the district, in which during the past two years, a goodly number of their children and youth, have enjoyed the advantages of Sabbath School instruction and have made, in proportion to these limited means, the most pleasing and encouraging proficiency. Your Petitioners beg to remind your Honourable House that it has been by a most marked and mysterious Providence, that they have been thrown into the arms of this Province, and compelled to look to its inhabitants generally, and to Your Honourable House in particular, for sympathy, protection, encouragement and instruction. By circumstances and events, to which it is most painful to refer but over which neither your Petitioners nor their forefathers could exercise any control, they have been transported from that warm and fruitful portion of the earth to whose climate their constitutions and complexion were adopted and have been conveyed to this distant and to them unfriendly region, and placed upon a stubborn and ungrateful soil, and forced to feel the severe pressure of poverty and to endure the rigors of the long, cold and dreary winters; and too long, alas! to suffer the still more cold and rigorous neglect and contempt of those in whose eyes we are an abomination, a reproach, and a byeword, who look down upon us as stronger aliens and intruders as a race of inferior and degraded beings, and upon those who are most kindly disposed towards us, are compelled by the customs and habits of society to deem it a most disgraceful crime to associate with us, and our children are not even allowed to receive instruction in company and under the same roof with others—since we are alas guilty of the notorious offence of wearing the hue enstamped upon us by the Allwise Creator and are found amidst the snows and paler faces of North America, instead of being where we freely confess we should be, among our own sable brethren under the burning suns of Africa, in the country originally assigned to us for our dwelling place by Him who made of one blood every nation under heaven and fixed the bounds of their habitation. But your Petitioners do not deem it necessary to refer either for the information or to move the compassion of your Honourable House, to their long, protracted hardships, sufferings, and wrongs. Long, long must it be, to all human appearance, before the unfortunate colored portion of Her Majesty's subjects inhabiting this Province can, even under the most favorable auspices rise up from that fearful degradation, and shake off that apathy ignorance and sloth inseparably connected with that degradation into which, without the pretext of an imputed crime, they have been plunged by the unjust and cruel hand of avarice and oppression. Your Petitioners cannot refrain from referring, and they do it with mingled emotions, to the pleasing fact, that they and their children are now enjoying the choice blessings of liberty and protection under the fostering wing of that very Power which formerly supported the oppression of their forefathers, but which, through the merciful interposition of Heaven is now putting forth its energies, and making the most noble exertions and sacrifices in order to redress our grievances and ameliorate the condition of our race. Most delightfully encouraging is it for us to know, that it is to that same Power, in thus applying to your Honourable House, that we now turn our imploring eyes and stretch out our hands for help, and we do it with the most confident assurance that the voice of our urgent necessities cannot be heard in vain.

Your Petitioners therefore humbly pray that your Honourable House would be pleased to take their case into careful consideration and to make such provision for the education of their children as you in your wisdom may deem meet.

And your Petitioners as in duty bound will ever pray—

Windsor, Feb. 6, 1845

David Williams

Colonel Cooper

Joseph Carter

Edward Pelote

Mark Taylor

Joseph Lewis

Pompey Johnson

Kenny Quory

Henry Upshaw

John Bowen

Lingard Pelote

Jules Finny

Lito Cooper

Abraham Green

PANS Assembly Petitions

RG5

Series P

Vol. 74

1845

ENDNOTES: SECTION A

CHAPTER ONE

1 Richard E. Leakey and Roger Lewin, *Origins*, Macdonald and Jane's Publishers, London, 1977, p. 8.

2 Roland Oliver, ed. *The Dawn of African History*, Oxford University Press, London, 1961, p. 41

3 Cited in *Patterns of Civilization: Africa*, p. 27

4 L.S.B. Leakey, *The Progress and Evolution of Man in Africa*, Oxford University Press, London, 1961, pp. 13 and 26

5 On this point, Leakey said: "......at a time when most so-called western civilized races still held that a man had such strong legal rights over his wife that he might with impunity force her to live with him physically, against her will and within the law, most African tribes gave women far greater freedom and greater rights to live their own lives as they chose, even to considerable sexual freedom, provided they remained with their husbands and looked after their children properly." *Op. cit.*, p. 19

CHAPTER TWO

1 Joseph E. Inikori, "The slave trade and the Atlantic economies, 1451-1870" in UNESCO, *The African slave trade from the fifteenth to the nineteenth century*, Paris, 1979, p. 71.

2 Quoted by Oliver Ransford, *The Slave Trade; The Story of Transatlantic Slavery*, London, 1971, p. 85.

3 Oliver Ransford, *op. cit*, p. 153

4 T. Watson Smith, "The Slave in Canada," *Collections of the Nova Scotia Historical Society* for the years 1896-1898, vol. x, 1899, p. 9

5 T. Watson Smith, *The Slave in Canada*, p. 32

CHAPTER THREE

1 Thomas H. Raddall, *Halifax Warden of the North*, 1977, pp. 19-20

2 Ellen Gibson Wilson, *The Loyal Blacks*, New York, 1976, p. 96

3 Ellen Gibson Wilson, *op. cit.*, p. 135.

4 It is common practice to consider the Black Loyalists as the first group of immigrants. In actual fact, free Black immigrants came out to Nova Scotia in the days following the settlement of Halifax in 1749 and therefore long before the arrival of the Black Loyalists. The Maroons would then constitute the third group.

5 Mavis C. Campbell, "From Nova Scotia to Sierra Leone: George Ross and the Trelawny Town Maroons of Jamaica." p. 24 (typescripts)

6 James W. St. G. Walker, *The Black Loyalists. The Search for a Promised Land in Nova Scotia and Sierra Leone 1783-1870.*

Endnotes: Section B

Chapter One

1. The spot on which Governor Wentworth built his house is still identifiable. In its place stands another house occupied in 1989 by one Mr. George Bundy. The house is located on what is referred to in 1989 as Colley's farm on Upper Governor's Road in East Preston.

2. The site of Maroon Hall can be seen in 1989 off Montague Road about three kilometres from the Black Cultural Centre on Highway 7, Westphal, Halifax County. In its place there is a new building which serves as a funeral house.

3. C.O. 217/70. Public Archives of Nova Scotia (PANS).

4. Brian Cuthbertson, *The Loyalist Governor, Biography of Sir John Wentworth*, 1983, p. 83.

4a. A few fugitives found their way into Nova Scotia via the New England states. One such person is John William Robertson who landed in Halifax through the help of the Boston Abolitionists. Reference to this person is contained in *The Book of Bible Against Slavery*. I am grateful to John Grant for this piece of information.

5. C.O. 217/93 PANS.

6. C.B. Fergusson, *A Documentary Study of the Establishment of the Negroes in Nova Scotia Between the War of 1812 and the Winning of Responsible Government*, 1948, p. 17 and John Norman Grant, "The Immigration and Settlement of the Black Refugees of the War of 1812 in Nova Scotia and New Brunswick," M.A. thesis of U.N.B., 1970, p. 51.

7. Fergusson, *op. cit.*, p. 21.

8. *Ibid.*, p. 23.

9. Grant, *op. cit.*, p. 62, f.n., 10.

10. C.O. 217/96, July 20, 1815, cited in Grant, *op. cit.*, p. 80.

11. PANS, Land Papers, Petition of Bazil Crowd, 1823, cited in Fergusson, *op. cit.*, p. 40.

12. PANS, Vol. 419, doc. 47, cited in Fergusson, *op. cit.*, p. 43.

13. Mrs. William Lawson, *History of the Townships of Dartmouth, Preston and Lawrencetown, 1893*, pp. 187-188.

14. Fergusson, *op. cit.*, p. 30.

15. Douglas F. Campbell, Ed., *Banked Fires—The Ethnics of Nova Scotia*, 1979, p. 109.

16. Robin W. Winks, *The Blacks in Canada. A History*, 1970, pp. 124-125.

17. Ellen Gibson Wilson, *The Loyal Blacks*, 1976, p. 219.

18. Ibid.

19. Interview, Charlotte Colley, November, 1988.

20. Fergusson, *op. cit.*, pp. 45-46.

21. *Ibid.*, p. 50.

22. *Ibid.*, p. 115.

23. The population of Preston in subsequent years was as follows: 1861: 641; 1871: 715; 1881: 794; 1891: 843; 1901: 498; 1911: 519; 1921: 572; 1931: 741; 1941: 909. Fergusson, *op. cit.*, p. 51.

24. Terrence M. Punch, *Sources for Research*, "The Black Population of Preston, Halifax County, in 1847," PANS, Vol. IV /1, p. 39.

25. Fannie Allison, et. al., "Early Pioneers, A Heritage of Faith and Courage, Upper Hammonds Plains, Nova Scotia," 1978, p. 1.

26. The population of Hammonds Plains in subsequent years was as follows: 1861: 770; 1871: 740; 1881: 785; 1891: 648; 1901: 691; 1911: 707; 1921: 682; 1931: 619; 1941: 696. Fergusson, op. cit., p. 54.

27. *Ibid.*, p. 55.

28. *Ibid.*, p. 129.

29. Donald H. Clairmont and Dennis William Magill, *Africville, The Life and Death of a Canadian Black Community*, 1987, p. 36.

30. The names were: Alcock, Alexander, Anderson, Brown, Byers, Berryman, Carvery, Cassidy, Downey, Dixon, Desmond, Emmerson, Farrell, Fletcher, Flint, Grant, Gannon, Hamilton, Howe, Izzard, Johnson, Jones, Kellam, Keelor, Lawrence, Macdonald, Mantley, Newman, Parris, Roan, Sparks, Steed, Skinner, Stewart, Thomas, Tolliver, Wearry, West and Williams. The committee members who compiled this list for the Africville cairn were Rev. Donald D. Skeir, Stanley Carvery, and Ruth Johnson. The other members were Rev. Dr. W.P. Oliver and Rev. Dr. J.C. Mack.

31. R.G. 5. Series P. Vol. 69/50, PANS.

32. Petition of David Williams and other settlers of Windsor, 1845.

33. G.A. Rawlyk, "The Guysborough Negroes: A Study in Isolation," *Dalhousie Review*, Vol. 48, No. 1, 1968, p. 25.

34. *Ibid.*

35. *Ibid.*, p. 28.

36. W.P. Oliver, "A Brief Summary of Nova Scotia Negro Communities," 1964, pp. 7-8.

37. PANS, Series P. Vol. 84/59.

38. Harriet Cunningham Hart, *History of the County of Guysborough*, Nova Scotia, 1975, p. 124.

39. I am grateful to my former Vice-Chancellor at the University of Malawi, Dr. Ian Michael, C.B.E., now in well-earned retirement in Bristol, England, for having arranged for copies of *The Methodist Magazine*, 1798, to be sent to me.

40. *The Methodist Magazine*, p. 283. Note his use of the word "Blacks" in the article. It is commonly held that this term is of very recent usage.

41. *Ibid.*, p. 264.

42. Selina Lani Pratt, "Black Education in Nova Scotia," M.A. Thesis, Dalhousie University, 1972, p. 32.

43. Fergusson, *op. cit.*, p. 118.

44. PANS, R.G. 5, Series P, Vol. 73, No. 21.

45. *Ibid.*, Vol. 74, No. 47.

46. *Baptist Annual Register*, Vol. 1, 1790-93, p. 480.

47. Stephen Eric Davidson, "Leaders of the Black Baptists of Nova Scotia, 1782-1832," B.A. Hon. thesis, Acadia University, 1975, p. 36.

48. *Ibid.*, p. 44.

49. *Ibid.*, p. 46 citing *The Novascotian*, Vol. 5, No. 26, June 27, 1832.

50. Davidson, *op. cit.*, pp. 59-65.

51. PANS, R.G. 5, Series P, Vol. 4, No. 51.

52. *Deacons in 1832*: Halifax: John Edwards, Jacob Ford, Prince William Sport. Dartmouth: Samuel Jones: Preston: Meredith Stanley; Beech Hill: James Morris; Hammonds Plains: Deal Whiley, William Marsman, Gabriel David.

Elders in 1832: Halifax: Thomas Bayley, Isaac Fletcher; Preston: John Collins; Beech Hill: John Maxwell: Hammonds Plains: Henry Whiley and Thomas Jones.

McKerrow, A Brief History of Blacks in Nova Scotia, 1783-1895. Introduced and Edited by Frank Stanley Boyd, Jr. p. 15.

53. Winks, op. cit., p. 340.

54. *Ibid.*, p. 363.

CHAPTER TWO

1. R. Preston, John Edwards, P. Wm. Sport, A. Dickson, Wm. Barrett, C. Hill, T. Connix, J. Cox [Halifax]; John Collins, George Carvery, John Thompson, Jas. Slaughter, Richard Crowd, William Dare, David Brown [Preston]; John Garry [Dartmouth]; John Hamilton, Deal Whiley, Nathan Goffican [Hammonds Plains]; Caesar Devine, Henry Bailey [Beech Hill]; Isaac Grant [Campbell Road]; Henry Jackson, Joseph Evans, Jas. Johnson [Bear River]; Charles Jordan, James Wilmot, J. Francis, I. Francis [Digby Joggins]; Isaac Johnson [Moose River]; C. Jackson, J. Kimbers, T. Wright [Granville Mountain]; Charles Langford [Weymouth]; David Dize, G. Dize [Yarmouth].

   Mc. Kerrow, *op. cit.*, pp. 25-26.

2. Savanah E. Williams. "Two Hundred Years in the Development of the Afro–Canadians in Nova Scotia, 1782-1982," in Jean Leonard Elliott, ed., *Two Nation, Many Cultures. Ethnic Groups in Canada*, p. 449, citing minutes of A.U.B.A., 1855 and 1861.

3. Pearleen Oliver, *op. cit.*, pp. 30-31; Savanah Williams, *op. cit.*, pp. 449-50; Mc. Kerrow, *op. cit.*, pp. 29-30.

4. Savanah Williams, *op. cit.*, pp. 450-451. This article was also published in Barry M. Moody, ed., *Repent and Believe: The Baptist Experience in Maritime Canada*, Lancelot Press, 1980.

5. Rev. A. Bailey, 1879-1880; Rev. W.R. Boone, 1880-1881; Rev. H.H. Johnson, 1880-1884; Rev. A.W. Jordan, B.D., 1884-1891; Rev. H.H. Johnson, 1892-1895; Rev. J.E. Jackson, 1895-1897; Rev. J.F. Robinson, 1897-1899; Rev. A. Clements, 1900-1902; Rev. Dr. Burch, 1902-1903; Rev. B.B.B. Johnson, 1903-1905; Rev. A. Clements, 1905-1908; Rev. M.B. Puryear, 1909-1917. There was no pastor in 1918. Rev. W.A. White assumed the pastorship in 1919. Pearleen Oliver, *op. cit.*, pp. 32 and 42.

6. *Ibid.*, p. 38.

7. Pearleen Oliver, "From Generation to Generation. Bicentennial of the Black Church in Nova Scotia, 1785-1985."

8. *Acadian Recorder*, October 26, 1917.

9. The author has made strenuous efforts for the past three years to obtain information on the location of the original building of the Home. St. Joseph's Home and Industrial School was the only one of its kind in Halifax. It opened on October 2, 1885 and closed down in 1955. The location mentioned by various respondents suggest the complex in present-day Mumford Road in Halifax occupied in part by the Halifax Shopping Centre. Another institution remembered is the Halifax Industrial School located in the Quinpool–Connaught Avenue area. One of these most certainly housed the original Home and School.

10. *Acadian Recorder*, October 26, 1917.

11. Robin Winks, *op. cit.*, p. 346.

12. Pearleen Oliver, *Brief History*, pp. 39-40; East Preston Ladies Auxiliary, Women at the Well. The other principal office-bearers were Rachael Upshaw, Secretary; Louisa Bundy, Treasurer; Bessie Wyse, Official Organizer; C.M. Saunders, Corresponding Secretary.

13. P.A.N.S., R.G. 1007.296 No. 48.

14. P.A.N.S., Micro: 935.J.86, Nova Scotia Assembly Journals, 1869.

14a. *Ibid.*

15. P.A.N.S. R.G. Series P, Vol. 78, pp. 2-3, Assembly Petitions, Education, 1883, cited in Boyd, *op. cit.*, p. 37.

16. James St. G. Walker, *A History of Blacks in Canada*, pp. 113-114.

17. *Acadian Recorder*, April 1, 1884.

18. *Halifax Morning Chronicle*, April 2, 1884.

19. *Ibid.*

20. *Ibid.*

21. Winks, *op. cit.*, p. 378.

22. *Halifax Morning Chronicle*, April 1 1884.

23. House of Assembly Debates, March 28, 1884.

24. Winks, op. cit., p. 379.

25. *Dartmouth Times*, May 10, 1884.

26. Legislative Assembly Journals, 1892, Education, p. 54.

27. *Ibid.*, 1895-96, pp. 55-56.

28. Bernice M. Moreau, "Adult Education Among Black Nova Scotians," Nova Scotia Department of Education, *Journal of Education*, No. 400, April, 1987, p. 34.

29. Noel H. Johnston Private Papers, East Preston.

30. Herbert H. Denton, "Nova Scotia Blacks Catching up on the Past," The *Washington Post*, September 25, 1986.

31. Nat Fleischer, Black Dynamite. *The Story of the Negro in Boxing*, Ring Athletic Library, Book No. 14, 1938, pp. 90-92.

32. Private communication, Preston E. Amos, 132—A.G. Street, S.W. Washington, D.C. 20024, July 16, 1985. Preston Amos is writing a book on black recipients of the Medal of Honour. In his communication, Mr. Amos pointed out that during the American Civil War [1861-1865], 78 known Blacks have received it. The official document in which this information appears is: Senate Committee Print No. 3, Medal of Honour Recipients, 1863-1978, February 4, 1979, p. 342.

33. Phyllis R. Blakeley, *The Dalhousie Review*, Vol. 37, No. 3, first page of unnumbered article.

34. Charles Bruce Fergusson, "William Hall, V.C.," *Journal of Education*, Nova Scotia Department of Education, December, 1967, p. 17.

35. *Ibid.*, p. 21. Of the six members of the "Shannon Brigade" who saved the entire corps from being wiped out, three died in the battle of Lucknow. The three who survived were Lieutenant Salmon and Seamen Hall and Robinson, all of whom were awarded the Victoria Cross for their bravery on November 16, 1857. See D.V. Warner," A Canadian Negro V.C.," *Canadian Magazine*, Vol. XVII, Number 2, June 1901, p. 115.

36. D.V. Warner, *op. cit.*, p. 115. The interview took place in September, 1900.

37. Fergusson, *op. cit.*, p. 21.

38. *Ibid.*, p. 21.

39. James W. St. G. Walker, *A History of Blacks in Canada*, p. 117.

40. S.M. Riley, "A Historical Review of Victoria Road United Baptist Church, 1844-1978," typescripts, privately held.

41. Belle Barnes, et al., *Traditional Lifetime Stories. A Collection of Black Memories*, vol. 1, pp. 64-65.

42. Mary Isobel Jones in "Early Pioneers. A Heritage of Faith and Courage," Upper Hammonds Plains, Nova Scotia, typescripts, 1978.

43. *Ibid.*

44. Willard Parker Clayton, *Whatever Your Will, Lord, Emmanuel Baptist Church, Upper Hammonds Plains, Nova Scotia, 1845-1984*, pp. 6-8.

45. Fannie Allison, et. al., "Early Pioneers," *op. cit.*, p. 1.

46. *Ibid.*, pp. 17-18.

47. Viola Parsons, *My Grandmother's Days*, 1988, p. 22.

48. Joan A. Brown, "A Study of Socio-Economic Patterns in Black Nova Scotia Communities, Sydney, N.S.," P.A.N.S. microfiche, B. 882, pp. 17-20.

49. *The Black Man*, Vol. 1, No. 9, August–September 1935, p. 3. Marcus Garvey was born on 17 August, 1887 in Jamaica and died in London on 10 June, 1940. In addition to the journal, *The Black Man*, the U.N.IA. published a weekly newspaper called *The Negro World*.

50. For information on Isaac Phills, I am grateful to his daughter, a retired school teacher and now real estate broker, Mrs. Gertrude Tynes and to Leo W. Bertley, *Canada and Its Peoples of African Descent*, 1977, p. 262.

51. *The Halifax Chronicle-Herald*, January 2, 1950.

52. *The Nova Scotia Gleaner*, Vol. 1, No. 3, 1929. I am grateful to Mr. Winston Ruck, himself the son of an immigrant from Barbados, who was born in Sydney, Nova Scotia, for a copy of this issue. Winston Ruck and his brother, Calvin Ruck, have both distinguished themselves as worthy first generation Nova Scotia-born descendants of West Indian immigrants.

53. Belle Barnes, et. al., *Traditional Lifetime Stories*, pp. 77-78.

54. Donald Clairmont and Dennis W. Magill, *Africville. The Life and death of a Canadian Black Community*, revised edition, 1987, p. 36.

55. McKerrow, *op. cit.*, p. 46.

56. Belle Barnes, *op. cit.*, p. 55.

57. Paul A. Erickson, *Halifax's North End*, 1968, pp. 121-122. The interviews were conducted by the present author for the Black Cultural Centre on 13 September, 1986. Dr. Erickson was invited to be present and permission was given to him to use the information in his book.

58. Interview by C. Michelle Sparks, Black Cultural Centre summer student researcher, 10 July, 1986.

59. P.A.N.S. R.G. 35-102 Series 1B, Vol. 1, 1906, Item 77, 26 February, 1906, Petition to Mayor.

60. *Ibid.*, Vol. 3, 1907, Item 22.

61. P.A.N.S. R.G. 35-102 Series 1B, Vol. 27, 191, Petition for police protection, June 19, 1919.

62. *Ibid.*, July 7, 1919.

63. Charles Saunders, *Sweat and Soul*, pp. 17-18, typescripts for forthcoming publication of the Black Cultural Centre for Nova Scotia, 1989. The reader is referred to this excellent book for the details of the life and accomplishments of Nova Scotia black boxers of distinction.

64. *Mail Star*, October 10, 1956.

65. Winks, op. cit., p. 315.

66. *Ibid.*

67. *Ibid.*, p. 317. See also Calvin W. Ruck, *Canada's Black Battalion, No. 2 Construction, 1916-1920*, 1986, Chapter 1, pp. 11-20.

68. James W. St.G. Walker, "Race and Recruitment in World War 1: Enlistment of Visible Minorities in the Canadian Expeditionary Force," paper presented to the Canadian Ethnic Studies Association Biennial Conference, Halifax, October, 1987.

69. The author had the pleasure of consulting the William White Diary in the office of the Black United Front, Halifax, in 1977.

70. Calvin Ruck, *op. cit.*, p. 44.

71. *The Truro Daily News*, August 17, 1917.

CHAPTER THREE

1. J. Murray Beck, *Politics of Nova Scotia, Vol. 2, 1896-1988*, pp. 66-7.

2. Copy dated December 22, 1918 supplied by Donna Sealey, Dartmouth, Nova Scotia.

3. P.A. Erickson, *Halifax's North End*, pp. 56-64. See also various testimonies in Traditional Lifetime Stories, Vol. 1.

4. Thomas H. Raddall, *Halifax Warden of the North*, pp. 255-56.

5. McKerrow, *A Brief History*, p. 101.

6. Belle Barnes. et. al., *Traditional Lifetime Stories*, pp. 70-71. John Pannill died on January 23, 1990.

7. *Ibid.*, p. 77.

8. Minutes of the 65th session of A.U.B.A., 7-10 September, 1918, p. 10.

9. Sylvia Hamilton, "Our Mothers Grand and Great: Black Women of Nova Scotia," *Canadian Women Studies*, Vol. 4, No. 2, Winter, 1982, p. 37.

10. Pearleen Oliver, *A Brief History*, p. 49.

11. *Ibid.*, p. 53.

12. Savanah E. Williams, "Two Hundred Years in the Development of the Afro-Canadians in Nova Scotia," in *Two Nations, Many Cultures*, edited by Jean Leonard Elliott, p. 448.

13. Donald Clairmont and Fred Wien, "Blacks and Whites: The Nova Scotia Race Relations Experience," in *Banked-Fires. The Ethnics of Nova Scotia*, edited by Douglas F. Campbell, p. 144.

14. *The Nova Scotia Gleaner*, Vol. 1, No. 3, October 5, 1929, pp. 4 and 6.

15. The author is indebted to Mr. Jack Desmond for the various interviews granted on 12 April, 1989 and on subsequent occasions, for a photograph, and for news clippings, notably the *Times*, Moncton, March 28, 1989 and the Mail Star, Halifax, May 31, 1986 and the *Chronicle-Herald*, Halifax, March 16, 1989.

16. *Halifax Chronicle-Herald*, March 16, 1989.

17. The information on this section dealing with black businesses was obtained from a number of sources: Crawley's Management Training Associates conducted a research entitled "Research on Black Businesses of the Past Metro Area" and from interviews with John Pannill, Jack Desmond, George Davis, Noel H. Johnston, Sydney Jones, Coulter States and Ruth Johnson, to all of whom the author is deeply indebted.

18. *The Nova Scotia Gleaner*, October 5, 1929.

19. PANS AG 35-102, 5A-6-334, letter dated January 27, 1944.

20. The author is grateful to Zina Williams, daughter of B.A. Husbands, for various interviews in 1989 and for information on her father. The Husbands family home was in Charles Street, Halifax. He was married to Iris Lucas of Lucasville who died in January, 1977 at the age of 93. The couple had fifteen children, eight sons and seven daughters. The surviving children in 1989 are Zina Williams in Halifax, Augusta Firmin in Boston and Kenneth Husbands in Montreal. B.A. Husbands attended the Joseph Howe School in Halifax. He was named to the Hall of Fame by Eboni Promotions, Halifax, on August 7, 1982. See also, *Halifax Chronicle-Mail Star*, June 20, 1968 and August 8, 1982, and *Barbados Advocate*, June 25, 1983. Other office-bearers of the League were Arthur Callendar, Keith Prevost, John Brown, Edith Gray and M.A. Ryan.

21. Oral interviews with Edith Gray, aged 76, Halifax; Jack Desmond, aged 84, Halifax; Deacon Sydney Jones, aged 88; Halifax, July 17, 1989.

22. Eugene Edward Williams, "An Historical Review of the Organization [NSAACP] and its Role in the Area of Education," Diploma in Social Work, Maritime School of Social Work, 1969, p. 6.

23. Minutes of the NSAACP, 1945, p. 3 cited by Jules Ramon Oliver, "An Historical Evaluation of the N.S.A.A.C.P. and the Role it Has Played in the Area of Employment," M.S.W. thesis, Maritime School of Social Work and Acadia University, 1969, p. 11.

24. Eugene Williams, op. cit., p. 8.

25. Jules Oliver, op. cit., p. 11.

26. Jeanette Poirier Arab, "The Struggle for Equal Rights for Porters and Questions it Suggests Regarding Canadian Racism," research paper made available by Coulter States, Dartmouth, N.S.

27. Belle Barnes, et. al., Traditional Lifetime Stories, pp. 73-74.

28. Personal interview, 18 March, 1989. For other studies on this subject see Agnes Calliste, "Sleeping Car Porters in Canada: An Ethnically Submerged Split Labour Market," Canadian Ethnic Studies, xix, 1, 87 and "Blacks on Canadian Railways," Canadian Ethnic Studies, xx, 2, 1988. In 1953, C.B. States was elected President of Division 132, Halifax, of the CBRE & OTW. The other officers were: Recording Secretary, Eugene Williams; Vice-President, Ernest Grosse; Financial Secretary, T.G. McDonald; Local Chairman, Booker Roache. See Canadian Railway Employees' Monthly, Vol. 39, No. 3, March, 1953, p. 83.

29. Personal interview, 21 December, 1977, 45 Albert Street, Dartmouth, N.S.

30. W.P. Oliver, "The Nova Scotia Home for Coloured Children," typed notes, privately held.

31. Ibid.

32. Minutes of the 67th meeting of A.U.B.A., New Glasgow, 4-7 September, 1920, p. 22.

33. D.E. Fairfax, "A Brief History of the Nova Scotia Home for Colored Children during the past 60 years," November 13, 1979, privately held.

34. PANS Vertical File, Nova Scotia Home for Colored Children, No. 2, December 16, 1977, Report for 1929.

35 A.D. Grayston to Phyllis Blakeley, September 3, 1969, PANS Vertical MSS File, Negroes No. 57, December 22, 1977. Dr. Melville Cumming died on 15 April, 1969.

36. D.E. Fairfax, op. cit.

37. Minutes of the 76th meeting of A.U.B.A., Hammonds Plains, 17-20 August, 1929, p. 1.

38. The Citizen, Halifax, May 29, 1936.

39. The Maritime Baptist, September 16, 1936.

40. The Diary of Rev. Dr. William Andrew White. Other sources consulted on W.A. White are Pearleen Oliver, A Brief History; The Maritime Baptist, September 16, 1936; Truro Daily News and Citizen-Sun, May 29, 1936; Dr. White's scrap book; Acadia University Baptist Records.

41. Halifax Herald, March 4, 1927.

42. Acadia University Baptist Church records, photocopies of obituary notices, May, 1927; Pearleen Oliver, op. cit., p. 44; Margaret Lawrence, Reverend and Mrs. Wellington States, research paper, Saint Mary's University, August 3, 1977. His three children were Leota, born 1910; Patricia, born 1912 and Coulter born 1914.

43. Pearleen Oliver, op. cit., p. 47.

44. Ibid.

45. Minutes of the 65th meeting of the A.U.B.A., Halifax, 7-10 September, 1918, p. 13.

46. Minutes of the 77th meeting of the A.U.B.A., Truro, 16-19 August, 1930, pp. 12-13.

47. Belle Barnes et. al., Traditional Lifetime Stories, pp. 21, 79, 82.

48. Ibid., p. 104.

49. I am grateful to Mrs. Doris Evans for the material compiled on black teachers for the Black Cultural Centre records, and to the many teachers who co-operated with the project.

CHAPTER FOUR

1. Interview, Jack Desmond, Halifax, 8 August, 1989.

2. *The National Black Awards of Canada.*

3. Alan Bundy's brother, Carl Bundy, also in the Air Force, both of whom were on leave from Canadian National Railways, as were Leo Brown, Douglas Bauld, John Riley, Coulter States and James Tynes and Austen Tynes. Other Dartmouthians on this roll of honour were: Murray Brown, William Kane, Alan Lucas, Gordon Lucas, Edgar Mansfield, Courtney Samuels, John Tynes, Frederick Tynes, Morris Tynes, Freeman Tynes, Wilfred Tynes, Rupert Tynes, Kenneth Tynes, and Byron Tynes and Francis Whalen. I am grateful to Coulter States for compiling this list on 28 August, 1,989.

4. I am grateful to Winston Ruck, Executive Director of the Black United Front for assistance in compiling this list, 25 August, 1989.

5. George Borden, written communication, 1987 entitled "Blacks in the Canadian Military."

6. Information on Oscar Seale and Thomas Miller gleaned from notes supplied by Winston Ruck, August 1989. The Thomas E. Miller Human Rights Award was inaugurated in Sydney on December 10, 1989.

7. H.A.J. Wedderburn, "From Slavery to the Ghetto. The Story of the Negro in the Maritimes," paper presented to the New Brunswick Human Rights Commission, March 25-26, 1968.

8. Jules Oliver, "An Historical Evaluation of the N.S.A.A.C.P. and the Role it Has Played in the Area of Employment," p. 8 citing W.P. Oliver, "Cultural Progress—Negro in Nova Scotia," *Dalhousie Review*, Vol. xxix, 1949, p. 297.

9. *The Dalhousie Review*, 1950, p. 297-98.

10. *Ibid.*

11. Dr. W.P. Oliver, "A Brief Summary of Nova Scotia Negro Communities," 1964.

12. *Ibid.* The family referred to is that of Isaac Phills, mentioned in this book; the successful politician is Thomas Miller, also mentioned in this chapter, and the medical doctor is Dr. A. Caldwell, also mentioned in this chapter.

13. Institute of Public Affairs, Dalhousie University, "The Condition of the Negroes of Halifax City, Nova Scotia," 1962, p. ii.

14. *Ibid.*, p. 10.

15. *Ibid.*, p. 21.

16. W.P. Oliver, "The Negro in Nova Scotia," *Journal of Education*, February, 1964, p. 19.

17. *Ibid.*, p. 20.

18. Gwendolyn V. Shand, *Adult Education Among the Negroes of Nova Scotia*, 1961, pp. 4-5.

19. *Ibid.*, pp. 4-13.

20. W.A. MacKay, "Combatting Discrimination Through Legislation." A paper for the Seminar on Inter-Group Relations sponsored by the Canadian Council of Christians and Jews, Halifax, February 1, 1967, p. 1.

21. *Ibid.*

22. W.P. Oliver, "The Role of Education in Improving Inter-Group Relations."
    Ibid.

23. The Negro Almanac. A Reference Work on the Afro-American, "Invention and Scientist," pp. 787-796. Bicentennial Edition, 1976.

24. "The Black Man in Nova Scotia," Teach-In Report, January, 1969, excerpt from Dr. W.P. Oliver's speech, pp. 5-6.

25. *Ibid.*, excerpt from Burnley (Rocky) Jones' speech, p. 18.

26. Judith H. Gold, "A Special University Program for Nova Scotian Blacks and Micmacs," in *Canadian Black Studies*, edited by Bridglal Pachai, 1979, pp. 182-183.

27. Cynthia M. Thomas, "Black Youth and Education," Ibid., pp. 186-193.

28. Cherry Paris, "Education and Human Rights," Ibid., p. 194.

29. Eleanor Dorrington, "Halifax Outreach Employment Project," Ibid., p.205.

30. Mohamed Abucar, *Struggle for Development: The Black Communities of North and East Preston and Cherry Brook, Nova Scotia 1784-1987, p. 25-26.*

31. Donald H. Clairmont and Dennis William Magill, *Africville. The Life and Death of a Canadian Black Community*, revised edition 1987, p. 44, fn. 25.

32. *Ibid.*, p. 86.

33. *Ibid.*, p. 87.

34. *Ibid.*, p. 89.

35. Robert A. Huttenback, *Racism and Empire White Settlers and Colored Immigrants in the British Self-Governing Colonies, 1830-1910*, 1976, pp. 15-16.

36. The sponsors of the Africville project are the Africville Genealogy Society, the Black Cultural Centre for Nova Scotia, Mount Saint Vincent University Art Gallery, and the National Film Board, Atlantic Centre. The principal author of the exhibition brochure is Charles Saunders, with short contributions by Donald Clairmont and Bridglal Pachai, while the book will have contributions by all three and will be published by Formac Publisher, Jim Lorimer.

37. *The United Church Observer*, December 1, 1963, pp. 14-15. Alan Borovoy's visit was written up by David Lewis Stein and published in Maclean's Magazine on October 20, 1962.

38. *Ibid.*, February 15, 1963, p. 6. Letter by F. Ian Gilchrist, MD.

39. I am indebted to Charles Saunders for coming up with the term "Africvilleans" in his writings on the 1989 Africville project alluded to in fn. 36.

40. Paul A. Erickson, *Halifax's North End*, pp. 119-122.

41. *Mail Star*, 12 January, 1970, article by Jim Robson. Aaron Carvery's grandfather was one of the black refugees who arrived in Nova Scotia between 1813 and 1816 and first settled in Preston, from where he moved to Africville. His father, William Carvery, a small contractor, was born in Africville and died in 1953. Aaron Carvery worked as a coal handler and stevedore on the Halifax waterfront, retiring in 1965. The Aaron Carvery incident was reported in various issues of the *Mail Star*. The N.S.A.A.C.P. protested against the strategy used by senior officials to induce Aaron Carvery to vacate his house when a suitcase containing cash was offered to Carvery in the presence of D.F. Murphy, City Solicitor, D.B. Hyndman, Director of Finance and City Treasurer, C.W. Smith, Internal Auditor, H.D. Crowell, Social Planner, Harry Carter, Special Projects Worker, Social Assistance Department, a former Africville resident himself. Also present were two plainclothes policemen. The N.S.A.A.C.P. demanded that the City tender an apology for its tactics. Its chairman, H.A.J. Wedderburn, who was a member of the N.S. Human Rights Commission suggested that the matter be referred to the Commission for investigation, a suggestion which was first made by Mayor Allan O'Brien. This was rejected on the grounds that the Commission, being a government agency, could not be relied upon to be impartial. In the end, the City admitted that the

356

whole thing was an "unintended mistake" and agreed to apologize, to accept the City Manager's settlement proposal, and thus to close the matter. See issues of the *Mail Star*, January 12, 1970, January 24, 1970, January 28, 1970, February 26, 1970.

42. Statement by Brenda Steed Ross.

43. Althea J. Tolliver and James A. Francois, *From Africville to New Road. How Four Communities Planned Their Development*, p. 10.

44. *The Daily News*, September 11, 1989, article by Sine MacKinnon, citing the President, Santosh Pachai.

45. *The Clarion*, Truro, July 16, 1947.

46. Minutes of the 114th Sessions, August 19-21, 1967, p. 17.

47. Ibid.

48. Report of the Rural and Urban Life Committee of the African United Baptist Association of Nova Scotia, August 17, 1968, p. 6, Deacon Richard Symonds Papers.

49. *The Canadian Bar Review*, Vol. xxv, 1947, p. 920. Viola Desmond was born in Halifax on July 6, 1914, the daughter of Mr. and Mrs. James Davis. She married Jack Desmond in 1936, studied hairdressing in Montreal and beauty culture in New York. She operated a beauty parlour on Gottingen Street in a building which she shared with her hairdresser husband, Jack Desmond. She died in 1965.

50. Originally designed as a church bulletin, the *Clarion* grew in size over the years. The Chairman of the paper's Board of Directors was Dr. A.E. Waddell, Halifax physician; the Vice-Chairman was A.T. Best and the Treasurer was L.B. Mills of New Glasgow.

51. *The Clarion*, April 1, 1947.

52. Speech delivered on the occasion of the opening of the North Preston Community Centre, November 6, 1976; "The Human Rights Act and its Effect on Improving Housing for Blacks in Nova Scotia," research paper, Maritime School of Social Work, March 21, 1979; "The Development of Human Rights in Nova Scotia," November 18, 1988, are among the many he has written or delivered over a period of over 20 years.

53. *The Mail Star*, October 26, 1968.

54. *The Mail Star*, December 6, 1969.

55. Martin Luther King, Jr., *Why We Can't Wait*, 1963, p. 22.

56. Winks, op. cit., pp. 452-458 for information on Halifax and Nova Scotia.

    See also the *United Church Observer*, December 1, 1963 for conditions in Nova Scotia.

57. Marvin Burke, "Halifax Has a White Problem," *The People*, November 21, 1968, p. 7. The writer was formerly co-ordinator of the Halifax Neighbourhood Centre which opened on 1 November, 1966 and whose one-time notable staff member was the well-known lightweight boxing champion of Canada, Delmore Buddy Daye. Marvin Burke is in 1989 the Director of the Nova Scotia Drug Dependency Commission.

58. *Contrast*, April 4, 1970.

59. *The Chronicle-Herald*, January 2, 1969. The Moderator of A.U.B.A. at the time, Ross Kinney, speaking for 24 churches in N.S. whose membership included 90% of the black population, said that the A.U.B.A. was opposed to the Black Panther movement. Rev. Donald Skeir, minister of the largest congregation of blacks in the Preston-Cherry Brook area supported the Moderator's position.

60. *Ibid.*, December 3, 1968.

61. *Dalhousie Gazette*, February 13, 1969.

62. *The People*, Vol. I, no. 9, March 20, 1969.

63. *The Mail Star*, June 18, 1969.

64. M. Loney, "Bankrolling the Revolution," *Canadian Dimension*, April 1977.

65. Colin Thomson, *Born with a Call. A Biography of Dr. William Pearly Oliver*, CM., pp. 121-133.
   The first President of B.U.F. was Carlyle Warner, the chief long-range planner for the City of Halifax.

66. The *Chronicle-Herald*, September 8, 1969.

67. The *Evening Telegram, Weekend Magazine*, Vol. 19, No. 8, February 22, 1969, p. 6.

68. M. Loney, *op. cit.*

69. On the very day these lines were written, October 31, 1989, the *Mail Star* reported as follows: "The Black United Front of Nova Scotia wants its $307,000 budget increased by $200,000, says the group's executive director, Winston Ruck. Black case workers are overloaded with work and there aren't enough of them to go around," he said. "B.U.F. wants more money so at least another six case workers can be hired to get projects off the ground in smaller communities throughout Nova Scotia where services to blacks are now limited or non-existent," he said.

70. Black Teachers Project, Black Cultural Centre, conducted by Doris Evans.

71. *Ibid.* Some of the Black teachers holding senior positions in 1989 are: Sandra Best, Principal, Caudle Park Elementary School; Joyce Clayton, Vice-Principal, Colby Village Elementary; Douglas Earle, Vice-Principal, Clayton Park Junior High; Ben Elms, Vice-Principal, Digby Regional Junior High; George Gray, Vice-Principal, Humber Park Elementary; Bill Jaggernathsing, Principal, Port-Mouton Consolidated; Vanroy Tobbitt, Vice-Principal, St. Stephens Highland Park; Gerald Tynes, Vice-Principal, Cole Harbour High; Gary Williams, Vice-Principal, Graham Creighton Junior High.

72. Cultural Education Centre proposals, 1972, Black Cultural Centre Library.

73. Anniversary Lectures: James Walker, *The Black Identity in Nova Scotia; Gilbert H. Scott, Cultural Pluralism, Multiculturalism and Community Development; Pamela C. Appelt, Citizenship, Culture and the Black Community;* Peter J. Paris, *The Moral, Political and Religious Significance of the Black Churches in Nova Scotia.*

   Books: Calvin Ruck, *Canada's Black Battalion No. 2 Construction Battalion 1916-1920; Colin Thomson, Born with a Call: The Biography of Dr. William Pearly Oliver; Traditional Lifetime Stories: A Collection of Black Memories Vol. I;* Mohamed Abucar, *Struggle for Development: The Black Communities of North and East Preston and Cherry Brook, Nova Scotia 1784-1987.*

74. The *Sunday Daily News*, March 20, 1989.

75. *The Rap*, Halifax, Vol. 2, No. 3, February 1988.

76. *The Reporter*, Port Hawkesbury, March 11, 1987.

77. *Atlantic Insight*, July, 1983, p. 41.

INDEX